Programming Jabber

Programming Jabber

DJ Adams

O'REILLY®

Beijing · Cambridge · Farnham · Köln · Sebastopol · Tokyo

Programming Jabber
by DJ Adams

Published by O'Reilly & Associates, Inc., 1005 Gravenstein Highway North, Sebastopol, CA 95472.

O'Reilly & Associates books may be purchased for educational, business, or sales promotional use. Online editions are also available for most titles (*safari.oreilly.com*). For more information, contact our corporate/institutional sales department: (800) 998-9938 or *corporate@oreilly.com*.

Editor: Chuck Toporek

Production Editor: Catherine Morris

Interior Designer: David Futato

Cover Designer: Ellie Volckhausen

Printing History:

> January 2002:   First Edition.

ISBN: 978-0-596-00202-2
[LSI]   [2011-04-01]

Table of Contents

Preface

What is Jabber? Depending on who you ask, the answer to that question could be any one (or all) of the following:

- Jabber is a technology.

- Jabber is a protocol (or set of protocols).

- Jabber is an XML-based Instant Messaging (IM) system.

- Jabber is an *implementation* of the set of protocols.

- Jabber is an idea whose time has come.

In fact, all these answers are right. Jabber is a set of protocols expressed within XML that allow people and applications to converse with one another. Sure, TCP sockets, STDIN/STDOUT, infrared, voice input, and teletype mechanisms all allow people and applications to converse; the difference is that Jabber provides a structured, extensible framework for exchanging all kinds of information.

This is all rather abstract, so what do we mean by "extensible framework for exchanging information"? Taking it one word at a time:

Extensible

Jabber's substrate is XML. XML is inherently extensible in the sense that tags can be added in a hierarchical sequence. Namespaces in XML allow us to keep track of the meaning and organization of these tags.

Framework

You can put together a system for exchanging information using many different tools. The point about the "framework" is that the information exchanged and the entities that are exchanging it are contextualized, bringing meaning and structure to the interactions.

Exchanging

> Conversation is two-way, and it takes many forms: question and answer, notification, compartmentalized discussion, and simple chat. Jabber supports all these different types of conversation and more.

Information

> One doesn't really say that *information* is exchanged in a conversation, but when you bring applications into the mix of conversing entities, it may well be the case. And it's not just information exchanged in the form of conversations but also information about the entities themselves that flows across this context framework.

It goes without saying: *Jabber is an instant messaging (IM) system.*

Instant messaging was Jabber's original raison d'être. Many deployments of Jabber software are to provide IM services, but Jabber is more than IM—certainly more than the phrase "instant messaging" represents. In this book you'll find out why this is so and how you can deploy solutions with Jabber that are more than mere chat. But most importantly, Jabber is fun!

Like chess, which has a small set of rules but countless game possibilities, the technologies employed in Jabber and the Jabber protocol itself are straighforward. The possibilities are almost limitless. Furthermore, because of a fundamental design feature* (you might call it a "philosophical" angle), implementing Jabber-based solutions to your problems can be fun—really!

The History of Jabber

Jeremie Miller started the Jabber project early in 1998, and it was announced to the public in January 1999. To understand why Jabber came about, and in the form it took, let's look briefly at what existed in the IM world before Jabber.

The Pre-Jabber History

While the concept of live chat systems has existed for many years, with commands such as Unix's *talk* and VMS's *phone*, IM as we know it today existed as a concept and a handful of systems from companies such as Mirabilis, AOL, Microsoft, and Yahoo!. These systems (ICQ from Mirabilis, AIM from AOL, MSN from Microsoft, and Yahoo!IM from Yahoo!) allowed their users to chat to one another and avail themselves of IM-related services. However, an AIM user couldn't chat with an ICQ user, and MSN users couldn't interact with Yahoo!IM users. Each system was effectively closed to the outside world.

---

* The complexity of a Jabber implementation should always remain in the *server*, leaving the clients simple and clean.

Furthermore, the protocols that these systems used were also mostly closed—proprietary—which meant it was difficult to find clients for these IM systems other than the ones supplied by the IM system owner.

Finally, the systems themselves were monolithic: multiple clients but a single server (or server farm). Although the companies were able to invest time and money into the problem, the fact remained that a monolithic architecture presented a scaling problem. Perhaps more relevant than that, companies that wanted to use IM services internally had to accept the fact that the conversations would be carried through the systems of a third party—namely the owners of these public IM systems. This was no more desirable than for a company to run its internal email using a public email service such as Hotmail.

Of course, these systems did have their advantages. The clients were accomplished and easy to learn and use, and as long as your correspondents were using the same IM system and you didn't mind your messages being carried by another organization (for private individuals these wouldn't be unique circumstances; again, we are led to the email services parallel), then you could leave the system management to someone else and get on with chatting.

Scratching an Itch

Having all your contacts use the same IM system is all well and good in theory but in practice is rarely the case. (If you're like me and have only a few friends, then this is not so much of a problem.) Jeremie Miller had correspondents in different IM systems and consequently had to have different IM clients running on his desktop to keep up with them all. Many great software projects stem from a personal "itch" that someone wanted to scratch. This was the primary itch that Jeremie had—a single client for all IM interaction: *panacea.*

Of course, one obvious solution would be to build a single client that supported all of the IM system protocols, but this approach had two drawbacks:

- The proprietary nature of the protocols made it harder to implement the support required and would make the client overly complicated.

- Every time the protocol, which wasn't under his control, changed or a new one came along, the client would have to be modified—a task not practical for a large user base.

On top of that, GUI programming isn't everyone's cup of tea, and Jeremie preferred a solution that allowed him to concentrate on the underlying problems at hand and let others build the GUIs.

Along Came Jabber

So Jeremie resolved to create a solution that had the following characteristics:

- It would have its own internal protocol, based upon XML.
- This protocol should be:
    - Simple to understand and implement
    - Easy to extend
    - Open
- The complexity of bridging the disparate proprietary IM protocols would remain at the server, each bridge being a plug-in module.
- All the clients would have to implement only the single, simple open protocol; everything else would be implemented at the server.

He called this solution "Jabber."

The main architectural feature for Jabber that Jeremie strived for was that it should be simple enough for anyone to implement a Jabber server of his own. Unlike a *centralized* server environment, with all of the traffic routed through a central point, Jeremie envisioned that Jabber would be *decentralized*, allowing individuals, companies, and public organizations to run their own servers. This is particularly relevant for internal-only, IM-style corporate communications. Just as email servers are used to exchange mail using the Simple Mail Transport Protocol (SMTP), the Jabber servers are able to connect and exchange IM traffic whenever necessary. Figure P-1 illustrates Jabber's distributed architecture, with two separate Jabber servers serving separate users.

Being *open* meant that Jabber could benefit from the help of anyone who wished to lend a hand, and administrators were empowered to be able to find and fix problems themselves if they so wished.

Being *XML-based*, as opposed to another binary format, for example, meant that the protocol streams were easy for humans to read, extensible, and readily integrated (a great range of XML parsing and construction tools is already available).

Being *distributed* meant that the Jabber system would belong to the people and that some of the scalability problems would be avoided. There remain some scalability issues, of course. Client-server communication that is TCP socket-based suffers from limitations of this technology. There are, however, initiatives to overcome these limitations with multiplexing techniques such as jpolld and dpsm (see *http://download.jabber.org*).

All of these features made for a good IM system design. But why stop at IM? Consider the client as an implementation of a simple protocol to exchange messages

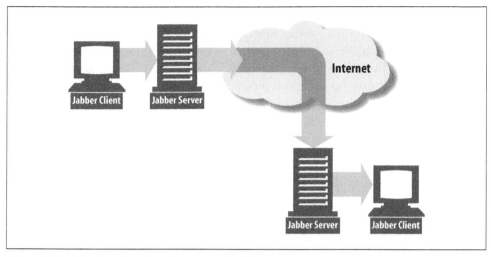

Figure P-1. The distributed architecture of Jabber

and presence information in XML structures and use plug-in services at the server, and what do you have? *A language- and platform-agnostic XML routing framework.*

Good grief, what a mouthful! This is why my response to "What is Jabber?" is usually just:

A really *great* technology!

IM System Features

This book assumes you have a basic knowledge of features commonly found in IM systems. In case you don't, here's a brief rundown of features relevant to what we'll be covering:

Presence

In many cases, there's not much point in sending a quick message to someone if they're not there. *Presence* is a term used in IM to describe the technique of exchanging information, in a controlled manner, about availability (or unavailability).

The idea is that when you connect to your IM server, your client sends an "I'm here" message that is relayed to your correspondents. It does the opposite when you disconnect. During the time you're connected, you can vary the information about your availability to reflect your immediate situation ("just popped out for coffee," "working on my resumé—don't disturb me!").

Buddy List™/roster

> Both terms (the former comes from the original IM systems, the latter from Jabber) refer to a list of correspondents with whom you regularly communicate and from whom you receive presence information. Depending on the IM system, the list may be stored on the client or on the server. Storing the list on the client has the (tenuous) advantage of being accessible when you're not connected to the server. Storing the list on the server means that you have a consistent roster content regardless of the client or workstation you happen to use—the list travels with you.

> Jabber stores the roster on the server.

Push and pull

> When you connect to an IM system, there may be information the client needs to retrieve—*pull*—from the server (the roster, for instance). This is under direct control of your client as it decides when to make the retrieval. During the course of the connection, you'll receive messages from your correspondents. You don't request these messages by making a *retrieve call* to the server, as you would with the Post Office Protocol (POP) or Internet Message Access Protocol (IMAP) to retrieve email messages from the mail server; they're *push*ed to you as they occur.

> In other words, you could say that the client must implement an event-based system, to listen out for and subsequently handle the incoming information, by displaying a pop-up window containing the chat message, for example.

> The push/pull system lends itself well to traffic other than IM traffic.

Client-server

> It almost goes without saying that, like other IM systems, Jabber has a client-server architecture. Clients and client libraries that implement the Jabber protocol, such as `Net::Jabber`, `Jabber::Connection`, `Jabberpy`, and `JabberBeans`, are available for many languages (here, for Perl, Python, and Java).

> With Jabber, it is especially relevant to stress that the "weight balance" in complexity terms, between the client and the server, comes down heavily on the server side. Not only does this mean that the complexity remains where it should be—on the server—but also makes the task of writing clients easier and the resulting software lighter.

Multiple versus single server

> We've already mentioned that the Jabber architecture does not dictate a single, centralized server. Not only does this mean that organizations can implement their own private system, but also that developers are free to install their own server and develop new plug-in services in addition to the IM bridges already available.

What's Inside

This book is not particularly about IM per se. Nor is it about the bridges to other IM systems. It's about the essence, the ideas, and the potential behind that concept and reality called *Jabber*.

You will learn about the Jabber protocol and how to use Jabber's technology to implement not only IM-based solutions but also solutions that don't involve inane chat. You'll learn how to install and configure your own Jabber server. You will discover more about the features of Jabber that give it its propensity for being an ideal messaging glue for many communication solutions; all of Jabber's technology features—the building blocks and the protocol itself—are explained; and you'll get to know how Jabber can be implemented in a variety of situations—some involving IM, others not—through a series of application and problem scenarios with fully working code examples, or *recipes*, in Perl, Python, and Java.

Here's a brief overview of what's in the book:

Part I, Getting Started with Jabber
> The first part of this book provides you with an introduction to Jabber; you'll learn about its features, why it's more than an IM system, and how to install and configure a Jabber server of your own.

Chapter 1, Introducing Jabber
> We begin with an imaginary conversation with human and application participants that shows how Jabber provides the supporting messaging "plasma." A short script shows how simple it is to make use of Jabber's power.

Chapter 2, Inside Jabber
> We take a look at some of the features—the nature—of Jabber, to understand why Jabber is more than just an IM system. The features introduced in this chapter will be revisited as core building material for our recipes in Part II.

Chapter 3, Intalling the Jabber Server
> Here you'll learn how to retrieve and install the Jabber server and perform minimal configuration, enough to be able to fire it up and use it as a basis for the recipes in Part II. Some troubleshooting and monitoring tips are also included.

Chapter 4, Server Architecture and Configuration
> Once we have our Jabber server installed and running, we take a closer look at how the server has been designed. We focus on the server makeup and the different ways it can be deployed. A detailed tour of the standard configuration is also in this chapter.

Part II, Putting Jabber's Concepts to Work

The second part of this book provides detailed information about the Jabber protocol and a series of recipes—practical solutions to everyday problems—deployed in Jabber. The recipes use various Jabber features as a way of illustrating parts of the protocol.

Chapter 5, Jabber Technology Basics

We take a detailed look at what Jabber looks like under the hood. We examine Jabber IDs (JIDs), resource and priority, and XML streams, and the basic Jabber building blocks (<message/>, <iq/>, and <presence/>).

Chapter 6, Jabber Namespaces

This chapter focuses on the standard Jabber namespaces used to accomplish IM-related and other tasks. A description for each one is given in turn.

Chapter 7, User Registration and Authorization

This chapter looks at the steps needed to create and authenticate with a user and examines the different types of authentication. We also build a utility to create users in order to generate users for our recipes.

Chapter 8, Using Messages and Presence

This chapter looks at some simple examples of Jabber deployment using basic features of message and presence, including presence subscription.

Chapter 9, Groupchat, Components, and Event Models

Extending the themes introduced in Chapter 8, we look at how messages can be extended to carry custom and compartmentalized data and how to write a 'bot that serves in a conference room. Furthermore, we look at how components are defined and written and examine how different event models can coexist with Jabber's.

Chapter 10, Pointers for Further Development

This chapter shows diverse applications of Jabber, from building an online address book using Jabber as infrastructure, through exchanging XML-RPC-encoded requests and responses over Jabber, to extending the client scope of SAP's R/3 business software.

Software Used in This Book

The recipes in this book come in varying flavors, some in Perl, some in Python, and some in Java. These examples—to a greater or lesser degree—make use of prewritten libraries that provide at least the basic services needed to connect to a Jabber server and exchange data with it. Here's a summary of the versions of the languages used in this book, along with those libraries that are used, what features they offer, and where they're available. In addition, references to all of these libraries can be found on the Jabber development web site, *http://dev.jabber.org*. The installation instructions for the libraries can be found in the library packages themselves.

Java

The Java recipes in this book are written in Java 2 (J2SE—the Java 2 Standard Edition), specifically with the 1.3.1 version of the Java Development Kit (JDK).

JabberBeans is the name of the Java library for Jabber used in this book. It offers comprehensive coverage of the features needed to write programs that interact with Jabber servers: connection, authentication, and the management of Jabber elements passed between your script and the Jabber server.

The JabberBeans library can be obtained from *http://jabberbeans.org*. The version used in this book is 0.9.0-pre4.

Perl

The recipes have been built and tested with Perl 5.6.0, although earlier and later versions of release 5 will probably work just fine.

Two libraries are available for programming Jabber solutions in Perl. Both come in the form of installable modules and are of the object-oriented persuasion.

Net::Jabber

> This module is available on the Comprehensive Perl Archive Network (CPAN), at *http://www.cpan.org*. Net::Jabber provides basic functionality for connecting to and interacting with a Jabber server, in addition to a host of higher-level features for manipulating all of the Jabber elements and making use of standard and custom namespaces.

> It relies upon a companion module XML::Stream, also available on CPAN, that provides the underlying mechanisms for creating connections to a Jabber server, as well as sending, receiving, and interpreting (parsing) the fragments of conversation between your script and that Jabber server.

> The version of Net::Jabber used in this book is 1.0022. The corresponding version of XML::Stream used is 1.12.

Jabber::Connection

> The Jabber::Connection module is available on CPAN and provides the same basic features Net::Jabber does, albeit in a more "RISC" (Reduced Instruction Set Computing) way. While it provides similar functionality for connecting to

and exchanging data with a Jabber server, it offers, via a companion module called `Jabber::NodeFactory`, a lower-level API—similar to that in the Jabber server itself—for constructing and manipulating the Jabber elements. There are no high-level features; instead, you build your own using the building blocks that the module provides.

The version of `Jabber::Connection` used in this book is 0.02.

Python

The Python examples have been written with Python 2.0.

`Jabberpy` is the name of the Python Jabber library used in the Python recipes in this book. As with Perl's `Net::Jabber` library set, `Jabberpy` provides its feature set from two separate libraries—`jabber`, which provides connectivity, authorization, and callback functions such as `Net::Jabber` and `Jabber::Connection`, and `xml-stream`, which provides the basic connectivity and parsing functions such as `Net::Jabber`'s companion `XML::Stream`.

The `Jabberpy` libraries are available from its project site, at *http://sourceforge.net/projects/jabberpy*.

The version of `Jabberpy` used in this book is 0.2.

Where to Go for More Information

There are plenty of places out there on the Net to find out more about Jabber in general and programming with Jabber in particular. The main web site at *jabber.org* has a number of faces:

http://www.jabber.org
> This is the main entry point for all things Jabber. Start here if you want to find out about Jabber generally.

http://dev.jabber.org
> You can find information on development efforts, both core and peripheral, here. There are lists of projects, discussion forums, and news items concerning new developments and initiatives in the Jabber world.

http://docs.jabber.org
> This is the place to go to if you want more information on Jabber's technology and protocols. It has a range of documents contributed by various members of the Jabber community.

In addition to the sites listed here, there are other resources available online for learning more about Jabber. Countless mailing lists, linked to from the *http://dev.jabber.org* page, cover subjects ranging from identity and profiles to security. The two main mailing lists are *jadmin* and *jdev*, covering administrative and development subjects, respectively. All newcomers are welcome!

Finally, there's a Jabber conference room called *jdev* where many of the Jabber developers hang out. Just point your Jabber client at *conference.jabber.org* and drop by for a chat.

Conventions Used in This Book

The following typographical conventions are used in this book:

Bold

> Used for commands, programs, and options. All terms shown in bold are typed literally.

Italic

> Used to show arguments and variables that should be replaced with user-supplied values. Italic is also used to indicate new terms, URLs, filenames, file extensions, directories, and to highlight comments in examples.

`Constant Width`

> Used to show the contents of files or the output from commands.

`Constant Width Bold`

> Used in examples and tables to show commands or other text that should be typed literally by the user.

`Constant Width Italic`

> Used in examples and tables to show text that should be replaced with user-supplied values.

These signify a tip, suggestion, or general note.

These indicate a warning or caution.

How to Contact Us

We have tested and verified the information in this book to the best of our ability, but you may find that features have changed (or even that we have made mistakes!). Please let us know about any errors you find, as well as your suggestions for future editions, by writing:

> O'Reilly & Associates, Inc.
> 1005 Gravenstein Highway North
> Sebastopol, CA 95472
> (800) 998-9938 (in the U.S. or Canada)
> (707) 829-0515 (international/local)
> (707) 829-0104 (fax)

You can also send us messages electronically. To be put on the mailing list or to request a catalog, send email to:

> *info@oreilly.com*

To ask technical questions or comment on the book, send email to:

> *bookquestions@oreilly.com*

We have a web site for the book, where we'll list examples, errata, and any plans for future editions. The site also includes a link to a forum where you can discuss the book with the author and other readers. You can access this site at:

> *http://www.oreilly.com/catalog/jabber*

For more information about this book and others, see the O'Reilly web site:

> *http://www.oreilly.com.*

Acknowledgments

To my dearest wife, Sabine, who patiently and quietly took on all the demands of daily life for us during this project, allowing me to devote myself to researching and writing. To my son, Joseph, who knew I was writing a book but also knew that helping him build train tracks, drawing, and going on bicycle rides was always good tonic for a mind congested with XML.

To my grandpa, Harold Lomax, who never tired of reading through what I had written to check and correct grammar and punctuation.

To my editor, Chuck Toporek, who not only has great taste in music, but also has a sense of humor to match his infinite patience. Chuck taught me a great deal about writing and thinking, without me even realizing it was happening. Also, many thanks to David Chu, Chuck's editorial assistant. It's easy to miss the people behind the scenes when they do such a good job, so thanks for pushing my SGML files through when they needed to be checked by Tools, for coordinating the technical review, and for assisting Chuck to make this book happen. Thanks also to Lenny Muellner, my SGML guru. He helped me with my SGML queries and always kept me on the right track.

To the reviewers of this book, Jens Alfke, Matthew Allum, Michael Bauer, Piers Harding, Jeremie Miller, and Thomas Muldowney, who gave up a lot of their time to provide me with wonderful feedback and great insights. Special thanks go to Piers, the best technical debating partner you could wish for; trying to keep up with him mentally is what drives me on.

And, of course, where would this book be without the very thing that captured my imagination and held it all this time? Thanks to Jeremie and the team of core Jabber developers for building something so fascinating. Thanks also to the Jabber developer community at large, a more friendly bunch of diverse people one could hardly hope to meet.

Finally, thanks to Tim O'Reilly and all of O'Reilly & Associates, Inc., for seeing Jabber for what it really is and for having confidence in me to write about it.

I

Getting Started with Jabber

This part of this book provides you with an introduction to Jabber; you'll learn about its features, why it's more than an IM system, and how to install and configure a Jabber server of your own.

Chapters in this part include:

- Chapter 1, *Introducing Jabber*
- Chapter 2, *Inside Jabber*
- Chapter 3, *Installing the Jabber Server*
- Chapter 4, *Server Architecture and Configuration*

1

Introducing Jabber

This book is about Jabber: the technology, protocols, ideas, and the philosophy. Jabber is about connecting things (users, applications, and so on) in an all-pervasive message plasma that flows between clients and servers, carrying content, structure, and conversations.

The spirit of Jabber lies in its openness, its extensibility, and its lean but generic nature. That it finds itself in the midst of all that technology that will provide the backdrop to the dawn of the next-generation Internet is no accident. Web services, peer-to-peer, XML encapsulation, presence, identity, distributed computing—these are all phrases that describe key intiatives and developments that lie at the core of the coming transition, and Jabber can and does play a central role.

This book will show you how Jabber works, what makes it tick, and how to bend and shape it into solutions that join applications and users together. This first part is a guide to Jabber's technology and server. Part II is an examination of Jabber's building blocks and a series of scenarios and scripts we call "recipes," to show you how to deploy Jabber in a variety of situations.

Imaginary Jabber Conversation

To help you better understand what transpires during a Jabber-based conversation, this section presents a conversation between two friends, Jim and John, and two "assistant" applications at their respective places of work.

Jim and John work at two different companies. Both of them invest in the stock market, and they use a Jabber-based service to check and monitor prices, to buy and sell shares, and to manage their portfolios. John's company also has a work-flow assistant that monitors incoming email and coordinates work items between colleagues.

Jim is notified that John is available:

```
<presence from='john@company-b.com/Desk'
    to='jim@company-a.com/home'>
  <status>Online</status>
  <priority>2</priority>
</presence>
```

Jim sends a quick chat message to John:

```
<message type='chat' from='jim@company-a.com/home'
    to='john@company-b.com'>
  <thread>01</thread>
  <body>Hey John, have you seen the latest story on Megacorp earnings?</body>
</message>
```

John responds:

```
<message type='chat' to='jim@company-a.com/home'
    from='john@company-b.com/Desk'>
  <thread>01</thread>
  <body>No, where is it?</body>
</message>
```

Jim sends John the URL:

```
<message type='chat' from='jim@company-a.com/home'
    to='john@company-b.com/Desk'>
  <thread>01</thread>
  <body>Here's the link</body>
  <x xmlns='jabber:x:oob'>
    <url>http://www.megacorp.co.uk/earnings3q.html</url>
    <desc>Third Quarter Earnings for Megacorp</desc>
  </x>
</message>
```

John receives an alert about the price of ACME Holdings (ACMH) falling below a threshold he previously set:

```
<message to='john@company-b.com' from='alert@stocks.company-b.com'>
  <subject>ACMH Fallen below 250p</subject>
  <body>ACME Holdings price 248p as at 10:20am today</body>
</message>
```

He checks the price of Megacorp stock (MEGC) by sending an empty message to the shares assistant application:

```
<message type='chat' to='MEGC@stocks.company-b.com'
    from='john@company-b.com/Desk'>
  <thread>T20</thread>
</message>
```

In reply, the shares assistant application sends the required information:

```
<message type='chat' from='MEGC@stocks.company-b.com'
    to='john@company-b.com/Desk'>
  <thread>T20</thread>
  <subject>MEGC Current Price</subject>
  <body>
    Megacorp price 1287p at 10:25am today
  </body>
</message>
```

John likes the price and decides to buy 100 more shares:

```
<message type='chat' to='MEGC@stocks.company-b.com'
    from='john@company-b.com/Desk'>
  <thread>T20</thread>
  <body>Buy 100 at 1287 now</body>
</message>
```

He sends a message to Jim telling him of his new investment. Jim checks his own portfolio:

```
<iq type='get' to='portfolio.company-a.com'
    id='port_01'
    from='jim@company-a.com/home'>
  <query xmlns='jabber:iq:browse'&sol;>
</iq>
```

He sees that he already holds 1200 Megacorp shares and decides against buying any more:

```
<iq type='result' from='portfolio.company-a.com'
    id='port_01'
    to='jim@company-a.com/home'>
  <portfolio xmlns='jabber:iq:browse' type='personal'
      jid='jim@portfolio.company-a.com'>
    <stock type='standard' name='Megacorp'
        jid='MEGC@portfolio.company-a.com' holding='1200'&sol;>
    <stock type='standard' name='ACME Holdings'
        jid='ACMH@portfolio.company-a.com' holding='500'&sol;>
  </portfolio>
</iq>
```

The workflow assistant application, *workassist*, sends John a notice that he's received an important email:

```
<message from='workassist@company-b.com'
    to='john@company-b.com/Desk'>
  <subject>New mail from: Alastair B</subject>
  <body>
      You have a new mail waiting; details are as follows:
      Subject: Incident last week
      From:   Alastair B
  </body>
</message>
```

He also receives an invite to a meeting:

```
<message from='joanne@company-b.com/laptop'
    to='john@company-b.com/Desk'>
  <body>
    Hey John, you're supposed to be helping us decide where to hold
    this year's Christmas party!
  </body>
  <x xmlns='jabber:x:conference' jid='room2@meeting.company-b.com'&sol;>
</message>
```

John decides to leave the mail until later and join the rest of his colleagues in the meeting room.

There's a great deal we see in this imaginary, but not unlikely, conversation:

- There are human and application participants involved in this conversation; Jabber makes no distinction nor holds any prejudice against either participant type.

- XML is used effectively to segregate the conversational chunks (Jim's opening gambit, John's response, the price alert, and so on) and to structure and identify data within those chunks (the URL for the earnings story, the portfolio information, the conference room invitation).

- Conversational strands are kept in context by use of a `<thread&sol;>` tag, so that Jim and John's clients have a chance to present what's said in an appropriate way.

- Each conversational chunk is a `<presence&sol;>`, `<message&sol;>`, or `<iq&sol;>` tag—the three Jabber building blocks on which everything is based.

- The conversation takes place across two Jabber servers; one server is located at `company-a.com` and the other at `company-b.com`.

- The conversation flow is asynchronous, in the sense that out of nowhere, a message alerting John to a stock price fall below threshold appears seemingly in the middle of John's conversation with Jim, as does the message from the *workassist* agent.

- All Jabber entities, human or otherwise, are identified by Jabber IDs such as John's (`john@company-a.com`) or the stock alert mechanism (`alert@stocks.company-b.com`).

- `company-b.com`'s stock system is multifaceted. As well as being able to send (and receive settings for) threshold alerts through the `alert@stocks.company-b.com` address, it can also interact using different identities to reflect the context of the stock being discussed. For example, `MEGC@stocks.company-b.com` represents the Megacorp (MEGC) stock.

In fact, this stock system is a Jabber component, a single entity that takes on each of the stock guises in the conversation.

The most common misconception about Jabber is that it's solely for instant messaging—Jabber is more than a bridge to other IM systems or a set of protocols. Instant messaging is just one of countless ways that an XML-based messaging technology such as Jabber's can be applied. Jabber is an extensible client/server architecture that *routes* XML data between clients and *services*, which plug into Jabber servers as *components*. The original and core set of components provide the IM features (and supporting services) that were briefly described in the Preface.

The XML structures that make up the Jabber protocol fall into three categories, each represented by a uniquely named top-level tag (also referred to as an *element*). These tags don't necessarily carry human-generated IM message content; as long as the resulting XML is well-formed, anything goes. Furthermore, the Jabber protocol design makes use of an XML feature that allows total flexibility of extension: *namespaces*.

To prevent flooding of the server with large amounts of data, there are mechanisms in place to "throttle" heavy connections. These mechanisms can be configured in the server configuration, described in the section "The io Section."

Bearing this in mind, it's clear that Jabber can be deployed to provide solutions far beyond the IM space as well as within it.

A Simple Script

Before moving on, let's have a look at how simple it is to interact with Jabber. Example 1-1 shows a simple Perl script that connects to a Jabber server, authenticates, checks who's online, and sends those people a reminder message. It uses the `Net::Jabber` library, which provides a high-level API to many Jabber-related functions such as handling the connection to the server (this is via another library that `Net::Jabber` uses—`XML::Stream`), authentication, events, and all the mechanisms to parse and create Jabber traffic.

Example 1-1. A simple Jabber script

```
#!/usr/bin/perl

use Net::Jabber qw(Client);
use strict;

# List of addressees for our reminder
```

Example 1-1. A simple Jabber script (continued)

```perl
our @addressees;

# What we want to send
my  $reminder = $ARGV[0] or die "No reminder!";

# Connect to our Jabber server
my $c= Net::Jabber::Client->new();
$c->Connect('hostname' => 'yak',
            'port'     => 5222);

# Authenticate
$c->AuthSend('username' => 'reminder',
             'password' => 'secret',
             'resource' => 'reminder');

# Set handler to deal with presence packets
# that might (will) be pushed to us (we're
# not interested in any other type of packet)
$c->SetCallBacks('presence' => \&handle_presence);

# Send out our own presence, and run an
# event loop for up to 5 seconds to
# catch any packets pushed to us
$c->PresenceSend();
$c->Process(5);

# Create a new message with our reminder text
my $m = Net::Jabber::Message->new();
$m->SetBody($reminder);

# Send the message to each of the addressees collected
# in the handle_presence() subroutine
foreach my $jid (@addressees) {

  $m->SetTo($jid);
  $c->Send($m);

}

# Disconnect from the Jabber server and exit
$c->Disconnect;
exit(0);


# Deal with presence packets
sub handle_presence {

  my ($sid, $presence) = @_;

  # Get the presence
  my $show = $presence->GetShow() || 'online';
```

Example 1-1. A simple Jabber script (continued)

```
# If the user is around, add to addressee list
push @addressees, $presence->GetFrom()
   if $show eq 'online' or $show eq 'chat';

}
```

The script is fairly self-explanatory. For now, we'll leave the script's description to the comments embedded within it; by the end of the book, you should have a good understanding of how to put together complete applications and utilities using Jabber libraries in Perl, Python, and Java.

2

Inside Jabber

Jabber has a number of features that are fundamental to its design philosophy. This *design philosophy* outlines Jabber as a much more flexible and generic solution to the original problem of connecting to disparate IM systems. These *features* give Jabber the potential to exist and act in the P2P (peer-to-peer, or person-to-person), A2P (application-to-person), A2A (application-to-application)—or in fact, any of the three-letter acronyms (TLAs) that have a 2 in the middle—spaces that have conversation at their core.

Understanding Jabber's features is fundamental to seeing how it fits into the bigger picture. In this chapter, we explore these features and discover in what ways Jabber is *not* simply a cross-IM mechanism. In this exploration, you'll get a feel for how capable Jabber is of being integrated into "conversational solutions."

In Part II of the book, we'll revisit each of these features and see how they can be used in many different programming scenarios.

XML-Based

Arguments abound for and against XML in the arena of data representation. XML is suited extremely well to Jabber, which is suited extremely well to XML. There are many reasons for this.

The alternatives for representing data in Jabber are binary and ASCII text. Binary? Well, perhaps binary data is more space efficient, but where is that advantage in the general scheme of things these days? Near the bottom of my list, anyway, especially as it's always at the cost of readability. ASCII? Well, yes, of course, ASCII is human readable, but since Jabber data flow consists of a series of conversational chunks—independent constructions in their own right—we need some sort of boundary mechanism to separate these chunks. XML affords us a very nice way of packaging individual chunks of data and giving their content meaning and context. These individual chunks of information have structure too, and this structure doesn't require any fixed-length madness either; XML allows the chunks, or fragments, to bend and stretch as required, while still retaining their meaning.

This flexibility also comes in the form of extensibility. It's straightforward to add distinct "extensions" to a fragment in a way that does not compromise the integrity of that fragment and provides a structure to the extension added.

So why reinvent the wheel when there are tools that can be taken off the shelf to parse the data? There are many tried and tested XML libraries out there, and to be able to receive (from the parser) the Jabber data in a native format of your choice is a definite advantage.

Some of these arguments, concerning XML fragments and extensibility, will become clearer in Chapter 5. Until then, consider that Jabber makes good use of an XML feature called *namespaces*. (See *http://www.w3.org/TR/REC-xml-names* for more details.) Namespaces are used in XML to segregate, or qualify, individual chunks of data, giving tags a reference to which they belong. What the reference is, in many ways, is of secondary importance; the point is the delineation that allows us to manage content within an XML fragment that is logically divided into subfragments. Consider Example 2-1, which shows a section of the imaginary conversation from Chapter 1.

Example 2-1. Qualifying a fragment extension with a namespace

```
<message type='chat' from='jim@company-a.com/home'
    to='john@company-b.com/Desk'>
  <thread>01</thread>
  <body>Here's the link</body>
  <x xmlns='jabber:x:oob'>
    <url>http://www.megacorp.co.uk/earnings3q.html</url>
    <desc>Third Quarter Earnings for Megacorp</desc>
  </x>
</message>
```

The main part of the fragment is the `<message/>` element containing the `<thread/>` and `<body/>` tags. The `<message/>` element is the "carrier" part of the fragment:

```
    <message type='chat' from='jim@company-a.com/home'
        to='john@company-b.com/Desk'>
      <thread>01</thread>
      <body>Here's the link</body>
    </message>
```

But the fragment has been embellished by an extension that is qualified by the
jabber:x:oob namespace:

```
<x xmlns='jabber:x:oob'>
  <url>http://www.megacorp.co.uk/earnings3q.html</url>
  <desc>Third Quarter Earnings for Megacorp</desc>
</x>
```

The xmlns attribute of the <x/> tag declares that the tag and any children of
that tag belong to, or are qualified by, the jabber:x:oob namespace. This namespace is used in Jabber to carry information about out-of-band (OOB) data: data
that moves *outside* of the main client-server-client pathways. When a client sends
a file directly to another client without sending that file via the server, this is said
to be "out of band." See the section "jabber:x:oob" in Chapter 6 for more details.
This namespace is different from the namespace that qualifies the carrier <mes-
sage/> tag and the other elements, <presence/> and <iq/>, that
appear at the same level. The namespace that qualifies *these* tags is not explicitly
specified as an xmlns attribute; rather, it is declared when the XML stream is established. It is over this XML stream that these elements flow. See Chapter 5 for more
details on XML streams and namespaces.

The general point is that the jabber:x:oob-qualified extension is recognizable as
an extension (by us and, more importantly, by the XML parser) and can be dealt
with appropriately—we are likely to want to handle the information contained in
the extension separately from the rest of the message.

So Jabber uses the extensible XML format to contain and carry data between endpoints.

"*XML between endpoints*"? That sounds rather generic to me—not something that's
limited to providing an IM experience. Indeed, that's the whole idea.

"XML Router" is a moniker often used to describe Jabber by people who have
made this logical leap. Remove the IM mantle, and underneath we find a system,
an architecture, capable of being deployed to exchange and distribute all manner
of XML-encoded data.

Asynchronous Nature

The exchange and distribution of information in real-world scenarios requires
more than a synchronous (sequenced) request/response framework. In IM, people
originate chat messages in a spontaneous and unpredictable manner (especially if
there's beer involved). In a loose network of independent applications, messages
originate on a similar "random" event basis. This asynchronous activity requires a
design equally asynchronous in nature—and that is what Jabber has.

To allow for the generation, and more importantly the receipt, of messages in an asynchronous fashion, Jabber's programming model for client and server alike is an *event-based* one. An event-based programming model is nothing to be afraid of. In simple terms, it's just a loop that iterates either doing nothing in particular or doing something regularly (like checking for user input and acting upon it if required) while waiting for something (an event) to happen. In Jabber's case, it will be the receipt of an XML fragment. Depending on what type of fragment it is, a *handler* will be called to deal with that fragment. We saw a simple example of this in the Perl script in Chapter 1.

In all but the simplest deployment examples of Jabber, the event model pervades. We will see the model in action in Part II. And while we've reduced the receipt of chat messages to a rather dry and generic event idea, let's also look at some concepts that often go hand in hand with event-based messaging systems.

Store and Forward

Depending on circumstances, if you send a message to someone who's not currently connected, that message will be held and passed to the recipient when he does connect.

Likewise, in the wider context of *application-to-application* (A2A) or *application-to-person* (A2P) messaging, this store-and-forward concept is often useful in non-time-critical situations, such as a centralized logging mechanism in which the log-writing component might be temporarily unavailable or a workflow scenario in which an application passes a message to a supervisor for approval (in this case, the message would be similar to an email).

Queuing

Indeed, in the case of the recipient being offline and messages being handled by a store-and-forward mechanism, or simply where the recipient cannot handle the messages as fast as they arrive, the nature of the XML stream in which these message fragments are transmitted (see Chapter 5 for details) means that the messages are naturally *queued*, to be handled in the order that they arrive.

Message Receipt

In many cases, it's not much use sending a message to an application and having it queued or stored offline, without knowing whether the recipient actually did (eventually) receive and handle it. Jabber supports the concept of *message receipt*, whereby the sender can request an acknowledgment of receipt from the recipient. This request is sent along with the message itself. Support for message receipt exists in the form of a namespace—`jabber:x:event`—which is described in the section "jabber:x:event" in Chapter 6.

Messaging

We've been using the term "message" in quite a general sense, to represent data passing from one Jabber entity to another. In fact, as we'll see in Chapter 5, there are different sorts of messages—and each one has a certain role within the whole context of the Jabber protocol. They are sometimes referred to as *elements*, and there are three of them: `<message&sol;>`, `<iq&sol;>`, and `<presence&sol;>`.

Actually, there are four, but the fourth, `<route&sol;>`, is only used in the server to route messages between the various components. More details on `<route&sol;>` can be found in the section "The service components" in Chapter 4.

The `<message&sol;>` element has five types—*normal, chat, groupchat, headline,* and *error*. The `<iq&sol;>` and `<presence&sol;>` elements also have types to distinguish and describe their usage and context. The `<iq&sol;>` element has the types *get, set, result,* and *error,* while the `<presence&sol;>` element has, among others, the types *available* and *unavailable*. Details can be seen in Table 2-1.

Furthermore, we already know that these elements can be extended using namespaces. Each element and type, and each of the pre-defined namespaces (those that begin `jabber:`) have been designed with specific scenarios in mind. An example of a *headline* `<message&sol;>` element containing an extension qualified by a pre-defined namespace is shown in Example 2-3.

Table 2-1. Jabber elements and types

Element	Tag	Types
Message	`<message>`	*normal, chat, groupchat, headline, error*
IQ	`<iq>`	*get, set, result, error*
Presence	`<presence>`	*available, unavailable, subscribe, subscribed, unsubscribe, unsubscribed, error*

There's a certain amount of consideration to be given in this respect when designing our messaging solutions and applications; how should we employ the basic message types, and do we need to create our own custom extensions qualified by our own namespaces?

For the most part, the answers to these questions will depend on what sort of solution needs to be developed; however, it is also important to consider what support is already available off the shelf in the form of Jabber clients. This is especially the case if the application is A2P or P2A. These Jabber clients provide varying levels of features supporting the different elements and types. For example, WinJab (for Win32 platforms) and Jarl (cross-platform, written in Perl/Tk) both support the *headline* type <message/> and can display URL information, which typically comes attached to the message in a jabber:x:oob-qualified extension, in a useful way. If you're writing a news headline alert mechanism, for example, you may want to consider aiming development with a target of WinJab or Jarl in mind; the alternative is to develop your custom news headline viewer client. (Indeed, we do just that, in the section "A Simple Headline Viewer" in Chapter 9.)

Payload Carrier

Earlier in this chapter we saw how a basic message was embellished with a structured and parseable "attachment" in the form of a jabber:x:oob-qualified <x/> tag and its child tags:

```
<x xmlns='jabber:x:oob'>
  <url>http://www.megacorp.co.uk/earnings3q.html</url>
  <desc>Third Quarter Earnings for Megacorp</desc>
</x>
```

How does this actually work in practice? Well, partly by requirement, partly by convention:

- All three of the elements, <message/>, <iq/>, and <presence/>, can carry these attachments.

- These attachments usually serve one of two purposes:

- To bring primary (or secondary) meaning to the element that contains it.

- To act as the driving force behind the element, such as that the element really exists only to carry the attachment.

This distinction is rather subtle, so let's look at a couple of examples.

Example 2-2 shows an attachment in the jabber:x:delay namespace. This works like a timestamp and in this context indicates when that presence element appeared—in other words, from what time Jim started on his break.

Example 2-2. A jabber:x:delay extension adds meaning to a <presence/> element

```
<presence from='jim@company-a.com/home' to='john@company-b.com'>
  <show>chat</show>
  <status>having a break from work</status>
  <priority>1</priority>
  <x xmlns='jabber:x:delay' from='jim@company-a.com/home'
     stamp='20010611T13:13:04'&sol;>
</presence>
```

Example 2-3 shows us a message element containing a URL attachment. In this case, the element serves to carry the URL attachment; there is not really any other purpose to it. Delivering the <message type='headline'/> carrier without the payload wouldn't make much sense.

Example 2-3. A jabber:x:oob extension is the heart of a <message/> element

```
<message type='headline' from='jabbercentral@news.company-b.com'
         to='john@company-b.com'>
  <x xmlns='jabber:x:oob'>
    <url>http://www.jabbercentral.com/news/view.php?news_id='989358658</url>
    <desc>
      Tomorrow, May 9th, a meeting regarding the Jabber Foundation
      will be held.
    </desc>
  </x>
</message>
```

The outermost tag of each attachment, by convention, is either <x/> or <query/> although they can be any valid XML tag name. The Jabber namespaces that are used to qualify these <x/> and <query/> attachments follow a convention, beginning with jabber:x: for those qualifying the <x/> attachments, and jabber:iq: for those qualifying the <query/> attachments.

The <x/> tag is used as a generic extension mechanism to add information to any of the Jabber elements, and <query/> is used to extend the <iq/> element.

The standard namespaces used in Jabber to qualify the <x/> and <query/> attachments are listed in Chapter 6. But we're not restricted to just those namespaces; we're free to build attachments qualified by custom namespaces, if we think that what we want to achieve isn't covered by anything out of the box. In this situation, there are two things to note:

- The namespaces cannot begin jabber:.
- The receiving recipient of the extended element must be able to appropriately interpret the attachments.

Request/Response

The HyperText Transfer Protocol (HTTP) is a great example of a simple, effective request/response model used on the Web to request and respond to requests for HTML and other content. Example 2-4 shows a typical HTTP request/response pairing, where GET /home.html HTTP/1.0 is the request, and everything else, starting with HTTP/1.1 200 OK, is the response.

Example 2-4. A typical HTTP request/response

```
GET /home.html HTTP/1.0

HTTP/1.1 200 OK
Date: Mon, 11 Jun 2001 13:43:13 GMT
Server: Apache/1.3.12 (Unix) mod_perl/1.24
Last-Modified: Fri, 09 Jun 2000 13:47:56 GMT
ETag: "8a69-6a-3940f58c"
Accept-Ranges: bytes
Content-Length: 306
Connection: close
Content-Type: text/html

<html>
<head>
...
```

It shows us the request verb GET and the specification of what to retrieve (the /home.html document), and it shows us what is returned in response.

While we've already seen that the Jabber protocol is asynchronous in nature, there is a similar request/response model available, too, which tends to the synchronous (i.e., first request, then response), although, unlike HTTP, the response is not guaranteed to *immediately* follow the request. Other unrelated Jabber fragments may be received in the stream in the time between request and response. This request/response model is called *Info/Query*, or IQ for short; the Jabber element employed in the implementation of this model is <iq/>.

This IQ model has many uses in providing Jabber's basic IM features. Figure 2-1 shows the element traffic in a typical IQ-based conversation.

Example 2-5, Example 2-6, and Example 2-7 show typical uses of the <iq/> element to effect the IQ request/response model.

Example 2-5. A simple client version query via the IQ model

```
SEND: <iq type='get' from='jim@company-a.com/home'
          to='mark@company-a.com/Laptop-7' id='v1'>
        <query xmlns='jabber:iq:version'&sol;>
      </iq>
```

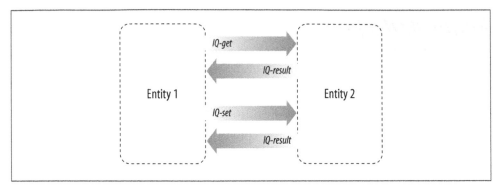

Figure 2-1. Element traffic in an IQ-based conversation

Example 2-5. A simple client version query via the IQ model (continued)

```
RECV: <iq type='result' to='jim@company-a.com/home'
        from='mark@company-a.com/Laptop-7' id='v1'>
      <query xmlns='jabber:iq:version'>
        <name>Jabber Instant Messenger</name>
        <version>1.7.0.14</version>
        <os>95 4.10</os>
      </query>
    </iq>
```

In Example 2-5 we see that the equivalent of HTTP's GET verb is the type='get' attribute of the <iq/> element and that the equivalent of *what* to get (/home.html) is our namespace specification in the <query/> tag.

Example 2-6 shows a two-stage request/response model. First, a query is made, using the IQ-get type with an ID of reg1 (the id attribute), to discover which fields are required for user registration. Then, the actual user registration attempt is made with the IQ-set (ID reg2). In this second stage, we can see a link with HTTP's POST verb, whereby data is sent along with the request.*

Example 2-6. A multiple-phase IQ to register a user

```
SEND: <iq type='get' id='reg1'>
        <query xmlns='jabber:iq:register'&sol;>
      </iq>

RECV: <iq type='result' id='reg1'>
        <query xmlns='jabber:iq:register'>
          <instructions>Choose a name and pass to register.</instructions>
          <username&sol;>
          <password&sol;>
        </query>
      </iq>
```

---

* Data can also be sent with an HTTP GET request, but let's just not go there, for the sake of the comparison.

Example 2-6. A multiple-phase IQ to register a user (continued)

```
SEND: <iq type='set' id='reg2'>
        <query xmlns='jabber:iq:register'>
          <username>helen</username>
          <password>tr0y</password>
        </query>
      </iq>
```

```
RECV: <iq type='result' id='reg2'&sol;>
```

While HTTP is primarily a client/server protocol (although these words have less and less meaning in a peer-to-peer environment in which each participating entity can be both client and server), Example 2-5 shows that the IQ model can be used in a client-to-client (or server-to-server, or server-to-client, for that matter) context as well.

Example 2-7 shows how an IQ-based conversation can extend beyond the *get ... result* or *set ... result* model. It shows how the IQ model can be used to deliver results of a search request in stages.

Example 2-7. Staggered response from IQ-based search request

The search request:

```
SEND: <iq type='set' to='ldap.company-a.com' id='801'>
        <query xmlns='jabber:iq:search'>
          <group>Support</group>
        </query>
      </iq>
```

The first part of the response is the first record found:

```
RECV: <iq type='set' from='ldap.company-a.com'
          to='jim@company-a.com/home' id='801'>
        <query xmlns='jabber:iq:search'>
          <name>John Aston</name>
          <phone>4701</phone>
          <group>Support</group>
        </query>
      </iq>
```

The second record found:

```
RECV: <iq type='set' from='ldap.company-a.com'
          to='jim@company-a.com/home' id='801'>
        <query xmlns='jabber:iq:search'>
          <name>Katie Smith</name>
          <phone>4711</phone>
          <group>Support</group>
        </query>
      </iq>
```

The last record found:

```
RECV: <iq type='set' from='ldap.company-a.com'
         to='jim@company-a.com/home' id='801'>
      <query xmlns='jabber:iq:search'>
        <name>Jeremy Taylor</name>
        <phone>4702</phone>
        <group>Support</group>
      </query>
    </iq>
```

No more records have been found, and no more results are sent; instead, an "end marker," signified by the `type='result'` attribute, is sent:

```
RECV: <iq type='result' from='ldap.company-a.com'
         to='jim@company-a.com/home' id='801'>
      <query xmlns='jabber:iq:search'&sol;>
    </iq>
```

Because of the inherently asynchronous nature of Jabber, we need some way of matching the responses received with the original request. After all, if we were to fire off two requests almost simultaneously to ask for the local time on our server and on a client in New Zealand:

```
SEND: <iq type='get' from='jim@company-a.com/home'
         to='piers@company-a.com/emacs'>
      <query xmlns='jabber:iq:time'&sol;>
    <iq&sol;>

SEND: <iq type='get' from='jim@company-a.com/home'
         to='company-a.com'>
      <query xmlns='jabber:iq:time'&sol;>
    <iq&sol;>
```

we might find that the responses come back out of sequence (in our view), because of the comparative network distances over which the two conversations must travel. First this:

```
RECV: <iq type='result' to='jim@company-a.com/home'
         from='company-a.com'>
      <query xmlns='jabber:iq:time'&sol;>
        <utc>20010611T17:59:13</utc>
        <tz>CET</tz>
        <display>Mon Jun 11 19:59:13 2001</display>
      </query>
    </iq>
```

and then this:

```
RECV: <iq type='result' to='jim@company-a.com/home'
         from='piers@company-a.com/emacs'>
      <query xmlns='jabber:iq:time'&sol;>
        <utc>20010611T17:59:14</utc>
```

```
            <tz>UTC+12</tz>
            <display>Tue Jun 12 06:59:14 2001</display>
        </query>
    </iq>
```

That's the reason for the id attribute in the examples earlier in this section. Between a request and a response, any id attribute value in the <iq/> element is preserved, allowing the requester to match up <iq/> request/response pairs. Using the id attribute, we can piece together related fragments of individual conversations, which in this case were a pair of client time queries.

Component/Service Architecture

The original problem for Jabber to solve was to provide bridges to different IM systems; the upshot of the solution was a server design that is ultimately as flexible as the imagination allows. Each of the IM bridges, or *transports* as they are often called, is a pluggable component; the Jabber server architecture, examined in detail in Chapter 4, is a component-based architecture. The standard Jabber server distribution comes with the components required to provide IM services, data storage, and server-to-server communication, for example. Each component is separately configurable and is made known to the server through the inclusion of that configuration into the main configuration structure.*

Components, also known as *services*, can be, to a large extent, platform agnostic. There are different methods by which components can connect to and interact with the Jabber server. One of these methods uses low-level Jabber library functions (in C) to bind the component (built in the form of a shared library) to the server. The other methods use either standard I/O (STDIO) in a process-spawning mechanism or TCP sockets.

Both the former library load method and the STDIO method require that the component runs on the same host as the Jabber server itself; this isn't in fact as restrictive as it sounds. As you'll find out in Chapter 4, it is possible to run multiple "instances" of a Jabber server across different hosts, each instance containing one or more components, in much the same way as, say, an SAP R/3 system can exist as multiple instances, each instance running on a separate host and providing different services (dialog, update, enqueue, message, background, gateway, spool) according to configuration.

Would it surprise you to learn that the binding fluid that flows between the Jabber server and components (and ultimately, of course, between Jabber clients and components) is XML? Of course not. In fact, it's the same XML that flows between Jabber clients and servers. There are extra message types that flow inside the

---

* XML is indeed all-pervasive in Jabber; the configuration is also written using XML.

server and between the components, including `<route&sol;>`, `<xdb&sol;>`, and `<log&sol;>`. These message types are explained in Chapter 4.

The `<message&sol;>`, `<iq&sol;>`, and `<presence&sol;>` elements can all flow to and from components—how a component handles or generates these elements reflects the purpose of that component. As we saw in the imaginary conversation in Chapter 1, components can also be addressed in the same way that other Jabber entities can be addressed:

- As a whole, the JID is simply the name of the component, for example, `stocks.company-a.com`.

- Using individual "users" as if they existed as separate entities within that component, for example, `MEGC@stocks.company-a.com`.

A version of this imaginary conversation will become reality in Part II as we learn how to build our own components and attach them to the Jabber server.

Although components are addressed in the same way that clients are addressed, and the interaction is similar, there is one significant difference between writing or using a *client* (which could just as well be a stub connector for a service) and writing or using a *component*.

This difference is rooted in the Jabber server architecture and becomes clear when we consider the nature of how the components provide their services. Messages sent to a client entity that is not connected will be stored and forwarded to that entity the next time it connects and becomes available. This is because the client's connection is inherently hosted, or managed, by the standard component that provides IM services such as availability handling and message queuing. This is the Jabber Session Manager (JSM) component. All clients are handled this way and automatically partake of these features. All entities that connect over a stream with the `jabber:client` namespace are considered clients, and their XML-based interaction is handled by the JSM.

Because other components connected to the Jabber server are peer components to the JSM component, no availability or message queueing is available, as the JSM is designed to handle only client-connected entities. The components that connect as separate entities (i.e., those that aren't written as shared libraries) do so over a stream that is described by one of two namespaces, each beginning `jabber:component:`. See Chapter 4 and Chapter 5 for more details. To put it another way:

- Send a message to a client that's not connected, and it will get stored until that client connects and becomes available again.

- Send a message to a component that's not connected, and an error will occur.

From a philosophical standpoint, this is fair enough, as you're trying to address a (temporarily) nonexistent feature of the server. From a practical standpoint, this is not usually a problem unless you're in the habit of restarting your Jabber server to randomly connect or disconnect components.

Custom Clients

Earlier in this chapter, we discussed features of off-the-shelf clients such as WinJab and Jarl, clients that natively support the `<message type='headline'&sol;>` element. Considering this, in combination with the features we know Jabber posesses and the solution potential that these features offer in presenting a wider deployment vista than IM services, we come to an interesting conclusion:

> A Jabber client is a piece of software that implements as much of the Jabber protocol as required to get the job done.

What does this mean? WinJab supports a Jabber feature called *browsing* (see later in this chapter); Jarl supports connections to the server via an HTTP proxy. Some clients merely support a limited subset of Jabber as we know it; for example, the sjabber client supports only the conferencing features of Jabber. (As a somewhat biased observer, I would, of course, call this "extremely focused.")

Our definition of a Jabber client deliberately omits any mention of a user interface (let alone a GUI!). Indeed, human interaction in a Jabber solution is only an assumption formed from the hangover of the IM idea. Various efforts are underway to use Jabber as a transport for A2A messaging—the Jabber As Middleware (JAM) project is one such effort (at *http://mailman.jabber.org/listinfo/jamdev*); an extension to one of the Perl libraries for Jabber (`Jabber::Connection`) to carry XML-RPC–encoded messages also exists (*http://www.pipetree.com/jabber/jrpc/*), which is shown in the section "Jabber-RPC in Perl" in Chapter 10.

So, a Jabber client doesn't *need* to follow any particularly conventional model, except if you're developing an IM client, of course, and even then, flexibility and fitness for purpose are key. We will see this philosophy in action in Part II of the book, where we develop just enough Jabber client code to be able to connect to a server, authenticate, and deal with one-way alert-style messages. This is a key idea: you use as much, or as little, of what Jabber has to offer to build your solutions. This doesn't refer to the Jabber building blocks, but also to the existing software, in particular the clients. For example, if you wanted to develop a Jabber IM-based approval cycle workflow process, you could carry the approval data in a custom namespace-qualified message extension. In this case, you're going to have to build a custom client to interpret that extension. However, if you carry the approval data inside the body of a normal message, then you can more or less take your pick of ready-made clients. Furthermore, if you include URLs in the message body—which many graphical clients can render into an active link—you can easily bind in the power of existing web-based interactivity to complete the solution. We see an example of this in the section "Building an ERP Connection" in Chapter 10.

XML-RPC and SOAP

Realizing that if Jabber is an XML router that can carry XML-based custom payloads in synchronous and asynchronous modes, we can immediately start to imagine scenarios in which Jabber fits as a transport glue in other already established application domains.

The XML Remote Procedure Call (XML-RPC) specification and the Simple Object Access Protocol (SOAP) both formalize method calls and responses in XML. The XML-RPC specification describes the use of HTTP to carry those encoded calls and responses between endpoints, and SOAP can use HTTP too. What if we carry XML-RPC or SOAP payloads in Jabber? We immediately see the step-change increase in contextual richness; XML-RPC interactivity becomes part of a wider, all-encompassing conversation between applications and humans. Indeed, the breadth of that interactivity increases too; Jabber affords a network transparency across traditional firewalls and Network Address Translation (NAT) mechanisms that often defeat HTTP-based calls.

Traditional IM-based clients, applications using client stub libraries, and components can all make use of the power these technologies have to offer, without having to leave the comfort of their Jabber environment, which can serve as a messaging plasma between all sorts of entities and services.

We will look at embedding XML-RPC–encoded calls in Jabber messages in the section "XML-RPC over Jabber" in Chapter 10.

Browsing

The more pervasive Jabber becomes and the more it is used, the larger the world of entities grows. And therein lies the challenge. How can we identify, organize, and navigate these entities in any useful way? Within the relatively narrow world of IM, the entities that exist (the IM users) and the hierarchies and relationships that are formed between them (where the only hierarchies are in the form of user rosters) don't really present much of a problem; as all the entities are users, there's no classification problem, and there's no hierarchical navigation problem. But within a system that regards users, applications, and services as equals (the unifying concept of a JID is an especially powerful device here), we need to have some way of searching, traversing, discovering, and querying these entities that is consistent regardless of what those entities are. Enter *Jabber Browsing*.

Browsing was introduced in Version 1.4 of the Jabber server to solve some specific problems with service discovery: how clients found out about what services (say, what IM transports) were available from the Jabber server that they were connected to. The namespace that supported the original discovery mechanism (jabber:iq:agents) was found to be too restrictive and, more importantly, too specific. A more generic way of describing entities in the Jabber world was needed.

Browsing has since grown from that single problem space and can now be found in Jabber software everywhere. Want to find out what a user's client is capable of (so you can interact with it) or what it otherwise offers? Just browse to it. Want to find out what conference rooms currently exist on a particular conference service? Browse that service. Want to take a peek to see who's in one of the rooms? Navigate down one level to browse to the room (if this is permitted by that room).

There are four key elements that make browsing so flexible and so powerful:

Categorization

> Browsing follows the MIME model in defining categories and subcategories, but rather than *content* being categorized (text/plain, image/png, and so on), the categorization in browsing is of entities that can be browsed to. Categories are used to describe users, services, agents, conferencing mechanisms, applications, and so on. Within these categories, the subcategories are used to make finer distinctions (service/pager, conference/private, user/device, and so on).

Identification

> Every entity described in browsing is identifiable by a JID; the world is homogenized, so to speak. The JID is the key to browsing navigation as, when listed in a browse result as identification for an entity, that JID can be used as the target of the *next* browse request.

Hierarchy

> Browsing describes entities in the Jabber world. But the world isn't *flat*—it's hierarchical! Relationships between entities are easily established and described by placing browse information in hierarchies. These hierarchies, these relationships, are represented in XML. A typical browse response might contain descriptions of entities on one or two levels. These levels can be navigated simply by choosing the JID of the desired node and making a further browse request, creating an instant "drill-down" method to access information.

Discovery

> It might be that the only information you have about any particular entity is its JID. You've been passed the JID from someone else, or you've found it when browsing a hierarchy of relationships. Browsing to that entity allows you to find out more—to *discover* what features and services it supports, through a list of namespaces returned in response to that browse request.

So, Jabber entities can be classified, given identities, organized into hierarchies, and navigated. What takes place from there is really up to the imagination. But what *is* a Jabber entity? For the sake of argument, let's say it's anything that has a JID. Does having a JID presume having an IM user account with a Jabber server? Not necessarily, as we'll see. So as long as we assign a JID to something we wish to include in the Jabber world, most anything goes. In the section "Browsing LDAP" in Chapter 10, we build an LDAP "reflector" service that enables us to browse LDAP information from within our Jabber clients.

Browsing is a combination—a culmination even—of many of the Jabber features. Browsing is carried out in the context of the IQ request/response mechanism and uses a namespace-qualified payload to carry the data whose hierarchy is naturally expressed in XML. Browsing bridges, philosophically and technically, the distances between the Jabber and non-Jabber spaces.

3

Installing the Jabber Server

This chapter explains what you have to do to obtain, install, configure, and start up a Jabber server of your own with the minimum of fuss.

It's certainly possible to learn about the Jabber protocols and technology and develop solutions using someone else's Jabber server, but for real understanding and control, it's definitely worth setting up one of your own. By installing and configuring a Jabber server, you will gain a valuable insight into how it and its components work together. Understanding how components are controlled and configured allows us to build Jabber solutions in the context of the "big picture."

Installations of earlier versions (1.0, 1.2) of the Jabber server were often complex affairs, and while the installation process has become much more straightforward, some people still shrink back from installing and configuring their own. This chapter shows how straightforward it is.

If you already have a server set up, you might want to skip this chapter and go on to Chapter 4, where the configuration and system architecture are explained in more detail.

Although the Jabber development platform is Linux, the Jabber server will compile and run on many flavors of Unix, including FreeBSD, Solaris, AIX, and IRIX.* Versions of the C compiler and *make* utility from the GNU project (at *http://www.gnu.org*) are recommended if you don't already have them installed.

The examples shown in this and other chapters are taken from Linux platforms (various Slackware and Red Hat distributions with 2.2 and 2.4 kernel versions); consult your local documentation for equivalent commands on your Unix OS.

---

* In fact, the next patch level version of the Jabber server, 1.4.2, which is available already, has the modifications necessary for it to be compilable under Mac OS X.

The incarnation of the Jabber server at the time of writing is Version 1.4, more specifically 1.4.1. Version 1.4 represents a major advance in the server code and brings increases in performance and reliability over earlier versions. Jabber server Version 1.4.1 is the one we will obtain and install here, and this will be used as the server for the recipes in the rest of this book.

Downloading the Jabber Server

The Jabber server package can be obtained from the Jabber project site, *http://www.jabber.org*; the 1.4.1 version is available in the downloads area:

> *http://download.jabber.org/dists/1.4/final/jabber-1.4.1.tar.gz*

The tarball *jabber-1.4.1.tar.gz* contains everything that you need to get a Jabber server up and running.* Previous versions of the Jabber server came in multiple packages; it was necessary to separately obtain and install GNU's portable threads library (*pth*) and the asynchronous DNS package (*ADNS*), as well as obtaining and installing various Jabber-specific libraries such as *libxode*, *libjabber*, and *libetherx*. Now some of these libraries and packages have become obsolete as far as the Jabber server is concerned (*ADNS* and *libetherx*) and others have been combined into the main Jabber server tarball.

If you don't want to compile the server yourself, you can also download prebuilt binaries for some of the platforms already mentioned, from *http://download.jabber.org*.

Installing the Server

Once you have downloaded the Jabber server tarball, you need to unpack it, configure the build environment, and compile the server. The general idea is that the Jabber server will be compiled and run from wherever you decide to unpack it; that is, there is no separate "install" step.

For this reason, and because it's also often useful to be able to install and start up a different version of the Jabber server for testing and comparisons, create a generic *jabber* directory somewhere central but local, for example in */usr/local/*:

```
yak:/usr/local# mkdir jabber
```

The Jabber server does not need to be and should not be run as *root*; so create a new user *jabber* (group *jabber*) to be used as the Jabber server administrator and make that user the owner of the generic Jabber server directory:

---

* If you want the Jabber server to support SSL connections, you will need to have installed an SSL package; see the next chapter for more details.

```
yak:/usr/local# groupadd jabber
yak:/usr/local# useradd -g jabber -d /usr/local/jabber jabber
yak:/usr/local# passwd jabber
Changing password for jabber
Enter the new password (minimum of 5, maximum of 127 characters)
Please use a combination of upper and lower case letters and numbers.
New password: ********
Re-enter new password: ********
Password changed.
yak:/usr/local# chown jabber:jabber jabber
yak:/usr/local#
```

Once you've created the generic Jabber server directory, switch to the new Jabber server administration user *jabber*, unpack the tarball you downloaded, and enter the resulting directory:

```
yak:/usr/local# su - jabber
yak:~$ tar xzf jabber-1.4.1.tar.gz
yak:~$ cd jabber-1.4.1/
yak:~/jabber-1.4.1$
```

Running the Configure Server

Examining the contents of the *jabber-1.4.1* directory, we see the following files:

- *configure* (the configuration script)
- *jabber.xml* (the server configuration file)
- *Makefile* (for compiling the Jabber server)
- *README* (some basic instructions)
- *UPGRADE* (information on upgrading from an earlier server version)

as well as a number of directories that contain the source code.

The first step is to run the *configure* script:

```
yak:~/jabber-1.4.1$ ./configure
```

to determine your platform's compiler settings.

If you want SSL support in the Jabber server, run the script with the *--enable-ssl* switch:

```
yak:~/jabber-1.4.1$ ./configure --enable-ssl
```

If you specified the *--enable-ssl* switch, the *configure* script looks for your SSL installation and adds the appropriate compiler flags. If it doesn't find your SSL installation, it says so and your Jabber server is compiled *without* SSL support.

Next, it will try to determine whether you have *pth* installed and if so will use the *pth-config* command to glean the extra compiler options for building the Jabber server. *pth* is required, so if it *isn't* already installed, it will be set up within your current *jabber-1.4.1* directory tree (as *pth* is included in the *jabber-1.4.1.tar.gz* tarball) and the appropriate compiler options added.

If *pth* is set up during the course of running *configure*, you may see a message: "Now please type 'make' to compile. Good luck.", which comes at the end of the *pth* configure procedure; you can ignore this because there is only one *make* step, for the Jabber server, that must be carried out as we are merely preparing the *pth* build environment for binding into the Jabber Server build.

Finally, after extra platform-specific compiler settings are determined, a shell script to set the build environment variables is created with the name *platform-settings*. This is used in the next step.

Example 3-1 shows typical output from the *configure* script.

Example 3-1. Typical output from configure

```
Running Jabber Configure
========================

Getting pth settings...        Done.
Setting Build Parameters...    Done.
Generating Settings Script...  Done.

You may now type 'make' to build your new Jabber system.
```

Running make

Once the platform settings have been determined by the *configure* script, we are ready to build the Jabber server with *make*:

```
yak:~/jabber-1.4.1$ make
```

Example 3-2 shows abbreviated typical output from the *make* command.

Example 3-2. Typical output from make

```
Making all in pthsock
make[1]: Entering directory '/usr/local/jabber/jabber-1.4.1/pthsock'
gcc -g -Wall -fPIC -I. -I.. -I/usr/local/include -I../jabberd/   -c client.c -o
client.o
gcc -g -Wall -fPIC -I. -I.. -I/usr/local/include -I../jabberd/ -shared -o pthsoc
k_client.so client.o -L/usr/local/lib -lpth -ldl -lresolv
make[1]: Leaving directory '/usr/local/jabber/jabber-1.4.1/pthsock'
Making all in xdb_file
make[1]: Entering directory '/usr/local/jabber/jabber-1.4.1/xdb_file'
gcc -g -Wall -fPIC -I. -I.. -I/usr/local/include -I../jabberd   -c xdb_file.c -o
```

Example 3-2. Typical output from make (continued)

```
xdb_file.o

...

gcc -g -Wall -fPIC -I. -I.. -I/usr/local/include -DHOME="\"/usr/local/jabber/jab
ber-1.4.1\"" -DCONFIGXML="\"jabber.xml\"" -o jabberd config.o mio.o mio_raw.o mi
o_xml.o mio_ssl.o deliver.o heartbeat.o jabberd.o load.o xdb.o mtq.o static.o lo
g.o lib/expat.o lib/genhash.o lib/hashtable.o lib/jid.o lib/jpacket.o lib/jutil.
o lib/karma.o lib/pool.o lib/pproxy.o lib/rate.o lib/sha.o lib/snprintf.o lib/so
cket.o lib/str.o lib/xmlnode.o lib/xmlparse.o lib/xmlrole.o lib/xmltok.o lib/xst
ream.o lib/xhash.o base/base_connect.o base/base_dynamic.o base/base_exec.o base
/base_stdout.o base/base_accept.o base/base_file.o base/base_format.o base/base_
stderr.o base/base_to.o -Wl,--export-dynamic -L/usr/local/lib -lpth -ldl -lresol
v
make[2]: Leaving directory '/usr/local/jabber/jabber-1.4.1/jabberd'
make[1]: Leaving directory '/usr/local/jabber/jabber-1.4.1/jabberd'
make[1]: Entering directory '/usr/local/jabber/jabber-1.4.1'
make[1]: Nothing to be done for 'all-local'.
make[1]: Leaving directory '/usr/local/jabber/jabber-1.4.1'
```

Running from the Build Environment?

You may be wondering where the *make install* step is—there isn't one. The Jabber server is run from within its build environment. One of the reasons for this is that additional components, such as transports, which may be installed at any time after the basic server installation, must be compiled with reference to various Jabber server header file information. One of the simplest ways of making this happen is to have the source for those components unpacked in a subdirectory within the *jabber-1.4.1* directory tree, and at compilation time component-level references to header files at the Jabber server level can be made using relative directory names that point back up the directory hierarchy.

Configuring the Jabber Server

The nature and behavior of a Jabber server is controlled by the contents of a configuration file (with a default name of *jabber.xml*), which you will find in the *jabber-1.4.1* directory. As you can probably guess from the filename's extension, the configuration is formatted in XML, which offers a very powerful way of expressing the nature and features of your Jabber server and associated services and components.

Details on how to navigate, interpret, and edit this configuration file are given in Chapter 4; here we will just look at the basic settings that can be modified before you start up the Jabber server.

For an experimental Jabber server (such as for the purposes of this book), there isn't actually anything you *need* to change in the configuration. The out-of-the-box configuration settings are pretty much what we need in order to experiment with our recipes later in the book; nevertheless, let's look at some of the settings you may wish to change right now:

Server hostname

The <host/> parameter specifies the Jabber server's hostname. As delivered, the *jabber.xml* configuration has this set to *localhost*:

```
<host><jabberd:cmdline flag="h">localhost</jabberd:cmdline></host>
```

You can change this to the name of your server hostname; in the case of our examples, this would be *yak*.

The *localhost* setting occurs elsewhere in the configuration too—as a literal in the welcome message that is sent to users after a successful registration with the server. You may wish to replace this occurrence of *localhost*; furthermore, you will find other occurrences, but they are within sections of the configuration that are commented out in the standard delivered version of *jabber.xml* (specifically, administration JIDs and definitions for various add-on agents and transports; we will cover these in the next chapter).

One other place that *localhost* occurs is in the <update/> section, which is explained next.

Server software update notification mechanism

The Jabber server development team offers a facility for servers to check for updated versions of the Jabber server software. The facility is addressed with this configuration setting:

```
<update><jabberd:cmdline flag="h">localhost</jabberd:cmdline></update>
```

which causes a versioning module, *mod_version*, in the Jabber Session Manager (JSM), to send a <presence/> packet (which carries the server version—in our case, 1.4.1) from the server to the Jabber ID *jsm@update.jabber.org* when the Jabber server starts up.

If your server is purely internal, and/or behind a firewall, it makes no sense to have this facility switched on (you can check for updates to the server on the *http://www.jabber.org* web site) as the <presence/> packet will never reach its intended destination. You can comment it out like this:

```
<!--
<update><jabberd:cmdline flag="h">localhost</jabberd:cmdline></update>
-->
```

Automatic user directory update

The configuration as delivered contains a directive:

```
<vcard2jud&sol;>
```

which means that any vCard data—a vCard is a virtual "business card" containing contact information and so on—that is maintained by a Jabber client will be automatically passed on to the central user directory (the Jabber User Directory, or JUD), defined elsewhere in the *jabber.xml* as the one at *jabber.org, users.jabber.org.*

If you've commented out the update notification mechanism because you're not going to be able to (or want to) reach the servers at *jabber.org*, then you might as well comment this out to avoid error messages being sent to Jabber clients when vCard data is modified:

```
<!--
<vcard2jud&sol;>
-->
```

Alternatively, instead of commenting out the <vcard2jud/>, you could comment out the definition of the JUD service in the <browse/> section:

```
<!--
<service type="jud" jid="users.jabber.org" name="Jabber User Directory">
  <ns>jabber:iq:search</ns>
  <ns>jabber:iq:register</ns>
</service>
-->
```

because the mechanism looks in the <browse/> section for a reference to a JUD service; if there isn't one there, no vCard update will be sent.

Some Jabber clients such as Jabber Instant Messenger (JIM) require vCard information to be entered when registering for a new account, which means that an attempt to contact *users.jabber.org* would be made the first time a user connects.

You may have noticed that the values for each of these two settings (<host/> and <update/>) were wrapped in another tag:

```
<jabberd:cmdline flag="h">...</jabberd:cmdline>
```

This means that you can override the setting with a command-line switch (or "flag"), in this case *-h*. So, in fact, you don't even need to modify the *jabber.xml* configuration at all, if you specify your hostname when you start the server up (the welcome message will not be changed, of course).

Starting and Stopping the Jabber Server

At this stage, we have a Jabber server with enough basic configuration to be able to start it up and have it do something useful (like accept client connections). If you're curious about the rest of the configuration you encountered while editing the *jabber.xml* file, you can jump to Chapter 4. Otherwise, let's start it up!

Starting the Server

The basic invocation looks like this:

```
yak:~/jabber-1.4.1$ ./jabberd/jabberd
```

but if you haven't bothered to change *localhost* anywhere in the configuration (as described earlier), you can use the *-h* switch to specify the hostname:

```
yak:~/jabber-1.4.1$ ./jabberd/jabberd -h yak
```

As it stands, there's a directive in the standard *jabber.xml* configuration file that specifies that any server error messages are to be written out to STDERR:

```
<log id='elogger'>
  <host&sol;>
  <logtype&sol;>
  <format>%d: [%t] (%h): %s</format>
  <file>error.log</file>
  <stderr/>
</log>
```

So either comment the directive out:

```
<!--
  <stderr&sol;>
-->
```

Or redirect STDERR to */dev/null*:

```
yak:~/jabber-1.4.1$ ./jabberd/jabberd -h yak 2>/dev/null
```

You won't lose the error messages—as you can see they're also written to the *error.log* file.

Assuming you wish to free up the terminal session after starting the server, you can send it to the background:

```
yak:~/jabber-1.4.1$ ./jabberd/jabberd -h yak 2>/dev/null &
```

Connecting a Client

Once the server is started, you're ready to start up a client and make a connection. The thing to remember at this point, when specifying which server to connect to, is to use the same hostname as you specified in the <host/> part of the configuration, described earlier in the section "Configuring the Jabber Server."

If your client supports the <alias/> mechanism, described in the section "Custom Configuration" in Chapter 4, this may not be necessary.

Stopping the Server

To stop the server, just kill the processes, and it will shut down:

```
yak:~/jabber-1.4.1$ killall jabberd
```

or:

```
yak:~/jabber-1.4.1$ kill `cat jabber.pid`
```

jabberd Command-Line Switches

We've seen the *-h* switch to specify the host when starting the server up. There are other switches available on the command line, too; they are listed in Table 3-1.

Table 3-1. Command-line switches

Switch	Relating to	Description
-c	Alternate configuration	Use this to specify an alternative configuration file if you don't want to use *jabber.xml*.
-D	Debugging info	Specifying this switch will cause (a large amount of) debugging information to be sent to STDERR.
-h	Hostname	The hostname of the Jabber server.
-H	Home folder	Used to specify "home" folder or directory.
-s	Spool area	The directory where the Jabber server stores data via the *xdb_file* module.
-v	Show version	Reports Jabber server version and exits.

Table 3-1. Command-line switches (continued)

Switch	Relating to	Description
-V	Show version	Same as *-v*.
-Z	Debugging info	Limits the debugging information to certain "zones" (comma-separated).[a]

[a] The "zones" are the filenames that immediately follow the timestamp in the debug log records, for example, *xdb_file* or *deliver*. Specifying one or more zones will limit debug output to lines that pertain to those zones.

Starting the Jabber server with any unrecognized switches will cause it to show you a list of valid switches:

```
[yak: ~/jabber-1.4.1]$ ./jabberd/jabberd -badswitch
Usage:
jabberd &
 Optional Parameters:
  -c            configuration file
  -D            enable debug output
  -H            location of home folder
  -v            server version
  -V            server version
```

Yes, the list that it shows isn't complete. If the common switch *-h* were present in the list, we could almost consider the unlisted switches as undocumented, but it isn't present, so we won't.

Monitoring and Troubleshooting the Server

We've already seen a glimpse of the configuration relating to logging of messages in the previous section. As standard, the Jabber server configuration describes two types of logging record and a recipient file for each type:

Error logging

Error log records are written to *error.log* in the current directory, as determined thus:

```
<log id='elogger'>
  <host&sol;>
  <logtype&sol;>
  <format>%d: [%t] (%h): %s</format>
  <file>error.log</file>
  <stderr&sol;>
</log>
```

Statistical logging

Statistical log records used for tracking purposes are written to *record.log* in the current directory, as determined thus:

```
<log id='rlogger'>
  <host&sol;>
  <logtype>record</logtype>
  <format>%d %h %s</format>
  <file>record.log</file>
</log>
```

Log records of this type are written when a client connects to the server and when a client disconnects.

Furthermore, we can use the debugging switch (*-D*) when we start the server and have debugging and trace output written to STDERR.

If Your Server Doesn't Start

A number of likely candidates might have prevented your server from starting.

Bad XML configuration

It is not difficult to make errors (typographical or otherwise) in the server configuration. The first line of defense is to be careful when editing your *jabber.xml* file. After that, the Jabber server isn't going to be too forthcoming with information if you have broken the well-formedness of the XML:

```
yak:~/jabber-1.4.1$ ./jabberd/jabberd -h yak
Configuration parsing using jabber.xml failed
```

Help is at hand in the shape of Perl and the XML::Parser module, which is a wrapper around the XML parser, *expat*.

Providing you have Perl and the XML::Parser module installed, you can get *expat* to give you a clue where the XML is broken:

```
yak:~/jabber-1.4.1$ perl -MXML::Parser
    -e 'XML::Parser->new->parsefile("jabber.xml", ErrorContext => 3)'

not well-formed (invalid token) at line 47, column 35, byte 1750:
    be on one line, the server doesn't like it otherwise! :)
    -->

    <host><jabberd:cmdline flag="h"yak</jabberd:cmdline></host>
==================================^

    &lt;!--
    This is the custom configuration section for the
 at /usr/local/lib/perl5/site_perl/5.6.0/i586-linux/XML/Parser.pm line 185
yak:~/jabber-1.4.1$
```

This shows us exactly where the problem is.* In this case, the close-tag symbol (>) had been inadvertently removed when replacing *localhost* with *yak*.

No XML Is Bad XML!

If you don't use the *-c* switch to specify which configuration file to use, the standard *jabber.xml* is used. If that file can't be found, you get *exactly the same error* as if your XML was not well-formed. You've been warned!

Unable to listen on port(s)

Taking the standard *jabber.xml* configuration, the Jabber server tries to bind to and listen on two ports: 5222 (for client connections) and 5269 (for server-to-server connections). If other processes are listening to these ports, then the Jabber server can't start and you'll see something like this in the *error log*:

```
20010407T12:11:06: [alert] (-internal): io_select unable to listen
    on 5222 [(null)]
20010406T12:11:06: [alert] (-internal): io_select unable to listen
    on 5269 [(null)]
```

If this is the case, use the *netstat* command to check the status of the ports:

```
yak:~/jabber-1.4.1$ netstat -an | grep -E '5222|5269'
tcp        0        0 0.0.0.0:5269            0.0.0.0:*              LISTEN
tcp        0        0 0.0.0.0:5222            0.0.0.0:*              LISTEN
```

If you see entries like this, it means that processes have been bound to these ports on *all* IP addresses.† For example, if 0.0.0.0:5222 is being listened to then you may have another instance of a Jabber server already running.

On some BSD systems, you cannot bind to the "default" null address; the same error messages will be issued as if the ports were already bound. In the standard *jabber.xml* configuration file, a bind to the null address is specified for each port as standard; you must change this and specify an explicit IP address for each of the ports in the configuration. That is, instead of:

```
<ip port="5222"&sol;>
```

do something like this:

```
<ip port="5222">127.0.0.1</ip>
```

---

* Better highlighting of problems in parsing the configuration file is available in Version 1.4.2 of the server. You're told where the configuration is broken or if there were problems opening the file.

† This "all" relates to the (null) shown in the unable-to-listen error messages shown earlier.

4

Server Architecture and Configuration

If you followed Chapter 3 through, you should now have a Jabber server of your own up and running. If you also made the configuration changes described there, you may be curious to find out about the other 99 percent of the configuration file contents—what it does, what sort of structure (if any) exists, and how you might modify the configuration to suit your own requirements.

On the other hand, if you want to press on with learning about the the protocol and looking at the recipes, you can safely skip this chapter right now and jump to Chapter 5. Whenever you want detail on specific server configuration, you can come back here at any time. Indeed, we'll be referring to parts of this chapter throughout the rest of the book.

Despite the initially daunting and seemingly random nature of the *jabber.xml* file contents, there *is* a structure to the configuration. This chapter will take you through that structure, explaining how all the pieces fit together and describing what those pieces do. In order to understand the configuration structure, we examine the nature of the server architecture itself. This architecture is reflected in that structure, and if we are to understand the latter, it helps to understand the former.

Indeed, in order to take the best advantage of what Jabber has to offer in terms of being a basis for many a messaging solution, it's important to understand how the server works and how you as a programmer fit in. Jabber programming solutions can exist at different levels within the Jabber architecture; understanding this architecture can help you make better decisions about what needs to be done to build a solution.

So in this chapter, we'll take a look at the Jabber server architecture and follow that by an in-depth tour of the server configuration in *jabber.xml*. Finally, we'll have a look at some of the server "constellation" possibilities—how you can organize parts of the server to run over different hosts and how you can make the server host multiple virtual server identities.

An Overview of the Server Architecture

In order to understand the configuration directives and how they work, it is necessary to take a step back and look at what the Jabber server really is.

jabberd and Components

The Jabber server is a daemon, *jabberd*, that manages the flow of data between various components that collectively make up the *Jabber service*. There are different components, each of which performs different kinds of tasks, and there is a basic set of components that is required for a simple Jabber server such as the one we configured and installed in Chapter 3.

The following list shows what the basic Jabber components are and what services they provide. It's worth considering the original and most well-known application of Jabber—instant messaging—and a Jabber design feature (distributed server architecture) to put this list into context and make better sense of it.

Session Management
  We need to be able to manage users' sessions while they're connected to the server. The component that does this is called the Jabber Session Manager (JSM), and it provides IM features such as message store and forward and roster management, as well as session management.

Client (to Server) Connections
  This is the component that manages the connections between clients and the server. It is known internally as c2s.

Server (to Server) Connections
  If there's a requirement to send a message from a user on one Jabber server to a user on another Jabber server, we need a way for the servers to connect to each other. This component establishes and manages server-to-server connections and is known internally as s2s.

Logging
  As in any server system, the ability to log events (error messages, notices, alerts, and so on) is essential. The logging component allows us do this.

Data Storage

There will be some server-side storage requirements, for example, to hold user authentication information and data such as last connect time (not to mention storage of rosters, personal details, and private data). The Data Storage component does this for us. It is known internally as the xdb component. xdb stands for "XML Database."

Hostname Resolution

Last but not least, we may need some way to resolve names of hosts that the Jabber server doesn't recognize as "local," as in the Server (to Server) connection context. This component is known internally as dnsrv.

Component Types

The relationship between *jabberd* and the components is shown in Figure 4-1. These components are the engines that serve and process XML messages, providing their services, and *jabberd* is the backbone along which messages are routed.

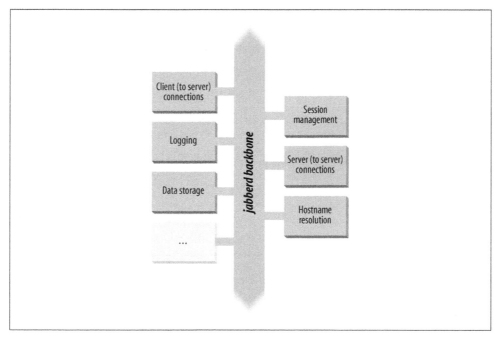

Figure 4-1. jabberd and the components

As seen in Figure 4-1, the *jabberd* backbone acts as the central artery or *hub*, managing the *peripheral* that are attached to it. The management of these components encompasses controlling and overseeing how they connect and coordinating the flow of data between them. Certain types of components receive only certain types of data. There is a distinction made between three different *types* of component:

- log
- xdb
- service

The different component types handle different types of data packets. Each packet is in the form of a distinct, fully formed XML fragment and is identified by the outermost element name in the XML fragment. This element name is matched up to a particular component type.

The log components

The log components handle `<log&sol;>` packets; you can guess that these are the components that provide *logging* services.

On receipt of a `<log&sol;>` data packet, a logging component will (hopefully) do something useful with it, like write it to a file or to STDERR.

The `<log&sol;>` packet shown in Example 4-1 is being used to record the successful connection and authentication of user *dj*, on *yak*, using the Jabber client JabberIM.

Example 4-1. A <log/> packet

```
<log type='record' from='dj@yak'>login ok 192.168.0.1 JabberIM</log>
```

The xdb components

The xdb components handle `<xdb&sol;>` packets. The `<xdb&sol;>` packets carry data and storage/retrieval requests to and from the xdb components that provide the Data Storage services.

On receipt of an `<xdb&sol;>` data packet, an xdb component will retrieve data from or write data to a storage system such as a collection of flat files or an RDBMS.

The `<xdb&sol;>` packet shown in Example 4-2 is carrying a request from the session manager to retrieve the preferences stored in a private namespace for the user *dj* (on Jabber server *yak* by the Jabber client JabberIM).

Example 4-2. An <xdb/> data packet

Example 4-2. An <xdb/> data packet (continued)

```
<xdb type='get' to='dj@yak' from='sessions' ns='jabberim:prefs' id='5'&sol;>
```

The service components

The service components handle the three main building blocks on which the Jabber functionality is based (the <message/>, <presence/>, and <iq/> packets). You can find out more about these building blocks in Chapter 5.

In addition, service components also handle the <route/> packets, which are used internally by *jabberd* to move packets around between components. For example, the Session Management component is the component that usually handles client authentication. It receives any incoming authorization requests received by and passed on from the Client (to Server) Connections component. However, it may be that the administrator has configured the Jabber server to use a different (third-party) component, developed by another group or company, to handle the authorizations. In this case, the request is *routed* from one component (Session Management) to another (the third-party authorization component).

So unlike the log and xdb components, which handle data packets whose element names match the component type (<log/> and <xdb/>), the service component is an umbrella component designed to handle packets with different element names (<iq/>, <message/>, <presence/>, and <route/>). Example 4-3 shows two typical service packets.

Example 4-3. Two service packets

```
<route to='dj@yak/81F2220' from='15@c2s/80EE868'>
  <presence>
    <status>Online</status>
  </presence>
</route>

<message id="jim_id_7" to="sabine@merlix" type="chat">
  <x xmlns="jabber:x:event">
    <composing&sol;>
  </x>
  <thread>3A378DF2B70F6A53A9C317CF526C6B7A</thread>
  <body>Hi there</body>
</message>
```

The first is an internal <route/> packet, which is carrying a <presence/> packet from the Client (to Server) Connections component, identified by the c2s part of the from attribute, to the Session Management component (where the session identifier 81F2220 is significant in the to attribute). This identifier is a hexadecimal representation of the user's session ID within the JSM, carried internally as a JID resource in the routing information. (The 15 is the identifier for the socket on which the pertinent client connection has been made.)

The second is a `<message&sol;>` packet, which contains the message itself ("Hi there"), as well as other information (a message event request and a conversation thread identifier; these are examined in detail in Part II of the book, particularly in Chapter 5 and Chapter 6).

It isn't necessarily the case, however, that all xdb components will handle all `<xdb&sol;>` packets or all service components will handle all `<presence&sol;>` packets. The configuration, described later in this chapter, determines how the components announce themselves and state their readiness to receive and handle packets.

Delivery trees

The phrase *delivery tree* is often used in Jabber terminology to signify a component or components that handle certain types of packet. The path a packet makes as it *descends* the collection of decision branches that guide it to the component or components that will handle it can be described in terms of such a delivery tree. For example, an xdb component type is sometimes referred to as an *xdb Delivery Tree*. Considering the division of components into different types that handle different packet types is perhaps easier to visualize as a tree, as shown in Figure 4-2.

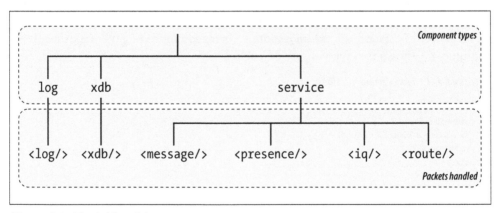

Figure 4-2. The Jabber delivery tree

The Jabber Delivery Tree shows which component types can handle what sorts of packets in the Jabber world. Furthermore, the log packets are distinguished by their log type (`error`, `notice`, or `record`), the xdb packets are distinguished by namespace, and all the packets are distinguished by hostname. This means, for example, multiple xdb components can be organized, and configured, to handle packets qualified by different namespaces, and intended for different hosts, while different log components can be set up to handle different log packet types. We'll see examples of this configuration later in this chapter.

Component Connection Methods

The notion of components providing distinct services and being coordinated by a central mechanism (*jabberd*) suggests a certain amount of independence and individuality—a plug-in architecture—and that is what Jabber is. The components described earlier, and others too, are "plugged in" to the Jabber backbone according to the requirements of the server.

The idea is that once you have the basic services like Session Management, Client (to Server) Connectivity, and Data Storage, you plug in whatever you need to suit the server's requirements. For example if you need conferencing facilities, you can plug in the Conferencing component. If you need user directory facilities, you can plug in the Jabber User Directory (JUD) component. If you need a bridge to the Yahoo! Instant Messaging system, you can plug in the Yahoo! Transport component. You can also connect to a component running on another Jabber server, as you'll see later in this chapter. You can write your own components and plug those in as well to provide services not available off the shelf. We build our own components in the section "An RSS News Agent" in Chapter 9 and the section "Browsing LDAP" in Chapter 10.

Components are *plugged in* to the Jabber server backbone in one of three ways:*

* Library load
* TCP sockets
* STDIO

Let's examine each one in turn.

Library load

The core components of a Jabber server providing IM services are connected using the library load method. This simply means that the component sources are compiled into shared object (*.so*) libraries and loaded into the main Jabber process (*jabberd*).

The components are written specially with the Jabber backbone in mind and contain standard component registration routines that utilize functions in the core Jabber libraries. These routines are used to bind the component relationship with *jabberd* (for example, there is a "heartbeat" mechanism through which the components are monitored) and to specify packet receipt requirements.

---

* The log component(s) are actually part of the backbone, and as such do not need to be plugged in.

Components receive packets based upon their type (log, xdb, or service) and upon a `<host&sol;>` configuration specification that we'll see later in this chapter and can also specify when in the delivery sequence they are to receive the packets

The library load method, which is also sometimes known as *dynamic load*, is represented in the configuration by the `<load&sol;>` tag, which wraps the library (or libraries) that should be loaded. Example 4-4 and Example 4-5 show how components can be plugged into the standard *jabber.xml* file using the library load. Example 4-4 shows the Client (to Server) Connections (c2s) component, which has been written and compiled as an *.so* library, being connected using the library load method.

Example 4-4. Loading of the c2s component with library load

```
<load>
  <pthsock_client>./pthsock/pthsock_client.so</pthsock_client>
</load>
```

In this example, we see the simpler form of the `<load&sol;>` tag. Inside the tag we have:

```
    <pthsock_client>./pthsock/pthsock_client.so</pthsock_client>
```

which specifies two things:

* Which library to load (in this case, *./pthsock/pthsock_client.so*).

* The name of the component registration routine that should be called by *jabberd* once the library has been loaded. The name of the routine is the name of the tag that wraps the library filename; in this example, it's `pthsock_client()`, denoted by the `<pthsock_client&sol;>` tag.

The second library load example, Example 4-5, shows multiple *.so* libraries being loaded when a component is connected—the form of the `<load&sol;>` tag is slightly more involved.

Example 4-5. Loading of the JSM component with library load

```
<load main="jsm">
  <jsm>./jsm/jsm.so</jsm>
  <mod_echo>./jsm/jsm.so</mod_echo>
  <mod_roster>./jsm/jsm.so</mod_roster>
  <mod_time>./jsm/jsm.so</mod_time>
  <mod_vcard>./jsm/jsm.so</mod_vcard>
  <mod_last>./jsm/jsm.so</mod_last>
  <mod_version>./jsm/jsm.so</mod_version>
  <mod_announce>./jsm/jsm.so</mod_announce>
```

Example 4-5. Loading of the JSM component with library load (continued)

```
  <mod_agents>./jsm/jsm.so</mod_agents>
  <mod_browse>./jsm/jsm.so</mod_browse>
  <mod_admin>./jsm/jsm.so</mod_admin>
  <mod_filter>./jsm/jsm.so</mod_filter>
  <mod_offline>./jsm/jsm.so</mod_offline>
  <mod_presence>./jsm/jsm.so</mod_presence>
  <mod_auth_plain>./jsm/jsm.so</mod_auth_plain>
  <mod_auth_digest>./jsm/jsm.so</mod_auth_digest>
  <mod_auth_0k>./jsm/jsm.so</mod_auth_0k>
  <mod_log>./jsm/jsm.so</mod_log>
  <mod_register>./jsm/jsm.so</mod_register>
  <mod_xml>./jsm/jsm.so</mod_xml>
</load>
```

Here we see multiple libraries being loaded to form the Session Management (the JSM) component, known as *jsm*.

This is what happens in a library load situation in which multiple libraries are involved:

1. *jabberd* loads the library in the tag that's pointed to by the `main` attribute of the `<load&sol;>` tag; in this example, it's the library *./jsm/jsm.so*:

   ```
   <jsm>./jsm/jsm.so</jsm>
   ```

2. *jabberd* then invokes the registration routine called `jsm()`, according to the name of the tag, as before.

3. The JSM loads the rest of the modules defined within the `<load&sol;>` tag (`mod_echo`, `mod_roster`, `mod_time`, and so on), invoking each module's registration routine (`mod_echo()`, `mod_roster()`, `mod_time()`, and so on) as they're loaded.

In case you're wondering, all the modules that belong to the JSM are actually compiled into a single *.so* library, which is why all the *.so* filename references in Example 4-5 are the same.

TCP sockets

Another method for connecting components to the Jabber backbone, in fact the most flexible method, uses a TCP sockets connection. This means that a component connected in this way can reside on the same or a different server than the one running *jabberd*. So instead of being loaded directly into the *jabberd* backbone, TCP sockets-connected components exist and run as separate entities and can be started and stopped independently.

It is possible to modify the contents of the configuration while the Jabber server is running and then send a hangup (HUP) signal to the *jabberd* processes. This causes the configuration file to be reread, allowing for any new library loaded components to be started and any old ones to be stopped. However, you may run into some problems with this; hopefully, these will be addressed in future bug fixes.

The configuration syntax for defining a connection point for a component that is going to connect to the backbone via TCP sockets looks like this:

```
<accept>
  <ip>127.0.0.1</ip>
  <port>9001</port>
  <secret>shhh</secret>
</accept>
```

The name for this TCP sockets tag configuration stanza is `<accept&sol;>`, reflecting the low-level socket library call `accept()` to which it directly relates. As `<load&sol;>` is to the library load method, so `<accept&sol;>` is to the TCP sockets method.

The `<accept&sol;>` tag usually has three child tags: `<ip&sol;>`, `<port&sol;>`, and `<secret&sol;>`. There is a fourth tag `<timeout&sol;>` with which you can control the heartbeat monitor of this component connection, which defaults to a value of 10 (seconds) if not explicitly specified (it seldom is).

To configure a TCP sockets stanza, specify an IP address (or hostname) and port to which the component will connect. If you want the socket to be network interface independent, you can write `<ip&sol;>` (an empty tag) to listen on your specified port on all (`INADDR_ANY`) IP addresses. The `<secret&sol;>` tag is used in the handshake when the component connects to the backbone, so that it can be authenticated.

More information on connecting components with `<accept&sol;>` can be found in Part II, in the section "The newsagent script as a component."

Standard I/O (STDIO)

The TCP sockets component connect method is used to connect an external component to the Jabber backbone via a socket connection through which streamed XML documents are exchanged. There is another way for components to connect and exchange XML document streams with the Jabber backbone—using the STDIO connection method.

While the TCP sockets method requires external components to be independently started and stopped, the STDIO method represents a mechanism whereby the

---

XML Streaming

Entity-to-entity connections in the Jabber world pass data to each other using *XML streams,* which is essentially the exchange of data in the form of XML fragments in "streaming" mode over a network connection.

During the lifetime of a connection between two entities, two complete XML documents will be passed between the entities. For example, if A connects to B, A will send B a document, fragment by fragment, and B will send A a document, fragment by fragment. The first things to be exchanged at the start of the connection are the document headers—the outermost (document root) XML tags. The root tag in each document is <stream/>.

XML namespaces are defined for the content of the XML documents to be exchanged. These namespaces represent what sort of entity connection is taking place. In the case of a Jabber-client-to-Jabber-server connection, the namespace is jabber:client. In the case of connections based on the TCP sockets connection method (using <accept/>), the namespace is jabber:component:accept.

To initiate a connection and conversation, the component will initiate the conversation by sending something like this to the Jabber server:

```
<?xml version="1.0"&quest;>
<stream:stream xmlns:stream="http://etherx.jabber.org/streams"
        xmlns="jabber:component:accept"
        to="component.name">
```

More detailed information on how XML streams work, and the namespaces that define them, can be found in Chapter 5.

---

jabberd process starts the external component itself. The component to start is specified inside an <exec/> tag. (Indeed the STDIO method is also known as the exec method.) Example 4-6 shows how the STDIO method is specified in the configuration.

Example 4-6. Invoking an external component with STDIO

```
<exec>/path/to/component.py –option a –option b</exec>
```

Here we see that the component is a Python program and is being passed some switches at startup.

So where's the socket connection in this method? There isn't one. The XML documents are exchanged through standard I/O (STDIO). The component writes XML fragments to STDOUT, and these are received on the Jabber backbone. The component receives XML fragments destined for it on STDIN, fragments that are written out from the Jabber backbone.

Just as a component connected using the TCP sockets method sends an opening document fragment, the component connected with this STDIO method sends an opening document fragment to initiate a connection and conversation:

```
<?xml version="1.0"&quest;>
<stream:stream xmlns:stream="http://etherx.jabber.org/streams"
               xmlns="jabber:component:exec"
               to="component.name">
```

Notice how the namespace that describes this type of conversation is:

```
jabber:component:exec
```

No secret is required in this case because it is assumed that the component can be trusted if it is specified in the configuration and execution is initiated by *jabberd* itself.

Server Configuration

At this stage, we should be fairly comfortable with the notion of a *jabberd* backbone and a set of components that combine to provide the features needed for a complete messaging system. We've looked at fragments of configuration in the previous section; now we'll examine the configuration directives in more detail.

It's not uncommon for people installing a Jabber server for the first time to be daunted (I was terrified!) by the contents of the *jabber.xml* configuration file. But really, for the most part, it's just a collection of component descriptions—what those components are, how they're connected, what packets they are to process, and what their individual configurations are.

Component Instances

There's a concept that encompasses Jabber's configuration approach that is taken from the object-oriented (OO) world—the concept of objects (and classes) and instances thereof. In Jabber server configuration, specifically the description of the components that are to make up a particular Jabber server, we talk about *instances* of components, not components directly.

In other words, a component is something generic that is written to provide a specific service or set of services; when we put that component to use in a Jabber server, we customize the characteristics of that component by specifying detailed configuration pertaining to how that component will *actually* work. We're creating an instance of that component.

A Typical Component Instance Description

Each component instance description follows the same approximate pattern:

- Declaration of the component type

- Identification (name) of the component

- Specification of the host filter for packet reception

- Definition of how the component is connected

- Custom configuration for the component

Of course, for any generalized rule, there's always an exception. The log component type, as mentioned earlier in this chapter, is defined slightly differently —while there is a host filter defined, a component connection definition is neither relevant nor present, and the custom configuration is limited; we'll see this later when we take a tour of the *jabber.xml*.

Let's have a closer look at the Client (to Server) Connections (c2s) component and how an instance of it is specified in the *jabber.xml*. We're going to use the one that is delivered in the Jabber 1.4.1 server distribution tarball. Example 4-7 shows how the c2s is defined. The definition includes details of how the component code is connected (using the library load method) and contains some custom configuration covering authentication timeout (the <authtime/> tag), traffic flow control (the <karma/> section), and what port c2s is to listen on (the <ip/> tag). We'll look at these custom configuration tags in detail later.

Example 4-7. The c2s instance configuration in jabber.xml

```
<service id="c2s">
  <load>
    <pthsock_client>./pthsock/pthsock_client.so</pthsock_client>
  </load>
  <pthcsock xmlns='jabber:config:pth-csock'>
    <authtime&sol;>
    <karma>
      <init>10</init>
      <max>10</max>
      <inc>1</inc>
      <dec>1</dec>
      <penalty>-6</penalty>
      <restore>10</restore>
    </karma>
    <ip port="5222"&sol;>
  </pthcsock>
</service>
```

Now let's arrange this instance configuration in diagram form. Figure 4-3 highlights the pattern we're expecting to see.

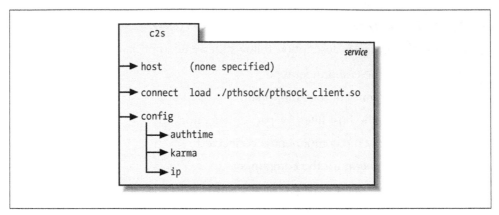

Figure 4-3. A diagram of the c2s instance configuration in jabber.xml

If we look at the component instance descriptions in this way, it's easy to understand how the configuration is put together, and we can begin to see the pattern
emerging. Taking each of the elements of the pattern in turn, let's examine what
the XML tells us.

Component type

The component type is *service*. We know that from looking at the outermost tag in
the XML:

```
<service id="c2s">
    . . .
</service>
```

So we know that this component instance will handle <message/>, <pres-
ence/>, <iq/>, and <route/> packets.

Identification

Each component instance must be uniquely identified within the space of a single
Jabber server (configuration). *jabberd* uses this identification to address the components and deliver packets to the right place. In this case, the identification of
this component instance is c2s; it's taken from the id attribute of the component
type tag:

```
<service id="c2s">
```

Host filter

The diagram shown in Figure 4-3 states "*none specified*" for the host specification—the host filter. So what happens now? Well, a host filter is usually one or
more <host/> tags containing hostnames to which the component instance

will "answer." It's a way of specifying that packets destined for a certain hostname will be received by that component instance.

However, if there are no <host/> tags specified as in this c2s example, then the component instance's identification is taken as the hostname specification. In other words, the <service id="c2s"> declaration in this example, coupled with the lack of any explicit <host/> tag, *implies* a host filter of c2s. This component instance wants to receive all packets with addresses that have c2s as the hostname. It's the equivalent of this host filter specification:

```
<host>c2s</host>
```

Packets and Hostnames

Each packet traveling within the Jabber universe has a destination address, in the form of a JID, which at the very least contains a hostname specification. This hostname can be a "real" hostname in the DNS sense, or it can be a Jabber-internal hostname, such as *jud.yak*.

When you send a packet, such as a <message/> element from your Jabber client, you're sending it as an XML fragment within the context of the jabber:client XML stream running between your client and the Jabber server. Apart from the initial activity to connect to the Jabber server's listening socket, there's no hostname resolution on the client's part—the hostname in the recipient address is just specified as a to attribute of the <message/> tag *inside* the stream.

Once a packet reaches the Jabber server, *jabberd* will try to deliver it to its destination. In doing so, it will check an internal list of component instances derived from the configuration file specified at startup and work out which instance (or instances; more than one may have registered to receive packets destined for the same hostname) should receive it.

If no matching instance can be found (i.e., there are no instances filtering for the hostname specified in the packet's destination address), then the Jabber server will assume it's for a nonlocal destination and attempt to resolve the hostname into an IP address using the Hostname Resolution component and send it on using the Server (to Server) Connections component.

The <host/> tag

There is some degree of flexibility in how you specify a hostname with the <host/> tag.

You can specify an absolute hostname like this:

```
<host>conference.yak</host>
```

You can specify more than one hostname like this:

```
<host>conference.yak</host>
<host>talk.yak</host>
```

For example, if this pair of <host/> tags appeared in an instance specification for the Conferencing component, you could address the component instance using either hostname.

You can use a wildcard character to specify all hostnames within a domain, for example:

```
<host>*.pipetree.com</host>
```

will match on all hosts with the domain name *pipetree.com*.

If you want the component instance to receive packets regardless of the hostname, you can specify an empty tag thus:

```
<host&sol;>
```

Component connection method

What is the component? Where do we load it from, or how does it connect to the Jabber backbone? There is a *component connection method* (see the section "Component Connection Methods," earlier in this chapter) specified in each of the component instance definitions. In our example of the c2s component instance, we see that the library load method is being used to load the *./pthsock/pthsock_client.so* shared object library and that the component registration routine pthsock_client() should be called once loading is complete:

```
<load>
  <pthsock_client>./pthsock/pthsock_client.so</pthsock_client>
</load>
```

Custom configuration

Once we've dealt with the (optional or implied) <host/> tag hostname filters and the component connection method, all that is left is the custom configuration for the component instance itself. This will look different for different components, but there is still a pattern that you can recognize. The configuration always appears in a "wrapper" tag that, like the <host/> and <load/> tags earlier, appears as an immediate child of the component type tag (that's <service/> in our c2s example):

```
<service id="c2s">
  ...
  <pthcsock xmlns='jabber:config:pth-csock'>
    ... [configuration here] ...
  </pthcsock>
</service>
```

There are two things to note here:

- The tag name (`<pthcsock&sol;>`)
- The namespace declaration (`xmlns='jabber:config:pth-csock'`)

The important part of the configuration wrapper tag is the namespace declaration:

```
xmlns="jabber:config:pth-csock"
```

because that is what the component actually uses to search for and retrieve the configuration.

As for the actual configuration elements for the c2s component instance that we see here (`<authtime&sol;>` and `<karma&sol;>`), we'll take a look at them in the section "Component Instance: c2s."

A Tour of jabber.xml

Now that we know what patterns to look out for, we're well prepared to dive into a *jabber.xml* configuration file. As an example, we'll take one that's very similar to the default *jabber.xml* installed with Version 1.4.1 of Jabber, but we'll plug in some extra components: the conferencing component and a local JUD component.

The entire configuration content, with comment lines dividing up each section, can be found in Appendix A. It's definitely worth turning briefly to have a look at the XML before continuing, to get a feel for how the configuration is laid out.

In order to deal with it without going crazy, let's break down the XML into manageable chunks. We'll build configuration diagrams for each of the top-level tags that are children of the root tag `<jabber&sol;>`. The opening tags for each of these chunks are as follows:

- `<service id="sessions">`
- `<xdb id="xdb">`
- `<service id="c2s">`
- `<log id="elogger">`
- `<log id="rlogger">`

- `<service id="dnsrv">`

- `<service id="jud">`

- `<service id="s2s">`

- `<service id="conf">`

- `<io>`

- `<pidfile>`

Most of these should be recognizable by now, but there are two chunks that we haven't come across yet: `<io>` and `<pidfile>`. These aren't components but nevertheless are part of the configuration for *jabberd*; there are also the two *Logging* component instances that we have not paid much attention to until now.

Figure 4-4 provides an overview of how the Jabber server is configured. It represents the contents, in diagram form, of the *jabber.xml* configuration file in Appendix A.

We can see that the bulk of the Jabber server functionality described here is in the form of components. Let's take each of these components—the chunks—one by one and have a closer look. The remainder of this chapter describes each of these chunks in detail.

Component Instance: sessions

The `sessions` component, described by the configuration XML shown in Example 4-8 and shown in diagram form in Figure 4-5, provides Session Management features for users (the word "users" is employed in the widest possible sense—a user could be a person or a script) connecting with Jabber clients, through XML streams identified with the `jabber:client` stream namespace.

The component also provides the services that give Jabber its IM capabilities— services such as roster management, message filtering, store-and-forward ("offline") message handling, and so on. These IM services are loaded individually as part of the component connection phase.

Example 4-8. jabber.xml configuration for the sessions component instance

```
<service id="sessions">

  <host><jabberd:cmdline flag="h">yak</jabberd:cmdline></host>

  <jsm xmlns="jabber:config:jsm">
    <filter>
        <default&sol;>
        <max_size>100</max_size>
        <allow>
```

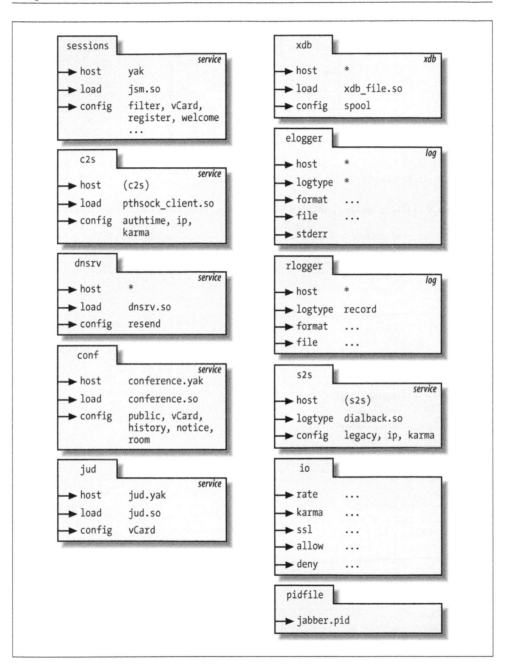

Figure 4-4. Configuration file in diagram form

Example 4-8. jabber.xml configuration for the sessions component instance (continued)

```
<conditions>
    <ns&sol;>
    <unavailable&sol;>
```

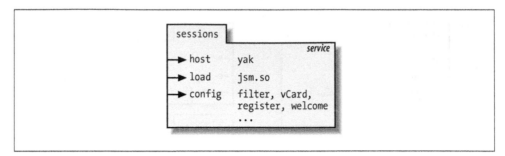

Figure 4-5. Diagram view of sessions component instance

Example 4-8. jabber.xml configuration for the sessions component instance (continued)

```
            <from&sol;>
            <resource&sol;>
            <subject&sol;>
            <body&sol;>
            <show&sol;>
            <type&sol;>
            <roster&sol;>
            <group&sol;>
        </conditions>
        <actions>
            <error&sol;>
            <offline&sol;>
            <forward&sol;>
            <reply&sol;>
            <continue&sol;>
            <settype&sol;>
        </actions>
    </allow>
</filter>
<vCard>
  <FN>Jabber Server on yak</FN>
  <DESC>A Jabber Server!</DESC>
  <URL>http://yak/</URL>
</vCard>
<register notify="yes">
  <instructions>Choose a userid and password to register.</instructions>
  <name&sol;>
  <email&sol;>
</register>
<welcome>
  <subject>Welcome!</subject>
  <body>Welcome to the Jabber server on yak</body>
</welcome>
<!--
<admin>
  <read>support@yak</read>
  <write>admin@yak</write>
  <reply>
    <subject>Auto Reply</subject>
```

Example 4-8. jabber.xml configuration for the sessions component instance (continued)

```
        <body>This is a special administrative address.</body>
      </reply>
    </admin>
    -->
    <update><jabberd:cmdline flag="h">yak</jabberd:cmdline></update>
    <vcard2jud&sol;>
    <browse>
      <service type="jud" jid="jud.yak" name="yak User Directory">
        <ns>jabber:iq:search</ns>
        <ns>jabber:iq:register</ns>
      </service>
      <conference type="public" jid="conference.yak" name="yak Conferencing"&sol;>
    </browse>

  </jsm>

  <load main="jsm">
    <jsm>./jsm/jsm.so</jsm>
    <mod_echo>./jsm/jsm.so</mod_echo>
    <mod_roster>./jsm/jsm.so</mod_roster>
    <mod_time>./jsm/jsm.so</mod_time>
    <mod_vcard>./jsm/jsm.so</mod_vcard>
    <mod_last>./jsm/jsm.so</mod_last>
    <mod_version>./jsm/jsm.so</mod_version>
    <mod_announce>./jsm/jsm.so</mod_announce>
    <mod_agents>./jsm/jsm.so</mod_agents>
    <mod_browse>./jsm/jsm.so</mod_browse>
    <mod_admin>./jsm/jsm.so</mod_admin>
    <mod_filter>./jsm/jsm.so</mod_filter>
    <mod_offline>./jsm/jsm.so</mod_offline>
    <mod_presence>./jsm/jsm.so</mod_presence>
    <mod_auth_plain>./jsm/jsm.so</mod_auth_plain>
    <mod_auth_digest>./jsm/jsm.so</mod_auth_digest>
    <mod_auth_0k>./jsm/jsm.so</mod_auth_0k>
    <mod_log>./jsm/jsm.so</mod_log>
    <mod_register>./jsm/jsm.so</mod_register>
    <mod_xml>./jsm/jsm.so</mod_xml>
  </load>

</service>
```

Component Type and Identification

The opening tag:

```
<service id="sessions">
```

identifies this component instance to the backbone as a *service* type component
and gives it a name (sessions) that can be used for internal addressing and to distinguish it from other component instances.

Host Filter

Assuming that our hostname isn't sessions, it's just as well that we have a
<host/> specification in this component instance description:

```
<host><jabberd:cmdline flag="h">yak</jabberd:cmdline></host>
```

which means that this Session Management component instance will handle packets addressed to the host yak.* The <jabberd:cmdline flag="h"> ... </jab-
berd:cmdline> wrapper around the hostname means that this value (yak) can be
overridden by specifying a switch *-h (hostname)* when *jabberd* is invoked, as is
described in Chapter 3. If you're sure you'll never want to override the hostname
setting here, this <jabberd:cmdline/> wrapper can safely be removed from the
configuration, to leave:

```
<host>yak</host>
```

As described earlier, you can specify more than one hostname; use a
<host> ... </host> pair for each one. This will effectively give you a virtual server
effect where Jabber will respond to different hostnames. This is useful in situations
such as deployment in an ISP where a single host serves multiple domains. The
client data stored on the server (such as rosters, offline messages, and so on) is
stored by the xdb component by hostname, so that a separate directory in the
spool area will be used for each specified hostname.

For example, if you specified the two hosts:

```
<host>a-domain.com</host>
<host>b-domain.com</host>
```

then the data for two users *jim@a-domain.com* and *john@b-domain.com* would
be stored as shown in Figure 4-6.

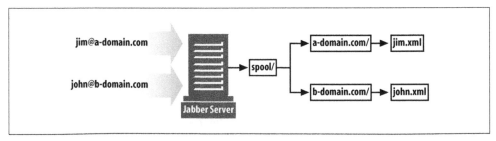

Figure 4-6. Storage of server-side user data by hostname

---

* Remember that if no <host/> is specified, the instance ID—in this case, sessions—is used
  instead.

Although specifying multiple hostnames for the Session Management component instance will effect a sort of virtual hosting, with separate data storage as described, the rest of the features of the component will be identical. For example, this means that the list of available services that the client can request—the *agent list* (old terminology) or *browse list* (new terminology)—and the session features such as roster management, administration functions, private data storage, and so on will be identical. If you want to offer different services for different hostnames from the same Jabber server, see the section "Managing the Configuration" later in this chapter.

You cannot use the catchall empty <host/> tag for the Session Management component—it needs to be given an explicit host identity in order to function.

Custom Configuration

In the section "A Typical Component Instance Description," we described the elements in this order: component type, component identification, host filter, connection method, custom configuration. Being XML, the configuration format is flexible enough to allow us to manage the ordering (but not the nesting!) of the configuration directives to suit our own layout purposes. In this instance, we come to the custom configuration—the connection method comes afterward.

The `sessions` component (i.e., the JSM) offers a lot of facilities, which means that in order to attach an instance of the JSM into our Jabber server we have a lot of configuring to do.

Our configuration wrapper tag for the JSM instance is:

```
<jsm xmlns="jabber:config:jsm">
```

The tag name `jsm` is simply representative of what the configuration pertains to; once loaded, the JSM will look for the configuration by the namespace identifier `jabber:config:jsm`. Within the wrapper tag, we have different sections that approximately relate to the different *services* that the JSM is going to provide.

Filter service

The message filter service, provided by the *mod_filter* module, allows clients to set up mechanisms that can control and manage incoming messages as they arrive at the recipient's Jabber server—before they start on the final leg of the journey to the recipient's client.

The service allows each user to maintain her own filter, which is a collection of *rules*. A rule is a combination of conditions and actions. For each incoming

---

Services and Modules

In the section "Component Connection Method," the method as to how these JSM services are loaded is described in detail. Generally, each service is represented by a tag that specifies a library to be loaded, and the tag name is what is used to refer to the service, thus giving it a name.

For example, the *echo* service that is used to test the Jabber server (any message sent to a special echo address servername/echo, which is the server name with a resource of echo, will be echoed back to the sender) is loaded in the <mod_echo/> tag and is referred to as the *mod_echo* module. So it can be said that the *mod_echo* module provides the echo *service*.

---

message, the message filter service kicks in and goes through the rules contained in the message recipient's filter one by one, checking the characteristics of the incoming message using the conditions defined in each rule. If one of the conditions matches, then the action or actions defined in that rule are carried out and the message filter service stops going through the rules—unless the action specified is continue—in which case the service goes on to the next rule. The continue action makes it possible to chain together a complex series of checks and actions.

Figure 4-7 shows what a filter definition looks like.

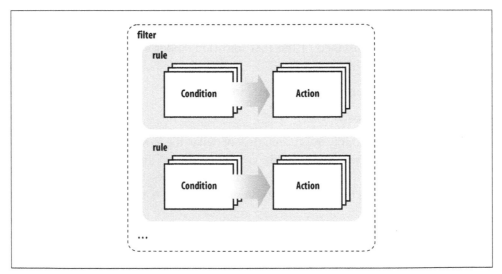

Figure 4-7. A message filter

Each user's filter is stored on the server using the xdb component (see later). What does a typical filter look like? Well, Example 4-9 shows a filter that contains two rules:

`holiday`

> Checks the message recipient's presence and sends a "holiday" notice back if the presence is set to Extended Away ("xa"—more detail on presence can be found in the section "The Presence Element") and forwards the incoming message to a colleague.

`custreply`

> Checks to see if the message is from someone who exists in certain groups in the recipient's roster and if so sends an auto-reply to that person, sets the incoming message type to `normal` (in case it was a `chat` message), and allows the message to reach its original intended destination.

> This could be useful in a customer support scenario in which the support representative could handle incoming queries in a queue of `normal` messages but have an auto reply sent out for each query telling the customer that her request will be dealt with shortly.

Example 4-9. A message filter with two rules

```
<query xmlns="jabber:iq:filter">
  <rule name="holiday">
    <show>xa</show>
    <reply>I'm on holiday - back on the 25th!</reply>
    <forward>mycolleague@yak</forward>
  </rule>
  <rule name="custreply">
    <group>CustomersNorth</group>
    <group>CustomersSouth</group>
    <reply>Thanks - an operator will attend to you shortly</reply>
    <continue&sol;>
  </rule>
</query>
```

Note that there is no nesting or grouping to distinguish conditions from actions. In the first rule, `holiday`, there is one condition (`<show&sol;>`) and two actions (`<reply&sol;>` and `<forward&sol;>`), and in the second rule, `custreply`, there are two conditions (two `<group&sol;>`'s) and two actions (`<reply&sol;>` and `<continue&sol;>`).

There are a few things to note from this example.

The action represented by the `<continue&sol;>` tag means that the filter checking will move on to the next rule that doesn't exist, meaning that the original message will still be delivered. No `<continue&sol;>` would have meant that the message would have been dropped (that is, it wouldn't have reached its final original destination), because when a rule matches the actions in that rule are carried out and a successful delivery is implied.

The conditions are OR'ed together—f *any* of the conditions in a rule match, then the rule has matched and all actions defined in the rule are carried out.

So with this in mind, let's examine the message filter service configuration:

```
<filter>
    <default&sol;>
    <max_size>100</max_size>
    <allow>
        <conditions>
            <ns&sol;>
            <unavailable&sol;>
            <from&sol;>
            <resource&sol;>
            <subject&sol;>
            <body&sol;>
            <show&sol;>
            <type&sol;>
            <roster&sol;>
            <group&sol;>
        </conditions>
        <actions>
            <error&sol;>
            <offline&sol;>
            <forward&sol;>
            <reply&sol;>
            <continue&sol;>
            <settype&sol;>
        </actions>
    </allow>
</filter>
```

Within the `<filter&sol;>` configuration wrapper, we have three children: `<default&sol;>`, `<maxsize&sol;>`, and `<allow&sol;>`.

`<default&sol;>`

The `<default&sol;>` tag allows the server administrator to specify default filter rules that will be applied for every user registered on that Jabber server. Specifying something like this:

```
<default>
  <rule name="server wide rule">
    <from>spammer@spamcity.com</from>
    <error>No spam please, we're British!</error>
  </rule>
</default>
```

will effectively filter out all messages from our friendly spammer.

The rules specified in the `<default&sol;>` tag will be *appended* to any personal rules the user may have defined himself. This is important when you consider the order in which the rules are tested and that, once a rule is matched, filter processing stops (unless the `<continue&sol;>` action is used).

`<maxsize&sol;>`

Filter rule matching is expensive. We don't want to let the user go overboard with filter rules—we can place an upper limit on the number of rules in a filter with the `<maxsize&sol;>` tag. (The default is large; anyone who can be bothered to create 100 rules deserves to have them all checked, in my opinion!)

`<allow&sol;>`

The `<allow&sol;>` tag specifies the `<conditions&sol;>` and `<actions&sol;>` that a user is allowed to use in building rules. Table 4-1 and Table 4-2 show the possible filter conditions and actions.

Table 4-1. Filter conditions

Condition	Example	Description
`<ns&sol;>`	`<ns>jabber:iq:version</ns>`	Matches the namespace (ns) of an `<iq&sol;>` packet[a]
`<unavailable&sol;>`	`<unavailable&sol;>`	Matches when the recipient's presence type is unavailable
`<from&sol;>`	`<from>spammer@spamcity.com</from>`	Matches the sender's Jabber ID (JID): *user@host*
`<resource&sol;>`	`<resource>Work</resource>`	Matches the recipient's resource
`<subject&sol;>`	`<subject>Work(!)</subject>`	Matches the message's subject (in the `<subject&sol;>` tag); must match exactly
`<body&sol;>`	`<body>Are you there?</body>`	Matches the message content (in the `<body&sol;>` tag); must match exactly
`<show&sol;>`	`<show>dnd</show>`	Matches the recipient's presence show—usually one of normal (the default), chat, away, xa (eXtended Away), or dnd (Do Not Disturb)
`<type&sol;>`	`<type>chat</type>`	Matches the type of the incoming message (in the type attribute) could be one of normal, chat, headline, or error
`<roster&sol;>`	`<roster&sol;>`	Matches whether the sender is in the recipient's roster
`<group&sol;>`	`<group>Friends</group>`	Matches whether the sender is in a particular group in the recipient's roster

[a] The name "message filter service" is slightly inaccurate as incoming `<iq&sol;>` (Info/Query) packets can also be filtered, and the matching takes place on the namespace described in the xmlns attribute.

Table 4-1. Filter conditions (continued)

Table 4-2. Filter actions

Action	Example	Description
<error/>	<error>Address defunct</error>	Sends an error reply to the sender.
<offline/>	<offline/>	Stores the incoming message offline. The recipient will receive it the next time she logs on.
<forward/>	<forward>colleague@server</forward>	The message will be forwarded to another Jabber ID (JID).
<reply/>	<reply>Be right back!</reply>	A reply will be sent to the sender.
<settype/>	<settype>normal</settype>	Changes the type of the incoming message (see <type/> in the previous table).
<continue/>	<continue/>	Special action to continue on to the next rule.

Server vCard

Every user, indeed every entity, can maintain a virtual "business card"—a vCard—which is stored server-side. vCards can be retrieved at any time by any user. The <vCard/> tag here in the JSM configuration gives the Jabber server an identity—its vCard can be retrieved also.

You can maintain the server's vCard data in this part of the JSM configuration:

```
<vCard>
  <FN>Jabber Server on yak</FN>
  <DESC>A Jabber Server!</DESC>
  <URL>http://yak/</URL>
</vCard>
```

All the vCard elements can be used for this vCard configuration, not just the ones shown here. More information on vCards can be found in the section "The vcard-temp Namespace."

Registration instructions

Registration instructions such as those defined here:

```
<register notify="yes">
  <instructions>Choose a userid and password to register.</instructions>
  <name&sol;>
  <email&sol;>
</register>
```

are available to whoever asks for them; in its most formal state, the procedure for creating a new user account on a Jabber server (specifically, in the JSM) includes a first step of asking the server what is required for the registration process.

The registration service is provided by the *mod_register* module.

In reply to such a request (which is made with an IQ-get request in the jabber:iq:register namespace—see the section "jabber:iq:register" and the section "User Registration" for details) the instructions and a list of required fields are returned by *mod_register*. Note that the list of fields provided in this <register/> section are over and above the standard fields in any case for registration:

- <username/>

- <password/>

so that in this particular configuration case both <name/> and <email/>, *and* <username/> and <password/> will be sent in the reply. The text inside the <instructions/> tag, also sent, is intended for display by the client if it supports such a dynamic process. Typically the client would request the registration requirements and build a screen asking the user to enter values for the required fields, while displaying the instructions received.

The notify="yes" attribute of the <register/> tag will cause a message to be automatically created and sent to the server administrator address(es) for every new account created. See the section "Administration" for details about specifying administration addresses.

If you want to prevent registration of new accounts on your Jabber server, comment out this <register/> section. The only standard module that handles <iq/> packets in the jabber:iq:register namespace, *mod_register*, will refuse to handle register requests if there is no <register/> section in the configuration, and so a "Not Implemented" error will be sent in reply to the request for registration details.

Welcome message

The welcome message defined here:

```
<welcome>
  <subject>Welcome!</subject>
  <body>Welcome to the Jabber server on yak</body>
</welcome>
```

will be sent to all new users the first time they log on. The <subject/> and <body/> contents are simply placed in a normal <message/> and sent off to the new Jabber ID (JID).

Administration

While the Unix user acts as the overall administrator for the Jabber server (for starting and stopping *jabberd*, for example), it is possible to specify administration rights for certain Jabber users that are local to the server. "Local" means users that are defined as belonging to the host (or hosts) specified in the <host/> tag within the same JSM component instance definition. If the host tag is:

```
<host>server.com</host>
```

then the JID's *dj@server.com* and *admin@server.com* are local, but *admin@anotherserver.com* is not.

The only difference between an administration JID and a "normal" JID is that the former is specified in tags in this section and the latter isn't. When a JID is specified between either the <read/> or <write/> tags, then it can be used to perform "administrative" tasks.

The <admin/> section as delivered in the standard *jabber.xml* that comes with Version 1.4.1 (see Appendix A) is commented out. Make sure that you remove the comment lines to activate the section if you want to make use of the administrative features:

```
<admin>
  <read>support@yak</read>
  <write>admin@yak</write>
  <reply>
    <subject>Auto Reply</subject>
    <body>This is a special administrative address.</body>
  </reply>
</admin>
```

If you want to specify more than one JID with administrative rights, simply repeat the tags, like this:

```
<read>admin1@yak</read>
<read>admin2@yak</read>
<read>admin3@yak</read>
```

Placing a JID inside of a <write/> tag implies that that JID also has <read/> administration rights. So there's not much point in doing something like this:

```
<read>admin@yak</read>
<write>admin@yak</write>
```

So what are the administrative features available to JIDs placed inside the <read/> and <write/> tags? For JIDs appearing in a <read/> tag in the <admin/> section, these are the features available:

Retrieve list of users currently online

By sending one of two possible types of query to the server, a JID can retrieve a list of users that currently have a session on the (local) Jabber server. The results come in one of two forms, depending on the query type. The first query version is of the "legacy" iq:admin type and the second is of the newer iq:browse type. (An example of the latter query can be seen in Example 5-1.)

The list of users in both sorts of results contains the user JID, for how long the user has been logged on (measured in seconds), how many packets have been sent from the user's session, and how many packets have been sent to the user's session. The first query version also contains presence information for each user in the list.

Receipt of administrative queries

Users normally send messages to other users—to other JIDs, where a JID is composed of a username and a hostname (a Jabber server name). The Jabber server itself is also a valid recipient, and the JID in this case is just the server name itself: no username and no @ sign.

If a user sends a message to the server, it will be forwarded to the JIDs listed in the <read/> (and <write/>) tags in this <admin/> section, and the reply defined in the <reply/> tag will be sent back to the user as an automated response.

For JIDs appearing in a <write/> tag in the <admin/> section, these are the features available:

Same as <read/>

JIDs listed in <write/> tags automatically have access to the same features as those JIDs listed in <read/> tags.

Configuration retrieval

In a similar way to how a list of online users can be requested by sending a query of the iq:admin variety, a copy of the JSM configuration can be requested by sending an iq:admin query to the server. The difference is that in the former user list request, a request tag <who/> is sent inside the query, and in this configuration request, a <config/> tag is sent.

The configuration XML, as it is defined in the JSM component instance section of the Jabber server being queried, is returned as a result.

Sending administrative messages

Two types of administrative messages can be sent: an announcement to all online users and a message of the day (MOTD). The announcement goes out to all users currently online. Similarly, the MOTD goes out to all users, but not only those online; when someone logs on and starts a session, the MOTD will be sent to them too, unlike the announcement, which will expire as soon as it is sent. The MOTD will not expire, unless explicitly made to do so. The MOTD can also be updated—those that had already received the MOTD won't receive the updated copy during their current session, but anyone logging on after the update will receive the new version of the message.

Update info request

The *mod_version* module provides a simple service that, at server startup, queries a central repository of Jabber software version information at *update.jabber.org*. The <update/> configuration tag:

```
<update><jabberd:cmdline flag="h">yak</jabberd:cmdline></update>
```

is used to control this query.

If the <update/> tag is present, the query is sent. If the update tag is not present, the query is not sent.

If you do intend leaving the <update/> tag in, you need to make sure that:

• The hostname specified as the value in the tag is resolvable and reachable as this is your Jabber server address to which the central repository will try to send back information (if there happens to be a newer version of the server software—specifically the JSM component—available).

• Your Jabber server is connected to the Internet to be able to reach *update.jabber.org*. You also need to be running instances of the Hostname Resolution and Server (to Server) Connections components so that your Jabber server can resolve the *update.jabber.org* host and send the query out.

The JSM component version releases are fortunately not so frequent that you require an automated mechanism to keep up with what's new; also you may wish to run an internal Jabber server with no connection to the outside world. So it is not uncommon for this section to be commented out. The JSM will still function without this piece of configuration.

It is worth noting here, however, that Jabber clients also use the central repository to find out about newer versions of themselves. As all Jabber client communication goes through the server,* you need to realize that commenting out the <update/> tag will not stop clients sending their queries.

---

* Actually, that's not true, it was just to catch those of you who were falling asleep. Not *all* communication goes through the Jabber server; for example, Jabber clients can use the out-of-band (OOB) namespace to negotiate client-to-client file transfers between themselves. See the section "jabber:iq:oob" for more details.

Autoupdate of JUD

The Jabber User Directory (JUD) is a service that provides a directory service of usernames and addresses. The service comes in the form of a component—we'll be looking at the component instance definition of a JUD later in the section "Component Instance: jud" later in this chapter. If a Jabber server is running a JUD service, then you can connect to it with your Jabber client and enter your name and address details and query it as you would any directory service to find details of other people.

At the same time, each user has the possibility of maintaining his own vCard—we discussed vCards earlier in the section "Server vCard. In the same way that the server's vCard can be requested and retrieved, you can request a user's vCard, and the user whose vCard is requested does not have to be connected at that moment for the request to be fulfilled—the vCards are stored server-side and the Jabber server (not the user's client) handles the request.

So in many ways it makes sense to align the data in the user vCard with data stored in a JUD. The `<vcard2jud&sol;>` configuration tag allows this alignment to happen automatically; if it appears in the configuration, it will cause any vCard updates (that would be typically performed by users changing their personal information via their Jabber clients) not only to be stored server-side in the vCard but also to be passed on to a JUD.

Which JUD? Well, the first one that's defined in the `<browse&sol;>` section of the configuration, which is described next. Effectively it means that if you run a local JUD but also connect to the JUD running on *jabber.org*, you can choose which JUD will be the recipient of the vCard updates by placing that one before any others in the `<browse&sol;>` list.

 The JUD is referred to here as a "local" JUD because there's a central JUD running on *jabber.org* that every Jabber user can connect to and use (even if they're on a different Jabber server); the word "local" makes the distinction that the JUD is running locally to the Jabber server to which the Jabber user is connected.

If you're not running a JUD locally, or you simply don't want your users' vCard updates going to a JUD, you can safely comment this tag out.

Browsable service information

As the Jabber server administrators, *we* know what services are available on our Jabber server: what components are connected and what features they offer. We know that we're running a JUD locally and have a Conferencing component.

But how do we let the Jabber clients know? If they're to be able to provide their users with an agreeable experience and expose them to all the server features and services available, we need some way to allow them to request information about what the server that they're connected to offers. Jabber has a powerful feature called *browsing* that allows one entity to query another entity for information. Browsing defines a simple request/response exchange and with that provides a singular and uniform way to retrieve (on the requester's part) and expose (on the requestee's part) feature information and availability.

Bearing that in mind, we can guess what the <browse/> section of the JSM custom configuration is for:

```
<browse>
  <service type="jud" jid="jud.yak" name="yak User Directory">
    <ns>jabber:iq:search</ns>
    <ns>jabber:iq:register</ns>
  </service>
  <conference type="public" jid="conference.yak" name="yak Conferencing"&sol;>
</browse>
```

Each child of the <browse/> tag defines a feature, in this case a "service," that the Jabber server offers. Of course, these services are the ones over and above the services provided by the basic components such as Session Management, Hostname Resolution, and so on.

Two services are defined ("exposed") in the <browse/> configuration:

• A local JUD:

```
<service type="jud" jid="jud.yak" name="yak User Directory">
  <ns>jabber:iq:search</ns>
  <ns>jabber:iq:register</ns>
</service>
```

• And a conferencing service:

```
<conference type="public" jid="conference.yak" name="yak Conferencing"&sol;>
```

The browsing features are covered in Part II, but briefly we can see here that each browsable item is identified by a JID (jid="jud.yak" and jid="conference.yak") and is classified using a category that is the combination of the item's outermost tag and the value of the tag's type attribute. So the JUD is classified as service/jud and has a JID of *jud.yak*, and the conferencing service is classified as conference/public and has a JID of *conference.yak*. The type and jid attributes are required. Each item has an optional name attribute for use when the item is displayed, for example.

Some services offer well-known facilities such as search and registration, which are commonly found across different services. These facilities can be described directly in the browse item, so that the entity requesting information about services receives information directly in the first request "hit" as to what facilities are available for each service:

```
<ns>jabber:iq:search</ns>
<ns>jabber:iq:register</ns>
```

The `ns` in the facility tagname (`<ns&sol;>`) stands for namespace; it is via namespace-qualified requests to a service that features are utilized. In this case, the search facility is represented by the `jabber:iq:search` namespace, and the registration facility is represented by the `jabber:iq:register` namespace.

Note also that the `<browse&sol;>` section can list services that are *not* local to the Jabber server in which that `<browse&sol;>` section occurs. See the section "Using Services on Other Jabber Servers" for details.

Component Connection Method

Phew! Now that we've got the configuration out of the way, we can have a look at how the JSM is loaded. And we can see immediately from the `<load&sol;>` tag that it's connected using the library load method:

```
<load main="jsm">
  <jsm>./jsm/jsm.so</jsm>
  <mod_echo>./jsm/jsm.so</mod_echo>
  <mod_roster>./jsm/jsm.so</mod_roster>
  <mod_time>./jsm/jsm.so</mod_time>
  <mod_vcard>./jsm/jsm.so</mod_vcard>
  <mod_last>./jsm/jsm.so</mod_last>
  <mod_version>./jsm/jsm.so</mod_version>
  <mod_announce>./jsm/jsm.so</mod_announce>
  <mod_agents>./jsm/jsm.so</mod_agents>
  <mod_browse>./jsm/jsm.so</mod_browse>
  <mod_admin>./jsm/jsm.so</mod_admin>
  <mod_filter>./jsm/jsm.so</mod_filter>
  <mod_offline>./jsm/jsm.so</mod_offline>
  <mod_presence>./jsm/jsm.so</mod_presence>
  <mod_auth_plain>./jsm/jsm.so</mod_auth_plain>
  <mod_auth_digest>./jsm/jsm.so</mod_auth_digest>
  <mod_auth_0k>./jsm/jsm.so</mod_auth_0k>
  <mod_log>./jsm/jsm.so</mod_log>
  <mod_register>./jsm/jsm.so</mod_register>
  <mod_xml>./jsm/jsm.so</mod_xml>
</load>
```

It's clear that the more complex version of the library load method is employed. The `jsm` module itself is loaded through the `<jsm>` . . . `</jsm>` tag pair and this in turn pulls in the other modules that are specified with the *mod_** module name tag pairs.

We've already become aquainted with some of the modules in this list; here's a quick summary of the modules that will be loaded into the JSM:

mod_echo
> This module provides a simple echo service that echoes back whatever you send it.

mod_roster
> This module provides roster management services; the roster is stored server-side.

mod_time
> You can request that the server send you a timestamp local to the server; this is the module that handles this request.

mod_vcard
> This is the module that handles requests for the Jabber server's vCard and also the user vCard management (such as submission to a JUD on change and storing/retrieving the data from the server-side storage).

mod_last
> *mod_last* provides facilities for returning last logout information for users or, in the case of a query on the server itself, server uptime.

mod_version
> This is the module that provides the version query service described in the section "Update info request."

mod_announce
> The serverwide announcements and MOTD facilities available to Jabber server administrators are provided by this module.

mod_agents
> The *mod_agents* module responds to requests for `agent` information made to the server. This is the module that returns the information in the `<browse&sol;>` tag in the JSM configuration. It can also return a summary of the server consisting of the server's vCard and whether new user registrations are open.
>
> When returning `<browse&sol;>` data, it gives similar information to *mod_browse* (see the next entry) and is provided for backward compatibility. The agent information is requested with two namespaces, `jabber:iq:agent` (for information on the server) and `jabber:iq:agents` (for information on a list of "agents"—the old name for "services"); these namespaces are being retired in deference to the new `jabber:iq:browse` namespace.

mod_browse

The *mod_browse* module responds to browsing requests made on the server or on users defined on that server. The module can also be used by users to modify the information returned if a browse request is made against them.

mod_admin

This module provides the administrative features described in the section "Administration." The module itself determines which JIDs are allowed access to which features (according to the configuration in the `<admin&sol;>` configuration block).

mod_filter

The services described in the section "Filter service" are provided by this module.

mod_offline

Being offline—which in this sense means not being connected to the Jabber server and having an (online) *session*—doesn't prevent a user receiving messages. They are merely stored offline and forwarded to the user when she logs on and starts a session. *mod_offline* provides these storage and forwarding services in conjunction with the xdb component. See the section "Component Instance: xdb."

mod_presence

The management of presence information—whether a user is online or offline, what his presence settings currently are, who should be sent the information, and so on. These facilities are provided by the *mod_presence* module.

mod_auth_*

Authentication must take place when a user connects to the Jabber server and wishes to start a session. There are currently three types of authentication supported by the Jabber server; the differentiation is in how the password exchange and comparison is managed:

plaintext

User passwords are stored in plaintext on the server and are transmitted from the client to the server in plaintext. A simple comparison is made at the server to validate.

If the connection between the client and the server is encoded using SSL, then the plaintext password travels through an encrypted connection.

digest

User passwords are stored in plaintext on the server, but no password is transmitted from the client to the server; instead, an SHA-1 digest is created by the client from the concatenation of the client's session ID and the password and sent to the server, where the same digest operation is carried out and the results compared.

zero knowledge
> User passwords are neither stored on the server nor transmitted from the client to the server. A combination of hash sequencing on the client side with a final hash and comparison on the server side allows credentials to be checked in a secure way.

There are three *mod_auth_** modules, one for each of these authentication types. More information on the authentication methods can be found in the section "User Authentication" in Chapter 7.

mod_log
> *mod_log* simply records the ending of each user session.

mod_register
> The *mod_register* module provides the services to register (create a new user), unregister (remove a user), and maintain user registration details with the server.

mod_xml
> Storage and retrieval of private and shared (public) data by users is made possible by this module.

Component Instance: xdb

The xdb component, described by the configuration XML shown in Example 4-10 and shown in diagram form in Figure 4-8, provides data storage for the server—it is the XML Database.

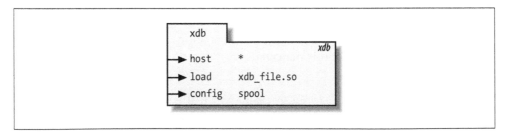

Figure 4-8. Diagram view of xdb component instance

All storage requirements by components connected to the Jabber backbone can be fulfilled by an xdb component. In normal configurations, there is a single instance, although it is possible to have more than one, each handling separate areas of storage, possibly using different storage mechanisms.

Example 4-10. jabber.xml configuration for the xdb component instance

```
<xdb id="xdb">

  <host&sol;>

  <load>
    <xdb_file>./xdb_file/xdb_file.so</xdb_file>
  </load>

  <xdb_file xmlns="jabber:config:xdb_file">
    <spool><jabberd:cmdline flag='s'>./spool</jabberd:cmdline></spool>
  </xdb_file>

</xdb>
```

Component Type and Identification

The opening tag identifies this component instance to the backbone as an xdb type component, as follows:

```
<xdb id="xdb">
```

This gives it a name, xdb, much in the same way that the sessions service has the name sessions.

Host Filter

For the host filter, we have an empty tag:

```
<host&sol;>
```

specified, which signifies that this xdb component instance will answer data storage and retrieval requests for all hosts. This, in turn, means that all data to be stored server-side will be stored using the same data storage mechanism, in this case xdb_file, which is a simple lowest common denominator storage system based upon directories containing files with XML content; these files are at a ratio of one per JID, plus "global" files where storage of data not tied to a JID is required. An example of this would be JUD's usage of xdb (and implicitly xdb_file in our configuration); a file called *global.xml* is used to store the user directory information that JUD manages.

If you want to use separate data storage mechanisms for your different virtual servers, you can define more than one xdb instance in your *jabber.xml* configuration and have the first use one storage system—say, xdb_file—and the second use another—say, a Relational Database Management System (RDBMS)-based system.*

You may also want to store data from different virtual hosts in different places on your system; by specifying more than one xdb instance, even if all of them use the same storage mechanism, you can specify a different spool directory in the configuration for each one.

As well as a host filter, there is another filter possible for xdb components. This is the namespace filter, represented by the <ns/> tag.

Every xdb storage and retrieval request is made with a namespace definition; for example, to retrieve the last logoff time for a user, the *mod_last* module makes a data retrieval request of the xdb component and specifies the jabber:iq:last namespace in that request, and to check if a user is using the zero-knowledge authentication method, the *mod_auth_0k* module makes a data retrieval request and specifies the jabber:iq:auth:0k namespace.

If you want an xdb component instance to handle only requests qualified with certain namespaces, specify them with the <ns/> tag. Example 4-11 shows the initial part of an xdb component instance definition that is to handle jabber:iq:roster and jabber:iq:last qualified storage and retrieval requests for the host *a-domain.com.*

Example 4-11. Host and namespace filters in an xdb definition

```
<xdb id="xdb">

   <host>a-domain.com</host>
   <ns>jabber:iq:roster</ns>
   <ns>jabber:iq:last</ns>


   . . .

</xdb>
```

No namespace filter in an xdb component instance definition implies the instance is to handle requests qualified by any namespace, the equivalent of an empty tag:

```
<ns&sol;>
```

---

* Some of these are being developed and are available right now.

To <ns/> or Not to <ns/>

If you are going to use namespace filters for xdb components, make sure you specify them for *every* xdb component instance definition; otherwise, you will receive an error message to the effect that packet routing will be incorrect and your Jabber server will not start.

Custom Configuration

The custom configuration section in our xdb component instance definition is specific to the data storage mechanism that we're going to be using. In this case, it's the xdb_file mechanism, and so we have the custom configuration wrapped by a tag qualified with a namespace to match:

```
<xdb_file xmlns="jabber:config:xdb_file">
  <spool><jabberd:cmdline flag='s'>./spool</jabberd:cmdline></spool>
</xdb_file>
```

Again, the tag name xdb_file is unimportant; the part that must be correct is the namespace jabber:config:xdb_file.

The configuration describes a single setting: where the spool area is. This, in the context of our xdb_file mechanism, is the root directory within which hostname-specific directories are created and used to store JID-specific and global XML datafiles. As the configuration stands here, the value (*./spool*) can be overridden at server startup time with the *-s* switch.

There is another configuration tag available for use here too. Using the configuration as it stands here, the xdb_file component would cache data indefinitely; if you were to modify data directly in the files in the spool area, the modifications wouldn't have any effect for data that had already been retrieved for a JID in the course of a server's uptime.* In other words, once data has been read from the file, it is cached until the server is stopped.

The <timeout/> configuration tag can be employed to control this caching. Used with a value that represents a number of seconds, the <timeout/> tag will force data in the cache to be purged (and therefore reread from file the next time it's requested) after that number of seconds of lifetime. Table 4-3 shows the effects of various values on caching.

---

* Do this only if you're sure you know what you're doing.

Table 4-3. Effect of <timeout/> tag

Tag value	Example	Effect
Less than 0	`<timeout>-1</timeout>`	No cache purge will be carried out and the cached data will live forever. This is the equivalent of having no explicit `<timeout&sol;>` tag set.
0	`<timeout>0</timeout>`	Cache will be purged immediately. This is the same as having no cache.
More than 0	`<timeout>120</timeout>`	Cached data will be purged after a certain lifetime specified (in seconds) as the value of the tag. In this example, it's 2 minutes. Don't bother setting a positive value less than 30; the cache purge check mechanism runs only every 30 seconds, so any resolution beyond 30 is meaningless.

Component Connection Method

The component connection method is library load:

```
<load>
   <xdb_file>./xdb_file/xdb_file.so</xdb_file>
</load>
```

The shared library *./xdb_file/xdb_file.so* is loaded and the `xdb_file()` function is called to initialize the component.

Component Instance: c2s

The `c2s` component, described by the configuration XML shown in Example 4-12 and shown in diagram form in Figure 4-9, provides the Client (to Server) Connections service—it manages Jabber client connections to the Jabber server.

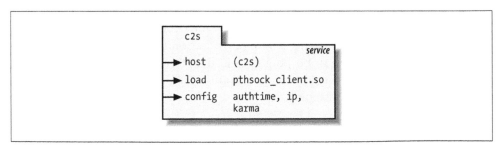

Figure 4-9. Diagram view of c2s component instance

Example 4-12. jabber.xml configuration for the c2s component instance

```
<service id="c2s">

  <load>
    <pthsock_client>./pthsock/pthsock_client.so</pthsock_client>
  </load>

  <pthcsock xmlns='jabber:config:pth-csock'>
    <authtime&sol;>
    <karma>
      <init>10</init>
      <max>10</max>
      <inc>1</inc>
      <dec>1</dec>
      <penalty>-6</penalty>
      <restore>10</restore>
    </karma>
    <ip port="5222"&sol;>
  </pthcsock>

</service>
```

Component Type and Identification

The opening tag:

```
<service id="c2s">
```

identifies this component instance to the backbone as a service type component and gives it the name c2s.

Host Filter

The c2s component has no explicit <host/> tag; the identification of the service with the id attribute is enough, and the value of the host filter will be taken as that identification. As long as the specified ID is unique within the context of the whole configuration, the component will be able to function correctly. It is normally set to c2s by convention.

Custom Configuration

The custom configuration for our c2s component contains three main tags:

`<authtime&sol;>`

The first tag, `<authtime&sol;>`, allows us to specify a time limit within which the connecting client has to have completed the authentication procedure. This includes sending the initial document stream identifier with the `jabber:client` namespace. Setting this to, say, 10 seconds:

```
<authtime>10</authtime>
```

will allow the client up to 10 seconds to authenticate, after which `c2s` will drop the connection. Setting the time limit to 0 seconds, which can be accomplished with an empty tag:

```
<authtime&sol;>
```

effectively gives the client an unlimited amount of time within which to authenticate.

`<karma&sol;>`

The next tag we find in the `c2s` component instance configuration is `<karma&sol;>`. This is a way of controlling bandwidth usage through the connections and will be explained in the section "The io Section" later in this chapter.

`<ip&sol;>`

Then we come to the `<ip&sol;>` configuration tag:

```
<ip port="5222"&sol;>
```

The standard port for client connections is 5222. This is where it is specified—in the `port` attribute. The `<ip&sol;>` tag itself can contain an IP address or hostname. If you specify something like this:

```
<ip port="5222">192.168.0.4</ip>
```

then only socket connections will be made to that specific combination of port and IP address. Not specifying an IP address means that the `c2s` service will bind to the port on all (`INADDR_ANY`) IP addresses on the host.

You can specify more than one combination of port and IP address using multiple `<ip&sol;>` tags:

```
<ip port="5222">
<ip port="5225">127.0.0.1</ip>
```

which here means client socket connections will be listened for on port 5222 on any IP address and port 5225 on the *localhost* address.

Three other configuration tags—`<rate&sol;>`, `<alias&sol;>`, and `<ssl&sol;>`—are not used here but are worth identifying now:

`<rate&sol;>`

> `<rate&sol;>`, like `<karma&sol;>`, is used to control connectivity and will be explained along with that tag in the section "The io Section" later.

`<alias&sol;>`

> `<alias&sol;>` is a way of providing alias names for your Jabber server. When a Jabber client makes a connection, the opening gambit is the root of the XML document that is to be streamed over the connection:

```
<stream:stream to="furrybeast" xmlns="jabber:client"
            xmlns:stream="http://etherx.jabber.org/streams">
```

> The use of *furrybeast* may be a DNS alias for *yak* and is specified by the client here in the to attribute of the document's root tag (`<stream&sol;>`).
>
> With the `<alias&sol;>` tag, we can "fix" the incoming host specification by replacing it with what we as the server want it to be. If this document root tag were to be sent to our Jabber server configured as *yak* and we had an `<alias&sol;>` tag thus:

```
<alias to="yak">furrybeast</alias>
```

> then the incoming hostname specification *furrybeast* would be recognized and translated to *yak* in the response:

```
<stream:stream xmlns:stream='http://etherx.jabber.org/streams'
            id='3AE71597' xmlns='jabber:client' from='yak'>
```

> Rather than specify a hostname to translate, a default alias name can be specified like this:

```
<alias to="yak"&sol;>
```

> meaning that *any* connections to the c2s component would have their Jabber hostname specification translated to *yak* if necessary. This is an indication to the client that the hostname *yak* should be used in any reference to that Jabber server.

`<ssl&sol;>`

> `<ssl&sol;>` is the equivalent of the `<ip&sol;>` tag and works in exactly the same way, with two exceptions:
>
> - An IP address *must* be specified, which means that something like `<ssl port="5223"&sol;>` is not allowed.
>
> - The connections are encrypted using SSL, which means that the Jabber server must have been configured to use SSL (see Chapter 3 and the section "The io Section" later in this chapter for details).

Component Connection Method

The component connection method is library load:

```
<load>
  <pthsock_client>. /pthsock/pthsock_client.so</pthsock_client>
</load>
```

The shared library *./pthsock/pthsock_client.so* is loaded and the `pthsock_client()` function is called to initialize the component.

Logging Definition: elogger

It has already been intimated that the log type components are exceptions to the general pattern when it comes to defining what they are in relation to the Jabber server. In fact, the logging "components" aren't really separate components at all—they are part of the *jabberd* backbone. Nevertheless, it is still worthwhile referring to them as components as they can be defined with different characteristics to perform different logging tasks.

The configuration XML for `elogger` is represented in diagram form in Figure 4-10 and is shown in Example 4-13.

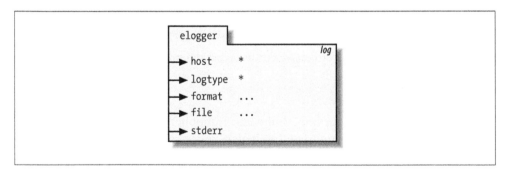

Figure 4-10. Diagram view of elogger

Example 4-13. jabber.xml configuration for elogger

```
<log id='elogger'>
  <host&sol;>
  <logtype&sol;>
  <format>%d: [%t] (%h): %s</format>
  <file>error.log</file>
  <stderr&sol;>
</log>
```

Component Type and Identification

The opening tag clearly denotes a log type component. The name given in the `id` attribute is `elogger`.

Host Filter

The `elogger` attribute will record log records for any hosts according to the empty host filter tag specified here:

```
<host&sol;>
```

Custom Configuration

Apart from the host filter declaration, every other tag within a `<log&sol;>` definition can be regarded as configuration. Taking each tag in turn, we have:

`<logtype&sol;>`

This tag declares which types of logging record will be handled by this logging definition. Actually, the `<logtype&sol;>` tag is more of a filter (like `<host&sol;>`) than configuration, but that's splitting hairs.

The tag can either be empty or contain one of the following values: `alert`, `notice`, `record`, or `warn`. You can specify more than one `<logtype&sol;>` tag to capture more than one log type. If you specify an empty tag (as is the case with the log component here), then all log types will be captured and handled apart from any log types that are explicitly declared elsewhere in other logging components. What does this mean? Well, in our case, since we have a second log type component, `rlogger` (described in the next section), that has an explicit declaration:

```
<logtype>record</logtype>
```

this log component won't receive `record` type log records to handle.

`<format&sol;>`

A logging component will typically write out the data it receives in a human-readable format. With the `<format&sol;>` tag, we can specify how the data appears. There are four variables that we can embellish with whatever text we like to form something that will be meaningful to us (and perhaps easily parseable for our scripts). The four variables are shown in Table 4-4.

Table 4-4. Logging component variables for <format/>

Variable	Description
%d	Timestamp
%t	Log type
%h	Host
%s	The actual log message

In elogger's <format/> tag, we have:

```
%d: [%t] (%h): %s
```

so a typical log record written by elogger might look like this:

```
20010420T21:38:30: [warn] (yak): dropping a packet to yak
   from jsm@update.jabber.org/1.4.1: Unable to deliver, destination unknown
```

<file/>

Typically the output from a logging component goes to a file. You can specify the name of the file with the <file/> tag, as follows:

```
<file>error.log</file>
```

<stderr/>

Additionally, it's possible to have the output from a logging component written to STDERR; place the empty <stderr/> tag in the logging component's definition to have this happen.

Logging Definition: rlogger

Logging definition elogger is a general catchall component that serves to direct all unhandled log records to a log file, *error.log*. The logging definition rlogger, on the other hand, has been defined specifically to capture and store (to a file—*record.log*) record type log records.

Components such as c2s, s2s, and sessions write record type log records, examples of which can be seen in Example 4-14. The "login ok" messages are from the c2s component, the "dialback" messages are from the s2s component, and the "session end" message is from the sessions component.

Example 4-14. Typical record type log records

```
20010811T14:27:19 dj@gnu.mine.nu login ok 213.122.45.3 home
20010811T14:28:25 piers@gnu.mine.nu login ok 213.122.128.174 yeha
20010811T14:29:20 conference.jabber.org out dialback 3 208.245.212.100 gnu.mine.nu
20010811T14:29:20 update.jabber.org out dialback 3 208.245.212.100 gnu.mine.nu
20010811T14:29:20 gnu.mine.nu in dialback 16 208.245.212.100 conference.jabber.org
20010811T14:29:20 jabber.org out dialback 55 208.245.212.100 gnu.mine.nu
20010811T14:35:25 dj@gnu.mine.nu session end 486 30 57 home
```

Example 4-14. Typical record type log records (continued)

```
20010811T14:36:39 dj@gnu.mine.nu login ok 213.122.45.3 home
20010811T14:56:50 gnu.mine.nu in dialback 2 216.109.164.2 obelisk.net
```

The configuration XML for `rlogger` is shown in Example 4-15 and is represented in diagram form in Figure 4-11.

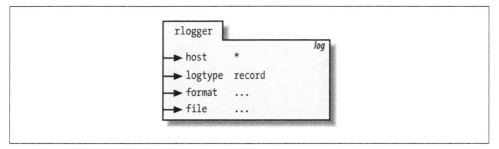

Figure 4-11. Diagram view of rlogger

Example 4-15. jabber.xml configuration for rlogger

```
<log id='rlogger'>
  <host&sol;>
  <logtype>record</logtype>
  <format>%d %h %s</format>
  <file>record.log</file>
</log>
```

Component Type and Identification

Like `elogger`, `rlogger` is identified as a log type component. It takes its name from the `id` attribute.

Host Filter

Again, like `elogger`, this logging definition will handle log records for any hosts.

Custom Configuration

The custom configuration of `rlogger` is very similar to that of `elogger`, except that the target file is called *record.log* (the `<file&sol;>` tag), the output format is slightly different (the `<format&sol;>` tag), and no output to STDERR is desired.

Component Instance: dnsrv

The dnsrv component, described by the configuration XML shown in Example 4-16 and shown in diagram form in Figure 4-12, provides routing logic and name resolution for packets that are destined for a nonlocal component, in other words, for a component that is running on another Jabber server.[*]

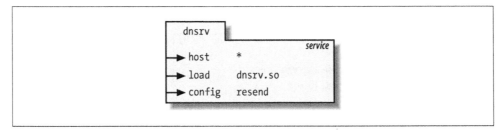

Figure 4-12. Diagram view of dnsrv component instance

Example 4-16. jabber.xml configuration for the dnsrv component instance

```
<service id="dnsrv">

  <host&sol;>

  <load>
    <dnsrv>./dnsrv/dnsrv.so</dnsrv>
  </load>

  <dnsrv xmlns="jabber:config:dnsrv">
        <resend service="_jabber._tcp">s2s</resend>
        <resend>s2s</resend>
  </dnsrv>

</service>
```

Once started, the component forks to spawn a child process that services the actual name resolution requests and the route determination. The component and its child communicate with a simple XML stream within which hostnames are passed to the child process in a "query" tag:

```
<host>update.jabber.org</host>
```

and answers are passed back in the form of attribute additions to the original query tag:

```
<host ip='208.245.212.100' to='s2s'>update.jabber.org</host>
```

---

[*] Or, for example, on a server offering another IM service (this is planned for the future).

Component Type and Identification

The component is a service and is identified with the name dnsrv:

```
<service id="dnsrv">
```

Host Filter

The dnsrv component is to provide hostname resolution and routing for all component activity within the Jabber server. For this reason, it needs to be open to all comers and has an empty host filter tag (<host/>).

Custom Configuration

The dnsrv component provides hostname lookup and dynamic routing services. To this end, the configuration concerns itself with defining how the routing is to be determined.

The configuration, identified with the jabber:config:dnsrv namespace, contains a list of entries that describe service types and next-delivery-point data. What does this mean? In hostname resolution, a lookup request can be made where a service and protocol, as well as a domain name, are specified. When more than one server shares the same domain name and services (such as Jabber) are managed across the servers, different host addresses can be returned, depending on the service requested. So far, so good; the resolution part of the deal is covered. But what happens once an IP address has been returned? The packet destined for the non-local component must be sent on its way—but via where? This is what the next-delivery-point data specifies.

If we examine the configuration, we see this:

```
<dnsrv xmlns="jabber:config:dnsrv">
  <resend service="_jabber._tcp">s2s</resend>
  <resend>s2s</resend>
</dnsrv>
```

The configuration is a list of services to try for during the resolution request. This list has two items. The first has the service="_jabber._tcp" attribute that says, "Try for the Jabber (via TCP) service when trying to resolve a name (using a SRV record lookup request) and, if successful, send the packet to the s2s component." The second is the default that says, "If you've reached here in the list and haven't managed to get a resolution for a particular service, just resolve it normally (using a standard resolver call) (gethostbyname()) and send it to the s2s component."

The value _jabber._tcp isn't Jabber configuration syntax; it's the prefix format to use with a domain name when making DNS SRV lookups. (See RFC 2782 for more details.)

Let's look at what happens in a typical request of dnsrv; to set the scene, a client connecting to the Jabber server to which this component instance is connected has requested software update information (see the section "Update info request" earlier in this chapter) and, as no local component with the identification or filter that fits the hostname *update.jabber.org* was found in the configuration, a request to resolve and route to this hostname is passed on to the dnsrv:

1. The component receives a request for *update.jabber.org*.

2. Resolution is attempted for the first <resend/> tag in the list; this is the one that implies an SRV lookup by specifying the _jabber._tcp service definition.

3. The SRV lookup fails—there are no SRV records maintained for the Jabber service for *update.jabber.org*.

4. Resolution is attempted for the second (and last) <resend/> tag in the list. No service is specified in this tag, so a normal resolution lookup is made.

5. The lookup is successful and returns an IP address.

6. The success means that we've got a match, and the packet destined for *update.jabber.org* can be passed on to the component specified as next in the chain, which is s2s, as specified in the tag:

```
<resend>s2s</resend>
```

Component Connection Method

The dnsrv component is loaded as a shared library with the library load method:

```
<load>
  <dnsrv>./dnsrv/dnsrv.so</dnsrv>
</load>
```

The dnsrv() function is called when loading is complete to initialize the service.

Component Instance: conf

The Conferencing component is a service that provides group chat facilities in a Jabber environment. Rooms can be created and people can join and chat, similarly to the way they do in IRC (Internet Relay Chat) channels. The component instance described by the configuration XML in Example 4-17 is shown in diagram form in Figure 4-13.

Example 4-17. jabber.xml configuration for the conf component instance

Example 4-17. jabber.xml configuration for the conf component instance (continued)

```
<service id='conf'>

  <host>conference.yak</host>

  <load>
    <conference>./conference-0.4.1/conference.so</conference>
  </load>

  <conference xmlns="jabber:config:conference">
    <public&sol;>
    <vCard>
      <FN>yak Chatrooms</FN>
      <DESC>This service is for public chatrooms.</DESC>
      <URL>http://yak/chat</URL>
    </vCard>
    <history>20</history>
    <notice>
      <join> has become available</join>
      <leave> has left</leave>
      <rename> is now known as </rename>
    </notice>
    <room jid="kitchen@conference.yak">
      <name>The Kitchen</name>
      <notice>
        <join> has entered the cooking melee</join>
        <leave> can't stand the heat</leave>
        <rename> now answers to </rename>
      </notice>
    </room>
  </conference>

</service>
```

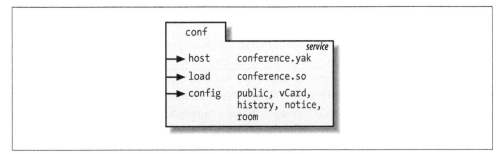

Figure 4-13. Diagram view of conf component instance

The component acts as a sort of third party, and all interaction between room participants is through this third party. This makes it possible to support privacy (such as using nicknames to hide users' real JIDs) and other features.

Component Type and Identification

The Conferencing component is identified to the backbone as a service:

```
<service id="conf">
```

and is given the identity `conf`, with which the component instance will register itself when loaded.

Host Filter

By convention, the Conferencing component often is addressed (by clients) as `conference.<hostname>`; we see that convention has been followed in that the host filter for this instance is:

```
<host>conference.yak</host>
```

which means that all packets destined to any JID at the hostname *conference.yak* will be sent to the `conf` component instance. This matches the identification of this service in the `<browse&sol;>` section of the JSM custom configuration.

Custom Configuration

Configuration of the Conferencing component is straightforward and is identified with the `jabber:config:conference` namespace:

```
<conference xmlns="jabber:config:conference">
  ...
</conference>
```

We can see from the contents of the custom configuration that there are a number of elements:

Public or private service
> Specifying (with the `<public&sol;>` tag) that a conference service is public means that users are allowed to browse the elements that the service is controlling, namely, the rooms. Rooms are either precreated or created on the fly by the first user to specify a new name when requesting to join a room. Specifying (with the `<private&sol;>` tag) that a conference service is private means that users are allowed to browse only rooms that they already know about, meaning rooms in which they're already present.

vCard
> The conference service component can have its own vCard information, which can be requested at any time. Here is where that vCard information can be maintained. Like the vCard for the JSM service, this particular definition uses only a few of the many possible vCard fields, for example:

```
<vCard>
  <FN>yak Chatrooms</FN>
  <DESC>This service is for public chatrooms.</DESC>
  <URL>http://yak/chat</URL>
</vCard>
```

Message history

When you join a room, it is sometimes useful to see some of the most recent messages from the room's conversation(s). The `<history&sol;>` tag allows you to specify how many previous messages are relayed to new room joiners.

If you don't specify a `<history&sol;>` tag, a default value of 10 will be used.

Action notices

Three main "events" can happen with users and rooms: a user enters a room; a user leaves a room; a user changes her nickname. When any of these events occurs, the conference service component sends some text to the room to notify the participants. You can modify the text that gets sent with the tags in the `<notice&sol;>` configuration element.

```
<notice>
  <join> has become available</join>
  <leave> has left</leave>
  <rename> is now known as </rename>
</notice>
```

Rooms

A room is normally created when a user requests to join a room that doesn't already exist, and the requesting user is determined to be the room's owner. Or a room may be precreated by using the `<room&sol;>` tag when the service starts up. Each room has a JID. Optionally, you can give the room a name (which may be displayed by clients as the room's title) and its own action notices:

```
<room jid="kitchen@conference.yak">
  <name>The Kitchen</name>
  <notice>
    <join> has entered the cooking melee</join>
    <leave> can't stand the heat</leave>
    <rename> now answers to </rename>
  </notice>
</room>
```

The other settings that can be specified within a `<room&sol;>` tag are shown in Table 4-5.

Table 4-5. Conference room settings

Setting	Description
<nick/>	This signifies that a nickname is required for entry to the room. If one is not specified (in the join request), a nickname will be constructed for the user dynamically, usually the JID with a numeric suffix to make it unique in the room.
<secret/>	Rooms can be protected from unauthorized entry by specifying a secret that will be required on entry.
<privacy/>	This tag signifies that a privacy mode is supported, which means that users' real JIDs will be hidden from browsing requests.

Component Connection Method

The Conferencing component is compiled into a shared object library (*./confer-ence-0.4.1/conference.so*) and is connected to the Jabber backbone with the library load method:

```
<load>
  <conference>./conference-0.4.1/conference.so</conference>
</load>
```

Once loaded, the function `conference()` is called to initialize the component and perform setup tasks, such as creating rooms specified in the configuration.

Component Instance: jud

As mentioned already, the JUD is a user directory service that provides storage and query facilities for the user's name and address data. The `jud` component instance described by the configuration XML in Example 4-18 is shown in diagram form in Figure 4-14.

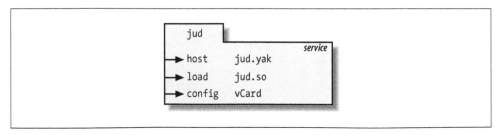

Figure 4-14. Diagram view of jud component instance

The JUD that is defined here relies upon the xdb component for data storage and retrieval services, which in turn means that, in this case, the data is stored in XML format in a file under the directory defined in the <spool/> tag in the xdb component instance's definition. All the data managed by the JUD is stored in one lump, with no specific JID associated with it; this means that xdb's engine, xdb_file, will store it as a single file called *global.xml* under the directory named after the JUD hostname *jud*.

Example 4-18. jabber.xml configuration for the jud component instance

```
<service id="jud">

  <host>jud.yak</host>

  <load>
    <jud>./jud-0.4/jud.so</jud>
  </load>

  <jud xmlns="jabber:config:jud">
    <vCard>
      <FN>JUD on yak</FN>
      <DESC>yak User Directory Services</DESC>
      <URL>http://yak/</URL>
    </vCard>
  </jud>

</service>
```

Component Type and Identification

JUD is clearly a service component and is identified as such with this tag:

```
<service id="jud">
```

The name given to the component instance is jud.

Host Filter

Requests of the JUD, such as searches or registrations (a user "registers" with the JUD and thereby causes his name and address details to be stored by the JUD), must be directed specifically at the JUD, which we have identified in the <browse/> area of our JSM configuration (see the next section) as *jud.yak*.

As we have identified the JUD in this way, requests will reach the JUD by way of this hostname, which is therefore what we want to filter on:

```
<host>jud.yak</host>
```

Requests to any other hostnames are not appropriate for the JUD to handle and will therefore be filtered out.

Custom Configuration

There is not much to configure in the JUD; it is a simple user directory service, and many of the features are currently hardcoded: where the data is stored, what data fields are stored per JID, and so on. The only configuration we can maintain is the JUD's vCard information. Just as the Jabber server itself and each user can have a vCard, components can have vCards too. These component vCards can be requested in the same way. (The vCard in this case is actually for the JSM, which is the heart of the Jabber server.)

```
<jud xmlns="jabber:config:jud">
  <vCard>
    <FN>JUD on yak</FN>
    <DESC>yak User Directory Services</DESC>
    <URL>http://yak/jud</URL>
  </vCard>
</jud>
```

The namespace that declares the JUD configuration is `jabber:config:jud`.

Component Connection Method

The JUD defined here is implemented as a set of C programs compiled into a shared object (*./jud-0.4/jud.so*) library. It is connected to the backbone with the library load connection method:

```
<load>
  <jud>./jud-0.4/jud.so</jud>
</load>
```

and the function `jud()` is called to initialize the component.

Component Instance: s2s

Just as the c2s component provides the Client (to Server) Connections service, so the s2s component provides the Server (to Server) Connections service. The XML configuration that describes the s2s component is shown in Example 4-19 and is represented in diagram form in Figure 4-15.

Example 4-19. jabber.xml configuration for the s2s component instance

```
<service id="s2s">

  <load>
    <dialback>./dialback/dialback.so</dialback>
  </load>

  <dialback xmlns='jabber:config:dialback'>
    <legacy&sol;>
```

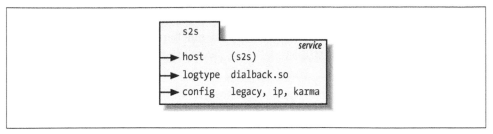

Figure 4-15. Diagram view of s2s component instance

Example 4-19. jabber.xml configuration for the s2s component instance (continued)

```
    <ip port="5269"&sol;>
    <karma>
      <init>50</init>
      <max>50</max>
      <inc>4</inc>
      <dec>1</dec>
      <penalty>-5</penalty>
      <restore>50</restore>
    </karma>
  </dialback>

</service>
```

Component Type and Identification

The component type is service, and the instance here is identified as s2s:

```
    <service id="s2s">
```

Host Filter

Like the c2s component instance definition, no explicit host filter is set for s2s. The identification of the component instance as s2s acts as a backup host filter.

Custom Configuration

The configuration for the s2s is similar to that of the c2s; after all, it is about managing connections to other hosts. The configuration namespace is, however, a little odd:

```
    <dialback xmlns="jabber:config:dialback">
```

Dialback? Well, in order to prevent spoofing on a connecting server's part, the s2s component implements an identity verification mechanism that is used to check that a connecting server is who it says it is. See the sidebar titled "Dialback" for more details.

As the namespace for the exchange of document streams in a client-to-server connection is `jabber:client`, so the namespace for the exchange of document streams in a server-to-server connection is `jabber:server`.

There are three immediate child tags in the configuration wrapper tag:

`<legacy&sol;>`

> This acts as a flag that allows "legacy" Jabber servers to connect (or disallows, if it is absent). A legacy Jabber server is one that has Version 1.0 and, of more relevance, no support for the dialback mechanism. Without the tag, an incoming connection from a Version 1.0 Jabber server that didn't support dialback would be refused.

`<ip&sol;>`

> While a normal Jabber server listens for client connections on 5222, it listens for connections from other Jabber servers on port 5269. This is specified with the `<ip&sol;>` tag, which has the same characteristics as the `<ip&sol;>` tag in the c2s configuration settings (more than one tag allowed, specific IP address optional).

`<karma&sol;>`

> Karma is used in the s2s component to control connection traffic, just as it is used in c2s. See the section "The io Section" later in this chapter for more details.

Component Connection Method

The library load method is used to connect the s2s component to the backbone:

```
<load>
  <dialback>./dialback/dialback.so</dialback>
</load>
```

The `dialback()` is called in the shared library after it has been loaded.

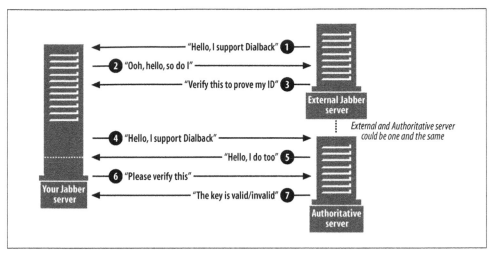

Figure 4-16. Dialback in action

Dialback

When an external Jabber server requests a connection to your Jabber server, the dialback mechanism ensures that the external Jabber server's identification can be verified. This is to prevent identity spoofing, the masquerading by one server or service under the name of another, and represents a big increase in security over earlier Jabber servers. To perform the identity check, your Jabber server "dials back" the external Jabber server to check credentials.

The sequence of events in a dialback conversation involves three (logical) parties and is roughly as shown in Figure 4-16.

Based on the validity of the key, your Jabber server can accept or refuse the incoming connection from the external Jabber server.

And, of course, the tables are turned and the shoe is on the other foot, to mix metaphors, if your Jabber server is the one trying to make a connection.

The io Section

The `<io&sol;>` section of the *jabber.xml* configuration file, shown in Example 4-20 and represented in diagram form in Figure 4-17, is where a number of settings relating to socket communication with the Jabber server are set.

Example 4-20. jabber.xml configuration for the io section

```
<io>

  <karma>
    <heartbeat>2</heartbeat>
    <init>64</init>
    <max>64</max>
    <inc>6</inc>
    <dec>1</dec>
    <penalty>-3</penalty>
    <restore>64</restore>
  </karma>

  <rate points="5" time="25"&sol;>

</io>
```

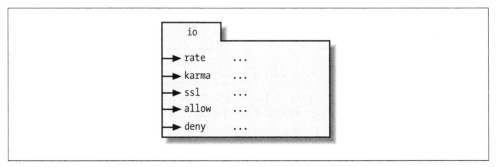

Figure 4-17. Diagram view of io section

Although a distinct section, io does not describe a component with custom configuration or a connection method; the contents are merely settings. Let's examine each of these settings here.

The <rate/> Tag

The <rate/> tag affords us a sort of connection throttle by allowing us to monitor the rate at which incoming connections are made and to put a hold on further connections if the rate is reached.

The rate is calculated to be a number of connection attempts—from a single IP address—within a certain amount of time. We can see these two components of the rate formula as attributes of the <rate/> tag itself:

```
<rate points="5" time="25"&sol;>
```

This means acceptance of incoming connections from an individual IP address will be stopped if more than five connection attempts (points) are made in the space of 25 seconds (time).

The "rating" (the throttling of connection attempts) will be restored at the end of the period defined (25 seconds in this case).

The effect of a `<rate&sol;>` tag in this io section is serverwide; all socket connections (for example, those of c2s and s2s) can be rate-limited. If there is no explicit `<rate&sol;>` specification in a particular service that listens on a socket for connections, then the specification in this io section is used. If no `<rate&sol;>` tag is specified in this io section, then the server defaults are used—these are actually the same as what's explicitly specified here.

The `<karma&sol;>` Tag

Like the `<rate&sol;>` tag, `<karma&sol;>` is used to control connectivity. Whereas rating helps control the number of connections, karma allows us to control the data flow rate per connection once a connection has been made.

The concept of karma is straightforward; each socket has a karma value associated with it. We can understand it better if we think of it as each entity (connecting through a socket) having a karma value. The higher the value—the more karma— an entity has, the more data it is allowed to send through the socket. So as rating is a throttle for connections, so karma is a throttle for data throughput.

There are certain settings that allow us to fine-tune our throughput throttle. Table 4-6 lists these settings, along with the values explicitly set in each of the c2s and s2s component sections in our *jabber.xml* file. Notice how the settings for the Server (to Server) Connections component are considerably higher than those for the Client (to Server) Connections—this is based on the assumption that server-to-server traffic will be greater than client-to-server on a socket-by-socket basis.

Table 4-6. Settings for karma control, with c2s and s2s values

Setting	c2s values	s2s values	Description
`<init&sol;>`	10	50	The initial value for karma on a new socket.
`<max&sol;>`	10	50	The maximum karma value that can be attained by a socket.
`<inc&sol;>`	1	4	By how much the karma value is incremented (over time).
`<dec&sol;>`	1	1	By how much the karma value is decremented in a penalty situation.
`<penalty&sol;>`	-6	-5	The karma value is plunged to this level once it falls to 0.
`<restore&sol;>`	10	50	The karma value is boosted to this level once it rises (after a penalty) to 0.

The relationship between an entity's karma and how much data it is allowed to write to the socket is linear; in fact, the amount is:

```
(karma value * 100)
```

and this every 2 seconds. The multiplier (100) and the karma period (2) are hard-coded into the server; a recompilation would be required to change these values.

Over time, an entity's karma value will increase, up to a maximum value (we need a ceiling on how much we're going to allow an entity to send!) every karma period (2 seconds).

The same karma formula is used to penalize an entity for sending too much data. If more than (karma * 100) bytes are sent within a certain period, the entity's karma value is decreased. Once the value reaches 0, it is plunged to a negative number, meaning that the entity must take a breather until the value grows back to 0 (over time, it will). At this point, the value will be restored to a value that gives the entity a chance to start sending data again.

The <ssl/> Tag

If you have compiled your Jabber server with SSL (see Chapter 3) and want to use SSL-encrypted connections, you will have to have specified the <ssl/> tags in the configuration of the c2s component instance. Furthermore, you must specify the location of your SSL certificate and key file. There is an <ssl/> tag in this io section for this purpose.

You can have separate files for each IP address specified in the c2s component instance configuration's <ssl/> tag. Example 4-21 shows the specification of two *.pem* files—one for each of two IP addresses.

Example 4-21. Specifying SSL certificate and key files per IP address

```
<ssl>
  <key ip="192.168.0.4">/usr/local/ssl/certs/ks1.pem</key>
  <key ip="192.168.9.1">/usr/local/ssl/certs/ks2.pem</key>
</ssl>
```

The <allow/> and <deny/> Tags

You can control at the IP address and network level who can connect to your Jabber server with the <allow/> and <deny/> tags.

The default (when no tags are specified) is to allow connections from everywhere. If you use <allow/> tags, then connections will be allowed *only* from the addresses or networks specified. If you use <deny/> tags, then connections will be denied from those addresses or networks specified. If you have both

`<allow&sol;>` and `<deny&sol;>` tags, the intersection of addresses between the two tag sets will be *denied*. In other words, `<deny&sol;>` overrides `<allow&sol;>`.

The tags wrap individual IP addresses, which are specified using the `<ip&sol;>` tag, or network addresses, which are specified using the `<ip&sol;>` tag in combination with the `<mask&sol;>` netmask tag. Example 4-22 shows connections to a Jabber server being limited to hosts from two internal networks with the exception of one particular IP address, and a specific host on the Internet.

Example 4-22. Using <allow/> and <deny/> to control connections

```
<allow>
  <ip>192.168.10.0</ip>
  <mask>255.255.255.0</mask>
</allow>

<allow>
  <ip>192.168.11.0</ip>
  <mask>255.255.255.0</mask>
</allow>

<allow>
  <ip>195.82.105.244</ip>
</allow>

<deny>
  <ip>192.168.11.131</ip>
</deny>
```

pidfile Section

The `pidfile` section simply specifies the name of the file to which the process ID (PID) of the Jabber server will be written at startup. In this case, the name of the file is *./jabber.pid*.

The XML describing this section is shown in Example 4-23 and is represented in diagram form in Figure 4-18.

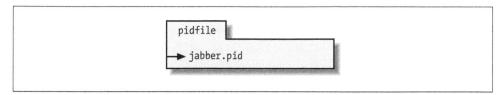

Figure 4-18. Diagram view of pidfile section

Example 4-23. jabber.xml configuration for the pidfile section

```
<pidfile>./jabber.pid</pidfile>
```

Managing the Configuration

Now that we've had a tour of the components and have an idea what sorts of configurations are possible, you may be wondering whether there's a way to retain some sort of overview of the actual XML. Dropping component instance definitions in and out of the configuration file is somewhat tedious, and certainly when editing such a large file, it's not difficult to lose sense of direction and comment out or edit the wrong section.

Help is at hand, in the form of the <jabberd:include> tag. This tag comes from the same stable as <jabberd:cmdline/> and provides the Jabber server administrator with ways to better manage the XML configuration.

The contents of a file specified with the <jabberd:include/> tag are imported (included) in the position that the <jabberd:include/> tag occupies. Depending on what the root tag in the file to be included is, the import is done in one of two ways:

- If the root tag matches the parent tag of <jabberd:include/>, the contents of the file minus the root tag are included.

- If the root tag does not match the parent tag of <jabberd:include/>, then the entire contents of the file are included.

For example, if we have a section like this in the *jabber.xml* file:

```
...
<conference xmlns="jabber:config:conference">
  <public&sol;>
  <vCard>
    <FN>yak Chatrooms</FN>
    <DESC>This is a public chatroom service.</DESC>
    <URL>http://yak/chat</URL>
  </vCard>
  ...
  <jabberd:include>./rooms.xml</jabberd:include>
</conference>
...
```

and the content of *./rooms.xml* looks like this:

```
<room jid="kitchen@conference.yak">
  <name>The Kitchen</name>
  <notice>
    <join> comes to add to the broth-spoiling</join>
    <leave> can't stand the heat</leave>
    <rename> is now known as </rename>
```

```
    </notice>
  </room>
  <room jid="cellar@conference.yak">
    <name>The Cellar</name>
    <secret>cellarsecret</secret>
  </room>
```

then these rooms will be defined to the Conferencing component as if the configuration XML had appeared directly inside of the `<conference&sol;>` configuration wrapper tag.

We can put the `<jabberd:include&sol;>` tag to good use and organize our configuration component instances as shown in Example 4-24.

Example 4-24. Configuration XML organized with <jabberd:include/>

```
<jabber>

  <!-- Core components -->

  <jabberd:include>./sessions.xml</jabberd:include>
  <jabberd:include>./config/standard/xdb.xml</jabberd:include>
  <jabberd:include>./config/standard/c2s.xml</jabberd:include>

  <!-- Testing -->

  <!--
  <jabberd:include>./config/local/conference.xml</jabberd:include>
  <jabberd:include>./config/test/test.service.xml</jabberd:include>
  -->

  <!-- Logging -->

  <jabberd:include>./config/standard/elogger.xml</jabberd:include>
  <jabberd:include>./config/standard/rlogger.xml</jabberd:include>

  <!--
  Internal-only server right now

  <jabberd:include>./config/standard/dnsrv.xml</jabberd:include>
  <jabberd:include>./config/standard/s2s.xml</jabberd:include>
  -->

  <!-- Misc -->

  <jabberd:include>./config/standard/jud.xml</jabberd:include>

  <!-- IO (incl. karma), PIDfile -->

  <jabberd:include>./config/standard/io.xml</jabberd:include>
  <jabberd:include>./config/standard/pidfile.xml</jabberd:include>

</jabber>
```

The XML in Example 4-24 gives us a great overview of which components are included in our Jabber server; we have the core components providing the Session Management, Client (to Server) Connections, and Data Storage services. There are a couple of components under test (Conferencing and a custom component we're calling `test.service`) that are currently deactivated. There are also Logging services in their standard configuration. The components providing facilities for connecting to other Jabber servers—Server (to Server) Connections and Hostname Resolution—are currently inactive, meaning that as configured, the Jabber server will be purely internal. There's a local JUD defined too; and finally we have the `io` and `pidfile` specifications—also abstracted out into separate XML chunks.

This works well especially if there are certain parts of the configuration—for example, certain component instance definitions—that don't normally change; you can see that many of the component configuration files are in a "standard" directory, which by convention could signify that they're the same as the XML configuration as delivered and are not likely to change.

The <jabberd:cmdline/> Tag

The `<jabberd:cmdline&sol;>` tag was mentioned in Chapter 3 as a way of providing a command-line hook into the configuration: values stored in the XML could be overridden by command-line switches used when invoking *jabberd*.

The tag is used in the standard XML configuration (see Figure 4-3) to allow replacement of the hostname and spool directory:

```
<host><jabberd:cmdline flag="h">yak</jabberd:cmdline></host>
```

and:

```
<spool><jabberd:cmdline flag='s'>./spool</jabberd:cmdline></spool>
```

In fact, this tag can be used in most places in the XML. So if, for example, you have a requirement to modify (respecify) the error and record log files for each *jabberd* invocation, you can do something like this:

```
<log id='elogger'>
  <host&sol;>
  <logtype&sol;>
  <format>%d: [%t] (%h): %s</format>
  <file><jabberd:cmdline flag="e">error.log</jabberd:cmdline></file>
  <stderr&sol;>
</log>
```

and then override the value `error.log` with something else at invocation time:

```
yak:~/jabber-1.4.1$ ./jabberd/jabberd -e error_log.txt &
```

Server Constellations

Throughout the discussion of components in this chapter and how they're arranged to form a "complete" Jabber server, we've really considered only a monolithic server, running in a single process. However, there may be good reasons (performance, administration, and manageability) to run the Jabber server in different configurations, or *constellations*.

> If the Hostname Resolution component is configured to run, then you will see two processes at startup, as the component—dnsrv—forks to have the resolver functionality run in a separate child process.

In this concluding section of this chapter, we take a look at some of the possible constellations and how they're constructed.

Multiple Servers on One Host

Although it's unlikely that this constellation would be of much use, it is possible to run more than one Jabber server on one host simply by creating multiple installations, maintaining each server's *jabber.xml* configuration file separately, and starting them up to listen to each other on different ports. Note that some Jabber clients don't support connections to anything other than port 5222, however.

As we have seen from examining the instance configuration for the Client (to Server) Connections and the Server (to Server) Connections components, the standard Jabber ports for client and server connectivity are 5222 and 5269, respectively. To run a second Jabber server on the same host, just ensure that its Connections component instances are configured to listen on different ports.

"Real" Virtual Jabber Servers

While looking at the section "Host Filter" earlier in this chapter, we saw how to use multiple <host/> tags to allow connection to the Jabber server under multiple hostnames. Although this simple feature might be useful in some circumstances, a better distinction of Session Management functionality might be more appropriate.

Taking our *a-domain.com* and *b-domain.com* hostname examples again, we might want to offer different welcome messages to new users and limit the authentication possibilities for the *b-domain.com* host to zero knowledge only. We also may wish to disable the message filtering service for the *a-domain.com* host. Furthermore, we might want to offer—in the <browse/> list—a different set of services for each of the hosts.

Let's have a look how this can be done. Using the <jabberd:include/> tag to organize our configuration XML by component instance definitions, we might have a *jabber.xml* configuration file that looks like Example 4-25.

Example 4-25. Virtual server jabber.xml configuration

```
<jabber>

  <!-- Common components -->
  <jabberd:include>./config/common/xdb.xml</jabberd:include>
  <jabberd:include>./config/common/c2s.xml</jabberd:include>
  <jabberd:include>./config/common/elogger.xml</jabberd:include>
  <jabberd:include>./config/common/rlogger.xml</jabberd:include>
  <jabberd:include>./config/common/dnsrv.xml</jabberd:include>
  <jabberd:include>./config/common/s2s.xml</jabberd:include>

  <!-- a-domain.com -->
  <jabberd:include>./config/a-domain/sessions.xml</jabberd:include>
  <jabberd:include>./config/a-domain/conference.xml</jabberd:include>

  <!-- b-domain.com -->
  <jabberd:include>./config/b-domain/sessions.xml</jabberd:include>
  <jabberd:include>./config/b-domain/conference.xml</jabberd:include>
  <jabberd:include>./config/b-domain/jud.xml</jabberd:include>

  <!-- IO, PIDfile -->
  <jabberd:include>./config/common/io.xml</jabberd:include>
  <jabberd:include>./config/common/pidfile.xml</jabberd:include>

</jabber>
```

What can we see here? First, *a-domain.com* and *b-domain.com* Jabber users will share the common facilities such as data storage (remembering that data will be stored by hostname within the spool area), Client (to Server) Connections, Logging, and so on.

 Don't forget that you can use two xdb component instances, specifying a different host filter in each, to store data in separate places—see the section "Component Instance: xdb" earlier in this chapter.

They also share the same `io` settings and `pidfile` definition; after all, there is still only one Jabber server that is hosting these two virtual servers, so we need only one `pidfile`.

But we also see that there are two *sessions.xml* files included—one for the *a-domain.com* host and another for the *b-domain.com* host. And with each of the *sessions.xml* files included, we have one or two other components—for Conferencing and JUD services.

Configuration for a-domain.com

The layout in the *jabber.xml* file indicates that there are separate definitions for each of the two hosts. Let's examine the contents of *./config/a-domain/sessions.xml*:

```
<service id="sessions.a-domain">

  <host>a-domain.com</host>

  <jsm xmlns="jabber:config:jsm">

    <!-- No filter config necessary -->

    <vCard>
      <FN>a-domain.com Jabber Services</FN>
      <DESC>Jabber 1.4.1 on a-domain.com</DESC>
      <URL>http://www.a-domain.com</URL>
    </vCard>

    <browse>
      <conference type="public" jid="conference.a-domain.com"
                  name="a-domain Conferencing"&sol;>
    </browse>

    <!--

    a-domain.com not open for self-service new user accounts

    <register notify="yes">
      <instructions&sol;>
      <name&sol;>
      <email&sol;>
    </register>

    -->

    <welcome>
      <subject>Welcome!</subject>
      <body>Welcome to the Jabber server at a-domain.com</body>
    </welcome>

    <admin>
```

```
          <write>admin@a-domain.com</write>
          <reply>
            <subject>Auto Reply</subject>
            <body>This is a special administrative address.</body>
          </reply>
        </admin>

    </jsm>

    <load main="jsm">
      <jsm>./jsm/jsm.so</jsm>
      <mod_echo>./jsm/jsm.so</mod_echo>
      <mod_roster>./jsm/jsm.so</mod_roster>
      <mod_time>./jsm/jsm.so</mod_time>
      <mod_vcard>./jsm/jsm.so</mod_vcard>
      <mod_last>./jsm/jsm.so</mod_last>
      <mod_version>./jsm/jsm.so</mod_version>
      <mod_announce>./jsm/jsm.so</mod_announce>
      <mod_agents>./jsm/jsm.so</mod_agents>
      <mod_browse>./jsm/jsm.so</mod_browse>
      <mod_admin>./jsm/jsm.so</mod_admin>

      <!--
      No filter service for a-domain.com
      <mod_filter>./jsm/jsm.so</mod_filter>
      -->

      <mod_offline>./jsm/jsm.so</mod_offline>
      <mod_presence>./jsm/jsm.so</mod_presence>
      <mod_auth_plain>./jsm/jsm.so</mod_auth_plain>
      <mod_auth_digest>./jsm/jsm.so</mod_auth_digest>
      <mod_auth_0k>./jsm/jsm.so</mod_auth_0k>
      <mod_log>./jsm/jsm.so</mod_log>
      <mod_register>./jsm/jsm.so</mod_register>
      <mod_xml>./jsm/jsm.so</mod_xml>
    </load>

</service>
```

We can see that this configuration file contains the definition of a JSM component instance. The instance is identified with the name `sessions.a-domain` and the host *a-domain.com* has been registered as what the JSM listens for—its "external identification."

We can also see that:

- The literal texts in the descriptions and in the welcome message are specific to *a-domain.com*.

- The administration section in the configuration describes a local user that is at *a-domain.com* as the administrator.

- The new user registration facility has been disabled.

- The *mod_filter* service has been commented out from the list of loaded modules in the component connection definition.

There is one service listed in the browse section—the Conferencing service, with the JID *conference.a-domain.com*; this is the service that's defined in the file *./config/a-domain/conference.xml*, which itself is specified in a `<jabberd:include&sol;>` tag in the main *jabber.xml* alongside this *sessions.xml* file.

Taking a look at this Conferencing service definition for *a-domain.com* in the *./config/a-domain/conference.xml* file, we see:

```
<service id='conf.a-domain'>
  <host>conference.a-domain.com</host>
  <load><conference>./conference-0.4.1/conference.so</conference></load>
  <conference xmlns="jabber:config:conference">
    <public&sol;>
    <vCard>
      <FN>a-domain Chatrooms</FN>
      <DESC>This service is for public chatrooms.</DESC>
      <URL>http://www.a-domain.com/chatrooms</URL>
    </vCard>
    <history>10</history>
    <notice>
      <join> is here</join>
      <leave> has left</leave>
      <rename> is now known as </rename>
    </notice>
    <room jid="bar@conference.a-domain.com">
      <name>The Bar</name>
    </room>
  </conference>
</service>
```

Similar to what we saw with the *./config/a-domain/sessions.xml* content, here we see *a-domain.com*–specific definitions: crucially the service identification as `conf.a-domain` and the `<host&sol;>` tag declaring the hostname that this service serves under.

Configuration for b-domain.com

Now that we've seen the *a-domain*–specific XML, let's have a look at the *b-domain*–specific XML:

```
<service id="sessions.b-domain">
  <host>b-domain.com</host>
  <jsm xmlns="jabber:config:jsm">

    ...

    <vCard>
```

```
        <FN>b-domain Jabber Server</FN>
        <DESC>Jabber 1.4.1 on b-domain.com</DESC>
        <URL>http://www.b-domain.com/</URL>
      </vCard>

      <browse>
        <conference type="public" jid="conference.b-domain"
                    name="b-domain Conferencing"&sol;>
        <service type="jud" jid="jud.b-domain" name="b-domain JUD">
          <ns>jabber:iq:search</ns>
          <ns>jabber:iq:register</ns>
        </service>
      </browse>

      <register notify="yes">
        <instructions>
          Choose a username and password to register with this server.
        </instructions>
        <name&sol;>
      </register>

      <welcome>
        <subject>Welcome!</subject>
        <body>Welcome to the Jabber server at b-domain</body>
      </welcome>

      <admin>
        <read>info@b-domain</read>
        <write>service@b-domain</write>
        <reply>
          <subject>Auto Reply</subject>
          <body>This is a special administrative address.</body>
        </reply>
      </admin>

    </jsm>

    <load main="jsm">
      <jsm>./jsm/jsm.so</jsm>
      <mod_echo>./jsm/jsm.so</mod_echo>
      <mod_roster>./jsm/jsm.so</mod_roster>
      <mod_time>./jsm/jsm.so</mod_time>
      <mod_vcard>./jsm/jsm.so</mod_vcard>
      <mod_last>./jsm/jsm.so</mod_last>
      <mod_version>./jsm/jsm.so</mod_version>
      <mod_announce>./jsm/jsm.so</mod_announce>
      <mod_agents>./jsm/jsm.so</mod_agents>
      <mod_browse>./jsm/jsm.so</mod_browse>
      <mod_admin>./jsm/jsm.so</mod_admin>
      <mod_filter>./jsm/jsm.so</mod_filter>
      <mod_offline>./jsm/jsm.so</mod_offline>
      <mod_presence>./jsm/jsm.so</mod_presence>
      <!--
```

```
      zero-knowledge authentication only

      <mod_auth_plain>./jsm/jsm.so</mod_auth_plain>
      <mod_auth_digest>./jsm/jsm.so</mod_auth_digest>
      -->

      <mod_auth_0k>./jsm/jsm.so</mod_auth_0k>

      <mod_log>./jsm/jsm.so</mod_log>
      <mod_register>./jsm/jsm.so</mod_register>
      <mod_xml>./jsm/jsm.so</mod_xml>
    </load>

  </service>
```

We can see we've fulfilled our requirements of the virtual server for *b-domain*: registration is open but authentication is limited to zero knowledge, and the services offered in the <browse/> list are unique to *b-domain*. That said, it *is* possible for someone registered to *b-domain* to connect to and use, say, the Conferencing service listening on conferencing.a-domain.com; see the section "Using Services on Other Jabber Servers" later in this chapter.

The Conferencing and JUD services associated with the *b-domain.com* hostname will be configured in a similar way to how the Conferencing service was configured in *./config/a-domain/conference.xml* for *a-domain*—crucially again the service IDs will be unique and the <host/> tags will be specific to *b-domain.com*.

As long as each component instance is uniquely identified and you have used separate hostname definitions, "real" virtual Jabber servers *all listening to the same Jabber standard client port of 5222 on a single host* can be a reality.

Splitting Up Jabber Server Processes

As well as being able to lump multiple Jabber server identities in the form of virtual hosting onto a single Jabber server and its corresponding monolithic process, you may also go in the opposite direction and split up a single Jabber server into multiple processes. These processes interact through TCP socket connections and so it's possible for them to run on the same or different physical hosts.

How is this achieved? Well, revisiting the ideas from the start of this chapter, we consider that a Jabber server is a daemon (*jabberd*) and a set of components that provide the services. Taking one step away from the "classic" Jabber server model, which contains components such as the ones described in the section "An Overview of the Server Architecture" at the start of this chapter, we can imagine a Jabber server where *jabberd* controls just one component, say the Conferencing component.

How much use is a Jabber server with a single Conferencing component? Not much. But when linked together with another Jabber server, we can see that this is a way to split off components and run them independently.

Taking the Conferencing component as an example candidate for ostracism, let's have a look at what we need to do.

Define the configuration for the satellite server

This is very straightforward. We've seen Conferencing configuration before, so we'll shorten it a bit here:

```
<jabber>

  <service id='conf.yak'>
    <host>conference.yak</host>
    <load><conference>./conference-0.4.1/conference.so</conference></load>
    <conference xmlns="jabber:config:conference">

       . . .

    </conference>
  </service>

</jabber>
```

This is the entirety of the configuration file so far for the satellite server—there's only one component instance—identified as `conf.yak`. Notice that the only other tag pair is the filewide `<jabber>` . . . `</jabber>`. Let's call it *jabber_conf.xml*.

Open a connection point in the main server

We've already seen a mechanism earlier in this chapter in the section "Component Connection Methods" that allows external components to connect into the Jabber server backbone by exchanging XML streams in the `jabber:component:accept` namespace. This is the TCP socket connection method.

We can prepare a connection point to the main Jabber server by specifying a component connection like this:

```
<service id="conflinker">
  <host>conference.yak</host>
  <accept>
    <ip>127.0.0.1</ip>
    <port>9001</port>
    <secret>confsecret</secret>
  </accept>
</service>
```

in the configuration for the main Jabber server.

There's no real difference between this XML and the XML shown in the <accept/> example earlier in this chapter. The clue lies in the service ID, which has been defined as conflinker. There's nothing special about the name; it simply gives the administrator a hint that there's some sort of link to a conference service from this point.

We're specifying acceptance of connections on IP address 127.0.0.1 (the same host as this main server), but it could just as easily be the IP address assigned to a network card, so that the connection could be made from a satellite server on a separate host.

List the service definition in <browse/>

While we're editing the main server's XML, we should add an entry for our satellite conference service:

```
<browse>
   ...
    <conference type="public" jid="conference.yak" name="yak Conferencing"&sol;>

   ...
</browse>
```

The JID defined here must match the host defined in the Conferencing component instance definition in the satellite server configuration.

Add a connector mechanism to the satellite server

Now that we've opened up a connection point in the main server, we need to add some corresponding configuration to the satellite server's XML—the "plug" that will attach to the connection point on the main server:

```
<jabber>
  <service id="conflinker">
    <uplink&sol;>
    <connect>
      <ip>127.0.0.1</ip>
      <port>9001</port>
      <secret>confsecret</secret>
    </connect>
  </service>
  <service id='conf.yak'>
    <host>conference.yak</host>
    <load><conference>./conference-0.4.1/conference.so</conference></load>
    <conference xmlns="jabber:config:conference">
       ...
    </conference>
  </service>
</jabber>
```

This new service (the "plug") with an ID of `conflinker` (which matches the ID of the corresponding "socket" in the main server)* contains two elements.

- The `<connect&sol;>` tag, which corresponds to the `<accept&sol;>` tag in the main server's configuration.

- The `<uplink&sol;>` tag, which serves as a conduit for all types of packets—those handled by each of the three delivery trees log, xdb, and service.

While we're looking at the satellite server's configuration again, it's worth pointing out that even in a situation in which the satellite server process would be running on a separate host (we're running it here on the same host—hence the localhost IP address of 127.0.0.1 in the `<accept&sol;>` tag), the value of the conference service's host filter is still *conference.yak*. In other words, the name of the host where the satellite server actually runs is irrelevant. This is because the conference service is still seen by the main Jabber server's *jabberd* as "local," through the accept/connect binding and the shared *logical* name yak is more appropriate.

Specify a different PID file location

If the satellite server is going to be running on the same host as the main server, and from the same directory (indeed, in this example, we've named the satellite server's configuration file *jabber_conf.xml* to distinguish it from the main server's *jabber.xml* file), make sure a different location for storing the PID file is specified:

```
<jabber>
  <service id="conflinker">
    ...
  </service>
  <service id='conf.yak'>
    ...
  </service>
  <pidfile>jabber_conf.pid</pidfile>
</jabber>
```

Starting the main server

Once everything is configured, start up the main server:

```
yak:~/jabber-1.4.1$ ./jabberd/jabberd -c jabber.xml &
```

The `<accept&sol;>` section should start listening on port 9001 for a connection:

```
yak:~/jabber-1.4.1$ netstat -an | grep 9001
tcp        0      0 127.0.0.1:9001          0.0.0.0:*               LISTEN
```

---

* Although the service ID's do not *need* to match.

Starting the satellite server

It's time to start up the satellite server, from the same directory in this example:

```
yak:~/jabber-1.4.1$ ./jabberd/jabberd -c jabber_conf.xml &
```

The satellite server should make a connection to the socket listening on 127.0.0.1:9001.

At this stage, you should have Jabber server services split between a main process and a separate process that runs a Conferencing component.

At the risk of stating the obvious, it is worth pointing out that this example shows that simply starting *jabberd* does not mean that any process will bind to and start listening on port 5222. It is the c2s component that makes this happen. So starting a second *jabberd* on the same host did not cause any socket listening problems because this second *jabberd* doesn't have a c2s component (because there's no JSM for clients to want to connect to) and so doesn't try to bind to port 5222.

Using Services on Other Jabber Servers

This section describes a technique that we've already seen used implicitly in the section "Splitting Up Jabber Server Processes." That is the use of services on *other* Jabber servers. In reality, the example of running a Conferencing module in a satellite Jabber server showed the technique in the context of local administrative control; we control the main and satellite servers, and the module in the satellite server may rely on services in the main server for support.

Consider the <browse/> section in the *jabber.xml* configuration file that comes with Jabber server 1.4.1:

```
<browse>
  ...
  <service type="jud" jid="users.jabber.org" name="Jabber User Directory">
    <ns>jabber:iq:search</ns>
    <ns>jabber:iq:register</ns>
  </service>
  ...
</browse>
```

What's this? A JID of *users.jabber.org*? How many Jabber server installations will be running with the *jabber.org* domain name? Yes, just one. This means that the <browse/> section is pointing to a JUD component running at *jabber.org* as *users.jabber.org*. If the Jabber server is running the Server (to Server) Connections and Hostname Resolution components, clients connecting to our server can transparently jump across the wire and avail themselves of the JUD services at *users.jabber.org*.

The entry doesn't have to be in the `<browse&sol;>` section. This is more for convenience, so that the clients can build a dynamic list of services from which the user
may choose. The client may of course offer a facility for the user to directly enter
the name (hostname, address) of the service she requires.

How does this procedure compare to the "satellite server" procedure? In this case,
the packets that originate from a Jabber client connected to our Jabber server
make their way to the JUD service on *users.jabber.org* by means of the Server (to
Server) service. That is, they travel through a connection described by the `jab-
ber:server` namespace. On the other hand, packets on our server destined for a
satellite conference service travel through a connection described by the `jab-
ber:component:accept` namespace.

II

Putting Jabber's Concepts to Work

This part of the book provides detailed information about the Jabber protocol and a series of recipes—practical solutions to everyday problems—deployed in Jabber. The recipes use various Jabber features to illustrate parts of the protocol.

Chapters in this part include:

- Chapter 5, *Jabber Technology Basics*
- Chapter 6, *Jabber Namespaces*
- Chapter 7, *User Registration and Authorization*
- Chapter 8, *Using Messages and Presence*
- Chapter 9, *Groupchat, Components, and Event Models*
- Chapter 10, *Pointers for Further Development*

5

Jabber Technology Basics

One of Jabber's strengths is its simplicity. Neither the technology employed to build Jabber networks nor the protocol used to facilitate conversations within those networks is complicated.

The aim of this chapter is to give you a good grounding in the technology and the protocol. In the Preface we likened Jabber to chess: a small set of rules but boundless possibilities. And, indeed, that is the case. In this chapter we cover identification within Jabber—how entities are addressed. Related to identity is the concept of *resources*; we look at how that relates to addressing, as well as its relationship to *presence* and *priority*.

The Jabber protocol is in XML, which is streamed between endpoints. We look at the details of these XML streams and see how they're constructed. Comprised of surprisingly few basic elements, the Jabber protocol is small but perfectly formed. Each element of Jabber's protocol will be reviewed in detail.

With this chapter under your belt, your understanding of Jabber fundamentals should be complete. Everything else is strategy, planning, and endgames.

Jabber Identifiers

An *entity* is anything that can be addressed in Jabber. A server, a component, a user connected with a client—these are all addressable entities. Every entity is identifiable by a *Jabber ID*, or JID. These JIDs give these entities their *addressability*. This is what a typical JID looks like:

```
qmacro@jabber.org/Laptop
```

This JID represents a user, connected to Jabber on a particular client. We can look at this JID in a more abstract way, by identifying its component parts:

```
username@hostname/resource
```

The *username* is separated from the *hostname* with an @ symbol, and the *resource* is separated from the *hostname* with a slash (/).

It's quite likely that the JIDs you may have encountered so far are those representing users' connections, such as the *qmacro@jabber.org/Laptop* example. This is not the only sort of entity that JIDs are used to represent. As a Uniform Resource Locator (URL) is fundamental to the HyperText Transport Protocol (HTTP), so a JID is fundamental in Jabber. JIDs are used to represent not only users connected to Jabber via their clients, but also every single entity in the Jabber universe that is to be addressed—in other words, that is to be the potential recipient of a message. Before looking at the restrictions that govern how a JID might be constructed (these restrictions are described in the section "Rules and Regulations"), let's first look at some examples in which a JID is employed to give entities their addressability:

A Jabber server

A Jabber server is identified by a JID that doesn't contain a *username*. For basic addressing, the JID is simply the *hostname*:

```
jabber.org
```

To address specific features of the server, a *resource* is often specified and reflects the feature being addressed:

```
jabber.org/admin
```

The JID *jabber.org/admin* is used by server administrators at *jabber.org* to obtain a list of online users.

Administrators can send an announcement to all online users on the Jabber server yak by sending a message to the JID:

```
yak/announce/online
```

In this case, the resource is *announce/online*. The first slash in the JID is interpreted as the separator; the second slash is simply part of the *resource*.

Unique identification of Jabber software

Jabber clients can make a request for information on new versions of themselves by sending a special packet to an update server that manages a software version database. The packet they send is a presence packet (see the section "Jabber's Building Blocks" later in this chapter for an explanation of packet types) to a JID that takes this form:

```
959967024@update.jabber.org/1.6.0.3
```

In this case, the important part of the JID is the *hostname* (*update.jabber.org*) which is the Jabber server to which the presence packet is destined. The *username* (95996702) is used to represent the unique identification of the client software requesting version information, and the *resource* (1.6.0.3) is set to be the current version of the client software.

A conference room

Jabber has a Conferencing component that provides group chat facilities akin to IRC. Whereas IRC has channels, the Conferencing component offers rooms. These rooms are addressed with JIDs in this form:

```
jdev@conference.jabber.org
```

The room name is specified in the *username* portion of the JID, and the *hostname* reflects the address of the conferencing component.

Browsing entities

Browsing is a powerful hierarchical navigation and entity discovery feature in Jabber. When a browse request is sent to an entity, that entity may return various pieces of information that reflect its component parts—how it's made up, what services it offers, what features it has, and so on.

The browse request is addressed to the entity via its JID, and the component parts that are returned in response are all identified with JIDs too. If we address a browse request to the JID yak/admin, we receive a list of online users. This is shown in Example 5-1.

Example 5-1: Querying the server yak for online users

```
SEND: <iq type='get' to='yak/admin'>
          <query xmlns='jabber:iq:browse'&sol;>
      </iq>

RECV: <iq type='result' to='dj@yak/console' from='yak/admin'>
          <item name='Online Users (seconds, sent, received)'
               xmlns='jabber:iq:browse' jid='yak/admin'>
            <user name='dj (548, 18, 15)' jid='dj@yak'&sol;>
            <user name='john (535, 11, 13)' jid='john@yak'&sol;>
            <user name='jim (488, 15, 17)' jid='jim@yak'&sol;>
          </item>
      </iq>
```

A further example of browsing is shown in Example 5-2, where a conference service running on the *jabber.org* server is queried for information.

Example 5-2: Querying a conference service

```
SEND: <iq to='conference.jabber.org' type='get'>
        <q xmlns='jabber:iq:browse'&sol;>
      </iq>

RECV: <iq type='result' to='qmacro@jabber.org/telnet'
          from='conference.jabber.org'>
        <conference xmlns='jabber:iq:browse'
          type='public' name='Jabber.org Conferencing Center'>
          <conference jid='help@conference.jabber.org'
                  type='public' name='Assistance Zone (2)'&sol;>
          <conference jid='jdev@conference.jabber.org'
                  type='public' name='Development Room (14)'&sol;>
          <conference jid='jabber@conference.jabber.org'
                  type='public' name='Users Area (6)'&sol;>
          <conference jid='chat@conference.jabber.org'
                  type='public' name='General Chat (1)'&sol;>
          ...
        </conference>
      </iq>
```

The JID `yak/admin` in Example 5-1 represents an administrative function in the Jabber server `yak`; it identifies the place—the service entry point—by Jabber address, from which this information can be retrieved.

Example 5-1 shows how pervasive the JID is as a mechanism for identification within Jabber. How we might use the information returned to us is not relevant at this point; the key thing to note is that the hooks used in conversations to jump from one point to another, to refer to other entities—services, users, transports, call-hooks into a server to obtain specific information—take the form of JIDs. Each one of the boldface attribute values in the example is a JID.

This administrative information about online users on a Jabber server can be retrieved by sending the IQ-get element shown in the example. However, the information is forthcoming only if the user making the request—sending the IQ-get element—is the *administrative* user. See the the section "Administration" in Chapter 4 for details on administrative users.

Taking another example from the conferencing area, JIDs are used to represent those present in a room in an abstracted way. Each room participant has an identity specific to that room, for example:

    jdev@conference.jabber.org/bd9505f766f98bd559d4c2d8a9d5ae78e3a7bbf5

As before, the room itself is represented by the *username* and *hostname* parts of the JID—in this case, it's the Jabber developers room (*jdev*) hosted on *conference.jabber.org*. The *resource* is the long hex number that represents an individual room participant. It's a hexadecimal SHA-1 message digest of the participant's JID, designed to be unique and calculated and assigned by the conferencing component as a user enters the room.*

Components, Hostnames, and Users

In the client software identification example of a JID being used to carry software version information, we have a presence packet addressed to a JID using the following form:

    959967024@update.jabber.org/1.6.0.3

But why doesn't the presence packet end up getting sent to a user called 959967024? The short answer is because the Jabber Session Manager (JSM) component isn't running at *update.jabber.org*.

Instead, the server is running a special component that provides a version information service and has no concept of user sessions as such. This component receives the presence packet—which doesn't go any further (i.e., it isn't passed on to somewhere else)—and then inspects the username and resource before performing the database lookup to see if their software needs to be updated.

So we see that just because a JID might have something defined for the username part, it doesn't necessarily mean there's a user at the end of the line. It just serves as a carrier of unique information embedded in the JID to whichever component is listening for packets to the hostname.

As you can see, JIDs are flexible identifiers used throughout Jabber to give addressability to various entities. In the context of the JSM and user management, the address structure *username@hostname* has many parallels with email addressing, and indeed not without reason. In the context of individual users, an email address represents a user on a specific email server. This server is the user's "home," the mailbox to which everything addressed to the user's email address is

---

* This is to shield the participant's real identity, which is the default setting for a conference room.

routed. Different email users have different home mailboxes. In the same way, the JIDs of different Jabber users reflect each user's home Jabber server, to which everything addressed to his JID is routed. A message addressed by a user based on one Jabber server to a user based on another Jabber server is automatically routed from the one server to the other.

Rules and Regulations

A JID *must* contain a hostname part to be valid. The username and resource parts are optional; circumstance and usage dictates when either of these parts is necessary. A username is specific to the hostname that it's paired up with. For example: `qmacro@jabber.org` is not the same as `qmacro@jabber.com`.

There are some restrictions on how each JID part is composed; Table 5-1 details these restrictions. Although you can be particular about the case of letters in a username, any operations (such as comparisons) at the Jabber server are case-insensitive. For example, if a user has registered `dj` as his username, then another user cannot register with the username `DJ`. However, the person who registered as `dj` can connect and send `DJ` when he authenticates, and for the duration of that session will be known as `DJ` not `dj`.

On the other hand, resources *are* case-sensitive.

Table 5-1. JID restrictions

JID part	Restrictions
username	A *username* can be up to 255 characters in length and may not contain any ASCII character under 33 (decimal),[a] nor can it contain any of the characters :, @, /, ", or '; also, whitespace (tabs, newlines, and carriage returns) and control characters are forbidden.
hostname	The same restrictions apply here as for normal DNS hostnames.
resource	There are no restrictions for the *resource* part of a JID.

[a] That is, it may not contain spaces or those considered to be control characters.

Resources and Priorities

In the previous section, we saw how the resource is used to "qualify" certain queries to a servername, to hold information such as version numbers, and to represent users in a conference room. However, the resource is traditionally seen as a way of making a distinction between simultaneous connections by a user to the same Jabber server. For example, if you connect to a Jabber server using the same username and password on three different machines (or *resources*), the Jabber server will look at the resource part of the JID to determine which client to route messages to.

For the purpose of this example, let's say that the three resources are a workstation, a laptop, and a PDA. Each client is connected to the same Jabber server, so the resource part of the JID can be used to distinguish between the three connections. They could also be used to differentiate between the three connections coming from the same client host.

The classic explanation serves us well here: In a work situation, I might be connected to my Jabber server using a client on my workstation. I might also be connected, with the same username, to my Jabber server on my laptop that's sitting next to my workstation. Furthermore, I might have a handheld device that runs a small Jabber client that I'm connected with, too.

On each client machine, I'm connecting using the same credentials (username and password) to the same Jabber server. So the resource part of a JID can be used to distinguish between my three connections. In this example, the three "resources" are my workstation, laptop, and handheld.

The resource part of a JID allows a user to be connected to Jabber (specifically the JSM, which manages users and sees user sessions as separate entities) multiple times.

Then the question becomes, what happens when someone sends you a message? To which client is the message sent?

This is where the concept of connection *priority* comes to our aid. Each Jabber client connection can be given a priority. When a user has more than one concurrent connection to a Jabber server, the priority is used to determine to which connection any messages intended for that user should be sent. IQ elements are *resource-bound*, that is, they are addressed to specific resources. In that sense, they are not affected by priority. (See the section "Jabber's Building Blocks" later in this chapter for information on the types of packets that are sent and received.) The connection with the highest priority value is the connection to which the messages are sent (priority values must be a positive integer and cannot be 0 or less).

Figure 5-1 shows priority in action. In this example, Sabine's message is sent to the Jabber client on the Desktop, as it has a higher priority. Note that with Jabber priority, 1 has a lower priority than, say, 5. The higher the number, the higher the priority.

In the event that there's a priority tie, the most recent connection to the Jabber server wins. For example, if DJ connects to the server first from a client running on his Laptop and then again later with a client running on his Desktop system, and both clients have their priority set to a value of 1, the client running on his Desktop would win and receive the incoming messages.

It is also possible to direct messages to a particular client. Taking the example from Figure 5-1, if *sabine@yak* were to specify *dj@yak/Laptop* instead of *dj@yak* as the recipient for a message, her message would go to Client 1 (Laptop), not Client 2 (Desktop), despite Client 1's lower priority value.

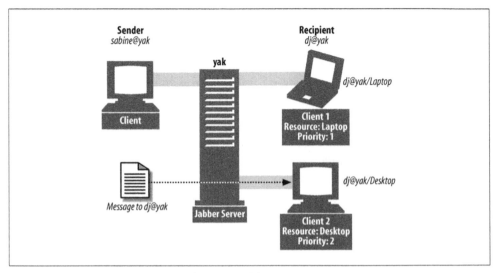

Figure 5-1. Resources, priority, and message delivery

 In the upcoming server Version 1.4.2, this resource-based routing facility has been made more flexible. Rather than relying upon exact matches (such as `Laptop` or `Desktop`), messages will be routed based on a subset of the resource value. For example, if logged in with the JID `sabine@yak/Laptop`, *sabine* would receive messages addressed to *sabine@yak/Laptop/foo*, *sabine@yak/Laptop/bar*, and so on. This allows clients to do flexible routing and delivery, based on the resource detail, once they've received the messages.

Priorities are specified when a user sends presence information. We will see this later in the section "Jabber's Building Blocks." It makes sense for the priority to be associated with a user's presence, rather than a user's client connection. For example, if the priority was specified at connection time, the user would have to disconnect and reconnect if she wanted to change priority. As it stands, she just has to send presence information containing a new priority value to change it. Figure 5-2 shows a WinJab client pop-up window used to change presence information. The value of the current priority can be changed.

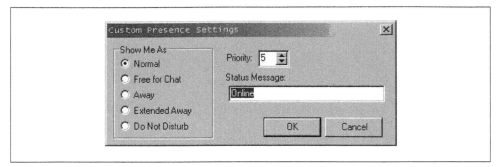

Figure 5-2. Changing presence and priority in the WinJab client

XML Streams

By now, you should already know that Jabber relies heavily on XML. XML courses through Jabber's veins; data sent and received between entities, and internally within the server itself, is formatted in XML *packets*.

However, the XML philosophy goes further than this. A connection between two Jabber endpoints, say, a client and a server, is made via a TCP socket, and XML is transferred between these endpoints. However, it's not just random fragments of XML flowing back and forth. There is a structure, a choreography, imposed upon that flow. The entire conversation that takes place between these two endpoints is embodied in a pair of XML documents.

The Conversation as XML Documents

The conversation is two-way, duplexed across a socket connection. On one side, the client sends an XML document to the server. On the other side, the server responds by sending an XML document to the client. Figure 5-3 shows the pair of XML documents being streamed across the TCP socket connection between client and server, over time.

But what do we mean when we say that the conversation is an XML document? To answer this, consider this simple XML document:

```
<?xml version="1.0"&quest;>
<roottag>
  <fragment1&sol;>
  <fragment2&sol;>
  <fragment3&sol;>
  ...
  <fragmentN&sol;>
</roottag>
```

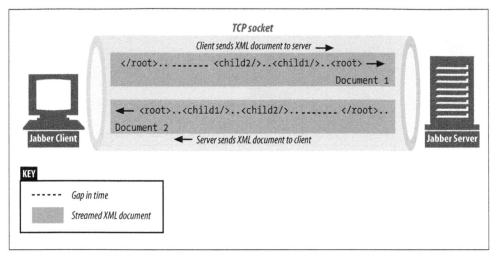

Figure 5-3. A conversation between client and server as a pair of streamed XML documents

The document starts with an XML declaration:

```
<?xml version="1.0"&quest;>
```

which is immediately followed by the opening root tag. This root tag is significant because there can be only one (and, of course, its corresponding closing tag) in the whole document. In effect, it wraps and contextualizes the content of the document:

```
<roottag>
  ...
</roottag>
```

The real content of the document is made up of the XML fragments that come after the opening root tag:

```
<fragment1&sol;>
<fragment2&sol;>
<fragment3&sol;>
...
<fragmentN&sol;>
```

So, taking a connection between a Jabber client and a Jabber server as an example, this is exactly what we have. The server is listening on port 5222 for incoming client-initiated connections. Once a client has successfully connected to the Jabber server, it sends an XML declaration and the opening root tag to announce its intentions to the server, which in turn responds by sending an XML declaration and opening root tag of its own.

From then on, every subsequent piece of data that the client sends to the server over the lifetime of the connection is an XML fragment (`<fragmentN/>`). The connection can be closed by the client by sending the matching closing root tag. Of course, the connection can be also closed by the server by sending the closing root tag of *its* XML document.

The fragments sent within the body of the XML document are the XML building blocks on which Jabber solutions are based. These XML building blocks are introduced and examined later in the chapter in the section "Jabber's Building Blocks."

Suffice it to say here that these fragments can come in any order within the body of the XML document, precisely because they're *in* the body. As long as an XML document has a root tag, and the fragments themselves are well-defined, then it doesn't matter *what* the content is. Because of the way the document is parsed— in chunks, as it appears—it doesn't matter if the fragments appear over a long period, which is the case in a client/server connection where messages and data are passed back and forth over time.

It should be fairly easy now to guess why this section (and the technique) is called *XML Streams*. XML is *streamed* over a connection in the form of a document and is parsed and acted upon by the recipient in fragments, as they appear.

The Opening Tag

Earlier, we said that the opening document tag was used by the client to "announce its intentions." The following is a typical opening document tag from a Jabber client that has made a socket connection to port 5222 on the Jabber server *jabber.org*:

```
<stream:stream
    xmlns:stream="http://etherx.jabber.org/streams"
    to="jabber.org"
    xmlns="jabber:client">
```

There are four parts to this opening tag:

The `<stream:stream>` *tag*
> Every streaming Jabber XML document must start, and end, with a `<stream:stream>` tag, qualified with the `stream` namespace.

The `stream` *namespace declaration*
> `xmlns:stream="http://etherx.jabber.org/streams"`
>
> The declaration of the `stream` namespace also comes in the opening `stream` tag. It refers to a URL (*http://etherx.jabber.org/streams*), which is a fixed value and serves to uniquely identify the `stream` namespace used in the XML document, rooted with `<stream&sol;>`, that is, streamed over a Jabber connection.
>
> The namespace qualifies only the tags that are prefixed `stream:`. Apart from `stream`, there is one other tag name used in these documents that is qualified

by this namespace, and that is `error`. The `<stream:error&sol;>` tag is used to convey Jabber XML stream connection errors, such as premature disconnection, invalid namespace specifications, incomplete root tag definitions, a timeout while waiting for authentication to follow the root tag exchange, and so on.

The to *attribute*

```
to="jabber.org"
```

There is a `to` attribute that specifies to which Jabber server the connection is to be made and where the user session is to be started and maintained.

We've already specified the *jabber.org* hostname, representing our Jabber server, when defining the socket connection (*jabber.org:5222*), so why do we need to define it again here? As indicated by the `to` attribute, you can see that we've made a *physical* connection to the *jabber.org* host. However, there may be a choice of *logical* hosts running within the Jabber server to which our client could connect.

When making the *physical* connection from our client to the Jabber server, we defined the hostname *jabber.org* for our socket connection (to *jabber.org:5222*). Now that we're connected, we're specifying *jabber.org* again as the *logical* host to which we want to connect *inside* Jabber. This is the logical host identity within the Jabber server running on the *jabber.org* host.

This "repeat specification" is required, because there's a difference between a *physical* Jabber host and a *logical* Jabber host. In the section "Server Constellations" in Chapter 4, we saw how a single Jabber server can be set up to service user sessions (with one or more JSMs) that are each identified with different logical hostnames. This is where the *physical/logical* hostname distinction comes from and why it's necessary to specify a name in the root `<stream:stream>` tag's to attribute.

It just so happens that in the example of an opening tag we've used, the *logical* hostname is the same as the *physical* one—*jabber.org*. In many cases, this will be the most commonplace. However, an Internet Service Provider (ISP), for example, may wish to offer Jabber services to its customers and dedicate a single host for that purpose. That host has various DNS names, which all resolve to that same host IP address. Only one Jabber server is run on that host. (If a second server were to be installed, it would have to listen on different—nonstandard—ports, which would be less than ideal.) To reflect the different names under which it would want to offer Jabber services, it would run multiple JSMs under different *logical* names (using different values for each `<host&sol;>` configuration tag, as explained in the section "A Tour of jabber.xml" in Chapter 4). When connecting to that Jabber server, it may well be that the *logical* name specified in the opening tag's to attribute would be different from the *physical* name used to reach the host in the first place.

The namespace of the conversation

```
xmlns="jabber:client"
```

In addition to the namespace that qualifies the `stream` and `error` tag names, which could be seen as representing the "outer shell" of the document, the `xmlns` attribute specifies a namespace that will qualify the tags in the body of the document, the conversation fragments of XML that will appear over time. This namespace is `jabber:client` and signifies that the *type* of conversation that is about to ensue over this document connection is a Client (to Server) conversation.

This namespace specification is required because a client connection is just one type of connection that can be made with a Jabber server, and different connections carry conversations with different content. Table 5-2 lists the conversation namespaces currently defined in the Jabber protocol.

Table 5-2. Conversation namespaces

Namespace	Description
jabber:client	This is the namespace that qualifies a connection between a Jabber client and a Jabber server.
jabber:server	This namespace qualifies a connection between two Jabber servers. *Dialback* (host verification mechanism) conversations also take place within the `jabber:server` namespace.
jabber:component:accept	When an external program connects to a Jabber server via a TCP sockets connection, this namespace is used to qualify the pair of XML documents exchanged over the connection.
jabber:component:exec	When an external program connects to a Jabber server via a STDIO connection, this namespace is used to qualify the pair of XML documents exchanged over such the connection.[a]

[a] For more details on external program connections to Jabber, see Chapter 4.

The Response

To complete our initial look at XML streams in a Jabber client/server conversation, let's have a look at what the Jabber server might send in response to the opening tag from the client:

```
<stream:stream
    xmlns:stream='http://etherx.jabber.org/streams'
    id='3AFD6862'
    xmlns='jabber:client'
```

```
from='jabber.org'>
```

There are a couple of differences between this opening tag from the server and the opening tag from the client—that is, above and beyond the fact that this response's opening tag is for a document that is going to be streamed along the socket in the opposite direction from that of the document to which the request's opening tag belongs. The first difference is that there's a `from` attribute instead of a `to` attribute. The second difference is that there's an extra attribute—`id`. Let's look at these in turn.

The from attribute

The `from` attribute is fairly straightforward; it normally serves to confirm to the client that the requested logical host is available. For example:

```
from="jabber.org"
```

If the host is available, the value of the `from` attribute from the server will match the value of the `to` attribute from the client. However, in some circumstances, the value can be different. The value sent in the `from` attribute is a *redirection*, or *respecification*, of the logical host by which the Jabber server (or more specifically the JSM component within the Jabber server) is actually known.

Logical host aliases can be defined in the Jabber server's configuration to "convert" a hostname specified in the incoming `to` attribute. The `<alias&sol;>` tag, which is used to define these logical host aliases, is described in the section "Component Instance: c2s" in Chapter 4. But how are these hostname conversions used? Here's an example.

Let's say that you're running a Jabber server on an internal network that doesn't have an available DNS server. The host where the Jabber server runs is called *apollo*, and its IP address is `192.168.1.4`. Some people will connect to the host via the hostname because they have it defined in a local */etc/hosts* file; others will connect via the IP address. Normally, the hostname (or IP address) specified in the connection parameters given to a Jabber client will be:

- Used to build the socket connection to the Jabber server.
- Specified in the `to` attribute in the opening XML stream to specify the logical host.

If the JSM section of the Jabber server is defined to have a hostname of *apollo*:

```
<host><jabberd:cmdline flag='h'>apollo</jabberd:cmdline></host>
```

then we need to make sure that the Jabber client uses that name when forming any JIDs for that Jabber server (e.g., the JID *apollo* used as an addressee for an IQ browse request). Having this:

```
<alias to='apollo'>192.168.1.4</alias>
```

in our c2s instance configuration would mean that any incoming XML stream header with a value of 192.168.1.4 in the to attribute:

```
<stream:stream
    to="192.168.1.4"
    xmlns="jabber:client"
    xmlns:stream="http://etherx.jabber.org/streams">
```

would elicit the following response:

```
<stream:stream
    from='apollo'
    id='1830EF6A'
    xmlns='jabber:client'
    xmlns:stream='http://etherx.jabber.org/streams'>
```

which effectively says: "*OK, you requested* 192.168.1.4, *but please use* apollo *instead.*" The client should use the value "confirmed" in the from attribute when referring to that Jabber server in all subsequent stream fragments. That is to say, when wanting to address the server, instead of sending something like this:

```
SEND <iq type='get' to='192.168.1.4'>
         <query xmlns='jabber:iq:version'&sol;>
     </iq>
```

it should address it like this:

```
SEND <iq type='get' to='apollo'>
         <query xmlns='jabber:iq:version'&sol;>
     </iq>
```

Not specifying an <alias/> tag in this example would result in problems for the client. Without any way of checking and converting incoming hostnames, the c2s component will by default simply transfer the value from the to attribute to the from attribute in its stream header reply.

Following this thread to its natural conclusion, it's worth pointing out that if we have an alias specification like this:

```
<alias to='apollo'&sol;>
```

then the value of the from attribute in the reply will *always* be set to *apollo* regardless of what's specified in the to attribute. This means that the to attribute could be left out of the opening stream tag. Although this serves well to illustrate the point, it is not good practice.

The id attribute

The `id` attribute is the ID of the XML stream and is used in the subsequent authorization steps, which are described in Chapter 7. For example:

```
id='3AFD6862'
```

The value is a random hexadecimal string generated by the server and is not important per se. What *is* important is that it's a value that is random and shared between server and client. The server knows what it is because it generated it, and the client knows what it is because the server sends it in the opening tag of the response.

The Simplest Jabber Client

Now that we know how a conversation with a Jabber server is started, let's try it ourselves. At a stretch, one could say that the simplest Jabber client, just like the simplest HTTP client, or the simplest client that has to interact with *any* server that employs a *text-based* protocol over a socket connection, is *telnet*.

Simply point *telnet* to a Jabber server, specifying port 5222, and send an opening tag. You will receive an opening tag, from the server, in response:

```
yak:~$ telnet localhost 5222
Trying 127.0.0.1...
Connected to localhost.
Escape character is '^]'.
<?xml version='1.0'&quest;>
<stream:stream xmlns:stream='http://etherx.jabber.org/streams' to='yak'
    xmlns='jabber:client'>
<?xml version='1.0'&quest;><stream:stream xmlns:stream='http://etherx.jabber.org/streams'
    id='3AFD839E' xmlns='jabber:client' from='yak'>
```

If you don't have a Jabber server to experiment with, see Chapter 3 on how to set one up.

Using *telnet* is a great way to find out more about the way the Jabber protocol works. Perhaps the next thing to do is try out the user registration and authentication steps described in Chapter 7. But watch out—send some invalid XML and the server will close the connection on you!

Jabber's Building Blocks

At this stage we've got a good impression of the structure of Jabber: what different elements make up a Jabber system, how entities in Jabber are addressed, and how communication between these entities is carried.

Now it's time to look at *what* gets carried—the fragments that we touched upon in the previous section. These fragments are the heart and soul of Jabber—the *lifeblood* that courses through Jabber's veins carrying information back and forth—these fragments in many ways define what Jabber is, what it stands for.

Surprisingly, when we look closely at these fragments, with Jabber's capabilities as a messaging platform in mind, we see that there are only three basic elements involved—<message/>, <presence/>, and <iq/>. Three different types of XML fragments, each with a different purpose. But with these three fragment types—these elements—all that Jabber promises, and more, can be achieved.

Now let's look at each of these Jabber elements in greater detail. But before we do, let's dive into the XML stream and pull out a handful of XML fragments to get us in the mood. Example 5-3 shows a chunk of conversation between a Jabber client and a Jabber server, which occurred immediately after the connection and authentication stages.

Although any conversation between two Jabber entities is contained within two XML documents exchanged in streams, the traditional way to represent both documents at the same time is to use prefixes to show whether a fragment is being sent (SEND:) or received (RECV:), by one of the two entities. When appropriate, the perspective is taken from the viewpoint of the entity that's *not* the Jabber server; in the case of Example 5-3, the viewpoint is of the Jabber client.

Example 5-3: A chunk of conversation between a Jabber client and a Jabber server

```
SEND: <iq id='roster_0' type='get'><id="iq"&sol;>
         <query xmlns='jabber:iq:roster'&sol;>
      </iq>

RECV: <iq id='roster_0' type='result' from='dj@yak/Work'>
         <query xmlns='jabber:iq:roster'>
          <item jid='sabine@yak' name='sabine' subscription='both'>
            <group>Family</group>
          </item>
         </query>
      </iq>

SEND: <presence><status>Online</status></presence><id="presence"&sol;>

      ... time passes ...

RECV: <message id='1' to='dj@yak' from='sabine@yak/winjab' type='chat'>
         <id="message"&sol;>
         <thread>3FE7392DDCA919CB49C73A2FFCE9901D</thread>
         <body>Hello</body>
      </message>
```

Example 5-3: A chunk of conversation between a Jabber client and a Jabber server (continued)

Example 5-3 shows three different elements in action, described as follows:

The <iq> elements
 The user's (*dj@yak*'s) contact list is requested and sent back by the server.

The <presence> element
 The client broadcasts the user's availability.

The <message> element
 The user receives a message from *sabine@yak*.

So, let's have a look at each of these elements, starting with arguably the most commonly occurring: <message/>.

The Message Element

It's obvious that in a messaging architecture such as Jabber, sending messages is fundamental. The <message/> element provides us with this facility. Any data, other than availability information or structured requests and responses (which are handled by the other two element types) sent from one Jabber entity to another, is sent in a <message/> element.

All things considered, the key word in that last sentence is "in." It's a good idea to regard Jabber elements as *containers*; the simile fits well as the elements themselves remain relatively static (save for the attributes) but the *content* can change to reflect the circumstances.

Message attributes

The <message/> element is a container, or envelope, which requires some form of addressing. The attributes of the <message/> element serve this purpose.

---

type   Optional

Synopsis
```
<message type='chat'>
```

The Jabber protocol defines five different message *types*. The message type gives an indication to the recipient as to what sort of content is expected; the client software is then able, if it wishes, to handle the incoming message appropriately.

Attribute Values

type='normal'

The normal message type is used for simple messages that are often one-time in nature, similar to an email message. If I send you a message and I'm not particularly expecting a response, or a discussion to ensue, then the appropriate message type is normal.

Some clients handle normal message types by placing them in a sort of message inbox, to be viewed by the user when he so chooses. This is in contrast to a chat type message.

Note that the normal message type is the default. So if a message is received without an explicit type attribute, it is interpreted as being normal.

type='chat'

The chat message type differs from the normal message type in that it carries a message that is usually part of a live conversation, which is best handled in real time with immediate responses—a chat session.

The handling of chat messages in many clients is done with a single window that displays all the chat messages both sent and received between the two parties involved—all the chat messages that belong to the same thread of conversation, that is. There's a subelement of the <message/> element that allows the identification of conversational threads so that the right messages can be grouped together; see the information on <thread/> later in the section "Message subelements."

type='groupchat'

The groupchat message type is to alert the receiving client that the message being carried is one from a conference (groupchat) room. The user can participate in many conference rooms and receive messages sent by other participants in those rooms. The groupchat type signifies to the receiving client that the address specified in the from attribute (see later in this section) is *not* the sending user's real JID but the JID representing the sending user, via her nickname, in the conference room from where the groupchat message originates.*

type='headline'

This is a special message type designed to carry news style information, often accompanied by a URL and description in an attachment qualified by the jabber:x:oob namespace. Messages with their type set to headline can be handled by clients in such a way that their content is placed in a growing list of entries that can be used as reference by the user.

---

* Also, groupchat type messages, such as those announcing entrances or exits of room participants, can be received from the room itself.

type='error'

The error message type signifies that the message is conveying error information to the client. Errors can originate in many places and under many circumstances. Refer to the description of the <error/> subelement in the next section for more details.

---

from   Set by server

Synopsis

    <message from='dj@yak/Desktop'>

The from attribute of the <message/> element shows the message originator's JID. In many cases this is the JID of a user, but with the message type groupchat, for example, it can be the JID of the conference room in the place where the message was originally sent.

The from attribute should not be set by the client. It is the Jabber server, to which the client from where the message originated is connected, that sets the attribute value. This is to prevent spoofing of JIDs. If a from attribute *is* set, it will be overriden by the server.

---

to   Optional

Synopsis

    <message to='qmacro@jabber.org'>

The to attribute is used to specify the intended recipient of the message and is a JID. The recipient may be another Jabber user, in which case the JID will usually be in the form *username@hostname* (with an optional */resource* if a message should be sent to a specific client connection), or it could be a Jabber server identity, in which case the JID will be in the form *hostname>* with an optional */resource* depending on the situation.

If no to attribute is specified, then the message will be directed back to the *sender*, or the server, depending on the circumstances. This may or may not be what you want.

This is also the case with the to attribute for the <iq/> element; however, it is not the case with the <presence/> element.* See the sidebar titled "Element Handling by the Jabber Server" for an explanation.

---

* Actually, it is, internally, but the effect is that it isn't. The packet is swallowed on its final delivery stage by the presence handler.

Element Handling by the Jabber Server

When elements (packets) make their way over the `jabber:client` XML stream and arrive at the Jabber server, they're delivered to the JSM that provides many of the services associated with Jabber's IM features, such as roster management, presence subscription, offline storage, and so on. Each packet received runs a gauntlet of handlers before being delivered to its ultimate destination specified by the value of the `to` attribute.

In some cases, a packet has no "ultimate destination" and is deemed to have been handled without reaching a final delivery point.

For example, in the case of a simple `<message&sol;>` packet with a JID specified in the `to` attribute, the packet will not be swallowed by a handler but will be delivered to that JID destination. On the other hand, in the case of a simple `<presence&sol;>` packet without a `to` attribute (a normal notification of availability), the packet will reach the *mod_presence* module in the JSM and be handled by that module, where the availability information will be distributed according to presence subscriptions. The `<presence&sol;>` packet itself, in its original form, will go no further.

---

id Optional

Synopsis

```
<message id='JCOM_12'>
```

When a message is sent, and a reply is expected, it is often useful to give the outbound message an identifier. When the recipient responds, the identifier is included in the response. In this way, the originator of the message can work out which reply corresponds to which original message.

At the Jabber server, this works because a reply is usually built from a copy of the original message, with the `from` and `to` attributes switched around. So the `id` attribute remains untouched and in place.

 Each `id` value within a session, represented by one streamed XML document, must be unique within that session, that is, within that one document.

Message subelements

While the <message/> element itself is a container for the information being carried, the subelements are used to hold and describe the information being carried. Depending on the circumstances and the message type, different subelements can be used.

subject   Optional

Synopsis

```
<message to='qmacro@jabber.org' from='piers@jabber.org/Home'>
  <subject>Time to meet?</subject>
  <body>What time to you want to meet this afternoon?</body>
</message>
```

The <subject/> subelement is used to set a message subject. Message subjects are not that common in chat type messages but are more appropriate in normal type messages in which the subject can be displayed in the style of a list of inbox items. This subelement is also used in groupchat type messages to set the subject (or "topic") of a conference room.

body   Optional

Synopsis

```
<message to='qmacro@yak' from='john@yak' type='chat'>
  <body>Hey - got a minute?</body>
</message>
```

The <body/> subelement carries the body of the message.

error   Optional

Synopsis

```
<message to='piers@pipetree.com/Home' from='qmacro@jaber.org' type='error'>
  <body>Are you there?</body>
  <error code='502'>Unable to resolve hostname.</error>
</message>
```

The <error> subelement is for carrying error information in a problem situation. In this example, the original message sent by *piers@pipetree.com* was a simple "Are you there?" to what he thought was qmacro's JID on the Jabber server at *jabber.org*. However, the to attribute was specified incorrectly (*jaber.org*), and the Jabber server on *pipetree.com* wasn't able to resolve the hostname. So Piers receives his message back with an additional <error/> subelement, and the message type has been switched to error (the type='error' attribute).

The <error/> subelement carries two pieces of related information: an error number, specified in the code attribute, and the error text. Table 5-3 lists standard error codes and texts. The entity generating the error can specify a custom error text to go with the error code; if none is specified, the standard text as shown is used.

Table 5-3. Standard error codes and texts

Code	Text
400	Bad Request
401	Unauthorized
402	Payment Required
403	Forbidden
404	Not Found
405	Not Allowed
406	Not Acceptable
407	Registration Required
408	Request Timeout
409	Conflict
500	Internal Server Error
501	Not Implemented
502	Remove Server Error
503	Service Unavailable
504	Remove Server Timeout
510	Disconnected

html Optional

Synopsis

```
<message id="3" to="dj@yak" type="chat">
  <html xmlns="http://www.w3.org/1999/xhtml">
    <body>
      <span style="font-family: Arial; font-size: 10pt">
        This is really <em>nice!</em>
      </span>
      <br/>
    </body>
  </html>
  <body>This is really nice!</body>
</message>
```

The <html/> tag is for support of messages formatted in Extensible HyperText Markup Language (XHTML). The normal <body/> tag carries plain text; text formatted with XHTML markup can be carried in <message/> elements inside the `<html&sol;>` subelement.

The markup must be qualified by the XHTML namespace `http://www.w3.org/1999/xhtml` (as shown in the example) and conform to the markup described in the XHTML-Basic specification defined at *http://www.w3.org/ TR/xhtml-basic*. This is despite the name of the tag being `html` and not `xhtml`.

Note that the content of the message must also be repeated in a normal `<body&sol;>` subelement without formatting, to comply with the "lowest common denominator" support for different Jabber clients—not all of them will be able to interpret the XHTML formatting, so they will need to receive the message content in a way that they can understand.

The `<html&sol;>` subelement effectively is a wrapper around a second, alternative, `<body&sol;>` subelement.

---

thread   Optional

Synopsis

```
<message to='qmacro@jabber.org' type='chat'>
  <thread>B19217AFEEBDC2611971DD1E8B23AAE4</thread>
  <body>Yes, they're at http://docs.jabber.org</body>
</message>
```

The `<thread&sol;>` subelement is used by clients to group together snippets of conversations (between users) so that the whole conversation can be visually presented in a meaningful way. Typically a conversation on a particular topic—a *thread*—will be displayed in a single window. Giving each conversation thread an identity enables a distinction to be made when more than one conversation is being held at once and `chat` type messages, which are component parts of these conversations, are being received (possibly from the same correspondent) in an unpredictable sequence.

Only when a new topic or branch of conversation is initiated must a client generate a thread value. At all other times, the correspondent client must simply include the `<thread&sol;>` tag in the response. Here the thread value is generated from a hash of the message originator's JID and the current time.

---

x   Optional

Synopsis

```
<message to='dj@yak' type='chat' from='sabine@yak/laptop'>
  <body>Hi - let me know when you get back. Thanks.</body>
  <x xmlns='jabber:x:delay' from='dj@yak' stamp='20010514T14:44:09'>
    Offline Storage
  </x>
</message>
```

The <x/> subelement is special. While the other subelements like <body/> and <thread/> are fixed into the Jabber building blocks design, the <x/> subelement allows <message/> elements to be extended to suit requirements. What the <x/> subelement does is provide an anchor point for further information to be attached to messages in a structured way.

The information attached to a message is often called the *payload*. Multiple anchor points can be used to convey multiple payloads, and each one must be *qualified* using a namespace.

Just as the content of XML streams is qualified by a namespace (one from the list in Table 5-2 earlier in this chapter), so the content of the <x/> *attachment* must be qualified. There are a number of Jabber-standard namespaces that are defined for various purposes. One of these, jabber:x:delay, is used in the example. These standard namespaces are described in Chapter 6. But there's nothing to stop you defining your own namespace to describe (and qualify) the data that you wish to transport in a <message/>. Namespaces beginning jabber: are reserved; anything else is OK.

Briefly, you can see how payloads are attached from the example. For every <x/> subelement, there's an xmlns attribute that qualifies it, and the data contained within the <x/> tag is formatted depending on the namespace.

In the example, the payload is carried in addition to the <body/> subelement. However, as the <body/> is actually *optional* in a message, it is possible to transmit structured payloads between Jabber entities without the need for "conventional" message content.

The Presence Element

The <presence/> element is used to convey a Jabber entity's availability. An entity can be *available*, which means that it's connected and any messages sent to it will be delivered immediately, or it can be *unavailable*, which means that it's not connected, and any messages sent to it will be stored and delivered the next time a connection is made.

For the large part, it is the entity itself, not the Jabber server to which it connects, that controls the availability information. The Jabber server will communicate an entity's *unavailability* if that entity disconnects from the server but will do that only if the entity has communicated its *availability* beforehand.

Availability information isn't a free-for-all. Presence in Jabber is usually exchanged within a subscription mechanism. See the section "Presence subscription" for an explanation.

Presence Management

It's worth noting that the *entities* referred to here are *client* entities, that is, clients (and therefore the users using those clients) connected to the Jabber server over an XML stream qualified by the `jabber:client` namespace (see the section "XML Streams"). Presence is a feature that is used throughout Jabber; the Jabber Session Manager (JSM) manages presence on behalf of clients. External components that connect to the Jabber server backbone are separate from the JSM and therefore don't have any concept of "managed" presence. That's not to say they can't partake in the sending and receiving of presence elements. They just have to manage everything themselves, as they don't have the JSM to do it for them.

Presence attributes

The attributes of the `<presence&sol;>` element are similar to those of the `<message&sol;>` element.

---

type   Optional

Synopsis

```
<presence type='unavailable'>
```

The `type` attribute of the `<presence&sol;>` element is used for many purposes. The basic usage is to convey availability. Two values are used: `available` and `unavailable`.* Another value is to signify that the `<presence&sol;>` packet is being used to query the packet recipient's presence (value is `probe`). The rest of the values (`subscribe`, `unsubscribe`, `subscribed`, `unsubscribed`) are used in the subscription structure, which is described in the section "Presence subscription."

Attribute Values

type='available'

> The `available` presence type is used by entities to announce their availability. This announcement is usually made to the Jabber server that manages the presence subscription mechanism (see the section "Presence subscription" for more details). However it can also be directed to a particular JID if the entity wants to control presence information itself.

---

* Technically speaking, there's no `available` value. The absence of a `type` attribute implies availability. However, for the purposes of discussion (it's easier to concentrate on something than to concentrate on a lack of something), we'll refer to `type='available'`.

The `available` presence isn't a simple binary "on/off"; varying degrees of availability are specified using subelements of the <presence/> packet. These include <show/> and <status/> and are described next.

If no `type` attribute is specified, then this value of `available` is assumed. It makes sense, as the most common type of <presence/> packet sent by entities is usually the `available` type, optionally qualified with the <show/> and <status/> subelements, as the user of the connected client changes her circumstances over time (off for a break, back, out to lunch, and so on).

type='unavailable'

The `unavailable` presence type is the antithesis of the `available` presence type. It is used to qualify an entity's unavailability. An entity is unavailable when its client has disconnected from the Jabber server. An `unavailable` presence type should be sent by clients before they disconnect.

How can we make sure that clients actually *send* such a packet when they disconnect (to keep the presence information equilibrium)? Well, we can't. If a client disconnects without sending an `unavailable` presence type, the Jabber server will send one out on its behalf when it disconnects. This is part of the presence service of the JSM and closely related to the presence subscription mechanism. See the section "Availability Tracker" for more details.*

While the <show/> and <status/> subelements qualify the `available` presence packet, there's no point in any embellishment of the fact that the entity is *unavailable*, so no subelements are used when the packet is of the `unavailable` type.

type='probe'

The `probe` presence type is a query, or probe, on another entity's availability. This probe is used by the Jabber server to determine the presence of entities in its management of the presence subscription mechanism. Under normal circumstances, this presence probe should not be used directly by a client— availability information is always pushed to the client by the server. Regardless, if a client insists on using a probe, there are two things to bear in mind:

* Information will be returned only in response to an availability probe if the probing entity already has a subscription to the entity being probed. This means that you can't bypass the subscription model and probe random entities for availability information; you can probe only those who have previously given you permission to be informed of their availability. See the section "Presence subscription" for more details.

---

* Not sending an `unavailable` presence type before disconnection means that the information held for a user in the `jabber:iq:last` namespace—see the section "jabber:iq:last" in Chapter 6—will not be stored.

- The <presence/> packet must be specified with a *from* attribute specifying the sender's JID in the form *username@hostname* before it is sent. The Jabber server does not add this attribute. The presence mechanism will use the full JID (including any *resource*) when working out whether the prober has permission. This will ultimately fail because permission is determined on a *username@hostname* basis, not a *username@hostname/ resource* basis.

Although possible right now, you should really avoid using the probe presence type in clients. Future versions of the Jabber server may block such packets.

---

type='subscribe'

This presence type is a request to subscribe to an entity's presence. ("Will you allow me to be sent your presence information by the server?") See the section "Presence subscription" for details.

type='unsubscribe'

This presence type is a request to unsubscribe from an entity's presence. ("I don't want to be sent your presence information anymore; please have the server stop sending it to me.") See the section "Presence subscription" for details.

type='subscribed'

This presence type is sent in reply to a presence subscription request, used to accept the request. ("OK, I accept your request; the server will send you my presence information.") See the section "Presence subscription" for details.

type='unsubscribed'

This presence type is sent in reply to a presence unsubscription request, used to accept the request. ("OK, I accept your unsubscription request; the server will stop sending you my presence information.")

It is also used to deny a presence subscription request. ("No, I don't accept your subscription request; I don't want the server to send you my presence information.")

These presence types are described in more detail in the section "Presence subscription."

from
Set by server

Synopsis
```
<presence from='dj@yak'/>
```

Similar to the attribute of the same name in the `<message&sol;>` element, here the `from` attribute is set by the server and represents the JID from which the availability information originates.

If you are sending a presence probe, `type='probe'`, you must set the `from` attribute yourself, as mentioned earlier.

---

to
Optional

Synopsis
```
<presence to='sabine@yak'/>
```

The `to` attribute is optional; if, as a user, you are just announcing availability (with the intention of having that announcement reflected to the appropriate members of your roster), then specifying a `to` attribute is not appropriate.* If you want to send your availability to a specific entity, then do so using this `to` attribute, specifying that entity's JID. Why might you want to do this? See the section "Availability Tracker" for an answer.

---

id
Optional

Synopsis
```
<presence id='p1'/>
```

All Jabber elements support an `id` attribute for tracking purposes. So, the `<presence&sol;>` packet is no different from the `<message&sol;>` packet in this respect. As presence notification is usually a one-way thing, it is very uncommon to see `<presence&sol;>` packets qualified with an `id` attribute.

---

* In fact, as in the cases for the other two elements, `<message&sol;>` and `<iq&sol;>`, not specifying a `to` attribute will cause the `<presence&sol;>` packet to be sent to the sender. However, in the case of the presence handler mechanism, the packet is swallowed before it can reach its destination, to prevent reflective presence problems.

Presence subelements

show   Optional
Synopsis

```
<presence>
  <show>xa</show>
  <status>Gone home for the evening</status>
</presence>
```

When an available presence is sent, it can be qualified with more detail. The detail comes in two parts and is represented by two subelements of the <presence/> element. The first part of the detail is in the form of a <show/> tag, which by convention contains one of five possible values. Table 5-4 lists these values and their meaning.

Table 5-4. Presence <show> values

Value	Meaning
away	The user is available but temporarily away from the client.
chat	This is similar to the normal value but suggests that the user is open to conversation.
dnd	"Do not disturb." Although online and *available*, the user doesn't want to be disturbed by anyone. Don't forget, unless the user is actually offline (unavailable or disconnected from the Jabber server), messages to that user will still be sent to the user immediately.
normal	This is the normal availability; there's nothing really special about this qualification—the user is simply available. If no <show/> tag is specified in an available <presence/> element, a value of normal is assumed.
xa	This is an extreme form of the away value—xa stands for "extended away" and is probably as near to an unavailable presence as you can get.

status   Optional
Synopsis

```
<presence>
  <show>dnd</show>
  <status>working on my book!</status>
</presence>
```

The other part of the detail that qualifies a user's availability is the <status/> subelement. It allows for a more descriptive remark that embellishes the <show/> data.

The examples for this subelement and the `<show&sol;>` subelement show how the `<status&sol;>` value is used as a textual description to explain the `<show&sol;>` value's "short code," or mnemonic.

---

priority   Optional
Synopsis

```
<presence>
  <show>chat</show>
  <status>coffee break</status>
  <priority>5</priority>
</presence>
```

Earlier in this chapter, the section "Resources and Priorities" described how a user's *priority* is used to determine the primary session to which messages should be sent.

As we see here, the priority is set using the `<presence&sol;>` element. In this example, we see that the user has set the priority high to make sure that messages are routed to him on the Jabber client running on this machine.

---

x   Optional
Synopsis

```
<presence from='dj@yak/Work' to='sabine@yak'>
  <status>Online</status>
  <priority>1</priority>
  <x xmlns='jabber:x:delay' from='dj@yak/Work'
     stamp='20011005T10:58:28'&sol;>
</presence>
```

Just as with the `<message&sol;>` element, extra information can be attached to the `<presence&sol;>` element by means of the `<x&sol;>` tag. In the same way, each `<x&sol;>` tag must be qualified with a namespace.

While there aren't many external uses for payloads in a `<presence&sol;>` packet, the Jabber server uses this facility to add information. In this example, we see that *dj@yak*'s notification of availability (remember, `type='available'` is assumed for `<presence&sol;>` packets without an explicit `type` attribute) is being sent to *sabine@yak*. While *dj@yak* connected to the Jabber server and sent his availability (which was stamped on receipt by the Jabber server) just before 11 a.m., *sabine@yak* is just logging on now (say, 30 minutes later). When she receives *dj@yak*'s presence, she knows how long that presence status has been valid for.

See the section "The X Namespaces" in Chapter 6 to find out what namespaces are available to qualify `<x&sol;>`-included payloads.

Presence subscription

Presence subscription is the name given to the mechanism that allows control over how entity presence information is made available to other entities. By default, the availability of an entity is unknown to other entities.

Let's put this into more concrete terms. For example, let's assume that you and I are both Jabber users. I'm registered with the Jabber server running at *jabber.org*, my JID is *qmacro@jabber.org*, and you are registered with a Jabber server running at your company, and your JID is *you@yourserver.com*.

If you want to know whether I'm available, you have to *subscribe* to my presence. This is done by sending a <presence/> packet to me with the type attribute set to subscribe. In the example that follows, the XML fragments are sent and received from *your* perspective:

```
SEND: <presence type='subscribe' to='qmacro@jabber.org'&sol;>
```

I receive the <presence/> packet, and when I receive it, it's been stamped (by your Jabber server) with a from attribute with the value *you@yourserver.com*. So, based upon who it is, I decide to accept the subscription request and send back a reply, which you receive:

```
RECV: <presence type='subscribed'
               from='qmacro@jabber.org/home'
               to='you@yourserver.com/work'&sol;>
```

This lets you know that I've accepted your subscription request. From now on, every time my availability changes (when I send a <presence/> packet or when I disconnect and the server generates an unavailable <presence/> packet on my behalf), that availability information will be relayed to you.

But how does this work? How does the Jabber server know that you've subscribed to my presence and I've accepted that subscription?

Enter the *roster*, stage right. The roster is a list of JIDs maintained for each user, stored server-side. A roster is similar to an AOL Buddy List; one could say that it's a sort of personal address book, but it's more than that. The presence subscription and roster mechanisms are tightly intertwined. We'll be examining the roster in more detail in the section "jabber:iq:roster" in Chapter 6. Here, we'll just look at the characteristics of the roster that are relevant for the presence subscription mechanism. The roster is managed using the third basic Jabber element—<iq/>—which will be explained in more detail later in this section. Ignore the tags that you aren't yet familiar with; it's just important to get the basic drift of what's going on.

While the roster is stored and maintained server-side, any changes to it made by the server are reflected in (pushed to) the client so it can be synchronized with a local copy.*

Let's expand the simple exchange of `<presence&sol;>` packets from earlier and see how the roster is used to record presence subscription information.

If you wish to subscribe to my presence and add my JID to your roster at the same time, these two actions are linked for obvious and practical reasons. Many Jabber clients use the roster as a basis for displaying availability information, and with the exception of an entity sending presence information directly to another entity regardless of roster membership, presence subscription information is stored by the user in the roster. Here's the order in which the subscription would take place:

1. A request is sent to the server to update your roster, adding my JID to it:

   ```
   SEND: <iq id="adduser1" type="set">
           <query xmlns="jabber:iq:roster">
             <item jid="qmacro@jabber.org" name="DJ Adams"&sol;>
           </query>
         </iq>
   ```

   You add an `id` attribute to be able to track the request and match up the response when it comes.

2. The server responds with a push of the updated (new) roster item:

   ```
   RECV: <iq type='set'>
           <query xmlns='jabber:iq:roster'>
             <item jid='qmacro@jabber.org' name='DJ Adams'
                   subscription='none'&sol;>
           </query>
         </iq>
   ```

   Note that in the update an additional attribute `subscription='none'` is sent, reflecting the presence subscription relationship between you and me. At this stage, the relationship is that I don't have a subscription to your presence and you don't have a subscription to my presence, hence the value `none`.

3. It also acknowledges the original update request, confirming its success:

   ```
   RECV: <iq id='adduser1' type='result'
             from='you@yourserver.com/Work'
             to='you@yourserver.com/Work'&sol;>
   ```

   Note the `id='adduser1'` identity is passed back so we can track the original request and find out where this response is being made.

---

* The local copy would exist only for the duration of the user's session and should always be regarded as a *slave copy*.

4. Meanwhile, you send the subscription request:

    ```
    SEND: <presence to="qmacro@jabber.org" type="subscribe"&sol;>
    ```

5. The server notes the subscription request going through and once more updates your roster and pushes the item out to you:

    ```
    RECV: <iq type='set'>
            <query xmlns='jabber:iq:roster'>
              <item jid='qmacro@jabber.org' name='DJ Adams'
                    subscription='none' ask='subscribe'&sol;>
            </query>
          </iq>
    ```

    The current subscription relationship is reflected with the `subscription='none'` attribute. In addition, we have a subscription request status, with `ask='sub-scribe'`. This request status shows that there is an outstanding presence subscription request to the JID in that roster item. If you've ever seen the word "Pending" next to a username in a Jabber roster, this is where that comes from. Don't forget that a subscription request might not get an immediate response, so we need to remember that the request is still outstanding.

6. Your subscription request is received and accepted, and a `subscribed` type is sent back to you as part of a `<presence&sol;>` packet:

    ```
    RECV: <presence to='you@yourserver.com'
                    type='subscribed' from='qmacro@jabber.org'&sol;>
    ```

7. The server also notices the subscription request acceptance and yet again updates your roster to keep track of the presence subscription. Again, it pushes the subscription information out to you so your client can keep its copy up-to-date:

    ```
    RECV: <iq type='set'>
            <query xmlns='jabber:iq:roster'>
              <item jid='qmacro@jabber.org' name='DJ Adams'
                    subscription='to'&sol;>
            </query>
          </iq>
    ```

    This time, the `subscription` attribute in the roster item has been set to `to`. This means that the roster owner (you) has a presence subscription *to* the JID in the roster item (i.e., me).

8. The server knows you've just subscribed to my presence; it generates a presence probe on your behalf that causes my presence information to be retrieved and sent to you:

    ```
    RECV: <presence from='qmacro@jabber.org/Work'
                    to='you@yourserver.com'>
            <status>Available</status>
            <priority>1</priority>
    ```

```
    <x xmlns='jabber:x:delay'
       from='qmacro@jabber.org/Work'
       stamp='20010515T11:37:40'&sol;>
</presence>
```

Of course, at this stage, our relationship is a little unbalanced, in that you have a subscription request to me, but I don't have a subscription request to you. So you are aware of my availability, but not the other way around. In order to rectify this situation, I can repeat the process in the opposite direction, asking for a subscription to your presence information.

The only difference to the sequence that we've just seen is that you will already exist on my roster because the server will have maintained an item for your JID to record the presence subscription relationship. While the item in your roster that represents my JID has a subscription attribute value of to (the roster owner has a presence subscription *to* this JID)—we've seen this in Step 7—the item in my roster that represents your JID has a subscription attribute value of from (the roster owner has a presence subscription *from* this JID).

Once I repeat this sequence to subscribe to your presence (and you accept the request), the value for the subscription attribute in the items in each of our rosters will be set to both.

The upshot of all this is that when an entity announces its presence, it does so using a single <presence/> packet, with no to attribute specified. All the members in that entity's roster who have a subscription to that entity's presence will receive a copy of that <presence/> packet and thereby be informed.*

Availability Tracker

The Jabber server (specifically, the presence handler within the JSM) has a mechanism called the *Availability Tracker.* As its name implies, its job is to track the availability of entities that have previously made an availability announcement (in a <presence/> element).

The concept of exchange of availability information via an exchange agreement recorded in the roster was introduced In the section "Presence subscription." This mechanism covers the automatic distribution of availability notification based upon prearranged presence subscriptions.

However, Jabber services (which are connected to the *jabberd* backbone; see the section "An Overview of the Server Architecture" in Chapter 4) may need to know

---

* That is, where there's a value of to or both in the roster item's subscription attribute.

an entity's availability or, more importantly, when they suddenly become *unavail-able*. These Jabber services usually won't have a prior presence subscription agreement recorded in anyone's roster.

The Conferencing service, which provides group chat facilities, allowing users to join discussion "rooms" and chat, is one of these services. The service maintains data for each room's participants, and, so that it can manage its memory usage effectively, needs to know when a user ends his connection with the Jabber server—in other words, when he becomes unavailable—so it can free that user's data. Normally, a user leaving a room is information enough for the service to know that data can be freed. But what if the user disconnects (or is disconnected) from his Jabber server without first leaving the room?

The availability tracker mechanism comes to the rescue. It maintains a list of JIDs to which an entity has sent his availability in a `<presence/>` packet containing a to attribute (i.e., a *directed* `<presence/>` packet). When the JSM notices that a user has ended his session by disconnecting, the presence handler invokes the availability tracker to send an *unavailable* `<presence/>` packet (with the `type='unavailable'` attribute) to all the JIDs to which the entity had sent directed availability information during the lifetime of that session.

How does this help in the Conferencing service case? Well, one of the requirements to enter a room is that presence must be sent to that room. Each room has its own JID, so a typical presence packet in room entry negotiation might look like this:

    SEND: <presence to='jdev@conference.jabber.org'/>

which would be for the `jdev` room running at the conferencing service at *conference.jabber.org.**

So, the availability tracker would have recorded this directed presence and will send an unavailable presence to the same JID if the user's session ends.

The IQ Element

The third and final element in the Jabber building block set is the `<iq/>` element ("iq" stands for "info/query"), which represents a mechanism for sending and receiving information. What the `<iq/>` element has over the `<message/>` element for this purpose is *structure* and *inherent meaning*. It is useful to liken the info/query mechanism to the request/response model of HTTP using GET and

---

* The example here contains a room JID with no resource specified; this is taken from the 0.4 version of the Conferencing protocol. An earlier version of the protocol (Groupchat 1.0) required that the nickname for the person entering the room be specified as a resource to the room's JID, for example, *jdev@conference.jabber.org/dj.*

POST.

The <iq/> element allows a structured conversation between two Jabber entities. The conversation exists to exchange data, to retrieve or set it, and to notify the other party as to the success (or not) of that retrieve or set action. There are four *states* that an <iq/> element can be in, each reflecting one of the activities in this conversation:

get Get information.

set Set information.

result
 Show the result when the get or set was successful.

error
 Specify an error if the get or set was not successful.

These states are reflected in the type attribute of <iq/> elements. The relationship between two entities in such a structured conversation that convey these states is shown in Figure 5-4.

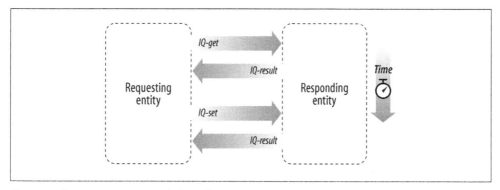

Figure 5-4. Entities in an <iq/>-based conversation

 As you can see, the combination of the <iq/> element specification and the type attribute is written like this:

IQ-*type*

For example, "IQ-get" refers to an <iq/> element with type='get', and so on.

Earlier in this chapter, we saw various elements in action in Example 5-3. The first two were <iq/> elements and showed a retrieval request and response for roster information.

First comes the request:

```
SEND: <iq id='roster_0' type='get'>
        <query xmlns='jabber:iq:roster'&sol;>
      </iq>
```

Then the response:

```
RECV: <iq id='roster_0' type='result' from='dj@yak/Work'>
        <query xmlns='jabber:iq:roster'>
          <item jid='sabine@yak' name='sabine' subscription='both'>
            <group>Family</group>
          </item>
        </query>
      </iq>
```

This snippet shows a number of things:

- The type of each info/query activity is identified by the `type` attribute.

- Each info/query activity contains a subelement (here, `<query&sol;>`), which is qualified by a namespace.

- The subelement is used to carry the information being retrieved.

- The response (`type='result'`) can be matched up to the request (`type='get'`) via the `id` tracking attribute.

So, if we look at the first `<iq&sol;>` element:

```
<iq id='roster_0' type='get'>
```

we can see that this "request" `<iq&sol;>` doesn't contain a `to` attribute. This is because the request is being made *of* the Jabber server (specifically the JSM), instead of a particular user. Next we see the response from the server:

```
<iq id='roster_0' type='result' from='dj@yak/Work'>
```

This "response" `<iq&sol;>` contains a `from` attribute stating that the result is coming back from the original requester! This is simply because the `from` attribute is a hangover from the original request to the Jabber server, which is stamped with its origin (*dj@yak/Work*) in the form of the `from` attribute. Here, as in many other places in the Jabber server, the response is simply built by turning the incoming request packet around and adding whatever was required to it before sending it back.

OK, let's examine the details of the `<iq&sol;>` element.

IQ attributes

The attributes of the `<iq&sol;>` element are the same as those of the `<presence&sol;>` and `<message&sol;>` elements and used pretty much in the same way.

type   Required

Synopsis

Example: <iq **type='get'**/>

As mentioned already, the `from` attribute is used to specify the activity.

Attribute Values

type='get'

This is used to specify that the <iq/> element is being used in *request* mode, to retrieve information. The actual subject of the request is specified using the namespace qualification of the <query/> subelement; see later in this section for details.

Using the HTTP parallel, this is the equivalent of the GET verb.

type='set'

While IQ-get is used to retrieve data, the corresponding `set` type is used to send data and is the equivalent of the POST verb in the HTTP parallel.

Very often, an IQ-get request will be made of an entity, to discover fields that are to be completed to interact with that entity. The Jabber User Directory (JUD) is a component that plugs into the *jabberd* backbone and provides simple directory services; users can register an entry in the JUD address book, on which searches can be performed.

Let's look at how IQ elements are used to interact with the JUD.

The registration conversation with the JUD starts with an IQ-get to discover the fields that can be used for registration, followed by an IQ-set filling those fields in the act of registration. Note how, each time, the JUD responds with an IQ-result to confirm each action's success.

Here we are requesting registration information from the JUD. Note the namespace that qualifies the <query/> subelement (and hence the <iq/>):

```
SEND: <iq type='get' to='jud.yak'
                id='judreg_ask'>
      <query xmlns='jabber:iq:register'&sol;>
      </iq>
```

The JUD responds with the fields to fill in. The response is basically a copy of the request, with new attributes and tags:

```
RECV: <iq type='result' to='dj@yak/Work'
          from='jud.yak' id='judreg_ask'>
      <query xmlns='jabber:iq:register'>
        <instructions>
          Complete the form to submit your details
```

```
                   to the User Directory
              </instructions>
              <name&sol;>
              <first&sol;>
              <last&sol;>
              <nick&sol;>
              <email&sol;>
            </query>
          </iq>
```

Now we know what to send:

```
SEND: <iq type='set' to='jud.yak' id='judreg_do'>
          <query xmlns='jabber:iq:register'>
            <name>DJ Adams</name>
            <first>DJ</first>
            <last>Adams</last>
            <nick>qmacro</nick>
            <email>dj@mailserver.org</email>
          </query>
        </iq>
```

And the JUD responds, saying the IQ-set request was successful:

```
RECV: <iq type='result' to='dj@yak/Work'
                    from='jud.yak' id='judreg_do'&sol;>
```

type='result'

As shown in the JUD conversation, the `result` type `<iq&sol;>` packet is used
to convey a result. Whether that result is Boolean (*it worked*, as opposed to *it
didn't work*) or conveys information (such as the registration fields that were
requested), each IQ-get or IQ-set request is followed by an IQ-result response,
if successful.

type='error'

If not successful, the IQ-get or IQ-set request is followed not by an IQ-result
response, but by an `error` type response. In the same way that a subelement
`<error&sol;>` carries information about what went wrong in a `<message
type='error'/>` element, so it also provides the same service for IQ-error
elements.[*]

Let's look at an IQ-error in action. A user, who is trying to join a conference
room, is notified that his entrance is barred because he hasn't supplied a
required password.

First, the user requests information on the room he wishes to join:

```
SEND: <iq type="get" id="conf1" to="cellar@conference.yak">
          <query xmlns="jabber:iq:conference"&sol;>
        </iq>
```

---

[*] Table 5-3 lists the standard Jabber error codes and their default descriptions.

The conference component instance, to which the IQ-get was addressed (with the to='cellar@**conference.yak**' attribute), responds with information about the cellar room, including the fact that a *nickname* and *password* must be specified to gain entrance:

```
RECV: <iq type='result' id='conf1' to='dj@yak/winjab'
                          from='cellar@conference.yak'>
       <query xmlns='jabber:iq:conference'>
         <name>Dingy Cellar</name>
         <nick&sol;>
         <secret&sol;>
       </query>
     </iq>
```

After sending availability to the room, to have the availability tracker kick in for that room's JID (see the section "Availability Tracker"):

```
SEND: <presence to="cellar@conference.yak"&sol;>
```

Entrance to the room is attempted with a nickname but without specifying a password:

```
SEND: <iq to="cellar@conference.yak" type="set" id="conf2">
       <query xmlns="jabber:iq:conference">
         <nick>dj</nick>
       </query>
     </iq>
```

The entrance attempt was unsuccessful. An IQ-error response is given with an <error/> subelement explaining what the problem was:

```
RECV: <iq to='dj@yak/winjab' type='error' id='conf2'
           from='cellar@conference.yak'>
       <query xmlns='jabber:iq:conference'>
         <nick>dj</nick>
       </query>
       <error code='401'>Unauthorized</error>
     </iq>
```

Again, the response is simply the request with modified attributes and data (the <error/> tag) added.

---

from Set by server

Synopsis

```
<iq from='dj@yak/Work'/>
```

Similar to the from attribute in the <message/> and <presence/> elements, this is set by the server and represents the JID where the <iq/> originated.

to   Optional

Synopsis
```
<iq to='jdev@conference.jabber.org'/>
```

This attribute is used to specify the intended recipient of the info/query action or response. If no to attribute is specified, the delivery of the packet is set to the sender, as is the case for <message/> packets. However, unlike the case for <message/> packets, <iq/> packets are usually dealt with en route and handled by the JSM.

What does that mean? Packets sent from a client travel over a jabber:client XML stream and reach the Jabber server, where they're routed to the JSM.*

A large part of the JSM consists of a series of packet handlers, in the form of modules, whose job it is to review packets as they pass through and act upon them as appropriate; some of these actions may cause a packet to be deemed to have been "delivered" to its intended destination (thus causing the packet routing to end for that packet) before it gets there.

So in the case of <iq/> packets without a to attribute, the default destination is the sender's JID, as we've already seen with the <message/> element. But because JSM handlers that receive a packet may perform some action to handle it and cause that packet's delivery to be terminated (marked complete) prematurely, the effect is that something sensible will happen to the <iq/> packet that doesn't have a to attribute and it won't appear to act like a boomerang. Here's an example:

The namespace jabber:iq:browse represents a powerful *browsing* mechanism that pervades much of the Jabber server's services and components. Sending a simple browse request without specifying a destination (no to attribute):

```
SEND: <iq type='get'>
          <query xmlns='jabber:iq:browse'&sol;>
       </iq>
```

will technically be determined to have a destination of the *sender's* JID. However, a JSM handler called *mod_browse* that performs browsing services gets a look-in at the packet before it reaches the sender and *handles* the packet to the extent that the query is deemed to have been answered and thereby the delivery completed. The packet stops traveling in the sender's direction, having been responded to by *mod_browse*:

---

* They're routed with the internal <route/> element; see the section "Component Types" in Chapter 4 for more details.

```
RECV: <iq type='result' to='dj@yak/sjabber' from='dj@yak'>
        <user name='DJ Adams' xmlns='jabber:iq:browse' jid='dj@yak'&sol;>
      </iq>
```

And while we're digressing, here's a meta-digression: we see from this example that a **browse** to a particular JID is handled at the server. The client doesn't even get a chance to respond. So, as one of browsing's roles is to facilitate resource discovery, how is this going to work if the client doesn't see the request and can't respond. The answer lies in the distinction of specifying the recipient JID with or without a *resource*. The idea is that you can query someone's client to find out what that client supports; for example, whiteboarding or XHTML text display.* As a resource is per client connection and in many ways *represents* that client, it makes sense to send a browse request to a JID including a specific resource:

```
SEND: <iq type='get' to='qmacro@jabber.org/sjabber'>
        <query xmlns='jabber:iq:browse'&sol;>
      </iq>
```

This time the destination JID is resource-specific and the packet passes by the *mod_browse* handler to reach the client (*sjabber*), where a response can be returned:

```
RECV: <iq type='result' to='piers@jabber.org/WinJab
                        from='qmacro@jabber.org/sjabber'>
        <user type='client' xmlns='jabber:iq:browse'
                        jid='qmacro@jabber.org/sjabber'>
          <whiteboard&sol;>
          <videochat&sol;>
          <PGP&sol;>
        </user>
      </iq>
```

---

id Optional

Synopsis
```
<iq type='get' id='roster1'/>
```

If we're going to rank the elements in terms of the importance of their being tracked, `<iq&sol;>` would arguably come out on top, as it inherently describes a request/response mechanism. So this element also has an id attribute for tracking purposes.

Don't forget that the pair of XML streams that represent the two-way traffic between Jabber client and server are independent, and any related packets such as

---

* Whiteboarding is collaborative sketching, not a form of surfing atop wave crests.

a request (traveling in one XML stream) and the corresponding response (traveling in the other) are asynchronous. So a tracking mechanism like the `id` attribute is essential to be able to match packets up.

IQ subelements

We've seen these two subelements of the `<iq&sol;>` element already in earlier examples—`<query&sol;>` and `<error&sol;>`. Here's a review of them.

---

query

Required

Synopsis

```
<iq type='get' to='yak'>
<query xmlns='jabber:iq:version'&sol;>
</iq>
```

We've already seen the `<query&sol;>` subelement performing the task of container for the info/query activity.

- For an IQ-get, the subelement usually just contains a qualifying namespace that in turn defines the essence of the *get* activity. This is evident in the example here, where the `<iq&sol;>` element is a retrieval of the server (*yak*) version information.

- For an IQ-set, it contains the qualifying namespace and also child tags that hold the data to be *set*, as in this example, in which a vCard (an electronic "business card") is being updated:

```
SEND: <iq type='set'>
          <vCard xmlns='vcard-temp' version='3.0'>
          ... [vCard information] ...
          </vCard>
      </iq>
```

- When `result` information is returned, it is enclosed within a `<query&sol;>` subelement qualified with the appropriate namespace, as in this IQ-result response to the earlier request for server version information:

```
RECV: <iq type='result' to='dj@yak/Work' from='yak'>
          <query xmlns='jabber:iq:version'>
            <name>jsm</name>
            <version>1.4.1</version>
            <os>Linux 2.2.12-45SAP</os>
          </query>
      </iq>
```

Of course, there are some results that don't carry any further information—the so-called Boolean results. When there's no information to return in a result, the `<query&sol;>` subelement isn't necessary. A typical case in which a Boolean result is returned is on successfully authenticating to the Jabber server (where the credentials are sent in an IQ-set request in the `jabber:iq:auth` namespace); the IQ-result element would look like this:

```
RECV: <iq type='result' id='auth_0'/>
```

- And for an **error** situation, while the actual error information is carried in an `<error/>` subelement, any context in which the error occurred is returned too in a `<query/>` subelement. This is usually because the service returning the error just turns around the IQ-set packet—which already contains the context as the data being *set*—and *adds* the `<error/>` subelement before returning it.

Here we see that the authentication step of connecting to the Jabber server failed because Sabine mistyped her password:

```
RECV: <iq type='error' id='auth_0'>
        <query xmlns='jabber:iq:auth'>
          <username>sabine</username>
          <password>geheimnix</password>
          <resource>pavilion</resource>
        </query>
        <error code='401'>Unauthorized</error>
      </iq>
```

Whoa! Hold on a minute, what's that **<vCard** xmlns='vcard-temp' version='3.0'> doing up there in the IQ-set example? Shouldn't it be **<query** xmlns='vcard-temp' version='3.0'>?

Actually, no. What it should be is defined, in each case, by the namespace specified in the `xmlns` attribute in the tag. It's important to note that while we specified the `<query/>` subelement as being *required*, it's actually the presence of the container itself that is required. Its *name*, while commonly `query`, really depends on the namespace qualifying it. So, while all of the containers qualified by the namespaces listed in the section "The IQ Namespaces" and the section "The X Namespaces," both in Chapter 6, have the tag name `query`, others, qualified by the namespaces in the section "Miscellaneous Namespaces," do not.

The critical part of the subelement is the namespace specification with the `xmlns` attribute. And we've seen this somewhere before—in the definition of component instance configuration in the section "Server Configuration" in Chapter 4, we learned that the tag wrapping the component instance's configuration, like that for the c2s service:

```
<service id="c2s">
  ...
  <pthcsock xmlns='jabber:config:pth-csock'>
    ... [configuration here] ...
  </pthcsock>
</service>
```

which is *pthcsock* here, is irrelevant, while the namespace defining that tag (jabber:config:pth-csock) is important, because it's what is used by the component to retrieve the configuration.

We've seen this feature in this chapter too; remember the <iq/> examples in the jabber:iq:browse namespace? The result of a browse request that returned user information looked like this:

```
RECV: <iq type='result' to='dj@yak/sjabber' from='dj@yak'>
        <user name='DJ Adams' xmlns='jabber:iq:browse' jid='dj@yak'&sol;>
      </iq>
```

Again, the query tag is actually <user/>. In fact, in browsing, the situation is extreme, as the <iq/> response's subelement tag name will be different, depending on what was being browsed. But what is always consistent is the namespace qualifying the subelement; in this example, it's jabber:iq:browse. See the section "jabber:iq:browse" in Chapter 6 for more details.

---

error   Optional

Synopsis

```
<iq type='error' from='dj@yak/Work' to='dj@yak/Work'>
  <query xmlns='jabber:iq:browse'>
  <error code='406'>Not Acceptable</error>
</iq>
```

The error subelement carries error information back in the response to a request that could not be fulfilled. Table 5-3 showed the standard error codes and default accompanying texts.

The example here shows the response to a browse request, but why might the request have been erroneous? Because the <iq/> type attribute had been specified as set instead of get. Browsing is a read-only mechanism.

6

Jabber Namespaces

While the building blocks of the Jabber protocol, described in Chapter 5, provide the groundwork for our solutions, for our chess rules, something is still missing.

A purity and elegance can be had with use of the three core elements, <message/>, <presence/>, and <iq/>, but a depth of meaning is missing. While the core elements define the moves we can make, it's the Jabber *namespaces* that provide us with the contextual set-moves that allow us to relate Jabber to the real world.

Namespaces provide a level of meaning, an environmental layer, above the basic "packet-shunting" world that would exist if our elements were to be passed back and forth bereft of context and application.

Basic activities such as user registration, authentication, roster management, and time-stamping are made possible by the application of standard Jabber namespaces to our elements. This chapter serves as a reference for all of Jabber's IQ and X namespaces. The IQ namespaces are used to qualify attachments to <iq/> elements, while the X namespaces are more ad hoc, and are used to add value, context, and information to any type of packet.

Namespace Usage

Chapter 5 frequently referred to *namespaces*. Jabber's namespaces are used within the message elements to qualify payloads (distinct content) within these elements. For example:

```
RECV: <iq id='roster_0' type='result' from='dj@yak/Work'>
        <query xmlns='jabber:iq:roster'>
          <item jid='sabine@yak' name='sabine' subscription='both'>
            <group>Family</group>
```

```
        </item>
      </query>
    </iq>
```

Here the `jabber:iq:roster` namespace is used to qualify a chunk of XML that contains roster information embedded in an `<iq&sol;>` element. A payload exists as a subelement of the main element (that is, a child tag of the parent `<message&sol;>`, `<presence&sol;>`, or `<iq&sol;>` tag) and, in XML terms, belongs to a different namespace than the main element.

The namespace of the *main* elements in the XML document that is streamed across the connection—`<message&sol;>`, `<presence&sol;>`, and `<iq&sol;>` and indeed their "standard" subelements, such as `<message&sol;>`'s `<subject&sol;>` tag—is defined in the root tag of the XML document and in this case is `jabber:client`. Namespaces like `jabber:client` that are used to qualify such XML document body fragments are described in the section "The Opening Tag" in Chapter 5. While the main elements in our client connection are qualified by `jabber:client`, each distinct payload ("attachment" is also a good way to think of these additional chunks of XML) is qualified by one of the specific namespaces listed in this chapter.

Standard Jabber namespaces begin `jabber:`, with a few exceptions. It could be argued that the exceptions aren't really Jabber standard since these are the namespaces that describe things like vCards and XHTML payloads. There's nothing to stop you from defining your own namespaces to qualify any sort of XML you'd like to attach to a Jabber element. The only rule is that, if you do, it *shouldn't* begin with `jabber:`.

Further to the rule that Jabber standard namespaces begin with `jabber:`, the categorization can be seen as falling into two distinct spaces. The first, the *iq space*, contains namespaces that qualify content within `<iq&sol;>`-based conversations. The second, the *x space*, contains namespaces that qualify extensions within all the elements (`<message&sol;>`, `<iq&sol;>`, and `<presence&sol;>`).

The IQ Namespaces

The namespaces that qualify attachments to `<iq&sol;>` elements are many and varied. After all, you could say that the raison d'etre of this request/response mechanism is to exchange structured information—and what better way to define that information than with namespaces?

This section looks briefly at each of the IQ namespaces in turn. Some of them will be covered in more detail in later chapters, as they will be used in examples that appear later in the book.

jabber:iq:agent

The jabber:iq:agent namespace is used to request and return information on an *agent*. An agent is a service running on a Jabber server, and it has a JID. To find out what features the particular agent offers, an IQ-get can be made using this namespace:

```
SEND: <iq type='get' to='yak/groups'>
        <query xmlns='jabber:iq:agent'&sol;>
      </iq>
```

Here, a request for features is being made of the agent with the JID yak/groups, which is the standard name for the Shared Groups service. The JID here is composed of a hostname (yak) and a resource (groups).

The response looks like this:

```
RECV: <iq type='result' to='dj@yak/Work' from='yak/groups'>
        <query xmlns='jabber:iq:agent'>
          <name>Jabber Server at yak</name>
          <url>http://yak</url>
          <service>jabber</service>
          <register&sol;>
        </query>
      </iq>
```

In reality, although the agent or service itself is specified as the recipient of the query, it is often a centralized mechanism that responds on behalf of the agent if the agent itself doesn't or can't respond. (This is the *mod_agents* module within the JSM.) This means that the results of the query might not be as helpful as you might expect. The only detail in the response shown here that might be of some use is the <register/> tag, but that's actually misleading as it's picked up from the general registration capabilities configuration and not anything particular to what was queried.

The main reason for this is actually also the answer to a question you might have right now: "How do I know which agent JIDs I can query on a particular Jabber server?" Indeed. It's very hit and miss to pick agent JIDs at random. The jabber:iq:agents (plural) namespace defines a *list* of agents. Usually what happens is that a query is made using the jabber:iq:agents namespace, and then further detail is requested with the jabber:iq:agent for a particular agent. However:

- The general information for both queries comes from the same place in the Jabber server configuration.

- That place is the <agents/> tag inside the JSM custom configuration, and is deprecated in favor of the <browse/> tag.

The `jabber:iq:agent`-based agent facility query is slowly but surely being replaced by the more generic but more powerful `jabber:iq:browse` mechanism (which is directly related to the `<browse&sol;>` configuration area of the JSM). That said, it is still supported for compatibility reasons; many Jabber clients still use the `jabber:iq:agent` and `jabber:iq:agents` namespaces in calls to discover services on the server. See the section "jabber:iq:browse" for more details on the `jabber:iq:browse` mechanism.

jabber:iq:agents

Whereas the `jabber:iq:agent` namespace is used in a query of an individual Jabber agent, or service, the `jabber:iq:agents` namespace is used in a query to retrieve a *list* of these agents.

As mentioned in the description for the `jabber:iq:agent` namespace, the Jabber server configuration (in the JSM custom configuration section) in earlier releases contained an `<agents&sol;>` tag, which was used to list the agents that were available on the Jabber server. The listing looked like this:

```
<agents>
  <!-- Note: this <agents&sol;> listing is not used in 1.4.1 -->
  <agent jid='users.jabber.org'>
    <name>Jabber User Directory</name>
    <description>
      You may register and create a public searchable profile,
      and search for other registered Jabber users.
    </description>
    <service>jud</service>
    <register&sol;>
    <search&sol;>
  </agent>
  <agent jid='...'>
    ...
  </agent>
  ...
</agents>
```

The `<agents&sol;>` listing has now been superseded by the `<browse&sol;>` tag. In fact, when responding to `jabber:iq:agents` *and* `jabber:iq:browse` queries, the Jabber server itself will refer to the same `<browse&sol;>` listing in both cases. Here's an example of a response to a `jabber:iq:agents` query:

```
RECV: <iq type='result' to='dj@yak/laptop' from='yak' id='agents'>
        <query xmlns='jabber:iq:agents'>
          <agent jid='users.jabber.org'>
            <name>Jabber User Directory</name>
            <service>jud</service>
            <register&sol;>
            <search&sol;>
```

```
        </agent>
      </query>
    </iq>
```

We can see that this response pretty much reflects the information in the `<agents&sol;>` configuration.

For more details on how this differs in response to a `jabber:iq:browse` query, see the section "jabber:iq:browse."

Further examples of `jabber:iq:agents` usage can be found in the section "An RSS News Agent" in Chapter 9.

jabber:iq:auth

The `jabber:iq:auth` namespace is used to qualify a structured authentication procedure between client and server.

Details of authentication are covered in Chapter 7; however, here we will look at the simplest authentication conversation between client and server. In this example, the client sends a username and password, and the server responds by sending a "successful" response, acknowledging the user's credentials, thus creating a session for that user:

```
SEND: <iq type='set' id='auth0'>
        <query xmlns='jabber:iq:auth'>
          <username>sabine</username>
          <password>geheimnis</password>
          <resource>WinJab</resource>
        </query>
      </iq>

RECV: <iq type='result' id='auth0'&sol;>
```

jabber:iq:autoupdate

The Update Info Request configuration description in the section "Update info request" in Chapter 4 describes a mechanism for Jabber servers to query a software version information repository to find out about new versions of the server.* This version information repository that responds to queries is also known as the Auto-Update service.

Not only can servers request software update information, clients can too. The procedure is the same in both cases and involves the `jabber:iq:autoupdate` and `jabber:x:autoupdate` namespaces. If clients support this software update information request, it will usually be in the form of a "silent" request that it sends out at

---

* By "Jabber server," we're referring to the JSM.

startup. The sending out of this request can often be switched on and off in the client's configuration.

The conversation starts with the requester sending a special availability packet to the information repository. Currently, there are two such public repositories: one running at *jabber.org* covering a wide range of Jabber software and the other running at *jabber.com* covering certain clients including JabberIM. This special availability packet looks like this:

```
SEND: <presence to='959967024@update.jabber.org/1.6.0.3'&sol;>
```

This is a *directed* <presence/> packet because it has a to attribute. What's even more interesting is that if we break down the JID, we're left with *959967024* as the username, *update.jabber.org* as the hostname, and *1.6.0.3* as the resource. This doesn't mean that the availability is destined for a user called *959967024* registered on the *update.jabber.org* Jabber server. While most presence packets are destined for users (within the presence subscription model), this one is destined for a service.

The service is running with the identification *update.jabber.org*—a component connected to the *jabberd* server backbone running at *jabber.org*. Therefore, the <presence/> packet will be routed to that service. Unlike the JSM, the *update.jabber.org* service has no concept of users or sessions. Instead, it receives the complete <presence/> packet, disassembles the JID in the destination address, and interprets component parts as it sees fit.

The service uses the username portion of the JID to identify the piece of software for which new version information is being requested. In our example, this is *959967024*. This value actually represents the JIM client and is the key to the client database kept on *http://www.jabbercentral.org*. Using a unique client database key to represent the piece of software allows the client's name to be changed without causing problems in the retrieval of version information by the Auto Update service.

The version information stored in the repository is compared to the current version of the requesting piece of software; in this case, our JIM Version 1.6.0.3. If a new version isn't available, nothing will happen. Because the initial part of the request was a <presence/> packet, no official response is expected (unlike a situation in which the initial part of the request was an IQ-get).

If there *is*, however, information stored in the repository about newer versions of the software, the query is replied to using a <message/> element, with a jabber:x:autoupdate attachment.

```
RECV: <message to='qmacro@jabber.org/Work' from='959967024@update.jabber.org'>
        <subject>Upgrade available for Jabber Instant Messenger</subject>
        <body>
            There is an update available for Jabber Instant Messenger.
            If your client supports the iq:autoupdate namespace, then
            you should see something in the client that will list the
            available files. If not, then go to http://www.jabbercentral.com
            and grab the new version.
        </body>
        <x xmlns='jabber:x:autoupdate'>959967024@update.jabber.org</x>
      </message>
```

The reply contains some text (in the <subject/> and <body/> tags) that could be displayed to the user.

Furthermore, the `autoupdate` attachment—an <x/> subelement qualified by the `jabber:x:autoupdate` namespace—contains information on where further information can be obtained in a programmatic way.*

This "programmatic way" involves sending an empty IQ-get, with the query part qualified by the `jabber:iq:autoupdate` namespace, to the address given in the `jabber:x:autoupdate` <message/> attachment:

```
SEND: <iq type="get" id="id_3" to="959967024@update.jabber.org">
        <query xmlns="jabber:iq:autoupdate"&sol;>
      </iq>
```

We're back on familiar ground; the Auto Update service responds to the request by sending version information for that piece of software:

```
RECV: <iq type='result' to='qmacro@jabber.org/Work'
                        from='959967024@update.jabber.org' id='id_3'>
        <query xmlns='jabber:iq:autoupdate'>
          <release priority='optional'>
            <url>http://www.jabber.com/download/jabbersetup.exe</url>
            <version>1.7.0.14</version>
            <desc&sol;>
          </release>
        </query>
      </iq>
```

The response contains information about the latest software release that prompted the version request. The release is either *required* or *optional* (as in this example). The tags within the `jabber:iq:autoupdate`-qualified query are fairly self-explanatory; note that the version description is empty in this example.

---

* Remember that the Jabber namespaces used to qualify <iq/> queries begin jabber:iq, while Jabber namespaces used to qualify general payloads to <message/>, <iq/>, or <presence/> begin jabber:x.

jabber:iq:browse

The `jabber:iq:browse` namespace is relatively new and could almost be seen as a departure from the traditional namespaces found elsewhere in Jabber. While namespaces such as `jabber:iq:agents` and `jabber:iq:register` define very strict content using specific tag names, `jabber:iq:browse` allows a more free-form containment of information. Both forms of *tight* and *loose* namespaces have a place in Jabber.

The real world contains countless types and classifications of information far more than you could ever reasonably cover with a finite collection of namespaces. And even if you did, that coverage would be out of date as soon as it was completed. The Jabber concept of *browsing*, introduced in Chapter 2, is an approach to being able to classify and exchange information of all kinds without the definitions being previously cast in stone.

More or less any hierarchical information can be represented in the `jabber:iq:browse` namespace. It can be seen as an open-ended way of describing structures in an almost ad hoc way. That said, the namespace comes with some general rules and some predefined classifications.

Information represented and described in a `jabber:iq:browse` extension is subject to classification. This classification is in two levels: *categories* and *subtypes*. The *category* is used to define the general area or type of information being represented. The *subtype* gives a more specific definition of that category. Table 6-1 shows a list of initial categories.

Table 6-1. jabber:iq:browse categories

Category	Description
application	Applications addressable via a JID can be described in this category. Initial suggestions for such application subtypes include `calendar` (calendar/schedule services), `whiteboard` (collaborative whiteboard tools), and `game` (multiplayer games).
conference	Used to describe elements in the conferencing (talk between three or more entities) world, such as private and public rooms. Subtypes of this category include `private` (private chat rooms), `irc` (IRC rooms), and `url` (for web-based conferences).
headline	Stock-ticker-style notification systems can be described using this category. Subtypes already defined include `rss`, `logger`, and `notice`.
item	A category placeholder, to effect hierarchies and lists in a `jabber:iq:browse` structure. You can fall back to this category for representation of pretty much any type of information in a navigable drill-down fashion.

Table 6-1. jabber:iq:browse categories (continued)

Category	Description
keyword	IRC-style utilities that are invoked from a chat-input command line; so-called keyword services such as dictionary lookups (subtype dictionary), DNS resolution (subtype dns), and FAQ answers (subtype faq) have their category in the jabber:iq:browse world.
render	Translation services such as English to French (subtype en2fr) or spelling tools (subtype spell) are defined in this category.
service	Maps to traditional Jabber services, such as IM transports and gateways to other systems, user directories, and so on. Typical subtypes within this category are irc (IRC gateway), aim (AIM transport), and jud (Jabber User Directory).
user	Various addressable elements of users, such as their clients (subtype client), inbox mechanisms (subtype inbox), and so on, find themselves in this category.

The categories listed in Table 6-1 are not exhaustive; the jabber:iq:browse namespace and the browsing idea were introduced with Version 1.4 of the Jabber server and are still evolving. The same goes for the category subtypes.

Any particular browsable entity can be described using the combination of the category and subtype, for example, user/client, in much the same way that Multipurpose Internet Mail Extensions (MIME) types are, for example, image/png. The category describes generally what the entity is, and the subtype further classifies the description. Following the MIME system further, we can define our own subtypes on the fly and specify them with an x- prefix, such as user/x-schedule.

Indeed, the browsing description model of category/subtype follows the MIME model; in places the category is often referred to in Jabber documentation as the *JID-type*. The JID is critical to browsing; it is a required attribute of all entities described in a jabber:iq:browse-based hierarchy. The JID is the key to navigating the hierarchy structure.

Earlier in this section we saw the results of making a query in the jabber:iq:agents namespace to retrieve information on the services available on a Jabber server. Now let's have a look at a similar query using the jabber:iq:browse namespace:

```
SEND: <iq type='get' to='yak'>
          <query xmlns='jabber:iq:browse'&sol;>
      </iq>

RECV: <iq type='result' to='dj@yak/home' from='yak'>
          <service name='Jabber Server' type='jabber'
                          xmlns='jabber:iq:browse' jid='yak'>
```

```
          <conference name='yak Conferencing'
                    type='public' jid='conference.yak'&sol;>
          <service name='yak User Directory' type='jud' jid='jud.yak'>
            <ns>jabber:iq:search</ns>
            <ns>jabber:iq:register</ns>
          </service>
          <service name='User Directory (Browsable)'
                    type='jud' jid='jud.merlix/users'&sol;>
        </service>
      </iq>
```

Notice how the information returned forms a hierarchy. The outermost item in the browse results represents the Jabber server as a whole (with the JID `yak`) and contains subitems that are services of that Jabber server (the `yak Conferencing` service, and the two forms of the JUD). Notice also the JID-types. Looking at the tag names and the `type` attributes, we see that the result represents a `service/jabber` entity, which itself contains a `conference/public` and two `service/jud` entities.

How many levels of hierarchy can we expect to receive (as a browsing information consumer) or provide (as a browsing information provider) in any given situation? It really depends on the application situation and the balance you want to achieve between shallow hierarchy responses and many IQ calls for navigational descent (light extensions but more traffic) and deeper hierarchy responses and few IQ calls for navigational descent (heavier extensions but less traffic).

Descending the browse hierarchy from an LDAP reflector

As an example, let's look at how we might perform a hierarchy descent in the navigation of Lightweight Directory Access Protocol (LDAP) information provided by a custom LDAP reflector in a `jabber:iq:browse` context.* Each time, the link to the next level is via the item's JID, which is the target of the browse query.

First, we send an initial query:

```
SEND: <iq type="get" id="browser_JCOM_15" to="ldap.yak">
        <query xmlns="jabber:iq:browse"></query>
      </iq>
```

In answer to the initial query to what is effectively the LDAP root represented by the JID of the LDAP component itself (`ldap.yak`, no username prefix), the initial hierarchy level containing `People` and `Groups` is returned, wrapped in a pseudo-root:

---

* In fact, one of the recipes in Chapter 10 is an LDAP reflector. Some background information on LDAP is given there.

```
RECV: <iq type='result' to='dj@yak/winjab' from='ldap.yak' id='browser_JCOM_15'>
        <query xmlns='jabber:iq:browse'>
          <item name='root entry' xmlns='jabber:iq:browse' jid='ldap.yak'>
            <item name='ou=People' jid='ou=People@ldap.yak'&sol;>
            <item name='ou=Groups' jid='ou=Groups@ldap.yak'&sol;>
          </item>
        </query>
      </iq>
```

We see the items presented to us and choose to descend the path marked `Groups`; our second browse request is made to the JID that represents that item, `ou=Groups@ldap.yak`:

```
SEND: <iq type="get" id="browser_JCOM_17" to="ou=People@ldap.yak">
        <query xmlns="jabber:iq:browse"></query>
      </iq>
```

The LDAP reflector component receives the IQ packet addressed to the JID `ou=People@ldap.yak` and interprets the username part of the JID (`ou=People`) as an LDAP RDN (*relative distinguished name*, a form of key within an LDAP structure that's further qualified by a common suffix), which returns the appropriate information from the next level in the LDAP hierarchy, the countries:

```
RECV: <iq type='result' to='dj@yak/winjab' from='ou=People@ldap.yak'
                                            id='browser_JCOM_17'>
        <item name='ou=People' xmlns='jabber:iq:browse'
                               jid='ou=People@ldap.yak'>
          <item name='ou=UK' jid='ou=UK,ou=People@ldap.yak'&sol;>
          <item name='ou=France' jid='ou=France,ou=People@ldap.yak'&sol;>
          <item name='ou=Germany' jid='ou=Germany,ou=People@ldap.yak'&sol;>
        </item>
      </iq>
```

The descent continues, via the JID `ou=UK,ou=People@ldap.yak`, which was specified as the unique identifier for that item (the country UK):

```
SEND: <iq type="get" id="browser_JCOM_18" to="ou=UK,ou=People@ldap.yak">
        <query xmlns="jabber:iq:browse"></query>
      </iq>
```

which continues:

```
RECV: <iq type='result' to='dj@yak/winjab' from='ou=UK,ou=People@ldap.yak'
                                          id='browser_JCOM_18'>
        <item name='ou=UK,ou=People' xmlns='jabber:iq:browse'
                                     jid='ou=UK,ou=People@ldap.yak'>
          <user name='cn=JanetAbrams' jid='JanetAbrams@yak'&sol;>
          <user name='cn=PaulAnthill' jid='PaulAnthill@yak'&sol;>
          ...
        </item>
      </iq>
```

The section of the actual LDAP hierarchy browsed is shown in Figure 6-1.

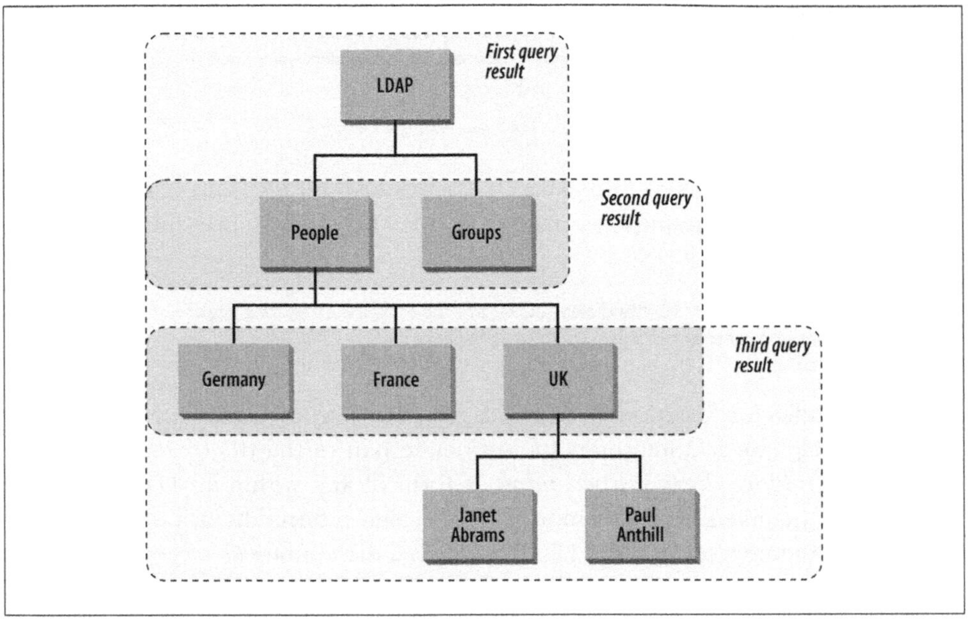

Figure 6-1. The example in the LDAP hierarchy browsed

Browse data isn't just something that can be retrieved; like presence, it can be pushed to an entity when required. In the same way that an alert in the form of a <message/> element might arrive at a client unannounced, so might browse information also appear. This is referred to as *live browsing*, as the information that is pushed is effectively *live*.

The Conferencing service uses this mechanism to push information on room participants to a new joiner. As the browse information is enveloped in an IQ element, it makes the most sense to use a type='set' (it might help to consider the parallel with the Hypertext Transfer Protocol (HTTP) verb POST as introduced in Chapter 2) to push this information. And this is what happens, as seen in this excerpt from information sent to a client as a conference room is joined:*

```
RECV: <iq type='set' to='qmacro@jabber.org/winjab'
                 from='jdev@conference.jabber.org'>
        <conference xmlns='jabber:iq:browse' name='Development Room'
                                      type='public'>
          <user name='piers'
                jid='jdev@conference.jabber.org/445d4b864bd6...'&sol;>
          <user name='pgmillard'
                jid='jdev@conference.jabber.org/1cffcbf43c75...'&sol;>
```

---

* The JIDs returned for the user entities in the room represent nicknames for those users in that room.

```
    <user name='reatmon'
          jid='jdev@conference.jabber.org/b3f3c19859de...'&sol;>
    ...
    </conference>
</iq>
```

As well as the LDAP browser recipe in the section "Browsing LDAP" in Chapter 10, an example of a simple `jabber:iq:browse` implementation can be found in the section "An RSS News Agent" in Chapter 9.

jabber:iq:conference

The Conferencing service provides facilities for entities to join rooms and chat with each other. The entry negotiations that take place between a room (via the service) and a potential participant are made using the `jabber:iq:conference` namespace. With this namespace, information on rooms can be requested, and attempts to enter rooms can be made.

The `jabber:iq:conference` namespace is currently in a state of flux, as more conferencing features (such as being able to eject users from rooms) are requested and added into the definition. Because of this, the examples that follow are deliberately innocuous. The *keyassist* recipe in the section "Keyword Assistant" in Chapter 9 describes and uses the older, but stable, conferencing protocol called "Groupchat."

The jabber:iq:conference namespace at work

Here we see a typical sequence of IQ elements that ensue in the entry negotiations for the *jdev* room hosted by the Conferencing service on *jabber.org*'s Jabber server. Information on the *jdev* room is requested:

```
SEND: <iq type="get" id="c2" to="jdev@conference.jabber.org">
        <query xmlns="jabber:iq:conference"&sol;>
      </iq>
```

The JID to which the IQ-get was sent—*jdev@conference.jabber.org*—works in a similar way to the LDAP reflector earlier in the section "Descending the browse hierarchy from an LDAP reflector." There's no real distinction between conferencing service *usernames* in the same way that there's a distinction in the JSM service, but that part of the JID is used to identify each room hosted by that service. In other words, **jdev** isn't a "real" user in the JSM sense.

The conferencing service replies with the relevant information:

```
RECV: <iq type='result' id='c2' to='qmacro@jabber.org/hailsham'
                          from='jdev@conference.jabber.org'>
    <query xmlns='jabber:iq:conference'>
      <name>Development Room</name>
      <nick&sol;>
    </query>
  </iq>
```

We see that the "friendly" name of the *jdev* room is "Development Room" and that we need to specify a nickname in order to gain entry. There are no other requirements (such as a secret password) that would have been identified inside an extra `<secret&sol;>` tag in the results.

We choose a nickname, and send this back in an IQ-set. However, before doing this, we must send our presence to the room to invoke the Availability Tracker, which is described in the section "Availability Tracker" in Chapter 5.

```
SEND: <presence to="jdev@conference.jabber.org"&sol;>

SEND: <iq to="jdev@conference.jabber.org" type="set" id="c3">
        <query xmlns="jabber:iq:conference">
          <nick>qmacro</nick>
        </query>
      </iq>
```

The Conferencing service acknowledges our entry to the room with our chosen nickname, having assigned us an anonymous handle in the `<id&sol;>` tag:

```
RECV: <iq to='qmacro@jabber.org/winjab' type='result' id='c3'
                        from='jdev@conference.jabber.org'>
        <query xmlns='jabber:iq:conference'>
          <nick>qmacro</nick>
          <name>Development Room</name>
          <id>jdev@conference.jabber.org/650e81de0fcc...</id>
        </query>
      </iq>
```

Closely linked with the `jabber:iq:conference` namespace is the `jabber:iq:browse` namespace, which is also used as a conduit for room-specific information and activity; see the section "jabber:iq:browse."

More information on joining and interacting with conference rooms can be found in the section "Keyword Assistant" in Chapter 9.

jabber:iq:gateway

The `jabber:iq:gateway` namespace is used to envelope a utility mechanism for converting external system identifiers (usernames and so on) to JID equivalents. The requirement for this grew out of the transport services to other IM systems

(AIM, Yahoo!, and so on), which have their own formats for user identification.

First, we know whether a service offers this utility from the namespace list that is returned if we *browse* that service. The next section shows how this might be done with the AIM Transport service.

Discovering and using the AIM Transport's jabber:iq:gateway utility

By browsing a service, we can tell whether it supports the `jabber:iq:gateway` utility:

```
SEND: <iq type="get" id="aim1" to='aim.jabber.org'>
        <query xmlns="jabber:iq:browse"&sol;>
      </iq>

RECV: <iq type='result' id='aim1' to='qmacro@jabber.org/winjab'
                                      from='aim.jabber.org'>
        <service xmlns='jabber:iq:browse' type='jabber'
                          jid='aim.jabber.org' name='AIM Transport'>
          <ns>jabber:iq:register</ns>
          <ns>jabber:iq:gateway</ns>
        </service>
      </iq>
```

We can now avail ourselves of this utility, to convert an AIM screen name test ScreenName to the equivalent JID to be used (in relation to the AIM Transport service) in a Jabber context:

```
SEND: <iq type='get' to='aim.jabber.org' id='conv5'>
        <query xmlns='jabber:iq:gateway'&sol;>
      </iq>

RECV: <iq type='result' to='qmacro@jabber.org/hailsham' id='conv5'
                                      from='aim.jabber.org'>
        <query xmlns='jabber:iq:gateway'>
          <desc>Enter the user's screen name</desc>
          <prompt&sol;>
        </query>
      </iq>
```

We can reply, with an IQ-set, with our screen name:

```
SEND: <iq type='set' to='aim.jabber.org' id='conf6'>
        <query xmlns='jabber:iq:gateway'>
          <prompt>test ScreenName</prompt>
        </query>
      </iq>
```

and receive the result of the transport-specific JID conversion:

```
RECV: <iq type='result' to='qmacro@jabber.org/Work' id='conf6'
                                              from='aim.jabber.org'>
        <query xmlns='jabber:iq:gateway'>
          <prompt>testScreenName@aim.jabber.org</prompt>
        </query>
      </iq>
```

jabber:iq:last

Like `jabber:iq:time` and `jabber:iq:version`, the `jabber:iq:last` namespace
allows a simple query on uptime, idletime, or last disconnect information to be
made on clients and servers.

Elapsed time information, in seconds, is returned in response to queries in the
`jabber:iq:last` namespace. If the query is made of a server element (the Jabber
server itself or a component connected to that server), then the information
returned represents the time since that element started, that is, the uptime:

```
SEND: <iq type='get' to='yak'>
        <query xmlns='jabber:iq:last'></query>
      </iq>

RECV: <iq type='result' to='dj@yak/Work' from='yak'>
        <query xmlns='jabber:iq:last' seconds='2339811'&sol;>
      </iq>
```

Not all components support the `jabber:iq:last` namespace; then again, in many
cases, the components—certainly those that are connected with the *library load*
mechanism (see Chapter 4)—will have the same uptime as the Jabber server
they're connected to. In other cases, for TCP sockets connected components that
can be attached while the Jabber server is running, the uptime may be less.[*]

When a *client* disconnects, the last (un)availability information in the closing
`<presence&sol;>` element is stored for that user, along with the current time:

```
SEND: <presence type='unavailable'>
        <status>Gone home for the evening!</status>
      </presence>
```

Making a `jabber:iq:last`-based query on a user's JID will return the information
that was stored from the `<status&sol;>` tag as well as the number of seconds representing the elapsed time since that disconnection (as a difference between the
time the query was made and the time stored for that user):

---

[*] There is a feature in the Jabber server Version 1.4.1 that allows dynamic starting and stopping of
library load components, but it is not completely developed at the moment.

```
SEND: <iq type='get' to='dj@yak' id='lastq'>
        <query xmlns='jabber:iq:last'&sol;>
      </iq>

RECV: <iq type='result' to='sabine@yak/Work' id='lastq' from='dj@yak'>
        <query xmlns='jabber:iq:last' seconds='4521'>
          Gone home for the evening!
        </query>
      </iq>
```

Notice that the JID of the user being queried is dj@yak and not dj@yak/Work. This, of course, is because the user was still disconnected. The query was addressed to the user with no resource specified and was answered on behalf of the user by the server (by the *mod_last* module—the same module that looks after storing this information). In a disconnected context, a resource is not appropriate for a user's JID (in the JSM); it is found only in a connected context.

The jabber:iq:last is also designed to support a similar client-targeted query (to be responded to by a client), this time requesting information on how long it has been since the user of that client was active (sent a message, changed her presence, and so on). In contrast to the previous jabber:iq:last query type, this query is designed to be made to a connected user:

```
SEND: <iq type="get" to="dj@yak/Work">
        <query xmlns='jabber:iq:last'&sol;>
      </iq>

RECV: <iq type='result' from='dj@yak/Work'>
        <query xmlns='jabber:iq:last' seconds='19'&sol;>
      </iq>
```

Here we see that the user is using a client that supports this type of jabber:iq:last query and was last active 19 seconds ago.

jabber:iq:oob

We've already seen a form of the oob—"Out-Of-Band"—namespace in action, in the imaginary conversation in Chapter 1, where jabber:x:oob was used to pass information about a third-party file location, in the form of a Uniform Resource Locator (URL). The word "band" here refers to the *bandwidth*, or connection, between the client and the server. The point of an *out-of-band* connection is that it's independent of that client-to-server connection (it typically is a connection from one client directly to another), and so doesn't impact the traffic or bandwidth on that connection. This makes sense when you consider that out-of-band connections are typically used for exchanging large volumes of data, such as binary files.

The jabber:iq:oob namespace is used for pretty much the same thing, except that its usage describes a very simple handshake between two Jabber clients to exchange a file between themselves. (Yes, *real* peer-to-peer for the purists.) The exchange is made using HTTP. Typically, the client sending the file will start listening for HTTP requests only at the beginning of the transfer process and stop listening at the end of the transfer process. The handshake is used to coordinate the process.

> It's worth pointing out here that HTTP-based peer-to-peer transfers are at the mercy of firewalls, Network Address Translation (NAT) mechanisms, and so on. There is some work underway to build a proxy mechanism—the Proxy Accept Socket Service (PASS). Details can be found at *http://foundation.jabber.org/jeps/jep-0003.html*.

The sender initiates the process by making the file available via HTTP on a specific (nonstandard) port and notifying the recipient of the URL:

```
SEND: <iq type='set' to='sabine@yak/winjab' id='file_2'>
        <query xmlns='jabber:iq:oob'>
          <url>http://192.168.0.7:5600/meetingnotes.txt</url>
          <desc>Meeting Notes</desc>
        </query>
      </iq>
```

The recipient retrieves the file and notifies the sender when the transfer is complete:

```
RECV: <iq type='result' to='dj@yak/Work' id='file_2' from='sabine@yak/winjab'&sol;>
```

jabber:iq:private

The `jabber:iq:private` namespace is traditionally a way of storing user-defined data that should be kept private. Persistency across sessions is achieved by storing the data in the user's records on the server. The data is, of course, formatted in XML.

> Private data stored by a user is accessible only to that user. Remember, however, that the private data is stored on the server. Unencrypted. If you're paranoid, encrypt it before storing it.

A typical use of the `jabber:iq:private` namespace is shown in Example 6-1. The JIM client stores countless user preferences on a per-user basis using this namespace. Once a user has connected and authenticated with a Jabber server, those user preferences are retrieved and used by the client to customize the settings.

Example 6-1. JIM retrieves user preferences stored in a jabber:iq:private namespace

```
SEND: <iq id="jabberim:prefs3860" type="get">
        <query xmlns="jabber:iq:private">
          <jabberIM xmlns="jabberim:prefs"&sol;>
        </query>
      </iq>

RECV: <iq id='jabberim:prefs3860' type='result' from='dj@yak/Work'>
        <query xmlns='jabber:iq:private'>
          <jabberim xmlns='jabberim:prefs'
                    UseAutoAway='true'
                    AwayTime='5'
                    XATime='30'
                    AwayStatus='Away (auto)'
                    XAStatus='Ext. Away (auto)'
                    WizardShown='false'
                    ... >
          </jabberim>
        </query>
      </iq>
```

In this example, you can see that a `private` namespace is used to qualify the particular chunk of stored data, `jabberim:prefs`. Also of interest is the difference between the tags—<jabberIM/> in the retrieval request and <jabberim/> in the response. Again we see evidence of an XML usage convention previously seen (for example, in the Jabber server component configuration stanzas; see Chapter 4 for more details). The namespace itself, not the enclosing tag name, is critical. If the preferences were originally stored using a tag name of <jabberim/>, then that's how they will be stored and returned.

To add (or change) private data, use the namespace in an IQ-set context:

```
SEND: <iq id="private-s3" type="set">
        <query xmlns="jabber:iq:private">
          <reminders xmlns="cal:events">
            <event date='20010617'>Father's Day</event>
          </reminders>
        </query>
      </iq>
```

Due to the way the `jabber:iq:private` storage mechanism is currently implemented, you can interact with only *one* private namespace-qualified chunk. In other words, a private store request like this:

```
SEND: <iq id="private-s4" type="set">
        <query xmlns="jabber:iq:private">
          <reminders xmlns="cal:events">
            <event date='20010617'>Father's Day</event>
          </reminders>
          <favorites xmlns='url:favorites'>
            <fav url='http://dev.jabber.org'>Jabber DevZone</fav>
```

```
            <fav url='http://www.scripting.com'>Scripting News</fav>
          </favorites>
        </query>
      </iq>
```

would result in the storage of only the `cal:events` chunk. The `url:favorites`
chunk would be ignored.

Storing public data

In the 1.4.1 release of the Jabber server, the JSM module *mod_xml* that services the
`jabber:iq:private` namespace has been extended to allow this server-side storage
to encompass nonprivate (i.e., publicly accessible) user data. The namespace in
this case is, fittingly, *not* `jabber:iq:private`. It can be anything you wish, provided
that it doesn't encroach on the standard Jabber namespace names—`jabber:*` and
`vcard-temp` are not allowed. However, anything else goes. The reason for the
`vcard-temp` namespace name is that there is an emerging but nevertheless not-yet-
established standard for vCard data. Until that standard is established, the Jabber
server developers have decided to handle this format in a temporary way.

The idea of publicly accessible data is just that; you can make information available to your fellow Jabber users (share URLs, contact lists, and so on). Of course,
this sharing is only one way; you write and others can only read. But how do they
find out *what* you've made available for them to read? The namespaces of any
data stored publicly (i.e., any namespace except for `jabber:iq:private`) are
returned by the Jabber server acting on behalf of the user in response to a `jab-
ber:iq:browse` request to that user's JID. That is, the JID without a specified
resource; otherwise, it would be passed on by the server to be handled by the
client connection with that resource.

Let's have a look at this in action. We'll also have a peek at how the storage of the
public and private information is structured in the user's spool file on the server to
understand how this works. The location of the spool files is defined in the `xdb`
component instances configuration—see the section "Component Instance: xdb"
in Chapter 4. In addition to the Father's Day event that was stored privately in the
previous example, we can also set some favorite URLs in a publicly accessible
namespace and receive an acknowledgment of successful storage from the server:

```
SEND: <iq type='set' id='setfavs'>
        <query xmlns='dj:public:favorites'>
          <item url='http://dev.jabber.org'>Jabber DevZone</item>
          <item url='http://www.scripting.com'>Scripting News</item>
        </query>
      </iq>

RECV: <iq type='result' from='dj@yak/Work' to='a1@yak/Work' id='setfavs'&sol;>
```

Now, the relevant section of dj@yak's spool file on the server looks something like that shown in Example 6-2.

Example 6-2. Section of user's spool storage showing public and private data

```
...

<foo xmlns='jabber:xdb:nslist' xdbns='jabber:xdb:nslist'>
  <ns type='private'>cal:events</ns>
  <ns>dj:public:favorites</ns>
</foo>

<reminders xmlns='cal:events' j_private_flag='1' xdbns='cal:events'>
  <event date='20010617'>Father's Day</event>
</reminders>

<query xmlns='dj:public:favorites' xdbns='dj:public:favorites'>
  <item url='http://dev.jabber.org'>Jabber DevZone</item>
  <item url='http://www.scripting.com'>Scripting News</item>
</query>

...
```

There are a few things to note in this example:

- The jabber:xdb:nslist namespace maintains a list of namespaces containing information stored for private and public reference.

- The private namespaces are marked in this list with a type='private' attribute.

- There is an additional flag (j_private_flag='1') that is held as an attribute of each of the privately stored fragments.

- Otherwise the information is stored exactly as it was set (additional xdbns attributes related to the xdb storage mechanisms notwithstanding).

The namespaces (<ns/> tags) in the jabber:xdb:nslist-qualified list are returned in any browse request to that user:

```
SEND: <iq type='get' to='dj@yak'>
        <query xmlns='jabber:iq:browse'&sol;>
      </iq>

RECV: <iq type='result' to='sabine@yak/Work' from='dj@yak'>
        <user name='DJ Adams' xmlns='jabber:iq:browse' jid='dj@yak'>
          <ns>dj:public:favorites</ns>
        </user>
      </iq>
```

and can be subsequently retrieved by anyone:

```
SEND: <iq type='get' to='dj@yak'>
        <query xmlns='dj:public:favorites'&sol;>
      </iq>

RECV: <iq type='result' to='sabine@yak/Work' from='dj@yak'>
        <query xmlns='dj:public:favorites'>
          <item url='http://dev.jabber.org'>Jabber DevZone</item>
          <item url='http://www.scripting.com'>Scripting News</item>
        </query>
      </iq>
```

Publicly stored data can contain multiple fragments qualified by different namespaces, such as:

```
SEND: <iq type='set'>
        <query xmlns='my:resume'>
          <education xmlns='resume:education'>
            <degree type='BA'>Classics</degree>
          </education>
          <employment xmlns='work:clients'>
            <client from='2001'>Author, O'Reilly & Associates, Inc.</client>
            <client from='1999'>Deluxe Video Services</client>
            <client from='1996'>Andersen Consulting</client>
            ...
          </employment>
        </query>
      </iq>
```

However, the retrieval *resolution* is still limited to all of the fragments defined by the top-level namespace (my:resume in this case).

jabber:iq:register

As the name suggests, the jabber:iq:register namespace is used to conduct registration exchanges between the client and server. The most obvious example of this is to create (*register*) a new user on the Jabber server. We cover user registration, including changes to user details such as passwords, in Chapter 7, so here we'll look at how to use the namespace to add or change an entry in the JUD.

First we request the fields for registration with an IQ-get:

```
SEND: <iq type='get' to='jud.yak' id='jud-2'>
        <query xmlns='jabber:iq:register'&sol;>
      </iq>

RECV: <iq type='result' to='dj@yak/Work' from='jud.yak' id='jud-2'>
        <query xmlns='jabber:iq:register'>
          <instructions>
            Complete the form to submit your searchable attributes
            in the Jabber User Directory
```

```
                    </instructions>
                    <name&sol;>
                    <first&sol;>
                    <last&sol;>
                    <nick&sol;>
                    <email&sol;>
                 </query>
              </iq>
```

and then send an IQ-set to set our information:

```
SEND: <iq type='set' to='jud.yak' id='jud-3'>
         <query xmlns='jabber:iq:register'>
           <name>DJ Adams</name>
           <first>DJ</first>
           <last>Adams</last>
           <nick>qmacro</nick>
           <email>dj.adams@pobox.com</email>
         </query>
      </iq>


RECV: <iq type='result' to='dj@yak/Work' from='jud.yak'&sol;>
```

This idiom—making a request to a service to return the fields appropriate for completion—is common in Jabber and is worth bearing in mind if you're intending to build a Jabber client. The nature of the form field requests means that the client application has to be flexible and accommodating, to bend itself around the dynamic server.

The recipe in the section "A Simple Jabber-Based Address Book" in Chapter 10 is an example of creating forms dynamically.

Services offering a registration mechanism are identifiable in the list returned from a jabber:iq:agents or a jabber:iq:browse query, as shown in Example 6-3.

Example 6-3. An agents or browse query reveals registration mechanisms

```
RECV: <iq to='dj@yak/Work' type='result' from='yak'>
         <query xmlns='jabber:iq:agents'>
           <agent jid='jud.yak'>
             <name>yak JUD (0.4)</name>
             <service>jud</service>
             <search&sol;>
             <register&sol;>
           </agent>
           ...
         </query>
      </iq>


      ...
```

Example 6-3. An agents or browse query reveals registration mechanisms (continued)

```
RECV: <iq type='result' to='dj@yak/Work' from='yak'>
         <service xmlns='jabber:iq:browse' type='jabber' jid='yak'
                 name='Jabber Server'>
           <service type='jud' jid='jud.yak' name='yak JUD (0.4)'>
             <ns>jabber:iq:search</ns>
             <ns>jabber:iq:register</ns>
           </service>
           ...
         </service>
       </iq>
```

There are a couple of extra elements that are fairly common across different implementations of the `jabber:iq:register` namespace:

`<remove&sol;>`

> When sent with an IQ-set request, the `<remove&sol;>` tag requests that the registration be canceled, revoked, or reversed.

`<registered&sol;>`

> When received in an IQ-result, the `<registered&sol;>` tag signifies that registration has already been made with the service, and any further registration IQ-sets will serve to modify the current registration details.

The `jabber:iq:register` namespace also defines a special `<key&sol;>` tag. This is a simple antispoofing mechanism that a piece of software responding to an IQ in this namespace can use to verify the sender of that IQ. This `<key&sol;>` tag can also be used in the `jabber:iq:search` namespace. See the following section for details on how this mechanism is used.

The <key/> tag

The `<key&sol;>` tag is used in registration and search sequences to add a simple form of security between the service and the entity requesting the service. It enables the service, the responder, to verify that the requester from whom it has just received an IQ-set is the same requester that had sent an IQ-get earlier.

This security mechanism predates the server-to-server dialback mechanism, described in Chapter 4. Since the advent of dialback, the relevance of the `<key&sol;>` tag usage has been reduced.

If a component wants to determine who ought to be allowed to partake of its registration or search services, it would make sense to make the determination when responding to an initial IQ-get, the "can I do this, and what do I have to do?" request. If the request is to be *denied*, the component can send back an IQ-error, say, with an error 405 "Not Allowed" (see Table 5-3).

If, however, the component determines that the requester should be allowed to use the service (with an IQ-set), it can send back an IQ-result containing a <key/> tag along with the rest of the instructions and fields. The <key/> tag contains a random string, such as a message digest of the requester's JID combined with a secret phrase. When the requester is ready to make the IQ-set, the "OK, I'd like to use this service, and here's the data" request, the <key/> tag must be included, with the contents intact. On receipt of the IQ-set, the component doesn't have to determine whether the requester is allowed to use the service, it just has to regenerate the string using the same algorithm as before and compare it with what the requester sent.

Example 6-4 shows the <key/> tag in action, based upon the same registration sequence shown earlier in this section.

Example 6-4. The <key/> tag in action

```
SEND: <iq type='get' to='jud.yak' id='jud-2'>
        <query xmlns='jabber:iq:register'&sol;>
      </iq>

RECV: <iq type='result' to='dj@yak/Work' from='jud.yak' id='jud-2'>
        <query xmlns='jabber:iq:register'>
          <instructions>
            Complete the form to submit your searchable attributes
            in the Jabber User Directory
          </instructions>
          <key>cff28e89afa94e734aabfb11ec1099780450d80e</key>
          <name&sol;>
          <first&sol;>
          <last&sol;>
          <nick&sol;>
          <email&sol;>
        </query>
      </iq>

SEND: <iq type='set' to='jud.yak' id='jud-3'>
        <query xmlns='jabber:iq:register'>
          <key>cff28e89afa94e734aabfb11ec1099780450d80e</key>
          <name>DJ Adams</name>
          <first>DJ</first>
          <last>Adams</last>
          <nick>qmacro</nick>
          <email>dj.adams@pobox.com</email>
        </query>
      </iq>

RECV: <iq type='result' to='dj@yak/Work' from='jud.yak'&sol;>
```

Another example of registration using the jabber:iq:register namespace is shown in the section "An RSS News Agent" in Chapter 9.

jabber:iq:roster

In the section "Presence subscription" in Chapter 5, we looked at the presence subscription mechanism used to coordinate and record information about the relationships between users and how they exchange availability information. This mechanism revolves around certain types of `<presence&sol;>` elements and storage of information in the users' *rosters*.

The roster structure is managed within the `jabber:iq:roster` namespace. Clients make roster requests when they connect to the Jabber server, to pull down the roster that is stored server-side. They also update the roster to add, change, or remove entries. However, roster updates aren't limited to just the client; there are certain attributes within each roster item that are maintained by the server, in response to presence subscription activity.

The roster in Example 6-5 contains five items. Three are friends, grouped together using `<group>Friends</group>`, which is used by clients to build the roster item display in a structured (hierarchical) way.

Example 6-5. A typical roster

```
<query xmlns='jabber:iq:roster'>
  <item jid='shiels@jabber.org' subscription='both' name='Robert'>
    <group>Friends</group>
  </item>
  <item jid='piers@jabber.org' subscription='both' name='Piers'>
    <group>Friends</group>
  </item>
  <item jid='sabine@pipetree.com' subscription='to' name='Sabine'>
    <group>Friends</group>
  </item>
  <item jid='jim@company-a.com' subscription='from' name='Jim'>
    <group>Work</group>
  </item>
  <item jid='jim@company-b.com' subscription='none'
        ask='subscribe' name='John'>
    <group>Work</group>
  </item>
</query>
```

The `subscription` attribute is used to store the presence subscription state between the roster owner and the particular item that holds that attribute. With two of the friends, Robert and Piers, the roster owner is subscribed to each of their presences, and each of them is subscribed to the presence of the roster owner. This is denoted by the `both` value in the `subscription` attribute, which means that the presence subscription flows both ways. Where the `subscription` attribute has the value `to` (as in Sabine's case) or `from` (Jim's case), the subscription flows in only one direction. Here, the roster owner is subscribed *to* Sabine's presence (but Sabine is not subscribed to the roster owner's presence), and Jim is subscribed to the roster owner's presence (i.e., the roster owner has a presence subscription *from* Jim).*

Where the value of the `subscription` attribute is `none` (as in John's case), neither party has a subscription to the other. In this case, a further attribute, `ask`, may be used to reflect that a presence subscription request is in progress.† The `ask` attribute can have one of two values:

`subscribe`
> Denotes that a request to subscribe to a user's presence has been made

`unsubscribe`
> Denotes that a request to unsubscribe from a user's presence has been made

In both cases, these requests are sent using a `<presence&sol;>` element with an appropriate value for the `type` attribute.

The server is responsible for maintaining the `subscription` and `ask` attributes; the client may maintain all the other elements. If an item is updated by the server— for example, as a result of a correspondent accepting a previous subscription request—the server will push the updated item to the client (all clients, if the user is connected multiple times with different resources) with an IQ-set:

```
SEND: <iq type='set'>
          <query xmlns='jabber:iq:roster'>
            <item jid='john@company-b.com' subscription='to' name='John'&sol;>
          </query>
      </iq>
```

Here, John has accepted the roster owner's subscription request by sending the following:

```
<presence to='dj@yak/Work' type='subscribed'&sol;>
```

The server will update the roster item accordingly by removing the `ask='sub-scribe'` and setting the value of the `subscription` attribute to `to`.

jabber:iq:search

The `jabber:iq:search` is closely related to the `jabber:iq:register` namespace, in that the dance steps are pretty much the same. As with `jabber:iq:register`, you can discover which entities (usually server components) support search features from the results of an agents or browse query, as shown in Example 6-3.

---

* In colloquial Jabber terms, Jim is known as a *lurker*, as he knows about the roster owner's availability, without the roster owner knowing about his.

† "Pending," in Jabber client parlance.

Also, as with the `jabber:iq:register` namespace, the fields to be used in the interaction are first retrieved with an IQ-get qualified by the `jabber:iq:search` namespace. Here we see an example of that with the JUD running on the *jabber.org* server:

```
SEND: <iq type='get' to='users.jabber.org' id='800'>
        <query xmlns='jabber:iq:search'&sol;>
      </iq>

RECV: <iq type='result' from='users.jabber.org'
          to='qmacro@jabber.org/laptop' id='800'>
        <query xmlns='jabber:iq:search'>
          <instructions>
            Fill in a field to search for any matching Jabber User
          </instructions>
          <first&sol;>
          <last&sol;>
          <nick&sol;>
          <email&sol;>
        </query>
      </iq>
```

To continue the similarity theme, an IQ-set is used to submit the search, sending back a value (or values) in the fields like this:

```
<email>pipetree.com</email>.
```

The only exciting feature of the `jabber:iq:search` namespace is perhaps the way it can return results in response to an IQ-set. This depends on the component and how the feature is implemented.

While the JUD component will return all results in one IQ element:

```
RECV: <iq type='result' from='users.jabber.org' to='qmacro@jabber.org/laptop'>
        <query xmlns='jabber:iq:search'>
          <item jid='qmacro@jabber.org'>
            <name>DJ Adams</name>
            <first>DJ</first>
            <last>Adams</last>
            <nick>qmacro</nick>
            <email>dj@pipetree.com</email>
          </item>
          <item jid='piers@jabber.org'>
            <name>Piers Harding</name>
            <first>Piers</first>
            <last>Harding</last>
            <nick>pxh</nick>
            <email>piers@pipetree.com</email>
          </item>
          ...
        </query>
      </iq>
```

the component providing transport services to the ICQ IM system returns the results item by item:

```
RECV: <iq type='set' from='icq.jabber.org' id='icqs8'
         to='qmacro@jabber.org/laptop'>
       <query xmlns='jabber:iq:search'>
         <item jid='4711471@icq.jabber.org'>
           <given>DJ</given>
           <family>Adams</family>
           <nick>qmacro</nick>
           <email>dj@pipetree.com</email>
         </item>
       </query>
      </iq>

RECV: <iq type='set' from='icq.jabber.org' id='icqs8'
         to='qmacro@jabber.org/laptop'>
       <query xmlns='jabber:iq:search'>
         <item jid='1234567@icq.jabber.org'>
           <given>Piers</given>
           <family>Harding</family>
           <nick>pxh</nick>
           <email>piers@pipetree.com</email>
         </item>
       </query>
      </iq>
```

The component signals the end of the search results with an empty IQ-result element:

```
RECV: <iq type='result' from='icq.jabber.org' id='icqs8'
         to='qmacro@jabber.org/laptop'>
       <query xmlns='jabber:iq:search'&sol;>
      </iq>
```

The *anti-spoofing mechanism* in the form of the <key/> tag, described in the earlier section titled "The <key/> tag," can also be used in conversations qualified by the jabber:iq:search namespace.

jabber:iq:time

The jabber:iq:time namespace qualifies an IQ-based conversation to make or respond to a query on time information.

To query the time at a particular entity, an IQ-get request like this is sent:

```
SEND: <iq type='get' id='time_19' to='conference.yak'>
        <query xmlns='jabber:iq:time'&sol;>
       </iq>
```

Three pieces of information—the time in UTC (coordinated universal time) format, the local time zone, and a nice display version of the local time—are returned in response to such a query:

```
RECV: <iq type='result' id='time_19' to='sabine@yak/Work'
         from='conference.yak'>
        <query xmlns='jabber:iq:time'>
          <utc>20010520T08:55:38</utc>
          <tz>GMT</tz>
          <display>Sun May 20 09:55:38 2001</display>
        </query>
      </iq>
```

The format of the <tz/> and <display> tags is not fixed. While this is what the Conferencing service returns, a response from the JIM client would give "GMT Standard Time" and "20/05/01 09:55:38," respectively.

 If you consider that certain components can be connected to the Jabber backbone but be running on different hosts in different time zones, communicating over TCP socket connections (as described in the section "Server Constellations" in Chapter 4), this may be more useful than you initially think.

Specifying clients as query targets

Many of these namespaces qualify queries that make just as much sense sent to a Jabber client as sent to a Jabber server or service. However, if you don't compose the recipient JID correctly, you could end up with an unexpected response.

Let's say you want to query the local time on Piers' client, which is connected to the Jabber server at *jabber.org*:

```
SEND: <iq type='get' id='time_21' to='piers@jabber.org'>
        <query xmlns='jabber:iq:time'&sol;>
      </iq>
```

You could get a response similar to this:

```
RECV: <iq type='error' id='time_21' from='piers@jabber.org'
         to='qmacro@jabber.org/home'>
        <query xmlns='jabber:iq:time'&sol;>
        <error code='503'>Service Unavailable</error>
      </iq>
```

Why? This query isn't addressed to a particular client or session. While <message/> elements can be addressed to a user JID in the form username@hostname and will be sent to the "primary" session according to presence priority, the recipients of <iq/> elements must be specified exactly. As we want to find out the time at Piers' client, which has the associated resource `desktop`, we must specify that resource in the JID:

```
SEND: <iq type='get' id='time_21' to='piers@jabber.org/desktop'>
        <query xmlns='jabber:iq:time'&sol;>
      </iq>
```

This will give us the response we're looking for:

```
RECV: <iq type='result' id='time_21' to='qmacro@jabber/home'
        from='piers@jabber.org/desktop'>
        <query xmlns='jabber:iq:time'&sol;>
          <utc>20010520T11:25:58</utc>
          <tz>CET</tz>
          <display>Sun May 20 13:25:58 2001</display>
        </query>
      </iq>
```

jabber:iq:version

Similar to the `jabber:iq:time` namespace, the `jabber:iq:version` namespace is used to make and respond to queries regarding the version of the particular piece of software being addressed. The query is formulated like this:

```
SEND: <iq type='get' id='ver-a' to='JID'>
        <query xmlns='jabber:iq:version'&sol;>
      </iq>
```

Responses depend on the entity being queried. Here are responses from three different entities:

- A client (*sjabber*):

```
RECV: <iq type='result' to='dj@yak/Work' from='sabine@yak/sjabber'>
        <query xmlns='jabber:iq:version'>
          <name>sjabber</name>
          <version>0.4</version>
          <os>linux</os>
        </query>
      </iq>
```

- The Jabber server itself (well, the JSM):

```
RECV: <iq type='result' to='dj@yak/Work' from='sabine@yak/sjabber'>
<query xmlns='jabber:iq:version'>
        <name>jsm</name>
        <version>1.4.1</version>
        <os>linux 2.2.12-45SAP</os>
</query>
</iq>
```

- And the JUD component:

```
RECV: <iq type='result' to='dj@yak/Work' from='sabine@yak/sjabber'>
<query xmlns='jabber:iq:version'>
        <name>jud</name>
        <version>0.4</version>
        <os>linux 2.2.12-45SAP</os>
</query>
</iq>
```

The `jabber:iq:version` namespace is used in the recipe in the section "An RSS News Agent" in Chapter 9.

The X Namespaces

While the IQ namespaces are used in exchanging structured information in semi-formalized conversations, the X namespaces are more ad hoc extensions that add value, context, and information to any type of packet.

jabber:x:autoupdate

The `jabber:x:autoupdate` namespace is used to carry information on where new version information can be found. Details and an example of this namespace's usage can be found in the description for the IQ version, `jabber:iq:autoupdate`, in the section "jabber:iq:autoupdate."

jabber:x:conference

Just as `jabber:x:autoupdate` is related to its big brother, `jabber:iq:autoupdate`, so too is the `jabber:x:conference` namespace related to `jabber:iq:conference`. The `<x&sol;>` version of the IQ-conference namespace is used to convey information about a conferencing room, usually attached to a message:

```
SEND: <message id='2113' to='robert@company-a.com'>
        <subject>Design Meeting</subject>
        <body>Robert - you're supposed to be at the meeting now!</body>
        <x xmlns='jabber:x:conference' jid='meeting1@meetings.company-a.com'&sol;>
    </message>
```

If supported by the receiving client, this will be interpreted as an invitation to the room and the procedure for joining the room (in this case, identified with the JID `meeting1@conf.company-a.com`) can be automatically initiated:

```
SEND: <iq type='get' id='c4' to='meeting1@meetings.company-a.com'>
        <query xmlns='jabber:iq:conference'&sol;>
    </iq>
```

jabber:x:delay

Messages are sometimes sent to entities that aren't available at that particular moment. If they are stored offline, they are timestamped, in the `jabber:x:delay` namespace, so that when they are finally received, the recipient can use this information to determine when they were originally sent:

```
RECV: <message to='sabine@yak/Work' from='yak'>
         <subject>Weekend at last!</subject>
         <body>Don't forget Father's Day on Sunday!</body>
         <x xmlns='jabber:x:delay' from='yak/announce/motd'
            stamp='20010615T09:00:01'>Announced</x>
      </message>
```

In this Message-Of-The-Day (MOTD) announcement, we see that, as well as the `stamp` attribute showing that the announcement was sent out on the Friday morning before Father's Day, a short text description, "Announced", is included.

The namespace is also used by the `xdb` component to timestamp various fragments of data stored in the user's records on the server. Here, we see that Sabine updated her user registration details (using a `jabber:iq:register` query during her session) at the beginning of March:

```
<query xmlns='jabber:iq:register' xdbns='jabber:iq:register'>
  <name>S. Reitz-Adams</name>
  <email>sabine@reitz-adams.org</email>
  <x xmlns='jabber:x:delay' stamp='20010302T12:15:42'>updated</x>
</query>
```

jabber:x:encrypted

You can use the relatively new `jabber:x:encrypted` namespace to implement message-level security. It allows the attachment of encrypted data Public Key Infrastructure (PKI) techniques, meaning that the data is encrypted using the message sender's private key and decrypted by the recipient using the sender's public key.

```
SEND: <message to='john@company-a.com' id='m221'>
         <body>Top Secret!</body>
         <x xmlns='jabber:x:encrypted'>
      lxG/K9tFGgtk9yUNRTWUMwtI2ty27s6M0VzwWQBCr6Irwu1CiHTG9o
      pSfX4ff3Yusa4Ah7ippuD9qcl/KgX4HEBJtt4Dt9SPb86jmaGN1gdd
      dxqxeTFvFat3mwO/DvU8CKULwMi7ejgn/ib0WhSM2cfsJEIUP=TsL6
      9HUY7eVvzKKe5CvMNnE/4UAQ41DfbqqXVSdCO8swLaG1los1zGP8io
      lZXjlaz75YwVVYucrFw7EXKa/wTGVjAPnkWBwv/AYx5poIyjqWQt6q
      kLZmk5YA44PxAGveOHhVDxUuRW8MTtMUqEENYZDwfugOEGCBWol8=X
      BaPqH5t4fS24OiqO2sJVJjIbORrBD0kYU2xhwcM3KSS/ffBAHEjoQ+
      WvxdFEtjYuzBtyI2a672oZvyA6IqIjpovvYtKFnP7ghKgpY3J9xhYg
      KKrWRIciH5rj3Imy2d87cCd8os5nWYkt8p1ZkebRoGPkIlvy0iL7m8
         </x>
      </message>
```

The Jabber server itself does not currently provide any mechanisms for key management or exchange; the namespace is for the time being purely a marked container to hold encrypted data.

jabber:x:envelope

The `jabber:x:envelope` namespace describes more complex message-addressing details than the simple `from` and `to` attributes in the `<message&sol;>` elements.

The first area in which this namespace is used is in server-side filtering, a service provided by the JSM's `mod_filter` module. For example, when a user sets a filter rule to forward all messages to someone else while he's not around:*

```
<rule name="absent">
  <show>xa</show>
  <forward>john@company-b.com</forward>
</rule>
```

a message such as this:

```
<message id='284' to='janet@company-b.com'>
  <body>Can you give me the sales figures for last quarter?</body>
</message>
```

will be passed on to *john@company-b.com* in this form:

```
<message id='284' to='janet@company-b.com'>
  <body>Can you give me the sales figures for last quarter?</body>
  <x xmlns='jabber:x:envelope'>
    <forwardedby jid='janet@company-b.com'>
    <from jid='mark@company-b.com'>
    <cc jid='john@company-b.com'>
  </x>
</message>
```

to add context information on where the message has come from.

jabber:x:event

Message *events* allow clients and servers alike to add information about the receipt and handling of messages at various stages of delivery. There are currently four types of events supported in this namespace:

Composing
> The composing event, represented by the `<composing&sol;>` tag within the `<x&sol;>` extension qualified by the `jabber:x:event` namespace, can be set by clients and signifies that the user is composing a reply to the message just

---

* The filter service is described in the section "Filter service" in Chapter 4.

sent.

Delivered

> When a message is received by a client, it can set the `<delivered&sol;>` flag to signify that the message has been received.

Displayed

> The displayed event is used to indicate that the message sent has been displayed to the user. This event is set, using the `<displayed&sol;>` tag, by clients.

Offline

> When a message recipient is not connected, the JSM module *mod_offline* will store the message and send it to the recipient when she is next available. This offline storage event can be set by the server, using the `<offline&sol;>` tag, to notify the sender that the message has been stored offline.

The `<composing&sol;>`, `<delivered&sol;>`, and `<displayed&sol;>` events are client events and are appropriate to be set only by the client. The `<offline&sol;>` event is a server event and appropriate to be set only by the server. In all cases, the events are set only if the message originator requests that they are. Adding a `jabber:x:event` extension to a message like this:

```
SEND: <message to='sabine@yak' id='M31'>
        <subject>Where are you?</subject>
        <body>Let me know when you get back.</body>
        <x xmlns='jabber:x:event'>
          <displayed&sol;>
          <offline&sol;>
        </x>
      </message>
```

is the way to request that we get notified:

- If and when the message is stored offline by the server in the eventuality that Sabine is not connected

- When the message is eventually displayed to Sabine

The former event will be set by the server; the latter by Sabine's client.

Setting an event is similar to *requesting* one and uses the `jabber:x:event` namespace. Here is what we would receive if the server did store our message to Sabine offline:

```
RECV: <message to='dj@yak/Work' id='M31' from='sabine@yak'>
        <x xmlns='jabber:x:event'>
          <offline&sol;>
          <id>M31</id>
        </x>
      </message>
```

That is, the <offline/> tag is sent back to the originator, along with an
<id/> tag that contains the id of the message that was stored offline. Example
6-6 shows the receipt of a chat message and the <composing/> event being
raised as Sabine starts to type her reply.

Example 6-6. Raising and canceling the <composing/> event

DJ sends a quick chat message to Sabine and requests that his client be notified
when she starts typing her response:

```
RECV: <message to='sabine@yak/Work' from='dj@yak/home' id='122' type='chat'>
        <body>hey, want a coffee?</body>
        <thread>ABAF6FC6521546A2B65B19EA391CB72A</thread>
        <x xmlns='jabber:x:event'>
          <composing&sol;>
        </x>
      </message>
```

Sabine starts to type, which fires the <composing/> event:

```
SEND: <message from='sabine@yak/Work' to='dj@yak/home'>
        <x xmlns='jabber:x:event'>
          <composing&sol;>
          <id>122</id>
        </x>
      </message>
```

Sabine is distracted, and her client decides she's abandoned the reply and sends a
cancellation of the <composing/> event, containing only the message id
included when the event was originally raised:

```
SEND: <message from='sabine@yak/Work' to='dj@yak/home'>
        <x xmlns='jabber:x:event'>
          <id>122</id>
        </x>
      </message>
```

jabber:x:expire

The jabber:x:expire is a simple namespace to add a "use by" or "read by" stamp
to a message. If you wish to send a message and impose a finite lifetime upon it,
attach an expiry extension thus:

```
SEND: <message to='piers@pipetree.com' id='M24'>
        <subject>Twinkies!</subject>
        <body>
          I've got some fresh Twinkies here, stop
          by for one before they all disappear!
        </body>
        <x xmlns='jabber:x:expire' seconds='1800'&sol;>
```

```
  </message>
```

If Piers was not connected when the message was sent, the *mod_offline* module would hold the message ready for when he reconnects. But before storing it, an extra attribute (`stored`) is added with the current time.

Example 6-7 shows what the relevant section of Piers' spool file would look like.

Example 6-7. Storage of an offline message with the jabber:x:expire extension

```
<foo xmlns='jabber:x:offline' xdbns='jabber:x:offline'>
  <message to='piers@pipetree.com' id='M24' from='dj@pipetree.com/kitchen'>
    <subject>Twinkies!</subject>
    <body>
      I've got some fresh Twinkies here, stop
      by for one before they all disappear!
    </body>
    <x xmlns='jabber:x:expire' seconds='600' stored='993038415'&sol;>
    <x xmlns='jabber:x:delay' from='dj@pipetree.com' stamp='20010620T12:00:15'>
      Offline Storage
    </x>
  </message>
</foo>
```

When Piers reconnects, *mod_offline* retrieves the message and compares the current time with the value in the `stored` attribute. If the difference exceeds the desired lifetime of the message, as specified in the `seconds` attribute, the message is discarded. Otherwise, the `seconds` attribute value is reduced to reflect the amount of time the message sat in storage, the `stored` attribute is removed, and the message is sent to Piers.

Furthermore, if Piers' client supports it, a further check of the message's lifetime can be made before display, in case the message was stored in an inbox-style mechanism. (With Piers' luck, he probably missed out on the Twinkies.)

jabber:x:oob

We've already seen the `jabber:x:oob` in action earlier in the book. It is used in a similar way to its big brother, the `jabber:iq:oob` namespace. Attaching URLs to messages, typically done by mechanisms that deliver news- and alert-style headines, is done like this:

```
SEND: <message type='headline' to='qmacro@jabber.org/laptop' id='h12'>
        <subject>Jabber Foundation Public Conference</subject>
        <x xmlns='jabber:x:oob'>
          <url>
            http://www.jabbercentral.com/news/view.php?news_id=989358658
          </url>
          <desc>
            Tomorrow, May 9th, a meeting regarding the Jabber
            Foundation will be held.
```

```
        </desc>
      </x>
    </message>
```

Multiple attachments can be made to a message, using multiple `<x&sol;>` tags qualified by this namespace.

The RSS Delivery Mechanism, described in the section "An RSS News Agent" in Chapter 9, and the Headline Viewer, described in the section "A Simple Headline Viewer," also in Chapter 9, both use the `jabber:x:oob` namespace.

jabber:x:roster

The `jabber:x:roster` namespace is related to its big brother, `jabber:iq:roster`; it is used to carry roster information as message attachments. This makes it straightforward for users to exchange contact information between themselves:

```
SEND: <message id='M91' to='shiels@jabber.org'>
        <body>Hi Robert - this is that fool I was telling you about...</body>
        <x xmlns='jabber:x:roster'>
          <item jid='qmacro@jabber.org' name='DJ Adams'>
            <group>Fools</group>
          </item>
        </x>
      </message>
```

Note that it is inappropriate to send the subscription-related attributes (`subscription` and `ask`, described in the section "jabber:iq:roster"). Instead, it is up to the recipient to negotiate his own presence subscription arrangements with the contact or contacts (more than one item can be sent in such an attachment) listed.

jabber:x:signed

The `jabber:x:signed` namespace is related to the `jabber:x:encrypted` namespace and is used to stamp `<presence&sol;>` and `<message&sol;>` elements with a PKI-based signature, thus providing reliable identification of the packet originator.

In generating the signature block, some relevant data must be used to pass into the signing algorithm so that an electronic signature is produced. In the case of `<presence&sol;>` elements, the contents of the `<status&sol;>` tag are used, and in the case of `<message&sol;>` elements, the contents of the `<body&sol;>` tag are used.

The presence of a `jabber:x:signed` signature in a `<presence&sol;>` packet is intended to signify that the client sending the packet supports such PKI infrastucture and, for example, is able to decrypt messages encrypted in the `jabber:x:encrypted` namespace.

Here's a `<presence&sol;>` packet containing a signature; the data "All present and correct" is what is fed into the algorithm:

```
SEND: <presence from='piers@jabber.org' to='qmacro@pipetree.com'>
  <status>All present and correct</status>
  <x xmlns='jabber:x:signed'>
    p/B8CuePDUvAAHPuacDb2OYjAHTGn4BbqChrhxwH8ZTKJxL
    9nUNH58OF=tl0VMDcSYizG5HFh
  </x>
</presence>
```

The X::IQ Relationship

As has been noted, some of the X namespaces—`autoupdate`, `conference`, `roster`, and `oob`—have cousins in the IQ space. If you're still confused about which to use where, there's a rule of thumb about context: the IQ namespaces generally are used to qualify a *conversation* that revolves around whatever the namespace represents, while the X namespaces apply more to one-off, ad hoc, information-laden messages.

For example, the `jabber:iq:conference` namespace qualifies much of the content of a conversation between a user and the conferencing service regarding entry to a specific room. The `jabber:x:conference` namespace is used to provide context and meaning to a pointer to a room.

Likewise, the `jabber:x:oob` namespace qualifies a pointer to some piece of information that is out of band, whereas the `jabber:iq:oob` namespace provides context to a negotiation that leads to the usage of that external bandwidth.

Miscellaneous Namespaces

In addition to the standard Jabber namespaces that begin `jabber:iq:` and `jabber:x:`, a couple of others are used often and are worthy of our attention.

They're both outside the `jabber:` namespace because they don't originate within Jabber. The vCard format, represented by the `vcard-temp` namespace, is an emerging Internet standard used in many different environments, not just within Jabber. XHTML is a World Wide Web Consortium (W3C) standard that Jabber has adopted to carry rich text in messages and is represented in Jabber with the `http://www.w3.org/1999/xhtml` namespace.

The vcard-temp Namespace

The `vcard-temp` namespace represents the vCard format. It's a format used to provide information about an entity—a person, company, or even, in Jabber's case, a piece of software—in the form of a virtual business card.

The idea behind the vCard format, which is an emerging but as yet incomplete standard, is that it can be used to hold information about something in a formalized and parcel-like way. vCards can be attached to email messages and extracted from user directories and address books. The fact that the format is not yet a standard is reflected in the "temporary" namespace (`vcard-temp`) used to qualify vCard exchanges.

> Jabber uses the vCard format to hold details about various parts of the Jabber server; each component can have a vCard, as seen in the section "A Tour of jabber.xml" in Chapter 4. Each Jabber user can have a vCard, too.

Retrievals of vCards, and updates, are made using IQs containing extensions qualified by the `vcard-temp` namespace. To *request* a vCard, send an IQ-get to the holder of the vCard you want, like this:

```
SEND: <iq type='get' to='qmacro@jabber.org' id='73'>
        <vcard xmlns='vcard-temp'&sol;>
      </iq>
```

Rather than the usual tag name of `query`, vCard `<iq&sol;>` extensions have the name `vcard` (this is sometimes seen in all caps or as `vCard`).

In response to this request, the vCard belonging to *qmacro* will be returned as shown in Example 6-8.

Example 6-8. A response returning qmacro's vCard

```
RECV: <iq id='73' to='dj@gnu.mine.nu/home'
         type='result' from='qmacro@jabber.org'>
        <vCard xmlns='vcard-temp' version='3.0'>
          <BDAY&sol;>
          <ORG>
            <ORGNAME&sol;>
            <ORGUNIT&sol;>
          </ORG>
          <TITLE&sol;>
          <ROLE&sol;>
          <TEL>
            <VOICE&sol;>
            <HOME&sol;>
          </TEL>
          <TEL>
            <fax&sol;>
            <HOME&sol;>
          </TEL>
          <TEL>
            <MSG&sol;>
            <HOME&sol;>
          </TEL>
```

Example 6-8. A response returning qmacro's vCard (continued)

```
            <ADR>
              <HOME&sol;>
              <EXTADD&sol;>
              <STREET&sol;>
              <LOCALITY&sol;>
              <REGION&sol;>
              <PCODE&sol;>
              <COUNTRY&sol;>
            </ADR>
            <FN>DJ Adams</FN>
            <TEL>
              <VOICE&sol;>
              <WORK&sol;>
            </TEL>
            <TEL>
              <fax&sol;>
              <WORK&sol;>
            </TEL>
            <TEL>
              <MSG&sol;>
              <WORK&sol;>
            </TEL>
            <N>
              <GIVEN>DJ</GIVEN>
              <FAMILY>Adams</FAMILY>
              <MIDDLE&sol;>
            </N>
            <ADR>
              <WORK&sol;>
              <EXTADD&sol;>
              <STREET&sol;>
              <LOCALITY&sol;>
              <REGION&sol;>
              <PCODE&sol;>
              <COUNTRY&sol;>
            </ADR>
              <EMAIL>dj.adams@gmx.net
              <INTERNET&sol;>
              <PREF&sol;>
            </EMAIL>
            <NICKNAME>qmacro</NICKNAME>
            <URL>http://www.pipetree.com/~dj/</URL>
          </vCard>
        </iq>
```

Obviously, *qmacro* has not added values for all of the fields that the vCard format defines. Nevertheless, the response gives us a good idea of what sort of information can be stored.

There are different versions of the vCard format, as it matures. The `version` attribute shown in the response in Example 6-8 signifies which version the vCard

Jabber uses the vCard format to hold details about various parts of
the Jabber server; each component can have a vCard, as seen in the
section "A Tour of jabber.xml" in Chapter 4. Each Jabber user can
have a vCard, too.

data returned conforms to. It's an optional attribute, and not all vCard requests will
return responses that include such an attribute.

In fact, it's not the only thing that's optional. Requesting the vCard belonging to a
Conferencing component called conf.gnu.mine.nu, for example, will elicit the
result shown in Example 6-9. Here, the vCard information consists of just three
fields: the full name of the component (<FN/>), the component's description
(<DESC/>), and a URL (<URL/>). Not all entities will have vCards containing
all the vCard elements, as this example shows. (If the vCard data for the Conferencing component looks familiar, that's because it is—we've seen how vCards for
components are maintained, in the *jabber.xml* configuration. See the section "Custom Configuration" in Chapter 4 for details.)

Example 6-9. Requesting a Conferencing component's vCard

```
SEND: <iq type='get' id='vc11' to='conf.gnu.mine.nu'>
         <vcard xmlns='vcard-temp'&sol;>
      </iq>

RECV: <iq type='result' id='vc11'
          from='conf.gnu.mine.nu'
          to='qmacro@jabber.org/home'>
          <vCard xmlns='vcard-temp'>
            <FN>gnu Chat</FN>
            <DESC>Conferencing Component</DESC>
            <URL>http://www.gnu.mine.nu/</URL>
          </vCard>
      </iq>
```

Notice also that the response shown in Example 6-8 seems to have come from
qmacro himself—the value in the <iq> element's from attribute seems to suggest
that. In fact, *qmacro* was never aware of the request. What actually happens,
when a request is made to retrieve a vCard belonging to a Jabber *user*, is that the
JSM responds to the request; it jumps in on behalf of the user registered with it to
answer the request. This means that Jabber user vCards can be retrieved whether
or not the user is connected and available at the time of the request.

This is in contrast to component vCards; it is the components themselves who
must respond to requests for vCards (in fact, to requests for *anything* addressed to
them). If a component is not connected, the request will fail, in that an IQ-error

(502, "Server Connect Failed") will be returned as the *jabberd* hub was unable to pass the request on.

That a user vCard can be retrieved independently of the user's availability highlights the fact that user vCards are stored on the Jabber server. The information is stored along with the rest of the user-specific information (such as private data and pending messages stored offline) in the user's spool file, in a similar way to how public and private data is stored, as shown in Example 6-2.

To *maintain* vCard information, an IQ-set is required:

```
<iq id='76' type='set'>
  <vCard xmlns='vcard-temp' version='3.0'>
    <BDAY>1966-09-03</BDAY>
    <ORG>
      <ORGNAME>Merlix</ORGNAME>
      <ORGUNIT&sol;>
    </ORG>
    <TITLE>Tea boy</TITLE>
    <ROLE>Making the tea</ROLE>
    ...
  </vCard>
</iq>
```

Not all of the vCard elements are shown to keep the example short, but don't assume that individual elements of a vCard can be maintained by sending only those elements back. The *whole* vCard must be sent in an IQ-set request for the vCard to be maintained. Whatever is received by the JSM is taken to be absolute, not relative, and replaces anything that was already stored in the spool.

Note that it's the maintainer's responsibility to specify a version attribute if one is required or desired.

The XHTML Namespace

As already shown in the section "Message subelements" in Chapter 5, the XHTML namespace, http://www.w3.org/1999/xhtml, is used to qualify an optional message tag <html/>, which can be used to carry a rich-text version of the message's <body/> contents.

Definitive information on the XHTML standard can be found at *http://www.w3.org/1999/xhtml*. As mentioned in the section "Message subelements" in Chapter 5, this namespace qualifies tags within <message/> elements that are optional. Jabber clients do not have to support rich-text formatting. If they do, a number of XHTML elements are *required*, and a number are *optional*. The protocol documentation section on Jabber's central documentation site at *http://docs.jabber.org* has full details.

7

User Registration and Authorization

With all of Jabber's building blocks at our fingertips, we can now take a look at two fundamental processes that revolve around Jabber users:

- The registration, or creation, of Jabber user accounts
- The authentication of a Jabber user account, including the different authentication methods

These processes involve some of the things we learned about in Chapter 5 and Chapter 6, so we'll take a look at them again along the way:

- The XML stream header
- The `jabber:iq:register` namespace
- The `jabber:iq:auth` namespace

At the end of this chapter, we will create a small utility program with which we can register users on a server. We can then use this utility program to create users as required for further recipes in this book.

XML Stream Flow

User registration and user authorization are two processes that take place at the start of an XML stream, immediately following the XML stream header exchange. The Jabber server is designed to check for and process any user registration request or authentication request *before* anything else.

This makes sense, as outside of a session (a session is created for a user when the authentication completes successfully), any other element—a <message/> element, a <presence/> element, or an <iq/> element that doesn't contain an extension qualified by the `jabber:iq:register` or `jabber:iq:auth` namespaces—is invalid. So if any of these other elements are sent *before* authentication has taken place (that is, before a session has been created for that connection), they are queued and processed *after* authentication.

Figure 7-1 shows the general flow within an XML stream, with regard to where the registration and/or authentication steps happen.

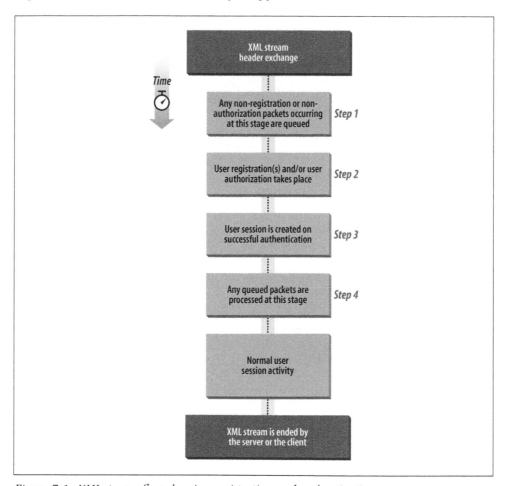

Figure 7-1. XML stream flow showing registration and authentication

User Registration

User registration with a Jabber *server* specifically means the creation (or modification) of a user account for the JSM component—the component that provides the basic IM services and has a notion of users and user sessions. It takes place at the start of a connection to a Jabber server, as does user authentication, as shown in Figure 7-1.

Let's take a look at the XML fragments involved in a typical user registration process. Example 7-1 shows the XML stream header exchange and the IQ packets in the `jabber:iq:register` namespace.

Example 7-1. A typical user registration process

First is the XML stream header exchange:

```
SEND: <?xml version='1.0'&quest;>
      <stream:stream to='yak' xmlns='jabber:client'
                     xmlns:stream='http://etherx.jabber.org/streams'>

RECV: <?xml version='1.0'&quest;>
      <stream:stream xmlns:stream='http://etherx.jabber.org/streams'
                     id='3B2DB1A7' xmlns='jabber:client' from='yak'>
```

Then the client sends a request to discover what information must be passed to the Jabber server to register a new user:

```
SEND: <iq type='get'>
        <query xmlns='jabber:iq:register'&sol;>
      </iq>

RECV: <iq type='result'>
        <query xmlns='jabber:iq:register'>
          <instructions>
            Choose a username and password to register with this server.
          </instructions>
          <name&sol;>
          <email&sol;>
          <username&sol;>
          <password&sol;>
        </query>
      </iq>
```

The client does as asked and sends the required information, which results in a successful new user registration:

```
SEND: <iq type='set'>
        <query xmlns='jabber:iq:register'>
          <username>leslie</username>
          <password>secret</password>
          <email>lel@plevna.com</email>
          <name>Leslie Hawke</name>
        </query>
      </iq>

RECV: <iq type='result'&sol;>
```

Configuration and Module Load Directives

Lets start by reviewing the relevant configuration in *jabber.xml*. User registration is a JSM feature, and we find two places of interest in that component instance definition. The first is in that instance's configuration, in the section qualified by the jabber:config:jsm namespace:

```
<register notify="yes">
  <instructions>
    Choose a username and password to register with this server.
  </instructions>
  <name&sol;>
  <email&sol;>
</register>
```

The second is in that instance's connection method, showing the *mod_register* module being loaded. The module plays a major part in handling the registration process, but there are others, too, as we will see:

```
<load main="jsm">
  <jsm>./jsm/jsm.so</jsm>
  <mod_echo>./jsm/jsm.so</mod_echo>
  <mod_roster>./jsm/jsm.so</mod_roster>
  <mod_time>./jsm/jsm.so</mod_time>
  <mod_vcard>./jsm/jsm.so</mod_vcard>
  <mod_last>./jsm/jsm.so</mod_last>
  <mod_version>./jsm/jsm.so</mod_version>
  <mod_announce>./jsm/jsm.so</mod_announce>
  <mod_agents>./jsm/jsm.so</mod_agents>
  <mod_browse>./jsm/jsm.so</mod_browse>
  <mod_admin>./jsm/jsm.so</mod_admin>
  <mod_filter>./jsm/jsm.so</mod_filter>
  <mod_offline>./jsm/jsm.so</mod_offline>
  <mod_presence>./jsm/jsm.so</mod_presence>
  <mod_auth_plain>./jsm/jsm.so</mod_auth_plain>
  <mod_auth_digest>./jsm/jsm.so</mod_auth_digest>
  <mod_auth_0k>./jsm/jsm.so</mod_auth_0k>
  <mod_log>./jsm/jsm.so</mod_log>
  <mod_register>./jsm/jsm.so</mod_register>
  <mod_xml>./jsm/jsm.so</mod_xml>
</load>
```

The <register/> configuration section looks familiar; the contents are very similar to the IQ-result returned in response to the IQ-get in the jabber:iq:register namespace in Example 7-1. Indeed, to respond to an IQ-get, the *mod_register* module looks for this <register/> section and formulates the contents into a reply, making a simple modification as it goes: it appends tags for the two fields <username/> and <password/> as these two are *always* required, regardless of configuration.

Removing the `<register&sol;>` section from the configuration effectively blocks the registration process and returns an appropriate error to the user:

```
SEND: <iq type='get'>
          <query xmlns='jabber:iq:register'&sol;>
      </iq>

RECV: <iq type='error'>
          <query xmlns='jabber:iq:register'&sol;>
          <error code='501'>Not Implemented</error>
      </iq>
```

Removing the reference to the *mod_register* module from the component instance's connection method:

```
<!--
  <mod_register>./jsm/jsm.so</mod_register>
-->
```

has the same effect.

More information on the configuration discussed here can be found in the section "Component Instance: sessions."

Step by Step

Taking the stream contents in Example 7-1 step by step, what do we see?

The XML stream header exchange

Although the XML declaration that is sent immediately preceding the opening `<stream:stream&sol;>` root tag is optional, it's not a good idea to leave it out. While the Jabber server currently does not enforce its presence, future implementations may do so.* The Jabber server will always send an XML declaration in response. In both cases—in both streamed XML documents—the encoding is assumed to be UTF-8.

For the most part, the rest of the `<stream:stream&sol;>` root tag is static. The namespace qualifying the stream content is `jabber:client` (which is the only namespace acceptable when making such an XML stream connection to the c2s— Client-to-Server—component listening on port 5222), and the namespace qualifying the stream itself is fixed at `http://etherx.jabber.org/streams`.[†]

The only thing that is going to be dynamic is the `to` attribute, which is used to specify the Jabber server name. Note that this is the *logical* name, the internal

---

* That said, for the time being, when you're testing against a Jabber server using *telnet*, it's 20 less characters that you have to type every time you create a new connection.

† The name "etherx" comes from an old library that implemented XML streams.

name, of the Jabber server. In our example, we've already resolved the physical hostname, yak, and connected to port 5222; the to attribute is to specify the virtual Jabber host, which in many cases—including an out-of-the-box *jabber.xml* configuration—has the same name as the physical host.

If our Jabber server has just a single virtual host, we can use an <alias/> configuration tag in the c2s component instance configuration, as described in the section "Custom Configuration," to remove the requirement of specifying the to attribute.

Using:

```
<alias to='yak'&sol;>
```

will set the *default* alias to yak and indeed override any value specified in the to attribute.

"Required" fields

The list of fields returned in the response to the IQ-get in the jabber:iq:register namespace is actually supposed to be a list of *mandatory* fields:

* <name/>
* <email/>
* <username/>
* <password/>

However, with the current version of the Jabber server (1.4.1, which is our reference version for this book), this is not the case.

The <username/> and <password/> fields *are* mandatory; not supplying them or supplying an invalid username or password will result in an error:

```
SEND: <iq type='set'>
         <query xmlns='jabber:iq:register'>
           <username>leslie</username>
           <email>lel@plevna.com</email>
           <name>Leslie Hawke</name>
         </query>
      </iq>

RECV: <iq type='error'>
         <query xmlns='jabber:iq:register'>
           <username>leslie</username>
           <email>lel@plevna.com</email>
           <name>Leslie Hawke</name>
         </query>
         <error code='406'>Not Acceptable</error>
      </iq>
```

However, currently, failing to supply any of the other fields—the fields that are
specified in the `<register&sol;>` section of the JSM instance's configuration—will
not result in an error. This may be fixed in a later release. In any case, it's no great
loss; the details are simply stored in the user's spool file on the server, and right
now there's only one situation where this information is subsequently used: in
answering a browse request made to a user's JID, the server looks up the
`<name&sol;>` tag from the registration data stored and uses the value there in the
browse response:

```
SEND: <iq type='get' to='dj@yak'>
          <query xmlns='jabber:iq:browse'&sol;>
      </iq>

RECV: <iq type='result' from='dj@yak' to='sabine@yak/Work'>
          <user name='DJ Adams' xmlns='jabber:iq:browse' jid='dj@yak'&sol;>
      </iq>
```

Set without get

In many of the examples of IQ throughout the book, we've seen a standard pattern: IQ-get -> IQ-result -> IQ-set -> IQ-result. This pattern isn't any different here,
but it's not essential. Bearing in mind that registration field requirements aren't
going to change that often, and even if they do, the only ones that are enforced
are `<username&sol;>` and `<password&sol;>`, you can get away with forgoing the IQ-
get and cutting straight to the chase with an IQ-set. This isn't a recommendation to
do that, merely an observation, as it's always good practice to ask first.

Still no connection

After registering a new user, note that there's still no session. Only after successful
authorization (see later in this chapter) is a session created. Although used in
authentication (and so implicitly in session creation), the value of the id attribute
in the XML stream header returned by the server (which has the value 3B2DB1A7 in
Example 7-1) is a *connection* ID, not a *session* ID.

So, what can we do at this stage? Well, one of two things: register another user
(yes!) or proceed to the authentication stage. Basically, reaching the end of the
registration process, we're back where we started; a "raw" connection where only
one of two sequences is valid: the `jabber:iq:register` or `jabber:iq:auth`
sequence.

Passwords

You may be wondering about the plaintext nature of the password sent in the registration process. Although the Jabber server offers different types of password-
based authentication, there's a "bootstrap" process required to get the password to

the server in the first place. There's currently no way around the fact that the server must at one time receive the password in all its plaintext glory. After receiving it, there are authentication processes that don't use the plaintext password again.

So if you're concerned about the security of this registration phase, consider doing it over a secure (SSL) connection to the server.

We will look at the detail of the different authentication mechanisms later in this chapter; however, it is worth noting here, in the context of the registration process, that the JSM modules that implement the mechanism are responsible for storing the password when it's received. The *mod_register* module actually registers the user, but it is the *mod_auth_plain* and *mod_auth_0k* modules that actually store the password when received.*

Passwords are stored on another occasion—when a user wishes to *change* his password. This procedure is also covered by the jabber:iq:register namespace, albeit in a different context—the context of a *session*. While a jabber:iq:register-based IQ conversation *outside* the context of a session is for registering a user, a similar conversation *within* the context of a session, that is, after a user has authenticated, is used to change the user's password and other registration details. Among other reasons, this is for security: a session context implies the user has identified and authenticated himself, and so has the authority to change the password.

Example 7-2 shows a typical IQ-set to change a password.

Example 7-2. Changing a password with jabber:iq:register

```
SEND: <iq type='set' id='pass_4' to='yak'>
        <query xmlns='jabber:iq:register'>
          <password>newsecret</password>
        </query>
      </iq>

RECV: <iq type='result' id='pass_4' from='yak' to='dj@yak/Work'&sol;>
```

The to attribute is required here, to make sure the query is handled by the server itself. We can also see evidence that the context of this exchange is within a session in the value of the to attribute on the IQ-result packet—the JID dj@yak/Work includes a resource suffix, which implies a session (a resource must be specified in the authentication process—see later in this chapter). And the specification of a <username/> is not necessary, as the server will stamp the incoming IQ-set anyway with the JID associated with the user's session.

---

* The *mod_auth_digest* module doesn't play a password-storing role, just a password-checking one, as the mechanism it provides uses the plaintext password that is stored by *mod_auth_plain*.

If you had made an IQ-get, as recommended earlier, before doing the IQ-set to change the password, the result would have looked like this:

```
RECV: <iq type='result' to='dj@yak/Work' id='pass_2' from='yak'>
        <query xmlns='jabber:iq:register'>
          <password&sol;>
          <instructions>
            Choose a username and password to register with this server.
          </instructions>
          <name&sol;>
          <email&sol;>
          <key>9a6957b7f69535274afa5c134fb4d916c5d5c20b</key>
          <registered&sol;>
        </query>
      </iq>
```

We see that, as in the registration IQ-get outside the session context, the contents of the `<register&sol;>` section of the JSM instance's configuration have been inserted (the `<instructions&sol;>`, `<name&sol;>`, and `<email&sol;>` tags). Additionally, we have a `<key&sol;>` tag, as a simple security token (described in the section "jabber:iq:register") and a `<registered&sol;>` tag. The `<key&sol;>` is not actually checked in the current implementation and therefore does not have to be supplied in the return IQ-set packet. And the `<register&sol;>` tag is merely a flag telling us that the user is already registered.

Use of the `jabber:iq:register` namespace in conversation with the JSM in a session context is not limited to changing passwords; you can modify the rest of the registration details supplied when the user was created—in this case, the `<name&sol;>` and `<email&sol;>` information. In fact, with the current implementation, because of the lack of checks, you can specify your own fields in the `jabber:iq:register` IQ-set, in both contexts. But don't do it; it's a habit that will probably be impossible to keep up in later releases of the server.*

It almost goes without saying that because IQs in the `jabber:iq:register` namespace are handled differently in a session context, you can't register a new user once your session has started; you must end it. To end it, the XML stream must be closed with a `</stream:stream>`, and a new connection and stream must then be created.

Reversing a user registration

The opposite of registering a user is *unregistering* a user. This is not the same as removing that user altogether. When the `<remove&sol;>` tag, described in the section "jabber:iq:register," is used in a `jabber:iq:register`-qualified IQ-set during a

---

* And no, you can't spoof someone else by specifying the `<username&sol;>` tag in a session context `jabber:iq:register` IQ-set; it is ignored, and the correct JID is taken from the `from` attribute stamp made as the packet hits the server.

user session, the user is *unregistered*. That is, all the information held in the user's spool file is removed. But the spool file itself is not removed until the Jabber server is shut down. This means that even if you <remove/> a user, the username will still exist until the server is cycled, causing an error if the same username is used in a new registration attempt:

```
RECV: <iq type='error'>
        <query xmlns='jabber:iq:register'>
          <username>dj</username>
          <password>secret</password>
        </query>
        <error code='409'>Username Not Available</error>
      </iq>
```

This may well be fixed in a later release of the Jabber server.

A note on error messages

Various errors can occur during user registration. They are, on the whole, fairly plain and easy to understand. But because of the way the server has been written, you might be surprised at *what* error message you receive in certain circumstances.

Because the required fields <username/> and <password/> are checked *before* looking to see whether or not there is a <register/> section in the JSM instance configuration, you will always receive a *406 "Not Acceptable"* instead of a *501 "Not Implemented"* if you don't supply those fields, even if the registration mechanism has been turned off.

Likewise, if you specify a username that already exists, you will receive a *409 "Username Not Available"* instead of a *501 "Not Implemented."*

Of course, if you do an IQ-get with the `jabber:iq:register` namespace beforehand, you *will* receive the "correct" error—good practice pays!

User Authentication

There are similarities between user registration and user authentication:

*   Authentication must take place outside of a session context (it doesn't really makes sense inside a session context, anyway). It is perfectly possible to perform a user registration step followed by a user authentication step (for any user) in the same XML stream.

*   Any packets sent before the authentication step (apart from user registration packets) are queued until after the authentication step has been completed.

- The IQ-get in the `jabber:iq:auth` namespace is not mandatory but is recommended (even more strongly than the recommendation for the IQ-get in the `jabber:iq:register` namespace).

Example 7-3 shows a typical authentication process, including the XML stream header exchange.

Example 7-3. A typical user authentication process

Here the authentication process immediately follows the initial XML stream header exchange:

```
SEND: <?xml version='1.0'&quest;>
       <stream:stream to='yak' xmlns='jabber:client'
                      xmlns:stream='http://etherx.jabber.org/streams'>

RECV: <?xml version='1.0'&quest;>
       <stream:stream xmlns:stream='http://etherx.jabber.org/streams'
                      id='1ED34A55' xmlns='jabber:client' from='yak'>
```

We ask the server about the authentication methods available for our specific user:

```
SEND: <iq type='get'>
         <query xmlns='jabber:iq:auth'>
           <username>dj</username>
         </query>
       </iq>

RECV: <iq type='result'>
         <query xmlns='jabber:iq:auth'>
           <username>dj</username>
           <password&sol;>
           <digest&sol;>
           <sequence>496</sequence>
           <token>3B2DEEC0</token>
           <resource&sol;>
         </query>
       </iq>
```

Because we're connecting here to the server with *telnet* and don't have any digest utilities handy, we decide to use the simplest authentication method and send our password in plaintext. The server checks the credentials and gives us the thumbs-up.

```
SEND: <iq type='set'>
         <query xmlns='jabber:iq:auth'>
           <username>dj</username>
           <password>secret</password>
           <resource>laptop</resource>
         </query>
       </iq>

RECV: <iq type='result' id='pthsock_client_auth_ID'&sol;>
```

At this stage, we have a session.*

Configuration and Module Load Directives

The c2s component contains a configuration directive related to the authorization process:

```
<service id="c2s">
  <load>
    <pthsock_client>./pthsock/pthsock_client.so</pthsock_client>
  </load>
  <pthcsock xmlns='jabber:config:pth-csock'>
    <alias to='yak'&sol;>
    <authtime&sol;>
    ...
  </pthcsock>
</service>
```

This <authtime/> tag is used to set the time limit, in seconds, within which authentication should be completed, starting to measure at the time the connection was made. See the section "Custom Configuration" for more details.

There is also an undocumented tag, <auth/>, which can be specified in the JSM instance configuration (for example, after the <register/> section) and with which you can specify an external component that is to handle authentication in place of the standard JSM modules (*mod_auth_*). The JSM module load directives specify the modules that handle authentication:

```
<load main="jsm">
  <jsm>./jsm/jsm.so</jsm>
  <mod_echo>./jsm/jsm.so</mod_echo>
  <mod_roster>./jsm/jsm.so</mod_roster>
  <mod_time>./jsm/jsm.so</mod_time>
  <mod_vcard>./jsm/jsm.so</mod_vcard>
  <mod_last>./jsm/jsm.so</mod_last>
  <mod_version>./jsm/jsm.so</mod_version>
  <mod_announce>./jsm/jsm.so</mod_announce>
  <mod_agents>./jsm/jsm.so</mod_agents>
  <mod_browse>./jsm/jsm.so</mod_browse>
  <mod_admin>./jsm/jsm.so</mod_admin>
  <mod_filter>./jsm/jsm.so</mod_filter>
  <mod_offline>./jsm/jsm.so</mod_offline>
  <mod_presence>./jsm/jsm.so</mod_presence>
  <mod_auth_plain>./jsm/jsm.so</mod_auth_plain>
  <mod_auth_digest>./jsm/jsm.so</mod_auth_digest>
  <mod_auth_0k>./jsm/jsm.so</mod_auth_0k>
  <mod_log>./jsm/jsm.so</mod_log>
  <mod_register>./jsm/jsm.so</mod_register>
```

---

* The pthsock_client_auth_ID value for the id attribute in the IQ-result is placed by the JSM as it processes the IQ-set request, when a value has not been specified.

```
    <mod_xml>./jsm/jsm.so</mod_xml>
  </load>
```

Each of these modules, *mod_auth_plain*, *mod_auth_digest*, and *mod_auth_0k* can play a role in the authentication process. As mentioned in the section "Component Connection Method," they provide different authentication methods, these methods being reflected in their names:

*   *mod_auth_plain*: plaintext

*   *mod_auth_digest*: digest

*   *mod_auth_0k*: zero-knowledge

You have a certain amount of flexibility as administrator to determine what methods are made available on your Jabber server. If you want to offer all three, do nothing. If you want to offer only the *zero-knowledge* method, comment out or otherwise remove the other two definitions from the list of module load directives:

```
  <!--
    <mod_auth_plain>./jsm/jsm.so</mod_auth_plain>
    <mod_auth_digest>./jsm/jsm.so</mod_auth_digest>
  -->
```

If you want to offer the *digest* method, you must include the module load directives for both *mod_auth_plain* and *mod_auth_digest*, as the latter is merely an extension—a "parasite"—upon the former.

Let's look at each of these authentication methods in turn.

Plaintext authentication method

The plaintext authentication method works as you would expect and is the default lowest common denominator method supplied with the Jabber server. It is provided by the *mod_auth_plain* module.

Method

> The password is transmitted in the XML stream, inside the `<password&sol;>` tag in the `jabber:iq:auth` IQ-set packet, from the client to the server in plaintext, where it is compared to the password stored, also in plaintext, on the server.

> When a password is changed, using a `jabber:iq:register` IQ-set as described earlier in this chapter, `mod_auth_plain` stores the password, as received, in the user's spool file.

Advantages

> This method is by far the simplest to implement on the client side. It is also useful for debugging and testing purposes as it can be used in a connection "by hand" via *telnet*, not requiring any extra computation such as the digest and zero-knowledge methods do.

Disadvantages

It's insecure, on two levels. First, the password is transmitted in plaintext across the wire from client to server. The risk can be minimized by encrypting the whole connection using SSL. Second, the password is stored in plaintext on the server, which may be compromised.

Digest authentication method

The module that provides the digest authentication method, *mod_auth_digest*, works in conjunction with the plaintext module, *mod_auth_plain*. It provides a way to avoid having to send the plaintext password across the wire.

Method

The digest method is similar to the plaintext method, in that the password sent by the client is compared to the password stored on the server. However, in this case, the password is first encoded using a hashing algorithm. It is encoded by the client before being sent across the wire, and it is encoded by the server (having retrieved it in plaintext) before making the comparison.

The algorithm used is the NIST SHA-1 message digest algorithm.* This algorithm takes arbitrary input and produces a fingerprint or "message digest" of it.† A random string, shared between the client and the server, is appended to the password before being passed to the hashing algorithm. This random string is the connection ID—the value of the id attribute in the server's XML stream header response that we saw in Example 7-3:

```
RECV: <?xml version='1.0'&quest;>
<stream:stream xmlns:stream='http://etherx.jabber.org/streams'
  id='1ED34A55' xmlns='jabber:client' from='yak'>
```

which means, in the case where the password is "secret," the string that will be hashed is:

```
secret1ED34A55
```

which is:

```
03ea09f012493415908d63dcb1f6dbdb9bfc09ba
```

The digested password is transmitted to the server inside the <digest/> tag. *mod_auth_digest* is unlike the other two modules in that it doesn't take any responsibility for storing passwords; it leaves that to *mod_auth_plain*, as the plaintext password must be rehashed with a new random suffix each time.

---

* More information on SHA-1 (Secure Hash Algorithm 1) can be obtained at *http://www.itl.nist.gov/fip-spubs/fip180-1.htm*.

† There are different types of message digest that can be produced with this algorithm: binary, hexadecimal, and base64. The hexadecimal format is used here and elsewhere in Jabber.

Advantages

No plaintext password is transmitted across the wire from client to server, and only a small amount of computation—a single SHA-1 hash process—is required.

Disadvantages

The password is still stored in plaintext on the server.

Zero-knowledge authentication method

The zero-knowledge authentication method is so-called as the server requires no knowledge of the password in order to check the credentials. It makes use of the same hashing algorithm used in the digest authentication method.

Method

Just as *mod_auth_plain* is responsible for storing the password (in plaintext) when a user is created or when the password is changed, so *mod_auth_0k* is responsible for storing *its version* of the password, actually, the information it needs (originally *based* on the password) to check the client's credentials in a zero-knowledge authentication process.

As we know from the user registration and password change processes, any new password is supplied to the server in plaintext. This is where a secure (SSL) connection is critical for complete security. While the *mod_auth_plain* module just stores that password as is, the *mod_auth_0k* module stores a sequenced hash of the password instead.

What does this mean? The server stores a value that is the password hashed with an arbitrary string token multiple (N) times, recursively. It doesn't store the password itself. It also remembers how many times it has been hashed (N).

Whenever a client wants to authenticate, the server sends the client the string token and the value of N. The client, having obtained the password from the user, performs the same iterative hashing sequence that the server performed when it was originally given the password but performs the sequence N-1 times. It passes the result of this sequence to the server, which does one more hash to go from N-1 to N, and compares what it gets with what it has stored. If they match, authentication is successful, and the server stores the N-1 hash passed from the client and decrements N, ready for next time.

The server sends the client the information it needs in two tags:

<sequence>

The value of N is sent in the <sequence/> tag.

The arbitrary string token to be hashed with the password is sent in the <token/> tag.

The *N*-1 hash value is passed by the client to the server in the <hash/> tag.

By way of illustration, Example 7-4 shows a small Perl script that a Telnet user can use to make the necessary hashing computations when wishing to authenticate with a Jabber server using the zero-knowledge method.

Example 7-4. A script implementing the client-side zero-knowledge process

```perl
#!/usr/bin/perl -w

use strict;
use Digest::SHA1 qw(sha1_hex);
use Getopt::Std;

our($opt_p, $opt_t, $opt_s);
getopt('pts');

unless ($opt_p and $opt_t and $opt_s)
{
  print "Usage: $0 -p <password> -t <token> -s <sequence>\n";
  exit;
}

# Initial hash of password
my $hash = sha1_hex($opt_p);

# Sequence 0: hash of hashed-password and token
$hash = sha1_hex($hash.$opt_t);

# Repeat N-1 times
$hash = sha1_hex($hash) while $opt_s--;

print "$hash\n";
```

To use the script, pass the data via the parameters, using the values obtained from the response to the initial IQ-get. The value that the script produces for the value to send in the <hash/> tag, like this:

```
$ ./0k
Usage: 0k -p <password> -t <token> -s <sequence>


$ ./0k -p secret -t ABCDE -s 400
01945b9b2c3207c4cce5dc99e50605779f570077
$
```

Advantages

No password is stored on the server. No (plaintext) password is transmitted from client to server.

Disadvantages

This method is slightly more compute-intensive than the other methods. There is still a security weak spot in the procedure, when the password is set or reset, as it must be passed in plaintext. A reset is required when N reaches 0, which is another disadvantage—a password can be used only N times before a plaintext reset.

Choosing the Authentication Method

Now that we know a little bit about the authentication methods, let's jump back to the initial IQ-get query in Example 7-3:

```
SEND: <iq type='get'>
        <query xmlns='jabber:iq:auth'>
          <username>dj</username>
        </query>
      </iq>

RECV: <iq type='result'>
        <query xmlns='jabber:iq:auth'>
          <username>dj</username>
          <password&sol;>
          <digest&sol;>
          <sequence>496</sequence>
          <token>3B2DEEC0</token>
          <resource&sol;>
        </query>
      </iq>
```

What we're actually seeing here is the result of the authentication modules announcing their readiness to authenticate the user dj. The query is passed to each of the modules. *mod_auth_plain* announces its readiness by inserting the <password/> flag, *mod_auth_digest* does the same with the <digest/> flag, and *mod_auth_0k* inserts the <sequence/> and <token/> tags and values, which is what the client will need if it wishes to authenticate using the zero-knowledge method. The <resource/> tag, which is required in any authentication, is finally added before the result is returned.

This way, the IQ-result can convey which authentication methods are available; if the *mod_auth_plain* and *mod_auth_digest* modules were to be commented out in the module load directive list, as we saw earlier, then the IQ-result would look like this without the <password/> or <digest/> tags:

```
RECV: <iq type='result'>
        <query xmlns='jabber:iq:auth'>
          <username>dj</username>
          <sequence>496</sequence>
          <token>3B2DEEC0</token>
          <resource&sol;>
        </query>
      </iq>
```

 At the beginning of this section, we strongly recommended using the IQ-get in the `jabber:iq:auth` namespace, before proceeding with the IQ-set. This was primarily to be able to check what authentication methods were supported. However, as you can see here, it is in fact *essential* in the case of the zero-knowledge authentication method, because without the `<sequence&sol;>` and `<token&sol;>` information, we cannot begin our hashing sequence.

Password Errors and Retries

If you don't supply all the required parameters, you are notified with a 406 *"Not Acceptable"* error:

```
SEND: <iq type='set'>
        <query xmlns='jabber:iq:auth'>
          <username>dj</username>
          <digest>03ea09f012493415908d63dcb1f6dbdb9bfc09ba</digest>
        </query>
      </iq>

RECV: <iq type='result' id='pthsock_client_auth_ID'>
        <query xmlns='jabber:iq:auth'>
          <username>dj</username>
          <digest>03ea09f012493415908d63dcb1f6dbdb9bfc09ba</digest>
        </query>
        <error code='406'>Not Acceptable</error>
      </iq>
```

In this case, no `<resource&sol;>` value was supplied. The `<resource&sol;>` value is required, as it is the key part of the JID that is used to distinguish between multiple connections as the same user on the same Jabber server.

If you get the password wrong, you receive a 401 *"Not Authorized"* error. There is currently no limit on the number of times an authorization attempt can be made, but the `<karma&sol;>` limits for the c2s connections (see Chapter 5) may slow the attempts down.

User Registration Script

Currently, the Jabber technology has no concept of *anonymous* users—users who can connect to the server with no previous registration requirement. Until this is possible, we have to make do with creating specific users for specific scenarios.

To this end, it would be useful to be able to run a quick script to register a new user, rather than grab an existing client, start it up, and go through the process of registering a new user with the Jabber server, with whatever window navigation and mouse clicking that might entail. All the script must do is interact with the Jabber server in the context of the `jabber:iq:register` namespace, specifically, pre-session. It must be able to make a registration *inquiry* by sending an IQ-get and returning the fields listed in the result and to make a registration *attempt*, when supplied with values for the registration fields.

We should be able to invoke our script, *reguser*, in one of two ways. The first, specifying merely a hostname (and optional port, which will default to 5222 if not specified), implies a registration *inquiry*, that we wish to make an inquiry of the Jabber server as to (a) whether registration is possible and (b) if so, what fields are required. The second way, specifying not only the host and optional port but also a list of field name and value pairs, implies a registration *attempt*. Example 7-5 shows both these ways in action.

Example 7-5. Uses of the reguser script

```
$ ./reguser yak:5222
[Enquiry] Fields: username password email name

$ ./reguser yak username=joseph password=spinach 'name=Joseph Adams'
    email=joseph@yak
[Attempt] (joseph) Successful registration

$ ./reguser yak username=dj password=secret 'name=DJ Adams' email=dj@yak
[Attempt] (dj) Error: 409 (Username Not Available)
```

As it's our first substantial script, let's take it step by step. It's written in Perl and uses the `Net::Jabber` module:

```
#!/usr/bin/perl

use strict;
use Net::Jabber 1.0022 qw(Client);

use constant NS_REGISTER => 'jabber:iq:register';

unless (@ARGV) {
  print usage();
  exit;
}
```

We start out with some basic start-of-script housekeeping: delaring our usage of
Net::Jabber, setting a constant for the jabber:iq:register namespace, and handling the case of being "wrongly" invoked by giving some help text from the
usage() subroutine. The specification of Client in the line:

```
use Net::Jabber 1.0022 qw(Client);
```

means that the connection is going to be client-based; in other words, the namespace that will be used to qualify the XML stream header that Net::Jabber will produce is jabber:client.

The Net::Jabber module has changed as it has matured over the recent versions
(1.0020, 1.0021, and 1.0022), and these changes do sometimes affect how the
scripts that use Net::Jabber should be written. So we explicitly specify in the use
statement which version of Net::Jabber we require, to avoid confusion.

```
my ($host, $port) = split(":", shift @ARGV);
$port ||= 5222;

my $c = Net::Jabber::Client->new();

defined($c->Connect(
            hostname => $host,
            port     => $port,
)) or die "Cannot reach Jabber server at $host:$port\n";

my ($iq, $query, $result);
```

We parse the hostname and port, defaulting the latter to 5222 if it wasn't specified.
Then we create a new instance of the Net::Jabber::Client object. The Net::Jab-
ber family of modules presents its collective functions in an object-oriented way.
The scalar $c represents the "client" mechanism with which we connect to the Jab-
ber server.

With the Connect() method, we make a connection to the Jabber server; the
namespace of the XML stream for this connection, sent to the Jabber server in the
stream header, is jabber:client.

```
# Registration attempt or inquiry?

if (scalar @ARGV) {

  # Attempt:
  # Send <iq type='set'>
  #         <query xmlns='jabber:iq:register'>
  #             <username>...</username>
  #             <password>...</password>
  #             ...
  #         </query>
  #     </iq>
```

```
print "[Attempt] ";

$iq = Net::Jabber::IQ->new();
$iq->SetType('set');
$query = $iq->NewQuery(NS_REGISTER);
```

We work out what we have to do by looking to see if any extra parameters beyond the hostname and port were specified. If there were, we need to build an IQ-set in the `jabber:iq:register` namespace to make a registration attempt.

The `Net::Jabber::IQ` module represents the IQ model and provides methods to manage IQ packets. With the `new()` constructor, we create a new, empty IQ packet in `$iq`, and set its `type` attribute to `set`.

As we know, the `<query&sol;>` part of an IQ packet is contained *within* the `<iq&sol;>` tag. The `NewQuery()` method, called on an IQ packet, creates a `<query&sol;>` tag as a child of that IQ packet and delivers us a handle on that `<query&sol;>` tag—which we store in `$query`—so that we can manipulate it independently of the IQ packet that wraps around it. The `jabber:iq:register` namespace value is passed as a parameter to the `NewQuery()` call to set the correct `xmlns` namespace attribute.

Figure 7-2 shows what the packet looks like at this stage and how the scalar object references `$iq` and `$query` relate to it.

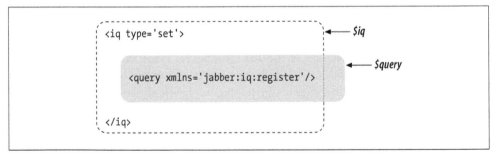

Figure 7-2. An IQ packet under construction by Net::Jabber::IQ

In our `foreach` loop, we run through the list of parameters, in the form *field-name=value*, and call a `Set` method on the `$query` object (the `<query&sol;>` packet) to add child tags:

```
foreach my $arg (@ARGV) {
  my ($field, $value) = split('=', $arg);
  print "($value) " if $field eq 'username';
  eval '$query->Set'.ucfirst($field).'($value)';
}

$result = $c->SendAndReceiveWithID($iq);
```

Net::Jabber::Query provides a number of SetXXXX methods that are available according to namespace. These "set" methods available for the jabber:iq:register namespace are plentiful and include SetName, SetEmail, SetPhone, and so on. Each method will create a child tag named after the method (e.g., SetName will create a <name/> tag, and SetPhone will create a <phone/> tag) and insert the value passed to the method into the tag.

For example:

```
$query->SetName('DJ Adams');
```

will insert (or amend) a tag in the <query/> thus:

```
<iq type='set'>
  <query xmlns='jabber:iq:register'>
    <name>DJ Adams</name>
  </query>
</iq>
```

We use eval to allow us to make our SetXXXX method calls dynamically, according to each field name specified. The ucfirst() function is used to change the first character of the field name to uppercase, to suit the SetXXXX method naming conventions.

Once we've added all the fields, we send the complete packet ($iq) to the server using the SendAndReceiveWithID() method on the connection ($c) object. This method is extremely powerful and does many things for us. It keeps the process of writing small scripts like this very simple. It adds a unique id attribute to the <iq/> packet, transmits the packet over the XML stream, *and waits for a response.*

"Hey, what about the event model that we read about?" you might ask. Of course, Net::Jabber supports an event-model programming style, but for now we can get away with keeping our code "procedural" (and short) using this high-level method that does everything we want. After all, in any one execution of the script, we wish to send only one packet to the Jabber server and receive one back. Nothing more complicated than that.

Recipes in later chapters will demonstrate the event model.

The response is stored in $result and is itself an IQ packet, as we expect. So $result is a handle on a Net::Jabber::IQ object that we can now manipulate:

```
# Success
if ($result->GetType() eq 'result') {
  print "Successful registration\n";
}

# Failure
```

```
    else {
      print "Error: ",
            $result->GetErrorCode(),
            " (",
            $result->GetError(),
            ")\n";
    }

  }
```

We check the type of the IQ returned from the server. If it's a `result`:

```
RECV: <iq type='result' id='1'>
        <query xmlns='jabber:iq:register'&sol;>
      </iq>
```

then great—the registration was successful. Otherwise, we can grab the error code
and description from the `<error&sol;>` element:

```
RECV: <iq type='error'>
        <query xmlns='jabber:iq:register'>
          <username>dj</username>
          <password>secret</password>
        </query>
        <error code='409'>Username Not Available</error>
      </iq>
```

using the `GetError()` and `GetErrorCode()` methods on the IQ object.

We go through a similar process if there are no further parameters following the
`host[:port]` specification:

```
  else {

    # Inquiry:
    # Send <iq type='get'><query xmlns='jabber:iq:register'&sol;></iq>

    print "[Inquiry] ";

    $iq = Net::Jabber::IQ->new();
    $iq->SetType('get');
    $query = $iq->NewQuery(NS_REGISTER);

    $result = $c->SendAndReceiveWithID($iq);
```

The only difference here is that we set the IQ type to `get`, not `set`, and we don't
insert any tags into the `$query` object, before sending the packet off and waiting
for a response:

If we receive a `result` type, like this:

```
RECV: <iq type='result'>
        <query xmlns='jabber:iq:register'>
          <instructions>
            Choose a username and password to register with this server.
          </instructions>
          <name&sol;>
          <email&sol;>
          <username&sol;>
          <password&sol;>
        </query>
      </iq>
```

then we need to extract the fields listed in the <query/> tag and return them
to the user.

```
# Success
if ($result->GetType() eq 'result') {
  $query = $result->GetQuery();

  my %contents = $query->GetRegister();
  delete $contents{'instructions'};
  print "Fields: ", join(', ', keys %contents), "\n";
}
```

While the NewQuery() method creates a new <query/> tag inside an IQ object,
the GetQuery() method retrieves an existing one, in the form of a Net::Jab-
ber::Query object whose handle we store in $query. We can call the GetRegister()
method on this query object, which returns a hash of the contents:

```
(
  'instructions' => 'Choose a username and password ...',
  'name'         => undef,
  'email'        => undef,
  'username'     => undef,
  'password'     => undef
)
```

And, after removing the "instructions," we can display them as the result.

When an error is returned in response to the IQ-get (perhaps no registrations are
allowed), we display the error in the same way as before:

```
# Failure
else {
  $query = $result->GetQuery();
  print "Error: ",
        $result->GetErrorCode(),
        " (",
        $result->GetError(),
        ")\n";
}

}
```

When we've finished, we close the connection and exit. Here we also have the usage() subroutine defined:

```
$c->Disconnect;

exit;


sub usage {

<<EOF
Usage:
Enquiry: reguser host[:port]
Attempt: reguser host[:port] field1=value1 [fieldN = valueN] ...
EOF

}
```

Using the Script

The script is very basic, but it gets the job done. It is suitable for calling from another script, for mass user generation, although you may wish to modify it so that a connection is not created and destroyed for every username that needs to be registered.*

It also illustrates how simple a Jabber client can be. In this case, the `Net::Jabber` libraries mask the bulk of the effort (socket connection, XML stream negotiation, XML fragment traffic management, and so on). We'll be making use of this script to create users for our recipes later on in the book.

---

* Otherwise, you may experience socket rating problems. See the section "The <rate/> Tag" in Chapter 4 for details.

8

Using Messages and Presence

Now that we have a decent grounding in the Jabber protocol and technology, let's put it to work for us. This chapter fits Jabber into solutions for two or three common problems and shows how the technology and features lend themselves very well to application-to-person (A2P) scenarios.

By way of introduction, we'll have a look at constructing and sending simple Jabber messages, to effect an "in-your-face" notification mechanism for a version control system. We'll also introduce a usage of the <presence/> element as an availability indicator for connecting systems. Finally we'll combine the two features (<message/> and the concept of *availability*) to make the notification mechanism "sensitive" to the presence of the person being notified.

CVS Notification via Jabber

CVS—the Concurrent Versions System—allows you to comfortably create and manage versions of the sources of your project. The most common use for CVS is to create and manage versions of program source code, but it can be readily used for any text files. For example, this book was written using DocBook SGML (*http://www.docbook.org*), and a CVS *repository* was used to manage different versions of the manuscript throughout the writing and editing process. CVS allowed us to maintain the original source files for the chapters, to compare those versions against edited files, and served as a place from which older versions could be retrieved. You can find out more about CVS at *http://www.cvshome.org*.

That's the "Versions System" part of CVS's name. The "Concurrent" part means that this facility is given an extra dimension in the form of group collaboration. With CVS, more than one person can share work on a project, and the various chunks of work carried out by each participant are coordinated—automatically, to a large extent—by CVS. Multiple changes by different people to the same file can be merged by CVS; any unresolvable conflicts (which may for example arise when more than one person changes exactly the same line of source code) are flagged and must be resolved by the participants involved.

The general idea is that you can create a project containing files and directories and have it stored centrally in a CVS repository. Depending on what sort of access is granted to this repository, other project participants can pull down a copy of the project—those files and directories—and work on it independently. In this way, each participant's work is isolated (in time and space) from the others. When the work is done, the work can be sent back to the repository and the changes will be merged into the central copy. After that, those merged changes are available to the rest of the participants.

CVS Watches and Notification

While CVS automatically handles most of the tedious merging process that comes about when more than one person works on a project, it also offers a facility that allows you to set a "watch" on one or more files in the project and be alerted when someone else starts to work on those watched files. This is useful if you wish to preempt any automatic merging process by contacting the other participant and coordinating your editing efforts with him.

There are two CVS commands involved in setting up watches and notifications. There are also a couple of CVS administrative files that determine how the notifications are carried out. Let's look at these commands and files in turn.

CVS commands

The CVS commands *cvs watch* and *cvs notify* are used, usually in combination, by project participants to set up the notification mechanism:

cvs watch on | off
> Assuming we have a CVS-controlled project called *proj1* and we're currently inside a local checked-out copy of the project's files, we first use *cvs watch* to tell CVS to watch a file ("turn a watch *on*") that we're interested in, which is *file4* in this example:
>
> ```
> yak:~/projects/proj1$ cvs watch on file4
> ```
>
> This causes CVS to mark *file4* as "watched," which means any time a project participant checks out the file from the central repository, the checked-out working copy is created with read-only attributes. This means the participant is (initially) prevented from saving any changes to that working copy. It is, in effect, a reminder to that participant to use the CVS command *cvs edit*, specifying *file4*, before commencing the edit session. Using *cvs edit* causes CVS to:

1. Remove the read-only attribute for the file

2. Send out notifications (to those who have requested them with the *cvs watch add*) that the participant has commenced editing it

cvs watch add | remove

While running *cvs watch on* against a file will set a marker causing the file to be replicated with the read-only attribute when checked out (which has the effect of "suggesting" to the participant editing the file that he use the *cvs edit* command to signal that he's to start editing), the actual determination of the notification recipients is set up using the *cvs watch add* command.

Running the command:

```
yak:~/projects/proj1$ cvs watch add file4
```

will arrange for the CVS notification to be sent to *us* when someone else signals their intention (via *cvs edit*) to edit *file4*.

CVS administrative files

A number of administrative files used to control how CVS works are kept in the central CVS repository. Two of these files, *notify* and *users*, are used to manage the watch-based notification process:

notify

The standard *notify* file contains a line like this:

```
ALL mail %s -s "CVS notification"
```

The ALL causes the formula described here to be used for any notification requirements (an alternative to ALL is a regular expression to match the directory name in which the edit causing the notification is being carried out).

The rest of the line is the formula to use to send the notification. It is a simple invocation of the *mail* command, specifying a subject line (-s "CVS notification"). The %s is a placeholder that CVS replaces with the address of the notification's intended recipient. The actual notification text, generated by CVS, is piped into the *mail* command via STDIN.

users

The *users* file contains a list of notification recipient addresses:

```
dj:dj.adams@pobox.com
piers:pxharding@ompa.net
robert:robert@shiels.com
...
```

This is a mapping from the user IDs (dj, piers, and robert) of the CVS participants, local to the host where the CVS repository is stored, to the addresses (*dj.adams@pobox.com, pxharding@ompa.net*, and *robert@shiels.com*) that are used to replace the %s in the formula described in the *notify* file.

The notification

If the contents of the *notify* and *users* files have been set up correctly, a typical notification, set up by DJ using the *cvs watch on file4* and *cvs watch add file4* commands, and triggered by Piers using the *cvs edit file4* command, will be received in DJ's inbox looking like the one shown in Example 8-1.

Example 8-1. A typical email CVS notification

```
Date: Fri, 8 Jun 2001 13:10:55 +0100
From: piers@ompa.net
To: dj.adams@pobox.com
Subject: CVS notification

testproject file4
---
Triggered edit watch on /usr/local/cvsroot/testproject
By piers
```

CVS Notifications via Jabber

While email-based notifications are useful, we can add value to this process by using a more immediate (and penetrating) form of communication: Jabber. Although mail clients can be configured to check for mail automatically on a regular basis, using an IM-style client has a number of immediately obvious advantages:

- It's likely to take up less screen real estate.

- No amount of tweaking of the mail client's autocheck frequency (which, if available, will log in, check for, and *pull* emails from the mail server) will match the immediacy of IM-style message *push*.

- In extreme cases, the higher the autocheck frequency of the mail client, the higher the effect on overall system performance.

- Depending on the configuration, an incoming Jabber message can be made to pop up, with greater effect.

- A Jabber user is more likely to have a Jabber client running permanently than an email client.

- It's more fun!

The design of CVS's notification mechanism is simple and abstract enough for us to put an alternative notification system in place. If we substitute the formula in the *notify* configuration file with something that will call a Jabber script, we might end up with something like:

```
ALL python cvsmsg %s
```

Like the previous formula, it will be invoked by CVS to send the notification, and the %s will be substituted by the recipient's address determined from the *users* file. In this case, the Python script *cvsmsg* is called. However, now that we're sending a notification via Jabber, we need a Jabber address—a JID—instead of an email address. No problem, just edit the *users* file to reflect the new addresses. Example 8-2 shows what the *users* file might contain if we were to use JIDs instead of email addresses.

Example 8-2. Matching users to JIDs in the notify file

```
dj:dj@gnu.pipetree.com
piers:piers@jabber.org
robert:shiels@jabber.org
```

As Jabber user JIDs in their most basic form (i.e., without a *resource* suffix) resemble email IDs, there doesn't appear to be that much difference. In any case, CVS doesn't really care, and it takes the portion following the colon separator and simply passes it to the formula in the *notify* file.

The cvsmsg Script

Let's now have a look at the script, called *cvsmsg*. It has to send a notification message, which it receives on STDIN, to a JID, which it receives as an argument passed to the script, as shown in Example 8-3.

Example 8-3. The cvsmsg Python script

```
import jabber
import sys

Server   = 'gnu.pipetree.com'
Username = 'cvsmsg'
Password = 'secret'
Resource = 'cvsmsg'

cvsuser  = sys.argv[1]
message  = ''

for line in sys.stdin.readlines(): message = message + line

con = jabber.Client(host=Server)

try:
    con.connect()
except IOError, e:
```

Example 8-3. The cvsmsg Python script (continued)

```
    print "Couldn't connect: %s" % e
    sys.exit(0)

con.auth(Username,Password,Resource)
con.send(jabber.Message(cvsuser, message, subject="CVS Watch Alarm"))
con.disconnect()
```

It's not that long but worth breaking down to examine piece by piece.

We're going to use the `Jabberpy` Python library for Jabber, so the first thing we do in the script is import it. We also import the `sys` module for reading from STDIN:

```
import jabber
import sys
```

As the usage of the script will be fairly static, we can get away here with hardcoding a few parameters:

```
Server   = 'gnu.pipetree.com'
Username = 'cvsmsg'
Password = 'secret'
Resource = 'cvsmsg'
```

Specified here are the connection and authentication details for the `cvsmsg` script itself. If it's to send a message via Jabber, it must itself connect to Jabber. The `Server` variable specifies which Jabber server to connect to, and the `Username`, `Password`, and `Resource` variables contain the rest of the information for the script's own JID (`cvsmsg@gnu.pipetree.com/cvsmsg`) and password.

```
cvsuser  = sys.argv[1]
message  = ''

for line in sys.stdin.readlines(): message = message + line
```

The `sys.argv[1]` refers to the notification recipient's JID, which will be specified by the CVS notification mechanism, as it is substituted for the `%s` in the *notify* file's formula. This is saved in the `cvsuser` variable. We then build up the content of our message body we're going to send via Jabber by reading what's available on STDIN. Typically this will look like what we saw in the email message body in Example 8-1:

```
testproject file4
---
Triggered edit watch on /usr/local/cvsroot/testproject
By piers

con = jabber.Client(host=Server)
```

Another `Jabberpy` module, `xmlstream`, handles the connection to the Jabber server. We don't have to use that module explicitly, however; the `jabber` module wraps and uses it, shielding us from the details—hence the call to instantiate a new `jabber.Client` object into `con`, to lay the way for our connection to the host specified in our `Server` variable: `gnu.pipetree.com`. If no port is explicitly specified, the standard port (5222), on which the `c2s` service listens, is assumed.

The instantiation causes a number of parameters and variables to be initialized, and internally an `xmlstream.Client` object is instantiated; various parameters are passed through from the `jabber.Client` object (for example, for logging and debugging purposes), and an XML parser object is instantiated. This will be used to parse fragments of XML that come in over the XML stream.

```
try:
    con.connect()
except IOError, e:
    print "Couldn't connect: %s" % e
    sys.exit(0)
```

A connection is attempted with the `connect()` method of the connection object in `con`. This is serviced by the `xmlstream.Client` object and an XML stream header, as described in the section "XML Streams," is sent to `gnu.pipetree.com:5222` in an attempt to establish a client connection. An `IOError` exception is raised if the connection cannot be established; we trap this, after a fashion, with the `try:` ... `except` as shown.

Once connected (meaning the client has successfully exchanged XML stream headers with the server) we need to authenticate:

```
con.auth(Username,Password,Resource)
```

The `auth` method of the `jabber.Client` object provides us with a simple way of carrying out the authentication negotiation, qualified with the `jabber:iq:auth` namespace and described in detail in the section "User Authentication. Although we supply our password here in the script in plaintext (`secret`), the `auth` method will use the IQ-get (`<iq type='get' ...>`) to retrieve a list of authentication methods supported by the server. It will try to use the most secure, "gracefully degrading" to the least, until it finds one that is supported. This is shown in Figure 8-1.

Note the presence of `Resource` in the call. This is required for a successful client authentication regardless of the authentication method. Sending an IQ-set (`<iq type='set' ...>`) in the `jabber:iq:auth` namespace without specifying a value in a `<resource&sol;>` tag results in a "Not Acceptable" error 406; see Table 5-3 for a list of standard error codes and texts.

We're connected and authenticated. "The world is now our lobster," as an old friend used to say. We're not necessarily *expecting* to receive anything at this stage, and even if we did, we wouldn't really want to do anything with what we

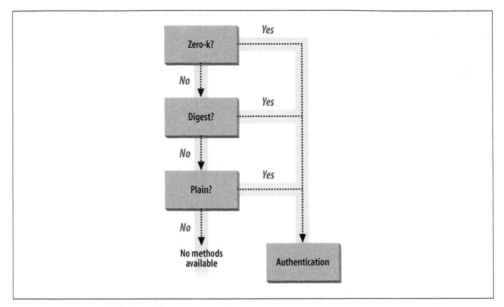

Figure 8-1. Graceful degradation in authentication

received anyway. So we don't bother setting up any mechanism for handling elements that might appear on the stream.

```
con.send(jabber.Message(cvsuser, message, subject="CVS Watch Alarm"))
```

The next step is to send the notification message (in `message`) to the user (in `cvsuser`). There are actually two calls here. The innermost call, `jabber.Message()`, creates a simple message element that looks like this:

```
<message to='[value in cvsuser variable]'>
  <subject>CVS Watch Alarm</subject>
  <body>[value in message variable]</body>
</message>
```

It takes two positional (and required) parameters; any other information to be passed (such as the `subject` in this example) must be supplied as *key=value* pairs. The outermost call, `con.send()`, sends whatever it is given over the XML stream that the `jabber.Client` object con represents. In the case of the `jabber.Message` call, this is the string representation of the object so created (i.e., the `<message&sol;>` element).

Once the notification message has been sent, the script's work is done. We can therefore disconnect from the server before exiting the script:

```
con.disconnect()
```

Calling the `disconnect()` method of the `jabber.Client` sends an *unavailable* presence element to the server on behalf of the user who is connected:

```
<presence type='unavailable'&sol;>
```

This is sent regardless of whether a `<presence&sol;>` element was sent during the conversation but does no harm if one wasn't.

After sending the unavailable presence information, the XML stream is closed by sending the stream's closing tag:

```
</stream:stream>
```

This signifes to the server that the client wishes to end the conversation. Finally, the socket is closed.

Dialup System Watch

These days, it's becoming increasingly common to have a server at home with a dialup connection to the Internet. Your data, your latest developments, and your mail are stored on there. This works really well when you're telecommuting and pulling those late night hacking sessions at home; you have access to all your information and can connect to the Net.

For many people, however, the reality is that it's not just at home where the work gets done. Consultants, freelancers, and people with many customers have their work cut out for them in traveling to different sites to complete jobs. One of the biggest issues in this respect, especially in Europe where dialup and pay-per-minute connections still outweigh fixed or flat-rate connections, is the accessibility of the information on the server at home, sitting behind a modem. In a lot of cases, the expense of leaving the server dialed up for the duration of the trip is far too great to be justified.

One solution is to have the server dial up and connect to the Internet at regular intervals, say, every hour or two, and remain connected for 5 or 10 minutes. If you need access to the information or need to log on to your server and run a few tests, you can hold the connection open, once you've connected to it, by running a *ping*, for example.

The problem here, though, is timing. Due to the inevitable synchronization problems between wristwatch and PC clock, eddies in the space-time continuum, and the fact that people simply forget to check the time, the online window of the server's dialup is often missed.

The essence of this problem is a *presence* thing. We need to know about the presence, the availability, of our server at home, with respect to the Internet.

Using Jabber as your IM mechanism at work, it's likely that you'll have a Jabber client of some sort on your laptop or desktop at the customer sites. Whether it's WinJab on Windows, Jarl in Command Line Interface (CLI) mode on a remote server over an SSH connection, or any other type of Jabber client and connection, the point is that the client turns out to be an ideal ready-made component for solving the dialup timing problem. Here's how it works:

- Get the server to dial up and connect to the Internet regularly.

- On connection, start a script that sends Jabber presence to you.

- On disconnection, get the script to end.

If you add to your roster a JID that represents the server at home, it would be possible to subscribe to the server's presence and know when it was available—connected to the Internet—and when it wasn't.

The script we're going to write to send Jabber presence is called *HostAlive*.

Making Preparations for Execution

Before diving into the script, it's necessary to do a bit of preparation. We're going to be using the *presence subscription* concept, which was described in Chapter 5 and is covered in more detail in the next section in this chapter. We're also going to have to get the script to run, and stay running, when the dialup connection is made and have it stop when the dialup connection is ended.

Presence

Rather than get involved in the nitty-gritty of presence subcriptions right now, let's use the tools that are around us to get things set up. In order for this to work, we need to be subscribed to the presence of the script that will be invoked when the server dials up and connects to the Internet. The script will connect to the Jabber server using a JID with a username that represents the Linux server: *myserver@gnu.pipetree.com*. My JID in this case is *dj@gnu.pipetree.com*, so we just use whatever Jabber client happens to be at hand, say, Jabber Instant Messenger (JIM), to effect both sides of the subscription.

Step 1: Create JID myserver@gnu.pipetree.com

We need to create the script's JID if it doesn't already exist. We can use the *reguser* script we wrote in the section "User Registration Script" to do this:

```
[dj@yak dj]$ ./reguser gnu.pipetree.com username=myserver password=secret
[Attempt] (myserver) Successful registration
[dj@yak dj]$
```

Step 2: Subscribe to myserver's presence

We start JIM with the JID *dj@gnu.pipetree.com* and then add *myserver@gnu.pipetree.com* to the roster. This should automatically send a presence subscription request to the JID. Adding the JID to the roster using JIM is shown in Figure 8-2.

Step 3: Accept presence subscription as myserver

Using the JIM client, we reconnect with the *myserver* JID and accept the presence subscription request from Step 2, so that *dj@gnu.pipetree.com* will automatically receive *myserver@gnu.pipetree.com's* availability information. Whether or not *myserver* subscribes to *dj's* presence is irrelevant in this case, as the script itself is not interested in the availability of anyone at all.

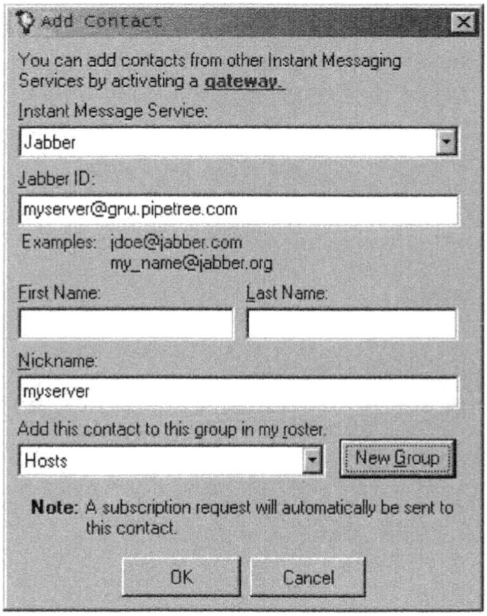

Figure 8-2. Adding myserver@gnu.pipetree.com to the roster

At this stage, the entry in *dj@gnu.pipetree.com's* roster that represents the Linux server will indicate whether the script run at dialup time is active. If we continue to use the JIM client, we will see that active status is shown by a yellow bulb and inactive by no icon at all.

Starting and stopping the script

The dialup connection is set up using the Point-to-Point Protocol daemon *pppd*. This uses a program such as *chat* to talk to the modem and get it to dial the ISP. The *pppd* mechanism affords us an ideal way to start and stop a script on the respective connection and disconnection of the line. When the connection has been made, the script */etc/ppp/ip-up* is invoked and passed a number of connection-related parameters. Similarly */etc/ppp/ip-down* is invoked when the connection is closed.

Some implementations of *pppd* also offer */etc/ppp/ip-up.local* and */etc/ppp/ip-down.local*, which should be used in place of the *ip-up* and *ip-down* scripts if they exist. These `.local` versions are intended to separate out system-specific connection-related activities from general connection-related activities, in a similar way to how the *rc.local* file allows system-specific startup activities to be defined in the */etc/rc.d/* Unix System V set of runlevel directories.

So what we want to do is start *HostAlive* with `ip-up[.local]` and stop it with `ip-down[.local]`. What these starter and stopper scripts might look like is shown in Example 8-4 and Example 8-5. They are simply shell scripts that share the process ID (PID) of the Jabber script via a temporary file. The starter starts the Jabber script and writes the PID of that script to a file. The stopper kills the script using the PID.

Example 8-4. An ip-up starter script

```
#!/bin/sh

# Change to working directory
cd /jabber/java/

# Call the Jabber script and put to background
/usr/java/jdk1.3.1/bin/java -classpath jabberbeans.jar:. HostAlive $5 &

# Write the running script's PID
echo $! > /tmp/HostAlive.pid
```

Example 8-5. An ip-down stopper script

```
#!/bin/sh

# Simply kill the process using the
# JID written by the starter script
/bin/kill `cat /tmp/HostAlive.pid`

# Remove the PID file
/bin/rm /tmp/HostAlive.pid
```

Example 8-4 shows that we're passing through one of the parameters that *pppd* gives to the *ip-up* script: the remote IP address—by which the server is known during its temporary connection to the Internet—in the $5 variable.* This IP address can be passed along as part of the availability information in the <presence/> element, so that the recipient (*dj*) can see what IP address has been assigned to the server.

The HostAlive Script

As you might have guessed from looking at Example 8-4, we're going to write *HostAlive* in Java, shown in Example 8-6. We'll use the JabberBeans library; see the section "Software Used in This Book" in the Preface for details of where to get this library and what the requirements are.

Example 8-6. The HostAlive script, written in Java

```java
import org.jabber.jabberbeans.*;
import org.jabber.jabberbeans.Extension.*;
import java.net.InetAddress;

public class HostAlive
{
  public static final String SERVER   = "gnu.pipetree.com";
  public static final String USER     = "myserver";
  public static final String PASSWORD = "secret";
  public static final String RESOURCE = "alive";

  public static void main(String argv[])
  {

    ConnectionBean cb=new ConnectionBean();

    InetAddress addr;

    try
    {
      cb.connect(addr=InetAddress.getByName(SERVER));
    }
    catch (java.net.UnknownHostException e)
    {
      //from getByName()
      System.out.println("Cannot resolve " + SERVER + ":" + e.toString());
      return;
    }
    catch (java.io.IOException e)
    {
      //from connect()
       System.out.println("Cannot connect to " + SERVER);
       return;
```

---

* The parameters that are passed from *pppd* to the *ip-up* script are: *interface-name, tty-device, speed, local-link-local-address, remote-link-local-address*, and *ipparam*. It's the *remote-link-local-address* that we're interested in here.

Example 8-6. The HostAlive script, written in Java (continued)

```java
}

InfoQueryBuilder iqb=new InfoQueryBuilder();
InfoQuery iq;
IQAuthBuilder iqAuthb=new IQAuthBuilder();

iqb.setType("set");


iqAuthb.setUsername(USER);
iqAuthb.setPassword(PASSWORD);
iqAuthb.setResource(RESOURCE);

try
{
   iqb.addExtension(iqAuthb.build());
}
catch (InstantiationException e)
{
   //building failed ?
   System.out.println("Fatal Error on Auth object build:");
   System.out.println(e.toString());
   System.exit(0);
}


try
{
   //build the full InfoQuery packet
   iq=(InfoQuery)iqb.build();
}
catch (InstantiationException e)
{
   //building failed ?
   System.out.println("Fatal Error on IQ object build:");
   System.out.println(e.toString());
   return;
}

cb.send(iq);

PresenceBuilder pb=new PresenceBuilder();
pb.setStatus(argv[0]);

try
{
   cb.send(pb.build());
}
catch (InstantiationException e)
{
   System.out.println("Fatal Error on Presence object build:");
   System.out.println(e.toString());
```

Example 8-6. The HostAlive script, written in Java (continued)

```
  return;
}

while (true) {
  try {
    Thread.sleep(9999);
  }
  catch (InterruptedException e)
  {
    System.out.println("timeout!");
  }
}
}
```

Step by Step

We'll examine the script a chunk at a time. We start by importing the libraries (the classes) we would like to use:

```
import org.jabber.jabberbeans.*;
import org.jabber.jabberbeans.Extension.*;
import java.net.InetAddress;
```

The `JabberBeans` library is highly modular and designed so we can pick only the features that we need; in this case, however, we're just going to import the whole set of classes within the `org.jabber.jabberbeans` and `org.jabber.jabberbeans.Extension` packages, for simplicity.

We're also going to be manipulating the Jabber server's hostname, so we pull in the `InetAddress` class for convenience.

The script must connect to the Jabber server on *gnu.pipetree.com* as the *myserver* user. We define some constants for this:

```
public class HostAlive
{
  public static final String SERVER   = "gnu.pipetree.com";
  public static final String USER     = "myserver";
  public static final String PASSWORD = "secret";
  public static final String RESOURCE = "alive";
```

In the same way as with the Python-based CVS notification script earlier in this chapter, we also start off by building a connection to the Jabber server. As before, it's a two-stage process. The first stage is to create the connection object:

```
public static void main(String argv[])
{

  ConnectionBean cb=new ConnectionBean();
```

A `ConnectionBean` object represents the connection between the script and the Jabber server. All XML fragments (Jabber elements) pass through this object.

Then it's time to attempt the socket connection and the exchange of XML stream headers:

```
InetAddress addr;

try
{
   cb.connect(addr=InetAddress.getByName(SERVER));
}
catch (java.net.UnknownHostException e)
{
   //from getByName()
   System.out.println("Cannot resolve " + SERVER + ":" + e.toString());
   return;
}
catch (java.io.IOException e)
{
   //from connect()
   System.out.println("Cannot connect to " + SERVER);
   return;
}
```

We create an Internet address object in `addr` from the hostname assigned to the `SERVER` constant. As the creation of the `addr` instance may throw an exception (*Unknown Host*), we combine the instantiation with the `connection()` call on the `ConnectionBean` object, which may also throw an exception of its own—if there is a problem connecting.

At this stage, we're connected and have successfully exchanged the XML stream headers with the Jabber server. So now we must authenticate:

```
InfoQueryBuilder iqb=new InfoQueryBuilder();
InfoQuery iq;
IQAuthBuilder iqAuthb=new IQAuthBuilder();

iqb.setType("set");


iqAuthb.setUsername(USER);
iqAuthb.setPassword(PASSWORD);
iqAuthb.setResource(RESOURCE);

try
{
   iqb.addExtension(iqAuthb.build());
}
catch (InstantiationException e)
{
   //building failed ?
```

```
                     System.out.println("Fatal Error on Auth object build:");
                     System.out.println(e.toString());
                     System.exit(0);
                  }


                  try
                  {
                    //build the full InfoQuery packet
                    iq=(InfoQuery)iqb.build();
                  }
                  catch (InstantiationException e)
                  {
                    //building failed ?
                    System.out.println("Fatal Error on IQ object build:");
                    System.out.println(e.toString());
                    return;
                  }

                  cb.send(iq);
```

Yes, that's an awful lot. Let's take it bit by bit.

Figure 8-3 shows how the objects in this section of code interrelate and represent various parts of what we're trying to do—which is to construct an authorization packet. This takes the form of an IQ-set containing a <query/> tag qualified by the jabber:iq:auth namespace like this:*

```
<iq type='set'>
  <query xmlns='jabber:iq:auth'>
    <username>myserver</username>
    <password>secret</password>
    <resource>alive</resource>
  </query>
</iq>
```

Constructing Jabber elements with the JabberBeans library uses so-called *builders* that allow individual element components to be created separately and then fused together into a final structure. In the code, we use two builders: an InfoQuery-Builder to construct the <iq/> envelope and an IQAuthBuilder to construct the <query/> content.

Taking the code step by step, we create or declare each of the three things, iqb, iq, and iqAuthb:

```
            InfoQueryBuilder iqb=new InfoQueryBuilder();
            InfoQuery iq;
            IQAuthBuilder iqAuthb=new IQAuthBuilder();
```

---

* We're not bothering in this example to ask the server for the authentication methods it supports and are just going ahead with a plaintext attempt.

iqb
>   This is the builder object with which we can build <iq/> elements.

iq   This is the <iq/> element that we're going to build.

iqAuthb
>   This is another builder object with which we can build IQ extensions
>   (<query/> tags) qualified by the jabber:iq:auth namespace.

The process of creating the authorization packet is detailed in Figure 8-3.

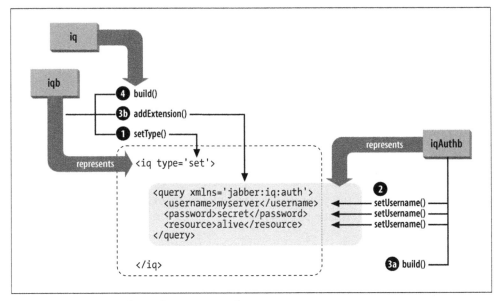

Figure 8-3. Creating the authorization packet

There are numbered steps in Figure 8-3; these follow what happens in the rest of
the authentication preparation:

Step 1: Set the type attribute of the IQ
>   We call the setType() method on the iqb object that represents the outer IQ
>   envelope to set the value of the type attribute:

```
iqb.setType("set");
```

Step 2: Set the values for the parts of the authorization section of the element
>   Having constructed the iqAuthb object, which represents the <query/>
>   portion of the element, we fill the values with these calls:

```
iqAuthb.setUsername(USER);
iqAuthb.setPassword(PASSWORD);
iqAuthb.setResource(RESOURCE);
```

Steps 3a and 3b: Generate iqAuthb *and add it to the* iqb *object*

Once the values inside the authorization <query/> tag are set, we can call the build() method on the object representing that tag in iqAuthb to generate an extension object (in other words, to *assemble* the tag) that can then be attached to the iqb object using the addExtension() method:

```
try
{
  iqb.addExtension(iqAuthb.build());
}
...
```

Step 4: Generate iqb *and assign it to the IQ object*

In the same way that we generated the authorization <query/> tag, we can generate the whole element and assign it to iq:

```
try
{
  //build the full InfoQuery packet
  iq=(InfoQuery)iqb.build();
}
...
```

Once we've constructed the authorization element, now held as the iq object, we can send it down the stream to the Jabber server with the send() method of the ConnectionBean object cb:

```
cb.send(iq);
```

Finally, once we've authenticated, we can construct the presence packet and send it using the same technique as before.* We construct a new object to represent the presence packet denoting general availability—<presence/>:

```
PresenceBuilder pb=new PresenceBuilder();
```

In this case, there are no namespace-qualified extensions to add to the <presence/> element, but we do want to add the IP address that was passed into the script and available in argv[0]. We can use the setStatus() method on the presence object to set the optional <status/> to contain that IP address:

```
pb.setStatus(argv[0]);
```

After this, we can go ahead and generate the element, which will look like this:

```
<presence>
  <status>123.45.67.89</status>
</presence>
```

---

* We're assuming the password is correct here, to keep this example straightforward. If it isn't correct, there's not much we can do at this point anyway.

After the generation with the build() call, we send it down the stream in the same way as the authorization <iq/> element:

```
try
{
  cb.send(pb.build());
}
catch (InstantiationException e)
{
  System.out.println("Fatal Error on Presence object build:");
  System.out.println(e.toString());
  return;
}
```

As for each of the build() calls, we must trap a possible exception that build() throws if it can't complete (for example, due to lack of information). This is the InstantiationException.

We can see the results of *myserver* sending such an information-laden <pres-ence/> element to *dj* in Figure 8-4. As the server connects to the Internet, the Java script is started via the *ip-up* script, and it relays the assigned IP address, which is shown in Jarl's status bar as the availability information reaches *dj* 's client.

Figure 8-4. myserver becoming available and relaying its IP address

All that remains for the script to do now is to hang around. While the XML stream to the Jabber server remains, and the connection is not broken, its availability will remain as it was as described by the simple <presence/> element we sent. So we simply go into a sort of hibernation. We have no hope of escaping, but it should be taken care of by the *ip-down* script as described earlier.

```
while (true) {
  try {
    Thread.sleep(9999);
  }
  catch (InterruptedException e)
  {
    System.out.println("timeout!");
  }
}
```

In fact, when the *ip-down* script kills the script, the socket connection will be closed, but there was no clean disconnect—no <presence type='unavailable'/> was sent by the script to the Jabber server. In this case, the Jabber server will notice that the socket was closed and generate an unavailable <presence/> element on behalf of the client.

Presence-Sensitive CVS Notification

In the section "CVS Notification via Jabber" early in this chapter, we replaced the email-based CVS notification mechanism with a Jabber-based one. The script used was extremely simple—it connected to the Jabber server specified, authenticated, and sent off the notification message to the recipient JID.

What if we wanted to make the script "sensitive"? Jabber's presence concept could help us here; if we extended the mechanism to allow for the building of presence-based relationships between the notification script and the notification recipients, we can make the sending of the notification message dependent on the recipient's availability. "Presence-based relationships" refers to the *presence subscription* mechanism described in the section "Presence subscription."

Here's how it would work:

*   Each potential recipient adds the JID used by the CVS notification script to his roster and sends a subscription request to it.[*]

*   The notification script, called *cvsmsg-s* ("cvsmsg-*sensitive*"), on receipt of the presence subscription from a recipient, accepts the request and reciprocates by sending a subscription request back to that recipient.

---

[*] The process of adding a JID to the roster and making a subscription request is an atomic action in many clients. It is generally assumed that adding a JID to your roster means that you're going to want to know when that entity is available, so the action of adding a JID to the roster will often generate a presence subscription request automatically.

- On receipt of the presence subscription from the notification script, the recipient accepts the request.

- When the notification script starts up to send a message, it announces its own availability with a `<presence&sol;>` element, which causes the availability of the JIDs to which it has a presence subscription to be sent to it. Based on these `<presence&sol;>` packets received, it can make a decision as to whether to send the notification message or not.

  The decision we're going to use here is an arbitrary one: if the recipient is online, we'll send the message, unless he's specified that he doesn't want to be disturbed, with the `<show>dnd</show>` element.

Subscription Relationships

This method will result in "balanced" subscription relationships between script and recipients. In other words, the script is subscribed to a recipient's presence, and vice versa.

Of the two presence subscription "directions," the one where the *notification script* subscribes to the *recipient's* presence (as opposed to the one where the *recipient* subscribes to the *notification script's* presence) is by far the most important. While it's not critical that the recipients know when the notification script is connected and active, it's essential that the notification script know about a recipient's availability at the time it wants to send a message.

So would it be more appropriate to create "unbalanced" subscription relationships?

An unbalanced relationship is one where one party knows about the other party's availability but *not* vice versa. The idea for sensitizing the notification script will work as long as the script can know about the availability of the recipients. Whether or not the opposite is true is largely irrelevant.

Nevertheless, it's worth basing the interaction on balanced, or reciprocal, presence subscriptions, primarily for simplicity's sake and also for the fact that most Jabber clients (and most *users* of these clients) tend to cope well and consistently with balanced subscriptions, whereby the representation and interpretation of unbalanced relationships is dealt with and understood in different manners. Some clients use a `lurker` group to classify one-way presence subscriptions from other JIDs (a "lurker" being one that can see you while you can't see it).

Far from being nebulous concepts, balanced and unbalanced subscription relationships are characterized technically by values of a certain attribute specified in each item—each JID—in a roster: the `subscription` attribute of the `<item&sol;>` tags within the roster. As we progress through the extensions to the CVS notification script, we'll be examining these values at various stages in this recipe description in the section "Taking the cvsmsg-s Script Step by Step."

Anthropomorphism

It's worth pointing out at this stage that adding a JID that's used by a *script* to connect to Jabber is slightly symbolic of the extension of the instant messaging world into the wider arena of A2P messaging. Adding a *service* JID to your roster and sharing presence information with that service immediately widens the scope of what's possible with a humble instant messaging client, and blurs the boundaries between people and applications.

The cvsmsg-s Script

The script, as it stands in the section "The cvsmsg Script," is what we want to extend and make sensitive to presence. Example 8-7 looks at the extended script, *cvsmsg-s*, and then walks through the additions.

Example 8-7. The cvsmsg-s script

```
import jabber
import sys
from string import split

Server   = 'gnu.pipetree.com'
Username = 'cvsmsg'
Password = 'secret'
Resource = 'cvsmsg'

cvsuser  = sys.argv[1]
message  = ''

def presenceCB(con, prs):

    type = prs.getType()
    parts = split(prs.getFrom(), '/')
    who = parts[0]

    if type == None: type = 'available'

    # Subscription request:
    # - Accept their subscription
    # - Send request for subscription to their presence
    if type == 'subscribe':
        print "subscribe request from %s" % (who)
        con.send(jabber.Presence(to=who, type='subscribed'))
        con.send(jabber.Presence(to=who, type='subscribe'))

    # Unsubscription request:
```

Example 8-7. The cvsmsg-s script (continued)

```
    # - Accept their unsubscription
    # - Send request for unsubscription to their presence
    elif type == 'unsubscribe':
        print "unsubscribe request from %s" % (who)
        con.send(jabber.Presence(to=who, type='unsubscribed'))
        con.send(jabber.Presence(to=who, type='unsubscribe'))

    elif type == 'subscribed':
        print "we are now subscribed to %s" % (who)

    elif type == 'unsubscribed':
        print "we are now unsubscribed to %s" % (who)

    elif type == 'available':
        print "%s is available (%s/%s)" % (who, prs.getShow(), prs.getStatus())
        if prs.getShow() != 'dnd' and who == cvsuser:
            con.send(jabber.Message(cvsuser, message, subject="CVS Watch Alarm"))

    elif type == 'unavailable':
        print "%s is unavailable" % (who)

for line in sys.stdin.readlines(): message = message + line

con = jabber.Client(host=Server)

try:
    con.connect()
except IOError, e:
    print "Couldn't connect: %s" % e
    sys.exit(0)

con.auth(Username,Password,Resource)

con.setPresenceHandler(presenceCB)
con.requestRoster()
con.sendInitPresence()

for i in range(5):
  con.process(1)

con.disconnect()
```

Taking the cvsmsg-s Script Step by Step

Now it's time to examine the script step by step. We'll concentrate mostly on the additions to the original *cvsmsg* script.

We bring in a string function that we'll be needing later in the script to chop up JIDs into their component parts (*username*, *hostname*, and *resource*):

```
import jabber
import sys
from string import split

Server   = 'gnu.pipetree.com'
Username = 'cvsmsg'
Password = 'secret'
Resource = 'cvsmsg'

cvsuser  = sys.argv[1]
message  = ''
```

Presence callback

The next addition to the script is a callback to handle `<presence&sol;>` elements. The callback in this script takes the form of a subroutine called `presenceCB()` ("presence callback"). Callbacks, in relation to programming with Jabber, are explained in the section "Jabber Programming and Callbacks."

This is what the callback for handling `<presence&sol;>` elements looks like:

```
def presenceCB(con, prs):

    type = prs.getType()
    parts = split(prs.getFrom(), '/')
    who = parts[0]

    if type == None: type = 'available'

    # Subscription request:
    # - Accept their subscription
    # - Send request for subscription to their presence
    if type == 'subscribe':
        print "subscribe request from %s" % (who)
        con.send(jabber.Presence(to=who, type='subscribed'))
        con.send(jabber.Presence(to=who, type='subscribe'))

    # Unsubscription request:
    # - Accept their unsubscription
    # - Send request for unsubscription to their presence
    elif type == 'unsubscribe':
        print "unsubscribe request from %s" % (who)
        con.send(jabber.Presence(to=who, type='unsubscribed'))
        con.send(jabber.Presence(to=who, type='unsubscribe'))

    elif type == 'subscribed':
        print "we are now subscribed to %s" % (who)

    elif type == 'unsubscribed':
        print "we are now unsubscribed to %s" % (who)

    elif type == 'available':
```

```
    print "%s is available (%s/%s)" % (who, prs.getShow(), prs.getStatus())
    if prs.getShow() != 'dnd' and who == cvsuser:
        con.send(jabber.Message(cvsuser, message, subject="CVS Watch Alarm"))

elif type == 'unavailable':
    print "%s is unavailable" % (who)
```

Phew! Let's take it a bit at a time. The first thing to note is what's specified in the subroutine declaration:

```
def presenceCB(con, prs):
```

As a handler, the subroutine `presenceCB()` will be passed the *connection object* in `con`, and the *presence node* in `prs`. `con` is the same connection object that is created later in the script (`con = jabber.Client(host=Server)`) and is passed in for convenience, as it's quite likely we're going to want to use it, say, to send something back over the stream.

The presence node in `prs` is an object representation of the XML fragment that came in over the stream and was parsed into its component parts. The object is an instance of the `jabber.Presence` class, which is simply a specialization of the more generic `jabber.Protocol` class, as are the other classes that represent the other two Jabber protocol elements that are to be expected: `jabber.Message` and `jabber.Iq`. The `jabber.Protocol` class represents protocol elements in general.

As such, there are a number of <presence/> element-specific methods we can call on the `prs` object, such as `getShow()` and `getStatus()` (which return the values of the <show/> and <status/> tags—children of the <presence/> element—respectively) and general element methods such as `getID`, which returns the value of any `id` attribute assigned to the element, and `setTo()`, which can be used to address the element—to set the value of the `to` attribute.

The first thing the handler does is to call a few of these element methods to determine the *type* of <presence/> element (presence types are described in the section "The Presence Element"), and who it's coming from:

```
type = prs.getType()
parts = split(prs.getFrom(), '/')
who = parts[0]
```

When the notification script is called, the JID found in the CVS *users* file is substituted for the `%s` in the formula contained in the CVS *notify* file. So if the user *dj* were to be notified, the JID passed to the script would be *dj@gnu.pipetree.com*.

The way JIDs are passed around *independently* of the context of a Jabber session is usually in the simpler form—*username@hostname*, that is, without the resource suffix—*username@hostname/resource*. As described in Chapter 5, the resource is primarily used to distinguish individual sessions belonging to one Jabber user.

But when the Jabber library—and subsequently a handler subroutine in the script—receives an element, it contains a `from` attribute whose value has been stamped by the Jabber server as it passes through. The value represents the session, the *connection*, from which the `<presence&sol;>` element was sent and, as such, includes a resource suffix. So in order to properly match up the source JID for any incoming `<presence&sol;>` element with the JID specified when the script was invoked (contained in the `cvsuser` variable), we need to strip off this resource suffix. The remaining *username@hostname* part is captured in the `who` variable.

There's one more step to determine the presence type. The `type` attribute is *optional*; its absence signifies the default presence type, which is `available`. So we effect this default substitution here to make the subsequent code clearer:

```
if type == None: type = 'available'
```

At this stage, we want to take different actions depending on what sort of presence information has arrived. Recalling the sequence of events in the reciprocal presence subscription exchange described earlier in this chapter, one of the activities is for a potential notification recipient to subscribe to the presence of the script's JID.

This subscription request is carried in a `<presence&sol;>` element, with a type of `subscribe`. Example 8-8 shows what a typical subscription request would look like.

Example 8-8. A presence subscription request from dj@gnu.pipetree.com

```
<presence type='subscribe' to='cvsmsg@gnu.pipetree.com'
                    from='dj@gnu.pipetree.com/work'&sol;>
```

At this stage, *dj@gnu.pipetree.com* has just sent a request to subscribe to the script's presence. The subscription relationship between the two parties is nondescript, and this is reflected in the details of the item in *dj* 's roster that relates to the script's JID:

```
<item jid='cvsmsg@gnu.pipetree.com' subscription='none' ask='subscribe'&sol;>
```

The relationship itself is reflected in the `subscription` attribute, and the current state of the relationship is reflected in the `ask` attribute.

If a subscription request is received, we want the script to respond by accepting the subscription request. Once the request has been accepted, a presence subscription request is made in return.

This incoming subscription request is handled here:

```
# Subscription request:
# - Accept their subscription
# - Send request for subscription to their presence
if type == 'subscribe':
    print "subscribe request from %s" % (who)
    con.send(jabber.Presence(to=who, type='subscribed'))
    con.send(jabber.Presence(to=who, type='subscribe'))
```

Each call to the `jabber.Presence` class constructor creates a node representing a `<presence&sol;>` element. The two parameters passed in the call are fairly self-explanatory: we specify *to whom* the `<presence&sol;>` element should be sent, and the *type*.

If the presence subscription request came in from the JID *dj@gnu.pipetree.com*, then the XML represented by the node created in the first call here (specifying a presence type of subscribed) would look something like that in Example 8-9.

Example 8-9. Acceptance of a presence subscription request from dj@gnu.pipetree.com

```
<presence type='subscribed' to='dj@gnu.pipetree.com'&sol;>
```

Addressing <presence/> Elements

It's worth pointing out here that there's a subtle difference between sending `<presence&sol;>` elements in a presence subscription conversation and sending general "availability" `<presence&sol;>` elements.

In the first case, we use a `to` attribute, because our conversation is one-to-one. In the second, we don't; our unaddressed availability information is caught by the server and in turn sent on to those entities that are subscribed to your presence.

Although you *can* send `<presence&sol;>` elements that convey availability information directly *to* a JID, it's not normal. However, explicitly addressing the elements in a subscription scenario is essential.

There's another situation in which such "directed" (explicitly addressed) `<presence&sol;>` elements are used—to partake of the services of the availability tracker. This is described in the the section "Availability Tracker."

Once constructed, each of the `jabber.Presence` nodes is sent back along the stream with the `con.send()` calls.

Now that the script has accepted *dj*'s subscription request, *dj*'s roster item for the script reflects the new relationship:

```
<item jid='cvsmsg@gnu.pipetree.com' subscription='to'&sol;>
```

`subscription='to'` denotes that the subscription relationship is currently one way—*dj* has a subscription to the script. There's no `ask` attribute as there's no current request going from *dj* to the script.

While *dj*'s roster item for the script shows a `subscription` value of `to`, the *script*'s roster item for *dj* shows a `subscription` value of `from`:

```
<item jid='dj@gnu.pipetree.com' subscription='from' ask='subscribe'&sol;>
```

which shows that the script has a subscription *from dj*.

Furthermore, remember that the script not only accepts *dj*'s subscription request, it sends a reciprocal one of its own. (Hence the `ask='subscribe'` status in the item.) When *dj* accepts this request, the roster item changes yet again to reflect the balanced relationship:

```
<item jid='cvsmsg@gnu.pipetree.com' subscription='both'&sol;>
```

We want the script to handle requests to `unsubscribe` from its presence in the same way:

```
# Unsubscription request:
# - Accept their unsubscription
# - Send request for unsubscription to their presence
elif type == 'unsubscribe':
    print "unsubscribe request from %s" % (who)
    con.send(jabber.Presence(to=who, type='unsubscribed'))
    con.send(jabber.Presence(to=who, type='unsubscribe'))
```

The only difference between this section and the previous one is that it deals with requests to `unsubscribe` as opposed to `subscribe` to presence. Otherwise it works in exactly the same way. A sequence of `<presence&sol;>` elements used in an "unsubscription conversation" between *dj* and the script, and the changes to the roster `<item&sol;>` tags on each side, is shown in Figure 8-5.

While we must take action on presence types `subscribe` and `unsubscribe`, we don't really need to do anything for their *acknowledgment* counterparts: `subscribed` and `unsubscribed` ("I have accepted your request, and you are now subscribed/unsubscribed to my presence").

Nevertheless, just for illustration purposes, we'll include a couple of conditions to show what's going on when the script runs:

```
elif type == 'subscribed':
    print "we are now subscribed to %s" % (who)

elif type == 'unsubscribed':
    print "we are now unsubscribed to %s" % (who)
```

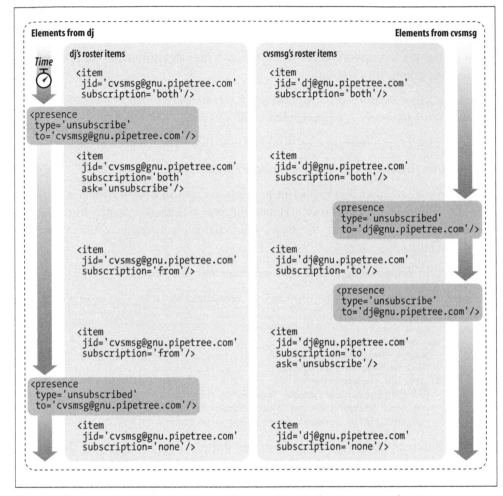

Figure 8-5. <presence/> elements and roster <item/>s in an unsubscription conversation

Apart from the types of <presence/> element covering the presence subscription process, we should also expect the basic availability elements:

```
<presence>...</presence>
```

and

```
<presence type='unavailable'&sol;>
```

It's an available <presence/> element that the functionality of the script hinges on:

```
elif type == 'available':
    print "%s is available (%s/%s)" % (who, prs.getShow(), prs.getStatus())
    if prs.getShow() != 'dnd' and who == cvsuser:
```

```
con.send(jabber.Message(cvsuser, message, subject="CVS Watch Alarm"))
```

This `presenceCB()` subroutine is set up to handle <presence/> elements. In a typical execution scenario, where the script is subscribed to the presence of many potential CVS notification recipients, the subroutine is going to be called to handle the availability information of all recipients who happen to be connected to Jabber at the moment of notification. We're interested in the availability information of only one particular recipient (`who == cvsuser`), and we want to check on the contents of the <show/> tag.

If we get a match, we can send the notification message by creating a `jabber.Message` node that will look like this:

```
<message to='dj@gnu.pipetree.com'>
  <subject>CVS Watch Alarm</subject>
  <body>
    testproject file4
    ---
    Triggered edit watch on /usr/local/cvsroot/testproject
    By piers
  </body>
</message>
```

As in the *cvsmsg* script, once created, the node can be sent with the `con.send()` method call.

Like the conditions for the presence subscription and unsubscription acknowledgments, we're including a final condition to deal with the case where a recipient disconnects from the Jabber server during the execution of the script: an `unavailable` <presence/> element will be sent:

```
elif type == 'unavailable':
    print "%s is unavailable" % (who)
```

We're simply logging such an event for illustration purposes.

Connection and authentication

Most of the main part of the script is the same as the nonsensitive version from the section "CVS Notification via Jabber": reading in the notification message, preparing a connection to the Jabber server, and trying to connect:

```
for line in sys.stdin.readlines(): message = message + line

con = jabber.Client(host=Server)

try:
    con.connect()
except IOError, e:
    print "Couldn't connect: %s" % e
    sys.exit(0)
```

```
con.auth(Username,Password,Resource)
```

Registration of <presence/> handler

While we've *defined* the `presenceCB()` subroutine to handle `<presence&sol;>` packets, we haven't actually told the Jabber library about it. The call to the `setPres-
enceHandler()` method of the connection object does this for us, performing the
"Register handler" step shown in Figure 8-6. The steps shown in Figure 8-6 are
described in the section "Jabber Programming and Callbacks."

```
con.setPresenceHandler(presenceCB)
```

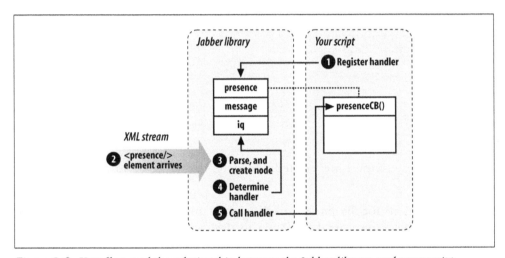

Figure 8-6. Handlers and the relationship between the Jabber library and your script

Request for roster

It's easy to guess what the next method call does:

```
con.requestRoster()
```

It makes a request for the roster by sending an IQ-get with a query qualified by
the `jabber:iq:roster` namespace:

```
<iq type='get' id='3'>
  <query xmlns='jabber:iq:roster'&sol;>
</iq>
```

to which the server responds with an IQ-result:

```
<iq type='result' id='3'>
  <query xmlns='jabber:iq:roster'>
    <item jid='dj@gnu.pipetree.com' subscription='both'&sol;>
    <item jid='piers@jabber.org' subscription='both'&sol;>
    <item jid='shiels@jabber.org' subscription='both'&sol;>
    ...
```

```
    </query>
  </iq>
```

However, as there are no explicit references to the roster anywhere in the script, it's not as easy to guess why we request the roster in the first place. We know that the client-side copy is merely a "slave" copy, and, even more relevant here, we know that subscription information in the roster <item/> tags is managed by the server—we as a client don't need to (in fact, *shouldn't*) do anything to maintain the subscription and ask attributes and keep them up to date.

So why do we request it? Basically, it's because there's a fundamental difference between <presence/> elements used to convey availability information and <presence/> elements used to convey presence subscription information. If John sends Jim availability information in a <presence/> element, whether directly (with a to attribute) or indirectly (through the distribution of that element by the server to Jim as a subscriber to John's presence), and Jim's offline on holiday, it doesn't make sense to store and forward the message to him when he next connects:

> Jabber server: *"Here's some availability information for John, dated 9 days ago."*

> Jim: *"Who cares?"*

The <presence/> elements conveying availability information are *not* stored and forwarded if they can't be delivered because the intended recipient is offline. What would be the point?

However, <presence/> elements that convey subscription information are a different kettle of fish. While it's not important that a user is sent out of date availability information when he next connects to his Jabber client, any subscription (or unsubscription) requests or confirmations that were sent to him *are* important. So they need to be stored and forwarded.

As we've already seen, the presence subscription mechanism and rosters are inextricably linked. And if we look briefly under the covers, we see how this is so. When a presence subscription request is sent to a user, it runs the gauntlet of modules in the JSM (see the section "Component Connection Method" for details on what these modules are). The roster-handling module *mod_roster* grabs this request, and, just in case the recipient turns out not to be connected, *stores* it.

And here's how intertwined the presence subscription mechanism and rosters really are: the request is stored as a cluster of attribute details within an <item/> tag in the roster belonging to the *recipient* of the presence subscription request. It looks like this:

```
<item jid='user@hostname' subscription='none' subscribe='' hidden=''&sol;>
```

On receipt of a presence subscription request, the *mod_roster* module will create the roster item if it doesn't exist already and then assign the attributes related to presence subscription—subscription='none' and subscribe=''—to it. There's no ask attribute, as this is assigned only to the item on the roster belonging to the *sender*, not the one belonging to the *receiver*, of the subscription request.

The subscribe attribute is used to store the reason for the request, that, if specified, is carried in the <status/> tag of the <presence/> element that conveys the request. If no reason is given, the value for the attribute is empty, as shown here. Otherwise, it will contain what was stored in the <status/> tag. Example 8-10 shows a presence subscription request that carries a reason.

Example 8-10. A presence subscription request with a reason

```
<presence to='dj@gnu.pipetree.com'>
  <status>I'd like to keep my eye on you!</status>
</presence>
```

The hidden attribute here:

```
<item jid='user@hostname' subscription='none' subscribe='' hidden=''&sol;>
```

is used internally by *mod_roster* to mark the item as nondisplayable; it effectively is a pseudo <item/> that, when brought to life, actually turns out to be a <presence/> element. So when a request for the roster is made, *mod_roster* makes sure that it doesn't send these "hidden" items. The hidden attribute always has an empty value, as shown here.

After storing the subscription request, *mod_roster* will actually send the original <presence/> element that conveyed that request to the recipient—that is, if the recipient is online *and* if the recipient has already made a request for his roster. As sending an availability presence packet:

```
<presence&sol;>
```

causes the *mod_offline* module to forward any messages stored offline in that user's absence, so requesting the roster:

```
<iq type='get'><query xmlns='jabber:iq:roster'&sol;></iq>
```

causes the *mod_roster* module to forward any subscription requests stored offline in that user's absence.

Sending of availability information

OK. We've connected, authenticated, defined, and registered the callback to handle <presence/> elements, and requested the roster, so *mod_roster* will send us any presence subscription (or unsubscription) requests. Now we need to make an availability announcement in the form of a simple <presence/> element:

```
<presence&sol;>
```

We can do this by calling the `sendInitPresence()` method on the connection object:

```
con.sendInitPresence()
```

This availability information will be distributed to all the entities that are subscribed to the script's presence and are online at that moment. It will also signify to the Jabber server that we are properly online—in which case it can forward to us any messages that had been stored up in our absence.

We're not really expecting any <message/> elements; indeed, we haven't set up any subroutine to handle them, so they'd just be thrown away by the library anyway. The real reason for sending presence is so that the server will actively go and probe those in a presence subscription relationship with the script and report back on those who are available (who have themselves sent their presence during their current session). This causes <presence/> elements to arrive on the stream and make their way to the `presenceCB()` handler.

Waiting for packets

Once everything is set up, and the script has announced its presence, it really just needs to sit back and listen to the <presence/> elements that come in. If one of these is from the intended notification recipient, and the availability state is right (i.e., not in `dnd` mode), we know that the circumstances are appropriate for sending the notification.

But the elements being sent over the stream from the server don't spontaneously get received, parsed, and dispatched; we can control when that happens from the script. This is the nub of the symbiosis between the element events and the procedural routines, and it's name is `process()`.

Calling `process()` will check on the stream to see if any XML fragments have arrived and are waiting to be picked up. If there are any, Steps 3 through 5, shown in Figure 8-6 and described in the section "Jabber Programming and Callbacks," are executed. The numeric value specified in the call to `process()` is the number of seconds to wait for incoming fragments if none is currently waiting to be picked up. Specifying no value (or 0) means that the method won't hang around if nothing has arrived. Specifying a value of 30 means that it will wait up to half a minute. We really want something in between, and it turns out that waiting for up to a second for fragments in a finite loop like this:

```
for i in range(5):
  con.process(1)
```

will allow for a slightly stuttered arrival of the <presence/> elements that are sent to the script as a result of the server-initiated probes.

Finishing up

We're just about done. The <presence/> elements that arrive and find their way to the callback are examined, and the CVS notification message is sent off if appropriate. Once the process() calls have finished, and, implicitly, the (potentially) multiple calls to presenceCB, there's nothing left to do. So we simply disconnect from the Jabber server, as before:

```
con.disconnect()
```

Jabber Programming and Callbacks

When programming all but the simplest Jabber scripts, you're going to be using *callbacks*, as we've seen in this recipe. Callbacks are also known as *handlers*.

Rather than purely procedural programming ("do this, then do that, then do the other"), we need a different model to cope with the *event-based* nature of Jabber or, more precisely, the event-based nature of how we converse using the Jabber protocol over an XML stream. Although we control what we *send* over the XML stream connection that we've established with the Jabber server, we can't control what we *receive*, and more importantly, we can't control *when* we receive it. We need an event-based programming model to be able to *handle* the protocol elements as they arrive.

The libraries available for programming with Jabber offer *callback* mechanisms. With these callback mechanisms, we can register subroutines with the part of the library that's handling the reception of XML document stream fragments. Then, whenever an element appears on the incoming stream (a fragment in the stream document that the Jabber server is sending to us), the library can pass it to the appropriate subroutine in the script for us to act upon—to be "handled." This passing of elements to be handled by callbacks is referred to as *dispatching*.

Figure 8-6 shows the relationship between the library and script, and the sequence of events surrounding registering a handler and having it called. Here are the steps shown:

Step 1: Register handler

The script uses a library function to register a subroutine—in this case, it's presenceCB()—as a handler with the library. In the registration, the subroutine is assigned as a handler for <presence/> elements.

Step 2: `<presence&sol;>` element arrives

An XML fragment arrives on the stream, sent by the Jabber server.

Step 3: Parse, and create node

The fragment is parsed into its component parts by an XML parser, and a node is created. A "node" is simply a term used to describe a succinct XML fragment—containing attributes, data, and child tags—that is usually in the form of an object that is programmatically accessible. The node creation step is theoretically optional; we could have the library pass on the fragment in a simple string representation form, but that would put the onus on the script to parse the string before being able to manipulate the fragment that the string represented.

Step 4: Determine handler

Once parsed, the library looks at what sort of element, or node, the fragment is and determines what (if any) handler has been registered. In this case, it's a `<presence&sol;>` element, and it finds that the subroutine `presenceCB()` has been registered as a handler for `<presence&sol;>` elements.

Step 5: Call handler

The library calls the handler `presenceCB()` in the script, passing in the node. It may pass in other information too (for example, the `Jabberpy` library also passes in the stream connection object, as we saw earlier, and the Perl library `Net::Jabber` also passes in a session ID relating to the stream).*

---

* This session ID is currently part of a new development within the `Net::Jabber` library and is currently not used for anything.

9

Groupchat, Components, and Event Models

By now, you should have a good idea of how scripts interact with Jabber and how the core elements such as <message/> and <presence/> can be constructed and handled.

This chapter builds upon what we've already seen in Chapter 8 and introduces new concepts. We build a nosy assistant that joins a conference room and alerts us to words and phrases that we want it to listen for. There are two popular conference protocols, as mentioned in the section "jabber:iq:conference"—the presence-based Groupchat protocol, and the `jabber:iq:conference`-based Conference protocol. The assistant recipe, a foray into the world of 'bots, takes a look at the original presence-based one.

As we've seen, programming within Jabber's event model is fairly straightforward. But what happens when you want to meld other components with event models of their own? We look at a couple of typical scenarios where this melding needs to happen. The first is a homage to the Trojan Room Coffee Machine (*http://www.cl.cam.ac.uk/coffee/coffee.html*), where we give life, or at least presence, to a coffeepot, using LEGO® MINDSTORMS™. The second is a Tk-based RSS headline viewer. Both the coffeepot and the Tk programming library have event loops of their own. With the coffeepot, we need to have a loop that polls the coffeepot's status, independently of the polling for incoming packets from the Jabber server. The Tk programming library's event model is similar to those of the Jabber programming libraries that are used in the recipes in this book, in that handlers are set up and a loop is started that listens for UI events. In both cases, we need to get these event loops to work in harmony with the Jabber libraries' event loops.

Building Jabber solutions without event loops is a Sisyphean task. The very nature of Jabber communication is event-based, and it's important to understand how to use the event features of the Jabber programming libraries and also how to be able to mesh those features with similar features in other libraries and systems.

We also look at extending messages and build a mechanism that delivers RSS headlines to clients who register with that mechanism. These headlines are carried using an extended message type. In fact, the RSS Delivery Mechanism is a *component*. The three recipes in Chapter 8 , were Jabber *clients*, in that they connected to the Jabber network via the Jabber Session Manager (JSM) service. We look at the differences between programming a client and programming a component in this chapter and build a complete component that can be queried and interacted with using the third of Jabber's building blocks—the <iq/> element.

Happy coding!

Keyword Assistant

Many of the Jabber core and peripheral developers hang out in a conference room called *jdev* hosted by the Conferencing component on the Jabber server running at *jabber.org*. While a lot of useful information is to be gleaned from listening to what goes on in *jdev*, it isn't possible to be there all the time. Conversations in *jdev* are logged to web pages, which can be used to visit after the fact to try to catch up with things; however, this can be a hopeless task. One solution is to build a 'bot that looks for specific keywords and Uniform Resource Locators (URLs) in the conversations in *jdev* and send those on as Jabber messages.

This script, *keyassist*, connects to a Jabber server, enters a conference room, and listens to the conversations, looking for certain words and phrases to be uttered. The *keyassist* script is given a bit of "intelligence" in that it can be interacted with and told, while running, to watch for (or stop watching for), certain words and phrases.

The *keyassist* script introduces us to programmatic interaction with the Conferencing component. Before looking at the script, however, let's have a brief overview of Conferencing in general.

Conferencing

The Conferencing component at *jabber.org* is conference.jabber.org. Details of the component instance configuration for such a Conferencing component can be found in the section "Component Instance: conf," where we see that the component exists as a shared object library connected with the library load component connection method. This component provides general conferencing facilities, oriented around a *conference room* and *conference user* model.

A Jabber user can *enter* (or *join*) a conference room, thereby becoming a conference user identified by a nickname that is chosen upon entering that room. Nicknames are generally used in conference rooms to provide a modicum of privacy— it is assumed that by default you don't want to let the other conference room members know your real JID.

The Conferencing component supports two protocols for user and room interaction: a simple one that provides basic features and a more complex one that provides the basic features plus facilities such as password-protected rooms and room descriptions—Groupchat and Conference.

 There is a third protocol, called *Experimental* `iq:groupchat`, which came between the Groupchat and Conference protocols. This reflected an experimental move to add features to the basic Groupchat protocol using IQ elements, the contents of which were qualified by a namespace `jabber:iq:groupchat`. This protocol has been dropped, and support for it exists only in certain versions of WinJab and JIM.

Groupchat

The Groupchat protocol is the simpler of the two and provides basic functions for entering and exiting conference rooms and choosing nicknames.

This Groupchat protocol is known as the *presence-based protocol*, because the protocol is based upon `<presence&sol;>` elements used for room entry, exit, and nickname determination. The Groupchat protocol has a nominal version number of 1.0.

Conference

The Conference protocol offers more advanced features than the Groupchat protocol and makes use of two IQ namespaces: `jabber:iq:conference` and `jabber:iq:browse`. It has a nominal protocol version number of 1.4, which reflects the version of the Jabber server with which it is delivered. Sometimes this version number is referred to as 0.4, such as in the downloadable tarball and in the value returned in response to a "version query" on the component itself, as shown in Example 9-1.

The version number isn't that important. The main thing to keep in mind is that the component that is called `conference.so` (see the reference to the *shared object library* in the section "Component Connection Method") supports both the Groupchat protocol and the Conference protocol. If you come across a shared object library called `groupchat.so`, this is the original Conferencing component that was made available with Jabber server Version 1.0. This library supports only the Groupchat protocol.

Example 9-1. Querying the Conferencing component's version

```
SEND: <iq type='get' to='conference.gnu.mine.nu'>
        <query xmlns='jabber:iq:version'&sol;>
      </iq>

RECV: <iq to='dj@gnu.mine.nu/jarl' from='conference.gnu.mine.nu'
        type='result'>
        <query xmlns='jabber:iq:version'>
          <name>conference</name>
          <version>0.4</version>
          <os>Linux 2.4.2-2</os>
        </query>
      </iq>
```

In this recipe we'll be using the simpler Groupchat protocol. It's widely used and easy to understand. Example 9-2 shows a typical element log from Groupchat-based activity. It shows a user, with the JID `qmacro@jabber.com`, entering a room called "cellar," hosted on the conference component at `conf.merlix.dyndns.org`, a room that currently has two other occupants who go by the nicknames `flash` and `roscoe`. The elements are from `qmacro`'s perspective, and are all explained following the example.

Example 9-2. The Groupchat protocol in action

The user `qmacro` tries to enter the conference room with the nickname `flash` and fails:

```
SEND: <presence to='cellar@conf.merlix.dyndns.org/flash'&sol;>

RECV: <presence to='qmacro@jabber.com/jarltk'
              from='cellar@conf.merlix.dyndns.org/flash'
              type='error'>
        <error code='409'>Conflict</error>
      </presence>
```

He tries again, this time with a different nickname, `deejay`, and is successful:

```
SEND: <presence to='cellar@conf.merlix.dyndns.org/deejay'&sol;>

RECV: <presence to='qmacro@jabber.com/jarltk'
              from='cellar@conf.merlix.dyndns.org/flash'&sol;>

RECV: <presence to='qmacro@jabber.com/jarltk'
              from='cellar@conf.merlix.dyndns.org/roscoe'&sol;>

RECV: <presence to='qmacro@jabber.com/jarltk'
              from='cellar@conf.merlix.dyndns.org/deejay'&sol;>

RECV: <message to='qmacro@jabber.com/jarltk'
              type='groupchat' from='cellar@conf.merlix.dyndns.org'>
        <body>deejay has become available</body>
      </message>
```

roscoe says hi, and qmacro waves back:

```
RECV: <message to='qmacro@jabber.com/jarltk'
              from='cellar@conf.merlix.dyndns.org/roscoe'
              type='groupchat' cnu=''>
         <body>hi</body>
      </message>

SEND: <message to='cellar@conf.merlix.dyndns.org' type='groupchat'>
         <body>/me waves to everyone</body>
      </message>
```

flash sends a private message to qmacro:

```
RECV: <message to='qmacro@jabber.com/jarltk'
              from='cellar@conf.merlix.dyndns.org/flash'
              type='chat'>
         <body>Is that you, qmacro?</body>
         <thread>jarl1998911094</thread>
      </message>
```

Feeling left out of the conversation, roscoe leaves the room:

```
RECV: <presence to='qmacro@jabber.com/jarltk' type='unavailable'
               from='cellar@conf.merlix.dyndns.org/roscoe'&sol;>

RECV: <message to='qmacro@jabber.com/jarltk' type='groupchat'
              from='cellar@conf.merlix.dyndns.org'>
         <body>roscoe has left</body>
      </message>
```

Let's take the stages in Example 9-2 one by one.

Failed attempt to enter room

qmacro makes an attempt to enter the room using the Groupchat protocol. This is done by sending a directed <presence/> element to a particular JID that represents the room and the chosen nickname. This JID is constructed as follows:

```
[room name]@[conference component]/[nickname]
```

In this example, the conferencing component is identified with the hostname conf.merlix.dyndns.org. qmacro's choice of nickname is flash:

```
cellar@conf.merlix.dyndns.org/flash
```

Thus the following element is sent:

```
SEND: <presence to='cellar@conf.merlix.dyndns.org/flash'&sol;>
```

The conference component determines that there is already someone present in the room cellar@conf.merlix.dyndns.org with the nickname flash, so qmacro is notified of this and receives a directed presence with an <error/> tag:

```
RECV: <presence to='qmacro@jabber.com/jarltk'
              from='cellar@conf.merlix.dyndns.org/flash'
              type='error'>
        <error code='409'>Conflict</error>
      </presence>
```

Note that the `<presence&sol;>` element has the type `error` and comes *from* the artificial JID constructed in the room entry attempt. The element is addressed to qmacro's real JID, of course—`qmacro@jabber.com/jarltk`—as otherwise it wouldn't reach him.

The error code 409 and text "Conflict" tells qmacro that the nickname conflicted with one already in the room. This is a standard error code/text pair; Table 5-3 shows a complete set of code/text pairs.

At this stage, qmacro is not yet in the room.

Successful attempt to enter room

qmacro tries again, this time with a different nickname, `deejay`:[*]

```
SEND: <presence to='cellar@conf.merlix.dyndns.org/deejay'&sol;>
```

This time, there is no conflict—no other user is in the room "cellar" with that nickname—and the conference component registers the entry. It does this by sending qmacro the presence of all the room occupants, including that of himself:

```
RECV: <presence to='qmacro@jabber.com/jarltk'
              from='cellar@conf.merlix.dyndns.org/flash'&sol;>

RECV: <presence to='qmacro@jabber.com/jarltk'
              from='cellar@conf.merlix.dyndns.org/roscoe'&sol;>

RECV: <presence to='qmacro@jabber.com/jarltk'
              from='cellar@conf.merlix.dyndns.org/deejay'&sol;>
```

These presence elements are also sent to the other room occupants so they know that `deejay` is present.

Conference component-generated notification

In addition to the presence elements sent for each room occupant, a general roomwide message noting that someone with the nickname `deejay` just entered the room is sent out by the component as a `type='groupchat'` message to all the room occupants:

---

[*] There's no rule that says the nickname can't be the same as the user part of your JID, if you're not concerned with hiding your true identity.

```
RECV: <message to='qmacro@jabber.com/jarltk'
            type='groupchat'
            from='cellar@conf.merlix.dyndns.org'>
         <body>deejay has become available</body>
      </message>
```

The text "has become available" used in the body of the message is taken
directly from the *Action Notices* definitions, part of the Conferencing component instance configuration described in the section "Custom Configuration."
Note that the identity of the room itself is simply a generic version of the JID
that the room occupants use to enter:

```
cellar@conf.merlix.dyndns.org
```

Roomwide chat

Once the user with the nickname roscoe sees someone enter the room, he
sends a greeting, and qmacro waves back:

```
RECV: <message to='qmacro@jabber.com/jarltk'
            from='cellar@conf.merlix.dyndns.org/roscoe'
            type='groupchat' cnu=''>
         <body>hi qmacro</body>
      </message>

SEND: <message to='cellar@conf.merlix.dyndns.org'
            type='groupchat'>
         <body>/me waves to everyone</body>
      </message>
```

As with the notification message, each message is a groupchat-type message.
The one received appears to come from cellar@conf.merlix.dyndns.org/
roscoe, which is the JID representing the user in the room with the nickname
roscoe. This way, roscoe's real JID is never sent to qmacro. The message dee-
jay sends is addressed to the room's identity cellar@conf.merlix.dyndns.org,
and contains a message that starts with /me. This is simply a convention that is
understood by clients that support conferencing, meant to represent an action
and displayed thus:

```
* deejay waves to everyone
```

Ignore the cnu attribute; it's put there and used by the component
and should never make it out to the client endpoints. The attribute
name is a short name for the conference user and refers to the internal structure that represents a conference room occupant within the
component.

One-on-one chat

The Conferencing component also supports a one-on-one chat mode, which is just like normal chat mode (where messages with the type `chat` are exchanged) except that the routing goes through the component. The intended recipient of a conference-routed chat message is identified by his room JID. So in this example:

```
RECV: <message to='qmacro@jabber.com/jarltk'
        from='cellar@conf.merlix.dyndns.org/flash'
        type='chat'>
      <body>Is that you, qmacro?</body>
      <thread>jarl1998911094</thread>
      </message>
```

the user nicknamed `flash` actually addressed the chat message to the JID:

```
cellar@conf.merlix.dyndns.org/deejay
```

which arrived at the Conferencing component (because of the hostname, `conf.merlix.dyndns.org` causes the `<message&sol;>` element to be routed there), which then looked up internally who `deejay` really was (`qmacro@jabber.com/jarltk`) and sent it on. This way, the recipient of a conference-routed message never discovers the real JID of the sender. In all other ways, the actual `<message&sol;>` element is like any other `<message&sol;>` element—in this case, it contains a message `<body&sol;>` and a chat `<thread&sol;>`. (See the section "The Message Element" for details on the `<message&sol;>` element.)

Leaving the room

In the same way that room entrance is effected by sending an `available` presence (remember, a `<presence&sol;>` element without an explicit `type` attribute is understood to represent `type='available'`), leaving a room is achieved by doing the opposite:

```
RECV: <presence to='qmacro@jabber.com/jarltk' type='unavailable'
            from='cellar@conf.merlix.dyndns.org/roscoe'&sol;>
```

The people in the conference room are sent a message that `roscoe` has left the room by the `unavailable` presence packet. This is by and large for the benefit of each user's client, so that the room occupant list can be updated. The component also sends out a verbal notification, in the same way as it sends a verbal notification out when someone joins:

```
RECV: <message to='qmacro@jabber.com/jarltk' type='groupchat'
            from='cellar@conf.merlix.dyndns.org'>
        <body>roscoe has left</body>
      </message>
```

Like the join notification, the text for the leave notification ("has left") comes directly from the component instance configuration described in the section "Custom Configuration."

The Script's Scope

The Keyword Assistant (*keyassist*) script will be written in Python using the Jabberpy library. As mentioned earlier, the script will perform the following tasks:

- Connect to a predetermined Jabber server

- Join a predetermined conference room

- Sit there quietly, listening to the conversation

- Take simple commands from people to watch for, or stop watching for, particular words or phrases uttered in the room

- Relay the context of those words or phrases to whomever requested them, if heard

In addition to setting the identity of the Jabber server and the conference room in variables, we'll also need to keep track of which users ask the assistant for words and phrases. We'll use a *dictionary* (*hash* in Perl terms), as shown in Example 9-3, because we want to manage the data in there by key, the JID of those users that the script will be assisting. Having a look at what this dictionary will look like during the lifetime of this script will help us to visualize what we're trying to achieve.

Example 9-3. Typical contents of the Keyword Assistant's dictionary

```
{
    'dj@gnu.pipetree.com/home':          {
                                            'http:': 1,
                                            'ftp:': 1
                                         },

    'piers@jabber.org/work':             {
                                            'Perl': 1,
                                            'Java': 1,
                                            'SAP R/3': 1
                                         },

    'cellar@conf.merlix.dyndns.org/roscoe': {
                                            'dialback': 1
                                            }
}
```

We can see from the contents of the dictionary in Example 9-3 that three people have asked the script to look out for words and phrases. Two of those people—dj and piers—have interacted with the script directly by sending a *normal* (or chat) <message/>. The other person, with the conference nickname roscoe, is in the "cellar" room and has sent the script a message routed through the Conference component in the same way that flash sent qmacro a private message in Example 9-2: the JID of the sender belongs to (has the hostname set to) the conference component. Technically, there's nothing to distinguish the three JIDs here; it's just that we know from the name that `conf.merlix.dyndns.org` is the name that identi-fies such a component.

If we dissect the dictionary, we can see that:

- `dj` wants to be notified if any web or FTP URLs are mentioned.

- `piers` is interested in references to two of his favorite languages and his favorite business software solution.

- `roscoe` is interested in any talk about dialback.

We said we'd give the script a little bit of intelligence. This was a reference to the ability for users to interact with the script while it runs, rather than having to give the script a static list of words and phrases in a configuration file. `dj`, `piers`, and `roscoe` have done this by sending the script messages (directly, not within the room) with simple keyword commands, such as:

dj: "*watch http:*"
script: "*ok, watching for http:*"

dj: "*watch gopher:*"
script: "*ok, watching for gopher:*"

dj: "*watch ftp:*"
script: "*ok, watching for ftp:*"

dj: "*ignore gopher:*"
script: "*ok, now ignoring gopher:*"

. . .

piers: "*list*"
script: "*watching for: Perl, Java, SAP R/3*"

. . .

roscoe: "*stop*"
script: "*ok, I've stopped watching*"

The keyassist Script

Example 9-4 shows the *keyassist* script in its entirety. The script is described in detail, step by step, in the next section.

Example 9-4. The keyassist Perl script

```
import jabber
from string import split, join, find
import sys

keywords = {}
```

Example 9-4. The keyassist Perl script (continued)

```
def addword(jid, word):
    if not keywords.has_key(jid):
        keywords[jid] = {}
    keywords[jid][word] = 1

def delword(jid, word):
    if keywords.has_key(jid):
        if keywords[jid].has_key(word):
            del keywords[jid][word]

def messageCB(con, msg):

    type = msg.getType()
    if type == None:
        type = 'normal'

    # Deal with interaction
    if type == 'chat' or type == 'normal':
        jid = str(msg.getFrom())

        message = split(msg.getBody(), None, 1);
        reply = ""

        if message[0] == 'watch':
            addword(jid, message[1])
            reply = "Okay, watching for " + message[1]

        if message[0] == 'ignore':
            delword(jid, message[1])
            reply = "Okay, now ignoring " + message[1]

        if message[0] == 'list':
            if keywords.has_key(jid):
                reply = "Watching for: " + join(keywords[jid].keys(), ", ")
            else:
                reply = "Not watching for any keywords"

        if message[0] == 'stop':
            if keywords.has_key(jid):
                del keywords[jid]
                reply = "Okay, I've stopped watching"

        if reply:
            con.send(msg.build_reply(reply))


    # Scan room talk
    if type == 'groupchat':
        message = msg.getBody()

        for jid in keywords.keys():
            for word in keywords[jid].keys():
```

Example 9-4. The keyassist Perl script (continued)

```
                if find(message, word) >= 0:
                    con.send(jabber.Message(jid, word + ": " + message))


def presenceCB(con, prs):

    # Deal with nickname conflict in room
    if str(prs.getFrom()) == roomjid and prs.getType() == 'error':
        prsnode = prs.asNode()
        error = prsnode.getTag('error')
        if error:
          if (error.getAttr('code') == '409'):
                print "Cannot join room - conflicting nickname"
                con.disconnect()
                sys.exit(0)

    # Remove keyword list for groupchat correspondent
    if prs.getType() == 'unavailable':
        jid = str(prs.getFrom())
        if keywords.has_key(jid):
            del keywords[jid]
Server   = 'gnu.mine.nu'
Username = 'kassist'
Password = 'pass'
Resource = 'py'

Room     = 'jdev'
ConfServ = 'conference.jabber.org'
Nick     = 'kassist'

con = jabber.Client(host=Server)
try:
    con.connect()
except IOError, e:
    print "Couldn't connect: %s" % e
    sys.exit(0)
else:
    print "Connected"

if con.auth(Username,Password,Resource):
    print "Logged in as %s to server %s" % ( Username, Server )
else:
    print "Problems authenticating: ", con.lastErr, con.lastErrCode
    sys.exit(1)

con.setMessageHandler(messageCB)
con.setPresenceHandler(presenceCB)

con.send(jabber.Presence())

roomjid = Room + '@' + ConfServ + '/' + Nick
```

Example 9-4. The keyassist Perl script (continued)

```
print "Joining " + Room
con.send(jabber.Presence(to=roomjid))

while(1):
    con.process(5)
```

Dissecting the keyassist Script

Taking *keyassist* step by step, the first section is probably familiar if you've seen the previous Python-based scripts in the section "CVS Notification via Jabber" and the section "Presence-Sensitive CVS Notification," both in Chapter 8.

```
import jabber
from string import split, join, find
import sys
```

Here, all of the functions and libraries that we'll need are brought in. We'll use the find function from the **string** library to help with the keyword searching.

Next, we declare the dictionary. This will hold a list of the words that the script will look for, as defined by each person, as shown in Example 9-3.

```
keywords = {}
```

Maintaining the keyword dictionary

To maintain this dictionary, we will use two subroutines to add words to and remove words from a user's word list. These subroutines are called when a command such as *watch* or *ignore* is recognized in the callback subroutine that handles incoming <message/> elements:

```
def addword(jid, word):
    if not keywords.has_key(jid):
        keywords[jid] = {}
    keywords[jid][word] = 1

def delword(jid, word):
    if keywords.has_key(jid):
        if keywords[jid].has_key(word):
            del keywords[jid][word]
```

A string representation of the JID (in jid) of the correspondent giving the command is passed to the subroutines along with the word or phrase specified (in word) by the user. The dictionary has two levels: the first level is keyed by the JID, and the second by word or phrase. We use a dictionary, rather than an array, at the second level simply to make removal of words and phrases easier.

Message callback

Next, we define the callback to handle incoming <message/> elements:

```
def messageCB(con, msg):

    type = msg.getType()
    if type == None:
        type = 'normal'
```

As usual, we're expecting the message callback to be passed the connection object (in con) and the message object itself (msg). How this callback is to proceed is determined by the *type* of message received. We determine the type (taken from the <message/> element's type attribute) and store it in the variable called type. Remember that if no type attribute is present, a message type of normal is assumed. (See the section "Message attributes" for details of <message/> attributes.)

The two types of incoming messages we're expecting this script to receive are those conveying the room's conversation—in groupchat-type messages—and those over which the commands such as *watch* and *ignore* are carried, which we expect in the form of normal- or chat-type messages.

The first main section of the messageCB handler deals with incoming commands:

```
# Deal with interaction
if type == 'chat' or type == 'normal':
    jid = str(msg.getFrom())

    message = split(msg.getBody(), None, 1);
    reply = ""

    if message[0] == 'watch':
        addword(jid, message[1])
        reply = "Okay, watching for " + message[1]

    if message[0] == 'ignore':
        delword(jid, message[1])
        reply = "Okay, now ignoring " + message[1]

    if message[0] == 'list':
        if keywords.has_key(jid):
            reply = "Watching for: " + join(keywords[jid].keys(), ", ")
        else:
            reply = "Not watching for any keywords"

    if message[0] == 'stop':
        if keywords.has_key(jid):
            del keywords[jid]
            reply = "Okay, I've stopped watching"

    if reply:
```

```
con.send(msg.build_reply(reply))
```

If the <message/> element turns out to be of the type in which we're expecting a potential command, we want to determine the JID of the correspondent who sent that message. Calling the getFrom() method will return us a JID object. What we need is the string representation of that, which can be determined by calling the str() function on that JID object:

```
jid = str(msg.getFrom())
```

Then we grab the content of the message by calling the getBody() on the msg object and split the whole thing on the first bit of whitespace. This should be enough for us to distinguish a command (*watch*, *ignore*, and so on) from the keywords. After the split, the first element (index 0) in the message array will be the command, and the second element (index 1) will be the word or phrase, if given. At this stage, we also declare an empty reply:

```
message = split(msg.getBody(), None, 1);
reply = ""
```

Now it's time to determine if what the script was sent made sense as a command:

```
if message[0] == 'watch':
    addword(jid, message[1])
    reply = "Okay, watching for " + message[1]

if message[0] == 'ignore':
    delword(jid, message[1])
    reply = "Okay, now ignoring " + message[1]

if message[0] == 'list':
    if keywords.has_key(jid):
        reply = "Watching for: " + join(keywords[jid].keys(), ", ")
    else:
        reply = "Not watching for any keywords"

if message[0] == 'stop':
    if keywords.has_key(jid):
        del keywords[jid]
        reply = "Okay, I've stopped watching"
```

We go through a series of checks, taking appropriate action for the supported commands:

watch
     Watch for a particular word or phrase.

ignore

Stop watching for a particular word or phrase.

list List the words and phrases currently being watched.

stop

Stop watching altogether; remove the list of words and phrases.

The addword() and delword() functions defined earlier are used here, as well as other simpler functions; one that lists the words and phrases for a particular JID:

```
keywords[jid].keys()
```

and one that removes them:

```
del keywords[jid]
```

If there was something recognizable for the script to do, we get it to reply appropriately:

```
if reply:
    con.send(msg.build_reply(reply))
```

The build_reply() function creates a reply out of a message object by setting to to the value of the original <message/> element's from attribute and preserving the element type attribute and <thread/> tag, if present. The <body/> of the reply object (which is just a <message/> element) is set to whatever is passed in the function call; in this case, it's the text in the reply variable.

Now that we've dealt with incoming commands, we need another section in the message callback subroutine to scan for the words and phrases. The target texts for this scanning will be the snippets of room conversation, which arrive at the callback in the form of groupchat-type <message/> elements:

```
# scan room talk
if type == 'groupchat':
    message = msg.getBody()
```

The message variable holds the string we need to scan; it's just a case of checking for each of the words or phrases on behalf of each of the users who have asked:

```
for jid in keywords.keys():
    for word in keywords[jid].keys():
        if find(message, word) >= 0:
            con.send(jabber.Message(jid, word + ": " + message))
```

If we get a hit, we construct a new Message object, passing the JID of the person for whom the string has matched (in the jid variable) and the notification, consisting of the word or phrase that was found (in word) and the context in which it was found (the sentence uttered, in message). Once found and constructed, the <message/> is sent to that user. By default, the Message constructor specifies no type attribute, so the user is sent a "normal" message.

Presence callback

Having dealt with the incoming <message/> elements, we turn to the <presence/> elements. Most of those we receive in this conference room will be notifications from people entering and leaving the room, as shown in Example 9-2. We want to perform housekeeping on our keywords dictionary so the entries don't become stale. We also want to deal with the potential problem of conflicting nicknames. Let's look at that first.

We want to check for the possibility of nickname conflict problems that may occur when we enter the room, and the chosen nickname (flash) is already taken.

Remembering that a conflict notification will look something like this:

```
<presence to='qmacro@jabber.com/jarltk'
          from='cellar@conf.merlix.dyndns.org/flash'
          type='error'>
  <error code='409'>Conflict</error>
</presence>
```

we test for the receipt of a <presence/> element with the following:

```
def presenceCB(con, prs):

    # Deal with nickname conflict in room
    if str(prs.getFrom()) == roomjid and prs.getType() == 'error':
        prsnode = prs.asNode()
        error = prsnode.getTag('error')
        if error:
          if (error.getAttr('code') == '409'):
              print "Cannot join room - conflicting nickname"
              con.disconnect()
              sys.exit(0)
```

The <presence/> element will appear to be sent from the JID that we constructed for the initial room entry negotiation (in the roomjid variable further down in the script); for example:

```
jdev@conference.jabber.org/kassist
```

We compare this value to the value of the incoming <presence/>'s from attribute, and also make sure that the type attribute is set to error. If it is, we want to extract the details from the <error/> tag that will be contained as a direct child of the <presence/>.

The Jabberpy library currently doesn't offer a direct high-level function to get at this tag from the Presence object (in prs), but we can strip away the presence object "mantle" and get at the underlying object, which is a neutral "node"—a Jabber element, or XML fragment, without any preconceived ideas of what it is (and therefore without any accompanying high-level methods such as getBody() or setPriority()).

 If this seems a little cryptic, just think of it like this: each of the Presence, Message, and IQ classes are merely superclasses of the base class Protocol, which represents elements generically.

The asNode() method gives us what we need—a Protocol object representation of the <presence/> element. From this we can get to the <error/> tag and its contents. If we find that we do have a nickname conflict, we abort by disconnecting from the Jabber server and ending the script.

The general idea is that this script will run indefinitely and notify the users on a continuous basis, so we need to do a spot of keyword housekeeping. No presence subscription relationships are built (mostly to keep the script small and simple; you could adapt the mechanism from the recipe in the section "Presence-Sensitive CVS Notification" if you wanted to make this script sensitive to presence), so notifications will get queued up for the user if he is offline with the use of the *mod_offline* module of the Jabber Session Manager (JSM). This makes a lot of sense for the most part; however, we still want to have the script send notifications even if the user is offline. Additionally, a command could be sent to the script to watch for a keyword or phrase from a user within the room. We would receive the command from a JID like this:

```
jdev@conference.jabber.org/nickname
```

This is a *transient JID*, in that it represents a user's presence in the *jdev* room for a particular session. If a word is spotted by the script hours or days later, there's a good chance that the user has left the room, making the JID invalid as a recipient. Although the JID is *technically* valid and will reach the conferencing component, there will be no real user JID that it is paired up with. Potentially worse, the room occupant's identity JID may be assigned to someone else at a later stage, if the original user left, and a new user entered choosing the same nickname the original user had chosen. See the upcoming sidebar titled "Transient and Nonexistent JIDs" for a short discussion of the difference between a transient JID and a nonexistent JID.

So as soon as we notice a user leave the room we're in, which will be indicated through a <presence/> element conveying that occupant's *unavailability*, we should remove any watched-for words and phrases from the dictionary:

```
# Remove keyword list for groupchat correspondent
if prs.getType() == 'unavailable':
    jid = str(prs.getFrom())
    if keywords.has_key(jid):
        del keywords[jid]
```

As before, we obtain the string representation of the JID using the `str()` function
on the JID object that represents the presence element's sender, obtained via the
`getFrom()` method.

The main script

Now that we have the subroutines and callbacks set up, all we need to do is
define the Jabber server and room information:

```
Server   = 'gnu.mine.nu'
Username = 'kassist'
Password = 'pass'
Resource = 'py'

Room     = 'jdev'
ConfServ = 'conference.jabber.org'
Nick     = 'kassist'
```

The `kassist` user can be set up simply by using the *reguser* script presented in the
section "User Registration Script":

```
$ ./reguser gnu.mine.nu username=kassist password=pass
[Attempt] (kassist) Successful registration
$
```

In the same way as in previous recipes' scripts, a connection attempt is made, followed by an authentication attempt:

```
con = jabber.Client(host=Server,debug=0,log=0)
try:
    con.connect()
except IOError, e:
    print "Couldn't connect: %s" % e
    sys.exit(0)
else:
    print "Connected"

if con.auth(Username,Password,Resource):
    print "Logged in as %s to server %s" % ( Username, Server )
else:
    print "Problems authenticating: ", con.lastErr, con.lastErrCode
    sys.exit(1)
```

Then the message and presence callbacks `messageCB()` and `presenceCB()` are
defined to the connection object in con:

Transient and Nonexistent JIDs

What happens when you send a message to a "transient" conference room JID? Superficially, the same as when you send one to a *nonexistent* JID. But there are some subtle differences.

A *transient JID* is one that reflects a user's alternate identity in the context of the Conferencing component. When you construct and send a message to a conference transient JID, it goes first to the conference component because of the hostname in the JID that identifies that component, for example:

```
jdev@conference.jabber.org/qmacro
```

The hostname `conference.jabber.org` is what the *jabberd* backbone uses to route the element. As mentioned earlier, the Conferencing component will relay a message to the real JID that belongs to the user currently in a room hosted by that component.

While the component itself is usually persistent, the room occupants (and so their transient JIDs) are not. When a message is sent to the JID `jdev@conference.jabber.org/qmacro` and there is no room occupant in the *jdev* room with the nickname `qmacro`, the message will still reach its *first* destination—the component—but be rejected at that stage, as shown in Example 9-5.

Example 9-5. A message to a nonexistent transient JID is rejected

```
SEND: <message to='jdev@conference.jabber.org/qmacro'>
        <body>Hello there</body>
      </message>

RECV: <message to='dj@gnu.mine.nu/jarl'
              from='jdev@conference.jabber.org/qmacro' type='error'>
        <body>Hello there</body>
        <error code='404'>Not Found</error>
      </message>
```

Although the rejection—the "Not Found" error—is the same as if a message had been sent to a JSM user that didn't exist, the difference is that the transient user always had the *potential* to exist, whereas the JSM user never did. Of course, if the JID referred to a nonexistent Jabber server, then the error returned wouldn't be a "Not Found" error 404, but an "Unable to resolve hostname" error 502.

```
con.setMessageHandler(messageCB)
con.setPresenceHandler(presenceCB)
```

After sending initial presence, informing the JSM (and anyone who might be subscribed to `kassist`'s presence) of the assistant's availability:

```
con.send(jabber.Presence())
```

we also construct—from the `Room`, `ConfServ`, and `Nick` variables—and send the `<presence&sol;>` element for negotiating entry to the *jdev* room hosted by the Conferencing component at `conference.jabber.org`:

```
roomjid = Room + '@' + ConfServ + '/' + Nick
print "Joining " + Room
con.send(jabber.Presence(to=roomjid))
```

The `con.send()` function will send a `<presence&sol;>` element that looks like this:

```
SEND: <presence to='jdev@conference.jabber.org/kassist'&sol;>
```

We're sending available presence to the room, to negotiate entry, but what about the initial presence? Why do we send that too if there are no users who will be subscribed to the `kassist` JID? If no initial presence is sent, the JSM will merely store up any `<message&sol;>` elements destined for `kassist`, as it will think the JID is offline.

The processing loop

Once everything has been set up, we simply need to have the script sit back and wait for incoming packets and handle them appropriately. For this, we simply call the `process()` function every 5 seconds to look for elements arriving on the XML stream:

```
while(1):
    con.process(5)
```

Connecting Devices to Jabber

LEGO MINDSTORMS. What a great reason to dig out that box of LEGO bricks you haven't touched in years. When I found out that LEGO was bringing out a programmable brick, the RCX,* , I went to my favorite toy shop and purchased the set. In addition to the RCX (shown in Figure 9-1), the MINDSTORMS set comes with an infrared (IR) port and an IR tower, which you can connect to the serial port of your PC, a battery compartment,† motors, touch and light sensors, and various LEGO Technic parts.

There are plenty of ways to interact with the RCX. The MINDSTORMS Robotics Invention System (RIS)™ set comes with Windows software with which you can build programs by moving blocks of logic around graphically on the screen and

---

* Contrary to popular belief, "RCX" stands for "Robotic Command Explorer," according to LEGO's official MINDSTORMS page.

† There's also a DC power socket for those of us without rechargeable batteries.

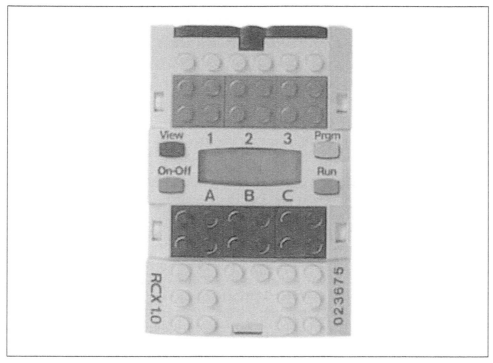

Figure 9-1. The LEGO MINDSTORMS RCX, or "programmable brick"

chaining them together. In addition, various efforts on the parts of talented individuals have come up with many different ways to program the RCX. *The Unofficial Guide to LEGO® MINDSTORMS™ Robots* (O'Reilly & Associates, Inc., 1999) tells you all you need to know about programing the RCX. What's important to know for this recipe is detailed in the sidebar titled "Programming the RCX."

What We're Going to Do

Everyone knows that one of the virtues of a programmer is *laziness*. We're going to extend this virtue (perhaps a little too far) and enhance it with a hacker's innate ability to combine two favorite pastimes—programming and playing with LEGO— to build contrived but fun devices.

Often being a key part of a programmer's intake, coffee figures highly on the daily agenda. It's important to have a good cup of coffee to keep the brain cells firing, but it's even more important to know whether there's actually any coffee left in the pot. Going over to the coffeepot to find out is time away from the keyboard and therefore time wasted. So let's put the RCX to good use and build a device to tell us, via Jabber, whether the coffeepot has enough for another cup.

Programming the RCX

There are two approaches to programming the RCX. One approach is to write a program on your PC, download it to the RCX, and start and stop the program using the buttons on the RCX itself.

The other approach is to control the RCX directly from a program that you write *and* execute on your PC, sending control signals and receiving sensor values over the IR connection.

Both approaches have their merits. How appropriate each one is boils down to one thing: connections. On the one hand, building autonomous machines that find their way around the kitchen to scare the cat and bring you a sandwich calls for the first approach, when, once you've downloaded the program to the RCX, you can dispense with any further connection with your PC because the entire logic is situated in your creation. On the other hand, if you want to build a physical extension to a larger system that, for example, has a connection to the Internet, the second approach is likely to be more fruitful, because you can essentially use the program that runs on your PC and talks to the RCX over the IR link as a conduit, a proxy of sorts, to other programs and systems that can be reached over the network. We're going to use the second approach.

The RIS software that comes as standard centers around an ActiveX control. While there are plenty of ways to talk to the RCX without using this control (the book mentioned earlier describes many of these ways), the features offered by the control—`Spirit.ocx`—are fine for many a project. And with Perl's `Win32::OLE` module, we can interact with this ActiveX control without having to resort to Visual Basic.

In building the device, a light sensor was connected to the RCX to "see" the level of coffee in the pot. Since the coffeepot is made of glass, light passes through it unless the coffee gets in the way, thus creating a simple binary switch:

- No (or a small amount of) light measured: there's coffee in the pot.
- Some (or a larger amount of) light: there's no coffee in the pot.

We want to be able to send the availability of coffee to all interested parties in a way that their off-the-shelf Jabber clients can easily understand and display.

Figure 9-2 shows the LEGO MINDSTORMS device in action. The brick mounted on the gantry is the light sensor, which extends to the glass coffeepot; a wire runs from it to the connector on the RCX. Behind the RCX is the IR tower, which is connected to the PC.

Figure 9-2. Our device "looking" at the coffeepot

Remembering that `<presence&sol;>` elements are a simple way of broadcasting information about availability *and* that they contain a `<status&sol;>` tag to describe the detail or context of that availability (see the section "The Presence Element" for details on the `<presence&sol;>` element), we have a perfect mechanism that's ready to be used. What's more, most, if not all, of the off-the-shelf Jabber client implementations will display the content of the `<status&sol;>` tag in the client user's roster next to the JID to which it applies. Figure 9-3 shows how the content of the `<status&sol;>` tag is displayed as a hovering "tooltip" in WinJab.

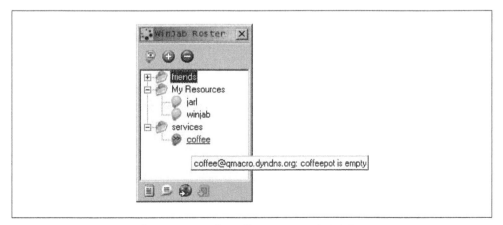

Figure 9-3. Receiving information on the coffee's status in WinJab

Here's what we need to do:

Step 1: Set up the RCX

We need to set the RCX up, with the light sensor, so that it's close enough to the coffeepot to take reliable and consistent light readings. Luckily the serial cable that comes with the MINDSTORMS set and connects to the IR tower is long enough to stretch from the computer to within the infrared line of sight to the RCX.

Step 2: Make the correct calibrations

There are bound to be differences in ambient light, sensitivity of the light sensor, and how strong you make your coffee. So we need a way of calibrating the setup, so that we can find the appropriate "pivot point" light reading value that lies between the two states of *coffee* and *no coffee*.

Step 3: Set up a connection to Jabber

We need a connection to a Jabber server and a client account there. We can set one up using the *reguser* script from the section "User Registration Script." We also need the script to honor presence from users who want to be informed of the coffee state.

Step 4: Set up a sensor poll/presence push loop

Once the RCX has been set up, the sensor calibrations taken, and the connection has been made, we need to monitor the light sensor on the RCX at regular intervals. At each interval, we determine the coffee state by comparing the value received from the sensor with the pivot point determined in the calibration step and send any change in that state as a new availability <presence/> element containing an appropriate description in the <status/> tag.

The Coffee Script

We're going to use Perl and the `Net::Jabber` libraries to build the script shown in Example 9-6. Perl allows us a comfortable way to interact with an ActiveX control, through the `Win32::OLE` module, so let's have a look at the *coffee* script as a whole, then we'll go back and look at the script in detail.

Example 9-6. The coffee script, written in Perl

```
use Net::Jabber qw(Client);
use Win32::OLE;
use Getopt::Std;
use strict;

my %opts;
getopt('ls', \%opts);

use constant SERVER   => "merlix.dyndns.org";
```

Example 9-6. The coffee script, written in Perl (continued)

```perl
use constant PORT     => 5222;
use constant USERNAME => "coffee";
use constant PASSWORD => "pass";
use constant RESOURCE => "perlscript";

use constant NOCOFFEE => 0;
use constant COFFEE   => 1;

use constant SENSOR   => defined($opts{'s'}) ? $opts{'s'} : 0;
use constant GRAIN    => 1;

my $current_status = -1;
my @status;
$status[NOCOFFEE] = 'xa/Coffeepot is empty';
$status[COFFEE]   = '/Coffee is available!';

my $rcx = &setup_RCX(SENSOR);

# Either calibrate if no parameters given, or
# run with the parameter given as -l, which will
# be taken as the pivot between coffee and no coffee
&calibrate($rcx) unless defined($opts{'l'});

# Determine initial status (will be either 0 or 1)
my $s = &set_status($rcx->Poll(9, SENSOR));

my $jabber = &setup_Jabber(SERVER, PORT, USERNAME, PASSWORD, RESOURCE, $s);

# Main loop: check Jabber and RCX
while (1) {
  defined($jabber->Process(GRAIN)) or
    die "The connection to the Jabber server was broken\n";
  my $s = &set_status($rcx->Poll(9, SENSOR));
  &set_presence($jabber, $s) if defined $s;
}


# Set up Jabber client connection, sending initial presence
sub setup_Jabber {
  my ($server, $port, $user, $pass, $resource, $initial_status) = @_;
  my $connection = new Net::Jabber::Client;

  # Connect
  my $status = $connection->Connect( hostname => $server,
                                     port     => $port );
  die "Cannot connect to Jabber server $server on port $port\n"
    unless $status;

  # Callbacks
  $connection->SetCallBacks( presence => \&InPresence );

  # Ident/Auth
```

Example 9-6. The coffee script, written in Perl (continued)

```perl
  my @result = $connection->AuthSend( username => $user,
                                      password => $pass,
                                      resource => $resource );
die "Ident/Auth failed: $result[0] - $result[1]\n"
  if $result[0] ne "ok";

# Roster
$connection->RosterGet();

# Initial presence dependent upon initial status
&set_presence($connection, $initial_status);

return $connection;
}


sub set_presence {
  my ($connection, $s) = @_;
  my $presence = Net::Jabber::Presence->new();
  my ($show, $status) = split("/", $status[$s], 2);
  $presence->SetPresence( show   => $show,
                          status => $status );
  print $status, "\n";
  $connection->Send($presence);
}


# Handle presence messages
sub InPresence
{
  my $presence = $_[1];
  my $from = $presence->GetFrom();
  my $type = $presence->GetType();

  if ($type eq "subscribe") {
    print "Subscribe request ($from) ...\n";
    $jabber->Send($presence->Reply(type => 'subscribed'));
  }

  if ($type eq "unsubscribe") {
    print "Unsubscribe request ($from) ...\n";
    $jabber->Send($presence->Reply(type => 'unsubscribed'));
  }
}


sub setup_RCX {
  my $sensor = shift;
  my $rcx = Win32::OLE->new('SPIRIT.SpiritCtrl.1');
  $Win32::OLE::Warn = 0;
  $rcx->{ComPortNo} = 1;
  $rcx->{InitComm};
```

Example 9-6. The coffee script, written in Perl (continued)

```
  $rcx->SetSensorType($sensor, 3);
  $rcx->SetSensorMode($sensor, 2);
  return $rcx;
}


sub calibrate {
  my $rcx = shift;

  print <<EOT;
Calibration mode.
Note the sensor values and decide on a 'pivot' value
above which 'no coffee' is signified and below which
'coffee' is signified.

End the calibration mode with Ctrl-C.

Press Enter to start calibration...
EOT

  <STDIN>;

  while (1) {
    print $rcx->Poll(9, SENSOR), " ";
    sleep 1;
  }

}


sub set_status {
  my $val = shift;

  my $new_status = $val < $opts{'l'} ? COFFEE : NOCOFFEE;

  if ($new_status != $current_status) {
    $current_status = $new_status;
    return $current_status;
  }
  else {
    return undef;
  }
}
```

Examining the Coffee Script Step by Step

Now that we've seen the *coffee* script as a whole, let's examine it step by step to see how it works.

Declaring the modules, constants, and variables

We first declare the packages we're going to use. In addition to Net::Jabber and Win32::OLE, we're going to use Getopt::Std, which affords us a comfortable way of accepting and parsing command-line options. We also want to use the strict pragma, which should keep us from making silly coding mistakes by not allowing undeclared variables and the like.

We specify Client on the usage declaration for the Net::Jabber package to specify what should be loaded. The package is a large and comprehensive set of modules, and only some of those are relevant for what we wish to do in the script—build and work with a Jabber *client* connection. Other module sets are pulled in by specifying Component or Server.

```perl
use Net::Jabber qw(Client);
use Win32::OLE;
use Getopt::Std;
use strict;
```

We're going to allow the command-line options *-l* and *-s*, which perform the following tasks:

No options specified (or just the -s options): calibration mode.
When we run the script for the first time, we need to perform the calibration and read values from the sensor to determine a midpoint value. A number above the midpoint signifies the presence of light and therefore the absence of coffee; below signifies the absence of light and therefore the presence of coffee. This step is necessary because not every environment (ambient light, sensitivity of the light sensor, and so on) will be the same. The upper and lower values, representing lightness and darkness, respectively, will vary across different environments. The point is to obtain a value in between these upper and lower values—the midpoint—with which we can compare a light value read at any particular time.

If we don't specify any options, the script will start up automatically in calibration mode:

```
C:\temp> perl coffee.pl
```

Figure 9-4 shows the script run in calibration mode. The values displayed, one each second, represent the values read from the light sensor. When the sensor was picking up lots of light, the values were 60. When the sensor was moved in front of some coffee, the values went down to around 45. Based upon this small test, the pivot point value was 50, somewhere in between those two values.

-l: Specify the pivot value.

Once we've determined a pivot point value, we run the script and tell it this pivot value with the *-l* (light pivot):

```
C:\temp> perl coffee.pl -l 50
```

-s: Specify the sensor number.

The RCX, shown in Figure 9-1, has three connectors to which you can attach sensors. They're the three gray 2-by-2 pieces, labeled 1, 2, and 3, near the top of the brick. The script assumes you've attached the light sensor to the one marked 1, which internally is 0. If you attach it to either of the other two, you can specify the connector using the *-s* (sensor) with a value of 1 (for the middle connector) or 2 (for the rightmost connector), like this:

```
C:\temp> perl coffee.pl -l 50 -s 2
```

You can specify the *-s* option when running in calibration or normal modes.

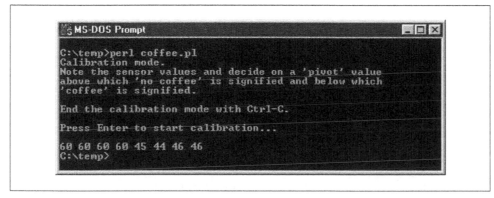

Figure 9-4. Running coffee in calibration mode

The options, summarized in Table 9-1, are defined with the Getopt::Std function:

```
my %opts;
getopt('ls', \%opts);
```

Table 9-1. Summary of the startup options

Option	Meaning
No option	Start the script automatically in calibration mode.
-l	Specify the pivot value.
-s	Specify the sensor number.

Next comes a list of constants, which describe:

- The script's Jabber relationship, including the server it will connect to and the username, password, and resource it will connect with.

- The representation of the two states of *coffee* and *no coffee*, which will be used to determine the content of the <status/> tag sent along inside any <presence/> element emitted.

- The identification of the connector to which the light sensor is attached and the polling granularity of the sensor (poll/presence push loop) described earlier. This item is measured in seconds.

```
use constant SERVER   => "merlix.dyndns.org";
use constant PORT      => 5222;
use constant USERNAME => "coffee";
use constant PASSWORD => "pass";
use constant RESOURCE => "perlscript";

use constant NOCOFFEE => 0;
use constant COFFEE   => 1;

use constant SENSOR   => defined($opts{'s'}) ? $opts{'s'} : 0;
use constant GRAIN    => 1;
```

The last part of the script's setup deals with the coffee state:

```
my $current_status = -1;
my @status;
$status[NOCOFFEE] = 'xa/Coffeepot is empty';
$status[COFFEE]   = '/Coffee is available!';
```

We use a two-element array (@status) to represent the two possible coffee states. The value of each array element is a two-part string, with each part separated by a slash (/). Each of these parts will be transmitted in a <presence/> element, with the first part (which is empty in the element representing the COFFEE state) representing the presence <show/> value and the second part representing the presence <status/> value. Example 9-7 shows what a <presence/> element looks like when built up with values to represent the NOCOFFEE state.

Example 9-7. A presence element representing the NOCOFFEE state

```
<presence>
  <show>xa</show>
  <status>Coffeepot is empty</status>
</presence>
```

Most Jabber clients use different icons in the roster to represent different <show/> values. In this case, we will use xa for *no coffee* and a blank (which represents "online" or "available") for *coffee* to trigger the icon change.

Initialization and calibration

Whenever we need to talk to the RCX, some initialization is required via the ActiveX control. That's the same whether we're going to calibrate or poll for values. The setup_RCX() function takes a single argument—the identification of which connector the light sensor is connected to—and performs the initialization, which is described later in the section "The setup_RCX() function." The function returns a handle on the Win32::OLE object that represents the ActiveX control, which in turn represents the RCX via the IR tower:

```
my $rcx = &setup_RCX(SENSOR);
```

If the *-l* option is not specified, it means we're going to be running calibration. So we call the calibrate() function to do this for us. We pass the RCX handle (in $rcx) so the calibration can run properly:

```
# Either calibrate if no parameters given, or
# run with the parameter given as -1, which will
# be taken as the pivot between coffee and no coffee
&calibrate($rcx) unless defined($opts{'l'});
```

As with the setup_RCX() function, calibrate() is described later.

Calibration mode will be terminated by ending the script with **Ctrl-C**, so the next thing we come across is the call to the function set_status(), which represents the first stage in the normal script mode; set_status() is used to determine the *initial* coffee status.

A value is retrieved by calling the ActiveX control's Poll() function. (Table 9-2 lists the ActiveX control's functions and properties used in this script.) We specify that we're after a sensor value (the 9 as the first argument) from the sensor attached to the connector indicated by the SENSOR constant:

```
# Determine initial status (will be either 0 or 1)
my $s = &set_status($rcx->Poll(9, SENSOR));
```

The value retrieved is passed to the set_status() function, which determines whether the value is above or below the pivot value and whether the new status is different from the current one. It's going to be something along the lines of one of the values displayed when the script was run in calibration mode. If it is (and in this case, it will be, because in this first call, the value of $current_status is set to -1, which represents neither the COFFEE nor the NOCOFFEE state), that status will be returned; otherwise, undef will be returned.

Table 9-2. RCX Spirit.ocx ActiveX control properties and functions used

Function/Property	Description
Poll(*SOURCE*, *NUMBER*)	Retrieves information from the RCX. In this script, the value for the *SOURCE* argument is always 9, which represents a sensor value (i.e., a value measured at a sensor), as opposed to an internal RCX variable or a timer. The *NUMBER* argument represents the connector to which the sensor we want to read is attached.
SetSensorMode(*NUMBER*, *MODE* [, *SLOPE*])	This function returns a value from the sensor. As with Poll() and SetSensorType(), *NUMBER* represents the sensor connector. The *MODE* argument can be used to determine the sensor mode, which can be *Raw* (mode 0), *Boolean* (mode 1), *Transitional* (mode 2), *Periodic* (mode 3), *Percentage* (mode 4), *Celcius* (mode 5), *Farenheit* (mode 6), or *Angle* (mode 7). The *SLOPE* argument qualifies the *Boolean* mode by specifying how *True* and *False* are to be determined.
SetSensorType(*NUMBER*, *TYPE*)	This function is used to specify the *type* of sensor the values will be read from. The *NUMBER* argument is the same as for the Poll() and represents the sensor connector. The *TYPE* argument represents the type of sensor that you want to set: *None* (type 0), *Switch* (type 1), *Temperature* (type 2), *Light* (type 3), or *Angle* (type 4).
property:ComPortNo	The serial port to which the IR tower is connected (e.g., 1 = COM1, 2 = COM2, and so on).
property:InitComm	When invoked, the serial communication port is initialized in preparation for the IR connection to the RCX.

Connecting to the Jabber server

At this stage, we're ready to connect to the Jabber server. The call to setup_Jabber() does this for us, returning a handle to the Jabber connection object that we store in $jabber. This handle will be used later in the script to send out <presence/> elements. The $jabber variable contains a reference to a Net::Jabber::Client object. This is the equivalent of the con variable used in the earlier Python scripts to hold the jabber.Client object and the ConnectionBean object (cb) in the earlier Java script.*

---

* For the Python scripts, see the section "CVS Notification via Jabber" and the section "Presence-Sensitive CVS Notification." For the Java script, see the section "Dialup System Watch."

```
my $jabber = &setup_Jabber(SERVER, PORT, USERNAME, PASSWORD, RESOURCE, $s);
```

In addition to passing the constants needed for the client connection to the Jabber server, we pass the initial coffee status, held in $s. We'll have a look at what the setup_Jabber() function does with this initial status a bit later when we get to the function's definition.

Sensor poll/presence push loop

Now that we've set everything up, determined the initial coffee status, and connected to the Jabber server, we're ready to start the main loop:

```
# Main loop: check Jabber and RCX
while (1) {
  defined($jabber->Process(GRAIN)) or
    die "The connection to the Jabber server was broken\n";
  my $s = &set_status($rcx->Poll(9, SENSOR));
  &set_presence($jabber, $s) if defined $s;
}
```

The while (1) loop is a bit of a giveaway. This script won't stop until you force it to by entering **Ctrl-C**—but that's essentially what we want. In the loop, we call the Process() method on the Jabber connection object in $jabber.

Process() is the equivalent of the Jabberpy's process() method in the Python scripts. Process() waits around for up to the number of seconds specified as the single argument (or not at all if no argument is specified) for XML to appear on the stream connection from the Jabber server. If complete fragments do appear, callbacks, defined in the connection object, are called with the elements (<iq/>, <message/>, and <presence/>) that the fragments represent. This is in the same way as, for example, callbacks are used in the Python scripts using the Jabberpy library. The setup_Jabber(), which will be discussed in the next section, is where the callback definition is made.

Net::Jabber's Process() method returns undef if the connection to the Jabber server is terminated while waiting for XML. The undef value is dealt with appropriately by ending the script.

The GRAIN constant, set to 1 second in the script's setup section, is used to specify how long to wait for any packets from the Jabber server. For the most part, we're not expecting to receive much incoming Jabber traffic—the occasional presence subscription (or unsubscription) request perhaps (see later), but other than that, the only packets traveling over the connection to the Jabber server will be availability <presence/> packets representing coffee state changes, sent from the script. This delay is normally set to 1 second. And because that's a comfortable polling interval for the light sensor, we can set that within the same loop.

Calling the ActiveX control's `Poll()` again with the same arguments as before ("get a sensor value from the sensor attached to the `SENSOR`th connector"), we pass the value to the `set_status()` to determine the coffee state. If the state was different from last time (if `$s` receives a value and not `undef`), then we want to emit a `<presence&sol;>` element to reflect that state. We achieve this by calling the `set_presence()` function, passing it the connection object and the state.

The setup_Jabber() function

Here we define the `setup_Jabber()` function, which is called to set up the connection to the Jabber server and authenticate with a predefined user:

```
# Set up Jabber client connection, sending intial presence
sub setup_Jabber {
    my ($server, $port, $user, $pass, $resource, $initial_status) = @_;
    my $connection = new Net::Jabber::Client;

    # Connect
    my $status = $connection->Connect( hostname => $server,
                                       port     => $port );
    die "Cannot connect to Jabber server $server on port $port\n"
      unless $status;

    # Callbacks
    $connection->SetCallBacks( presence => \&InPresence );

    # Ident/Auth
    my @result = $connection->AuthSend( username => $user,
                                        password => $pass,
                                        resource => $resource );
    die "Ident/Auth failed: $result[0] - $result[1]\n"
      if $result[0] ne "ok";

    # Roster
    $connection->RosterGet();

    # Initial presence dependent upon initial status
    &set_presence($connection, $initial_status);

    return $connection;
}
```

First, we instantiate a new `Net::Jabber::Client` object. `Net::Jabber` distinguishes between client- and component-based connections to Jabber; the component-based equivalent of this class is `Net::Jabber::Component`. The `Connect()` method is passed arguments that specify the hostname and port of the Jabber server to connect to. It returns a 0 status if the connection could not be made.

We can register handlers for Jabber elements received over the XML stream carried by the connection we just made. Here we are interested in incoming presence subscription or unsubscription requests, as we'll see in the definition of the `InPresence()` function.

The single method, `SetCallBacks()`, does what the collective `jabber.Client` methods `setPresenceHandler()`, `setMessageHandler()`, and `setIqHandler()` do in a single call—taking a list of element types and subroutine references, in the form of a hash.

After registering the callback for `<presence&sol;>` elements, it's time to authenticate, passing the username, password, and resource defined in the list of constants at the start of the script. If authentication is successful, the result of the call to the `AuthSend()` method is a single string with the value `ok`. If not, that value is replaced with an error code and the descriptive text is available in a further string. (This is why we catch the results of a call in an array, called `@result`.) A complete list of Jabber error codes and texts can be found in Table 5-3.

Why `RosterGet()`? We're not subscribing to anyone, and we're not really interested in anything but the values we're polling from our brick. So theoretically there's no reason to make a request to retrieve our roster from the server. However, because we want the script to receive and process subscription and unsubscription requests, we need to request the roster beforehand; otherwise, the JSM won't send such requests to us. See the section "Request for roster" in Chapter 8 for an explanation as to why.

Once we've requested the roster, so as to receive presence subscription and unsubscription requests, the job is almost done. The last thing to do in setting up the Jabber connection is to send initial availability information. The `setup_Jabber()` function receives the initial coffee status as the last argument in the call (in `$initial_status`), which it passes on to the function that sends a `<presence&sol;>` element, `set_presence()`. Along with the initial coffee status, we also send the `$connection` object that represents the connection to the Jabber server that we've just established (referred to outside of this function with the `$jabber` variable). This is so the `set_presence()` function can use the connection handle to send the element down the stream.

The set_presence() function

This function is used by `setup_Jabber()` to send the script's (and therefore the coffee's) initial presence. It's also used within the main sensor poll/presence push loop to send further presence packets if the coffee's state changes.

```
sub set_presence {
  my ($connection, $s) = @_;
  my $presence = Net::Jabber::Presence->new();
  my ($show, $status) = split("/", $status[$s], 2);
  $presence->SetPresence( show    => $show,
```

```
                            status => $status );
    print $status, "\n";
    $connection->Send($presence);
}
```

On receipt of the Jabber connection object and the coffee status, which will be 0
(NOCOFFEE) or 1 (COFFEE), set_presence() constructs a new Net::Jabber::Presence
object. This object represents a <presence/> element, upon which we can
make method calls to hone the element as we wish. SetPresence() is one of these
methods, with which we can set values for each of the <show/> and <sta-
tus/> tags. We retrieve the values for each of these tags by pulling the strings
from the appropriate member of the @status array, as described earlier in the section "Declaring the modules, constants, and variables."

We print the coffee's status (remember, this function is called only when the status
changes, not every time the sensor is polled) and send the newly built <pres-
ence/> element down the XML stream to the Jabber server. This is accomplished by passing the presence object as an argument to the Send() method of
the connection object in $connection. This works in the same way as the send()
function in Jabberpy and the send() function in JabberBeans. Everyone who has
subscribed to the script user's presence, and who is available, will receive the coffee status information.

Figure 9-3 shows the status information received in the WinJab client. The string
sent in the <status/> tag is shown in the tooltip that appears when the mouse
hovers over the "coffee" roster item.

The InPresence() subroutine

Our presence handler, the callback subroutine InPresence(), honors requests for
subscription and unsubscription to the script user's (and therefore the coffee's)
presence. This callback is designed to work in the same way as the presenceCB()
callback in the Python recipe described in the section "Presence-Sensitive CVS
Notification."

However, while the Python Jabberpy library hands to the callbacks a jab-
ber.Client object and the element to be handled, the Perl Net::Jabber library
hands over a session ID and the element to be handled. Don't worry about the
session ID here; it's related to functionality for building Jabber servers, not clients,
and we can and should ignore it for the purposes of this recipe. What is important
is the element to be handled, which appears as the second argument passed to the
subroutine collected by the $presence variable from $_[1].

What is common between the two libraries is that the element that is passed to be
handled as the subject of the callback is an instance of the class that the callback
represents. In other words, a callback is used to handle <presence/> elements,

and the element received is an instance of the Net::Jabber::Presence class (just as the element received by a Jabberpy presence callback is an instance of the jabber.Presence class).

```
# Handle presence messages
sub InPresence
{
  my $presence = $_[1];
  my $from = $presence->GetFrom();
  my $type = $presence->GetType();

  if ($type eq "subscribe") {
    print "Subscribe request ($from) ...\n";
    $jabber->Send($presence->Reply(type => 'subscribed'));
  }

  if ($type eq "unsubscribe") {
    print "Unsubscribe request ($from) ...\n";
    $jabber->Send($presence->Reply(type => 'unsubscribed'));
  }
}
```

With an object in $presence, we can get information from the element using data retrieval methods such as those used here: GetFrom() and GetType(), which extract the values from the from and type attributes of the <presence/> element, respectively.

If the <presence/> element type represents a subscription request (type='subscribe'), we unquestioningly honor the request, by sending back an affirmative reply. The Reply() method of the presence object is one of a number of high-level functions that make it possible to turn elements around and send them back. In this case, the method replaces the value of the <presence/>'s to attribute with the value of the from attribute, and preserves its id. It also allows us to pass arguments as if we were calling the SetPresence() method described earlier. Rather than set the <show/> and <status/> tags as we did earlier in the set_presence() function, we merely set the element's type attribute to subscribed or unsubscribed, depending on the request.

So, with an incoming <presence/> element in $presence that looks like this:

```
<presence from='qmacro@jabber.org/office' type='subscribe'
          to='coffee@merlix.dyndns.org' id='21'>
```

calling the Reply() method would cause the element in $presence to change to this:

```
<presence to='qmacro@jabber.org/office' type='subscribed' id='21'>
```

Remember, the from attribute on elements originating from the client is set by the *server*, not by the *client*. The script doesn't ask for a subscription to the user's presence in return. The script isn't interested in whether the people who have sub-scribed to its presence are available—its purpose is to let people know whether there's any coffee left in the pot.

The setup_RCX() function

This function is called once every time the script is started and is required to ini-tialize the RCX:

```
sub setup_RCX {
    my $sensor = shift;
    my $rcx = Win32::OLE->new('SPIRIT.SpiritCtrl.1');
    $Win32::OLE::Warn = 0;
    $rcx->{ComPortNo} = 1;
    $rcx->{InitComm};
    $rcx->SetSensorType($sensor, 3);
    $rcx->SetSensorMode($sensor, 2);
    return $rcx;
}
```

A `Win32::OLE` object representing the RCX's ActiveX control `Spirit` is instantiated. A `Win32::OLE` function is used to suppress warnings, and the RCX is initialized by setting the COM port to COM1 for serial communications. The sensor type and mode are set for the light sensor attached to the connector identified by the value passed into the `$sensor` variable. Table 9-2 shows us that sensor type 3 represents *Light*, and sensor mode 2 specifies a *Transitional* measurement mode, the upshot of which is that the values returned on a poll are all within a certain restricted range, which makes it easier to decide whether there's any coffee in the pot.

We return the `Win32::OLE` RCX object to be used elsewhere in the script for cali-bration and polling.

The calibrate() function

The `calibrate()` function is called if the script is started without the *-l* option. This function simply prints a message, waits for the user to press **Enter**, and then goes into a a gentle loop, emitting whatever value was polled from the light sensor so the user can determine the pivot point:

```
sub calibrate {
    my $rcx = shift;

    print <<EOT;
Calibration mode.
Note the sensor values and decide on a 'pivot' value
above which 'no coffee' is signified and below which
'coffee' is signified.

End the calibration mode with Ctrl-C.
```

```
Press Enter to start calibration...
EOT

  <STDIN>;

  while (1) {
    print $rcx->Poll(9, SENSOR), " ";
    sleep 1;
  }


}
```

The output produced from this function can be seen in Figure 9-4.

The set_status() function

The set_status() function receives the latest light value as polled from the sensor and compares it with the pivot value. If the status defined in $new_status is differ-ent from the *current* status (in $current_status), then the current status is updated and returned; otherwise, undef is returned:

```
sub set_status {
  my $val = shift;

  my $new_status = $val < $opts{'l'} ? COFFEE : NOCOFFEE;

  if ($new_status != $current_status) {
    $current_status = $new_status;
    return $current_status;
  }
  else {
    return undef;
  }
}
```

If this function returns a status value, a new <presence/> element is generated and emitted by the script. Otherwise, there's no change ("the coffee's still there," or "there's still no coffee!") and nothing happens.

An RSS News Agent

While the Jabber clients available off the shelf are orientated toward receiving (and sending) messages from other people, the possibilities don't stop there, as is clear from the recipes we've seen already. In this recipe, we're going to build a Jabber component that retrieves news items from various sources on the Web and sends them on to Jabber users who have expressed an interest in receiving them. We're going to use the Web for our news sources, but they could just as easily be sources within a corporate intranet. The key thing is that the sources are available in a readily parseable format.

RSS (RDF* Site Summary or, alternatively, Really Simple Syndication) is an XML format used for describing the content of a web site, where that site typically contains news items, diary entries, event information, or generally anything that grows, item by item, over time. A classic application of RSS is to describe a news site such as JabberCentral (*http://www.jabbercentral.org*). JabberCentral's main page (see Figure 9-5) consists of a number of news items—in the "Recent News" section—about Jabber and its developer community. These items appear in reverse chronological order, and each one is succinct, sharing a common set of properties:

Title
> Each item has a title ("JabberCon Update 11:45am - Aug 20").

Short description
> Each item contains a short piece of text describing the content and context of the news story ("JabberCon Update - Monday Morning").

Link to main story
> The short description should be enough to help the reader decide if he wants to read the whole item. If he does, there's a link ("Read More") to the news item itself.

It is this collection of item-level properties that are summarized in an RSS file. The formality of the XML structure makes it a straightforward matter for:

* Automating the retrieval of story summaries for inclusion in other sites (syndication)

* Combining these items with items from other similar sources (aggregation)

* Checking to see whether there is any new content (new items) since the last visit

Example 9-8 shows what the RSS XML for JabberCentral's news items shown in Figure 9-5 looks like.

Example 9-8. RSS source for JabberCentral

```
<?xml version="1.0" encoding="ISO-8859-1"&quest;>

<!DOCTYPE rss PUBLIC "-//Netscape Communications//DTD RSS 0.91//EN"
    "http://my.netscape.com/publish/formats/rss-0.91.dtd">

<rss version="0.91">

  <channel>

    <title>JabberCentral</title>
```

---

* RDF stands for "Resource Description Framework."

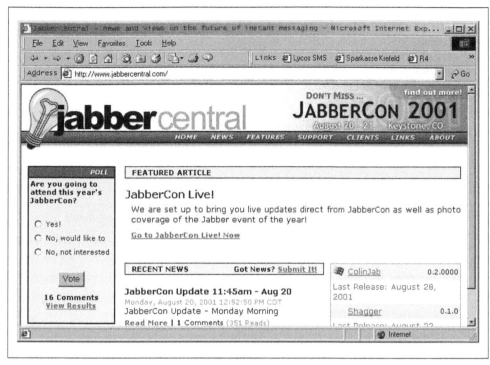

Figure 9-5. JabberCentral's main page

Example 9-8. RSS source for JabberCentral (continued)

```
<description>
    JabberCentral is the premiere Jabber end-user news and support
    site. Many Jabber developers are actively involved at JabberCentral
    to provide fresh and authoritative information for users.
</description>

<language>en-us</language>
<link>http://www.jabbercentral.com/</link>
<copyright>Copyright 2001, Aspect Networks</copyright>

<image>
    <url>http://jabbercentral.com/images/jc_button.gif</url>
    <title>JabberCentral</title>
    <link>http://www.jabbercentral.com/</link>
</image>

<item>
    <title>JabberCon Update 11:45am - Aug 20</title>
    <link>http://www.jabbercentral.com/news/view.php?news_id=998329970</link>
    <description>JabberCon Update - Monday Morning</description>
</item>

<item>
    <title>Jabcast Promises Secure Jabber Solutions</title>
```

Example 9-8. RSS source for JabberCentral (continued)

```
        <link>http://www.jabbercentral.com/news/view.php?news_id=998061331</link>
        <description>
          Jabcast announces their intention to release security
          plugins with their line of products and services.
        </description>
      </item>

      ... (more items) ...

    </channel>

</rss>
```

The structure is very straightforward. Each RSS file describes a *channel*, which is defined as follows:

Channel information

The channel header information includes the channel's title (`<title/>`), short description (`<description/>`), main URL (`<link/>`), and so on. The channel in this case is JabberCentral.

Channel image

Often RSS information is rendered into HTML to provide a concise "current index" summary of the channel it describes. An image can be used in that summary rendering, and its definition is held in the `<image/>` section of the file.

Channel items

The bulk of the RSS file content is made up of the individual `<item/>` sections, each of which reflects an item on the site that the channel represents. We can see in Example 9-8 that the first `<item/>` tag:

```
      <item>
        <title>JabberCon Update 11:45am - Aug 20</title>
        <link>http://www.jabbercentral.com/news/view.php?news_id=998329970</link>
        <description>JabberCon Update - Monday Morning</description>
      </item>
```

describes the most recent news item shown on JabberCentral's main page—"JabberCon Update 11:45am - Aug 20." Each of the news item properties are contained within that `<item/>` tag: the title (`<title/>`), short description (`<description/>`), and link to main story (`<link/>`).

Channel interactive feature

There is a possibility for each channel to describe an interactive feature on the site it represents; often this is a search engine fronted by a text input field and Submit button. The interactive feature section of an RSS file is used to describe how that mechanism is to work (the name of the input field and the Submit button and the URL to invoke when the button is clicked, for example). This is so HTML renderings of the site can include the feature otherwise available only on the original site.

 This interactive feature definition is not shown in the RSS example here.

RSS information lends itself very well to various methods of viewing. There are custom "headline viewer" clients available—focused applications that allow you to select from a vast array of RSS sources and have links to items displayed on your desktop (so, yes, the personal newspaper—of sorts—is here!). There are also possibilities for having RSS items scroll by on your desktop control bar.

And then there's Jabber. As described in the section "The Message Element," the Jabber `<message&sol;>` element can represent something that looks suspiciously like an RSS item. The message type "headline" defines a message that carries news headline information. In this case, the `<message&sol;>` element itself is usually embellished with an *extension*, qualified by the `jabber:x:oob` namespace (described in the section "jabber:x:oob"). Example 9-9 shows what the element would look like if the first news item from the JabberCentral site were carried in a headline message.

Example 9-9. A headline message carrying a JabberCentral news item

```
<message type='headline' to='dj@qmacro.dyndns.org'>
  <subject>JabberCon Update 11:45am - Aug 20</subject>
  <body>JabberCon Update - Monday Morning</body>
  <x xmlns='jabber:x:oob'>
    <url>http://www.jabbercentral.com/news/view.php?news_id=998329970</url>
    <desc>JabberCon Update - Monday Morning</desc>
  </x>
</message>
```

The `jabber:x:oob` namespace carries the crucial parts of the RSS item. Clients, such as WinJab and Jarl, can understand this extension and display the content in a clickable list of headlines, each representing a single RSS item, similar to the headline viewer clients mentioned earlier.

Of course, we could send RSS items to clients in nonheadline type messages:

```
<message type='headline' to='dj@qmacro.dyndns.org'>
  <subject>JabberCon Update 11:45am - Aug 20</subject>
  <body>
    JabberCon Update - Monday Morning
    http://www.jabbercentral.com/news/view.php?news_id=998329970
```

```
    </body>
    </x>
</message>
```

where the complete item information is transmitted in a combination of the `<subject&sol;>` and `<body&sol;>` tags. This works, but the clients can only display the message, as with any other message. However, if we send formalized *metadata*, the value of the message content increases enormously. (Figure 9-8 shows Jarl displaying RSS-sourced news headlines.)

Distributing RSS-sourced headlines over Jabber to standard Jabber clients is a great combination of off-the-shelf technologies. In fact, we'll see in the next section that it's not just standard Jabber clients that fit the bill; we'll write a Jabber-based headline viewer to show that not all Jabber clients are, nor should they be, made equal.

Writing the News Agent

We're going to write an RSS news agent, which we'll simply call *newsagent*. The *newsagent* is a mechanism that checks predefined sources for new RSS items and sends (or pushes) them to people who are interested in receiving them. For the sake of simplicity, we'll define the list of RSS sources in *newsagent* itself. See the section "Reviewing the RSS News Agent Script Step by Step" later in this chapter for details on how to further develop this script.

The newsagent script as a component

Until now, the examples we've used, such as *cvsmsg*, *HostAlive*, and *keyassist* (shown in Chapter 8), have all existed as Jabber *clients*. That is, they've performed a service while connected to the Jabber server via the JSM. There's nothing wrong with this. Indeed, it's more than just fine to build Jabber-based mechanisms using a Jabber client stub connection; that way, your script, through its *identity*—the user JID—can avail itself of all the IM-related functions that the JSM offers—presence, storage and forwarding of messages, and so on. Perhaps even more interesting is that the mechanism needs only an account, a username, and a password on a Jabber server to be part of the big connected picture.

However, we know from Chapter 4 that there are other entities that connect to Jabber to provide services. These entities are called *components*. You can look at components as philosophically less "transient" than their client-connected brethren and also closer to the Jabber server in terms of function and connection.

We know from the section "jabberd and Components" that there are various ways to connect a component: library load, STDIO, and TCP sockets. The first two dictate that the component will be located on the same host as the *jabberd* backbone to which it connects, although a Jabber server could consist of a *collection* of *jabberds* running on separate hosts. The TCP sockets connection type uses a socket connection between the component and the *jabberd* backbone, over which streamed XML documents are exchanged (in the same way they are exchanged in a client connection). It allows us to run components on any host and connect them to a Jabber server running on another host if we wish. This approach is the most desirable because of the connection flexibility. But it's not just the flexibility that matters: because the component is abstracted away from the Jabber server core libraries, it's up to us to decide how the component should be written. All the component has to do to get the Jabber server to cooperate is to establish the socket connection as described in the component instance configuration, perform an authenticating handshake, and correctly exchange XML stream headers.

Let's review how a TCP socket-based component connects. We'll base the review on what we're actually going to have to do to get *newsagent* up and running.

First, we have to tell the Jabber server that it is to expect an incoming socket connection attempt, which it is to *accept*. We do this by defining a component instance definition (or "description"—see the section "Component Instances") for our component. We include this definition in the main Jabber server configuration file, usually called *jabber.xml*. Example 9-10 shows a component instance definition for the RSS news agent, known as `rss.qmacro.dyndns.org`.

Example 9-10. A component instance definition for the RSS news agent

```
<service id='rss.qmacro.dyndns.org'>
  <accept>
    <ip>localhost</ip>
    <port>5999</port>
    <secret>secret</secret>
  </accept>
</service>
```

The name of the host on which the main Jabber server is running is `qmacro.dyndns.org`; it just so happens that the plan is to run the RSS news agent component on the same host. We give it a unique name (`rss.qmacro.dyndns.org`) to enable the *jabberd* backbone, or hub, to distinguish it from other components and to be able to route elements to it.

An alternate way of writing the component instance definition is shown in Example 9-11. The difference is simply in the way we specify the name. In Example 9-10, we specified an `id` in the `<service/>` tag with the value `rss.qmacro.dyndns.org`. In the absence of any `<host/>` tag specification in the definition, this `id` value is used by the *jabberd* routing logic as the identification for the component when determining where elements addressed with that destination should be sent. In Example 9-11, we have an explicit `<host/>` specification that will be used instead; we simply identify the service with an `id` attribute value of `rss`. In this latter case, it doesn't really matter from an addressability point of view what we specify as the value for the id attribute.

Example 9-11. An alternative instance definition for the RSS news agent

```
<service id='rss'>
  <host>rss.qmacro.dyndns.org</host>
  <accept>
    <ip>localhost</ip>
    <port>5999</port>
    <secret>secret</secret>
  </accept>
</service>
```

The instance definition contains all the information the Jabber server needs. We can tell from the <accept/> tag that this definition describes a TCP sockets connection. The socket connection detail is held in the <ip/> and <port/> tags. In this case, as we're going to run the RSS News Agent component on the same host as the Jabber server itself, we might as well kill two related birds—performance and security—with one stone by specifying localhost in the <ip/> tag:*

Performance

 Connecting over the loopback device, as opposed to a real network interface, will give us a slight performance boost.

Security

 Accepting only on the loopback device is a simple security measure that leaves one less port open to the world.

The <secret/> tag holds the secret that the connecting component must present in the authentication handshake. How the secret is specified is described later on in this section.

Now let's look at the component's view of things. It will need to establish a socket connection to 127.0.0.1:5999. Once that connection has been established, *jabberd* will be expecting it to announce itself by sending its XML document stream header. Example 9-12 shows a typical stream header that the component will need to send.

Example 9-12. The RSS component's stream header

```
SEND: <?xml version='1.0'&quest;>
      <stream:stream xmlns='jabber:component:accept'
                     xmlns:stream='http://etherx.jabber.org/streams'
                     to='localhost'>
```

---

* Despite the tag name, you can specify an IP address or a hostname in the <ip/> tag.

This matches the description of a Jabber XML stream header (also known as a stream "root" as it's the root tag of the XML document) from the section "XML Streams." The namespace that is specified as the one qualifying the *content* of the stream is `jabber:component:accept`. This namespace matches the component connection method (TCP sockets) and the significant tag name in the component instance definition (`<accept&sol;>`). Likewise, the namespace `jabber:component:exec` matches the *STDIO* component connection method and the significant tag name in *its* component instance definition format: (`<exec&sol;>`)—see the section "Standard I/O (STDIO)." The value specified in the `to` attribute matches the hostname specified in the configuration's `<ip&sol;>` tag.

After receiving a valid stream header, *jabberd* responds with a similar root to head up its own XML document stream going in the opposite direction (from server to component). A typical response to the header (Example 9-12) received from the server by the component is shown in Example 9-13.

Example 9-13. The server's stream header reply

```
RECV: <?xml version='1.0'&quest;>
      <stream:stream xmlns:stream='http://etherx.jabber.org/streams'
                     id='3B8E3540'
                     xmlns='jabber:component:accept'
                     from='rss'>
```

The stream header sent in response shows that the server is confirming the component instance's identification as `rss`. This reflects whatever was specified in the `<service&sol;>` tag's `id` attribute of the component instance definition. Here, the value of the `id` attribute was `rss` as in Example 9-11.

It also contains an ID for the component instance itself (`id='3B8E3540'`). This ID is a random string shared between both connecting parties; the value is used in the next stage of the connection attempt—the authenticating handshake.

The digest authentication method for clients connecting to the JSM is described in the section "Digest authentication method." This method uses a similar shared random string. On receipt of the server's stream header, the component takes the ID and prepends it onto the secret that it must authenticate itself with. It then creates a NIST SHA-1 message digest (in a hexadecimal format) of that value:

```
SHA1_HEX(ID+SECRET)
```

After the digest is created, it is sent in a `<handshake&sol;>` element as the first XML fragment following the root:

```
SEND: <handshake id='1'>14d437033d7735f893d509c002194be1c69dc500</handshake>
```

On receipt of this authentication request, *jabberd* combines the ID value with the value from the `<secret&sol;>` tag in the component instance definition and performs the same digest algorithm. If the digests match, the component is deemed to have authenticated itself correctly, and it is then sent back an empty <handshake/> tag in confirmation:

```
<handshake&sol;>
```

The component may commence sending (and being sent) elements.

If the component sends an invalid handshake value—the secret may be wrong or the digest may not have been calculated correctly—the connection is closed: *jabberd* sends a stream error, ending the conversation:

```
RECV: <stream:error>Invalid handshake</stream:error>
```

Working out who gets what newsfeeds

Definitions of the RSS sources are held within the *newsagent* itself, but there's no reference to who might want to receive new items from which sources. We need a way for the component to accept requests, from users, that say things like:

> "I'd like to have pointers to new items from Slashdot sent to me, please."

or:

> "I'd *also* like pointers to new items on Jon Udell's site, please."

or even:

> "Whoa, information overflow! Stop all my feeds!"

There's a common theme that binds together components such as the Jabber User Directory (JUD), and the transports to other IM systems such as Yahoo! and ICQ. This theme is known as *registration*. We've seen this before in the form of *user registration*, described in the section "The XHTML Namespace." This is the process of creating a new account with the JSM. Registration with a *service* such as the JUD or an IM transport, however, follows a similar process, and both types of registration have one thing in common: the jabber:iq:register namespace.

The jabber:iq:register namespace is used to qualify the exchange of information during a registration process. The registration process to create a new user account with the JSM uses the jabber:iq:register namespace to qualify registration data exchanged. The registration process with the JSM to modify the account details (name, email address, and so on) also uses jabber:iq:register to qualify the account amendment data exchanged. Both types of registration requests are addressed to the JSM. The difference, which allows the JSM to distinguish between *what* is being requested, is that no session is active on the stream between client and server in the new user registration process, whereas in the account amendment process, a session *is* active. This is also mentioned in the section "Passwords" Chapter 7.

The `jabber:iq:register` namespace is described in the section "jabber:iq:register" in Chapter 6. It shows us how a typical conversation between requester and responder takes place:

1. The client sends an IQ-get: "*How do I register?*"

2. The component sends an IQ-result: "*Here's how: follow these instructions to fill in these fields.*"

3. The client then sends an IQ-set with values in the fields: "*OK, here's my registration request.*"

4. To which the component responds, with another IQ-result: "*Looks fine. Your registration details have been stored.*"

It's clear that this sort of model will lend itself well to the process of allowing users to make requests to receive pointers to new items from RSS sources chosen from a list. Example 9-14 shows this conversational model in Jabber XML. There are many fields that can be used in a registration request; the description in the section "jabber:iq:register" in Chapter 6 includes a few of these—`<name&sol;>`, `<first&sol;>`, `<last&sol;>`, and `<email&sol;>`—but there are more. We'll take the `<text&sol;>` field to accept the name of an RSS source when a user attempts to register his interest to receive pointers to new items from that source. The conversational model is shown from the component's perspective.

Example 9-14. A registration conversation for RSS sources

"*How do I register?*"

```
RECV: <iq type='get' id='JCOM_3' to='rss.qmacro.dyndns.org'
        from='dj@qmacro.dyndns.org/basement'>
        <query xmlns='jabber:iq:register'&sol;>
      </iq>
```

"*Here's how:*"

```
SEND: <iq id='JCOM_3' type='result' to='dj@qmacro.dyndns.org/basement'
        from='rss.qmacro.dyndns.org'>
        <query xmlns='jabber:iq:register'>
          <instructions>
            Choose an RSS source from: Slashdot, Jon Udell[, ...]
          </instructions>
          <text&sol;>
        </query>
      </iq>
```

"*OK, here's my registration request:*"

```
RECV: <iq type='set' id='JCOM_5' to='rss.qmacro.dyndns.org'
        from='dj@qmacro.dyndns.org/basement'>
        <query xmlns='jabber:iq:register'>
          <text>Slashdot</text>
```

```
    </query>
  </iq>
```

"Looks fine. Your registration details have been stored."

```
SEND: <iq id='JCOM_5' type='result' to='dj@qmacro.dyndns.org/basement'
      from='rss.qmacro.dyndns.org'>
      <query xmlns='jabber:iq:register'>
        <text>Slashdot</text>
      </query>
  </iq>
```

After some time passes . . .

"Whoa, information overflow! Stop all my feeds!"

```
RECV: <iq id='JCOM_11' to='rss.qmacro.dyndns.org' type='set'
      from='dj@qmacro.dyndns.org/basement'>
      <query xmlns='jabber:iq:register'>
        <remove&sol;>
      </query>
  </iq>
```

"OK, you've been removed. All feeds stopped."

```
SEND: <iq id='JCOM_11' to='dj@qmacro.dyndns.org/basement' type='result'
      from='rss.qmacro.dyndns.org'>
      <query xmlns='jabber:iq:register'>
        <remove&sol;>
      </query>
  </iq>
```

A lightweight persistent storage system is used for the user/source registrations—
DataBase Manager (DBM)—to keep the script fairly simple.

The bigger question here is: how will the user know he can register to a particular
RSS feed? Or more importantly: how can he determine if the RSS News Agent system exists? Most clients, having connected to the server and established a session
with the JSM, make a request for a list of *agents* (old terminology) or *services* (new
terminology) available from the Jabber server with the following IQ-get method:

```
SEND: <iq id="wjAgents" to="qmacro.dyndns.org" type="get">
      <query xmlns="jabber:iq:agents"&sol;>
  </iq>
```

The response to the request looks like this:

```
RECV: <iq id='wjAgents' to='dj@qmacro.dyndns.org/basement'
      type='result' from='qmacro.dyndns.org'>
      <query xmlns='jabber:iq:agents'>
        <agent jid='conf.qmacro.dyndns.org'>
          <name>Public Chatrooms</name>
          <service>public</service>
          <groupchat&sol;>
```

```
          </agent>
          <agent jid='users.jabber.org'>
            <name>Jabber User Directory</name>
            <service>jud</service>
            <search&sol;>
            <register&sol;>
          </agent>
        </query>
      </iq>
```

which reflects the contents of the <browse/> section in the JSM configuration as shown in Example 9-15.

Example 9-15. The JSM configuration's browse section

```
<browse>
  <conference type="public" jid="conf.qmacro.dyndns.org"
      name="Public Chatrooms"&sol;>
  <service type="jud" jid="users.jabber.org" name="Jabber User Directory">
    <ns>jabber:iq:search</ns>
    <ns>jabber:iq:register</ns>
  </service>
</browse>
```

If we *add* a stanza that describes the component for the RSS News Agent to the <browse/> section of the JSM configuration:

```
<service type="rss" jid="rss.qmacro.dyndns.org" name="RSS News Agent">
  <ns>jabber:iq:register</ns>
</service>
```

we get an extra section in the jabber:iq:agents response from the server:

```
<agent jid='rss.qmacro.dyndns.org'>
  <name>RSS News Agent</name>
  <service>rss</service>
  <register&sol;>
</agent>
```

The client-side effect of the agents response is exactly what we're looking for. Figure 9-6 shows WinJab's Agents menu displaying a summary of what it received in response to its jabber:iq:agents query.

We can see that the stanza for the RSS news agent was present in the <browse/> section and the component is faithfully displayed in the agent list, along with Public Chatrooms and Jabber User Directory. In the main window of the screenshot we can see the Supported Namespaces list; it contains the namespace that we specified in the stanza. By specifying:

```
<ns>jabber:iq:register</ns>
```

we're effectively telling the client that the component will support a registration conversation.

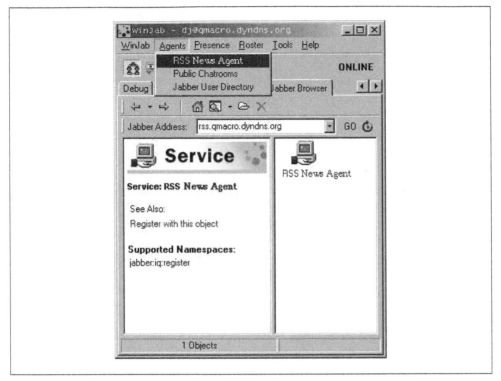

Figure 9-6. WinJab's Agents menu

But that's not all—we've advertised the RSS news agent in the <browse/> section of the configuration for the JSM on the Jabber server running on qmacro.dyndns.org. That's why we got the information about the RSS news agent when we connected as user dj to qmacro.dyndns.org (see the window's titlebar in Figure 9-6). You may have noticed something odd about the definition of the other two agents, or services, in the <browse/> section earlier or in the corresponding jabber:iq:agents IQ response. Let's take a look at this response again, this time with the extra detail about the component:

```
RECV: <iq id='wjAgents' to='dj@qmacro.dyndns.org/basement'
       type='result' from='qmacro.dyndns.org'>
       <query xmlns='jabber:iq:agents'>
         <agent jid='rss.qmacro.dyndns.org'>
           <name>RSS News Agent</name>
           <service>rss</service>
           <register&sol;>
         </agent>
         <agent jid='conf.qmacro.dyndns.org'>
           <name>Public Chatrooms</name>
           <service>public</service>
           <groupchat&sol;>
         </agent>
```

```
            <agent jid='users.jabber.org'>
              <name>Jabber User Directory</name>
              <service>jud</service>
              <search&sol;>
              <register&sol;>
            </agent>
          </query>
        </iq>
```

While the `jid` attribute values for the RSS news agent and Public Chatroom agents show that they are components connected to the Jabber server (i.e., they both have JIDs in the `qmacro.dyndns.org` "space," and so are connected to the Jabber server running at `qmacro.dyndns.org`), the `jid` attribute for the Jabber User Directory points to a name in the `jabber.org` "space"! This is a side effect of the power and foresight of Jabber's architectural design. If we connect a component— whether it's one we've built ourselves or one we've downloaded from *http://download.jabber.org*—we can give it an *internal* or *external* identity when we describe it in the *jabber.xml* configuration.

Example 9-8 and Example 9-9 show two examples of an instance definition for the RSS news agent component. Both specify potentially *external* identities. If the hostname `rss.qmacro.dyndns.org` is a valid and resolvable hostname, the component can be reached from anywhere, not just from within the Jabber server to which it is connected. If the hostname wasn't resolvable by the outside world, by having a simple name such as `rss`, it could be reached only from the Jabber server to which it was connected.

So let's say `rss.qmacro.dyndns.org` *is* a valid and resolvable hostname. If your client is connected to a Jabber server running on `yourserver.org`, this is what would happen if you were to send a registration request (an `<iq&sol;>` element with a query qualified by the `jabber:iq:register` namespace) addressed to `rss.qmacro.dyndns.org`:

Packet reaches JSM on `yourserver.org`.
You send the IQ from your client, which is connected to your Jabber server's JSM. This is where the packet first arrives.

Internal routing tables consulted.
This is how `yourserver.org`'s *jabberd* looks in its list of internally registered destinations and doesn't find `rss.qmacro.dyndns.org` in there.

Name resolved and routing established.
`yourserver.org`'s `dnsrv` (Hostname Resolution) service is used to resolve the `rss.qmacro.dyndns.org`'s address. Then, according to `dnsrv`'s instance configuration (specifically the `<resend>s2s</resend>` part—see the section "Component Instance: dnsrv"), the IQ is routed on to the s2s (Server to Server) component.

Server to server connection established.

> yourserver.org establishes a connection to qmacro.dyndns.org via s2s and sends the IQ across the connection.

Packet arrives at the RSS News Agent component on qmacro.dyndns.org.

> jabberd on qmacro.dyndns.org routes the packet correctly to rss.qmacro.dyndns.org.

So, what do we learn from this? As exemplified by the reference to the JUD running at users.jabber.org that comes predefined in the standard *jabber.xml* with the 1.4.1 version of the Jabber server, you can specify references to services, components, *on other Jabber servers*. If you take this RSS News Agent script and run it against your own Jabber server, there's no reason why you can't share its services with your friends who run their own Jabber servers.

The key is not the reference in the <browse/> section; it is the resolvability of component names as hostnames and the ability of Jabber servers to route packets to each other. The stanza in <browse/> just makes it easier *for the clients* to automatically know about and be able to interact with services in general. Even if a service offered by a public component that *wasn't* described in the result of a jabber:iq:agents query, it wouldn't stop you from reaching it. The agent browser is another client, Gabber (shown in Figure 9-7), which is a GTK-based Jabber client that allows you to specify a Jabber server name, in the Server to Browse field, so that you can direct the jabber:iq:agents queries to whatever server you want.

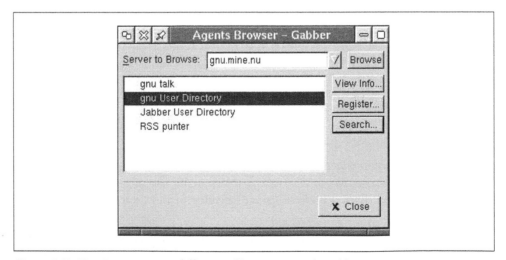

Figure 9-7. Viewing agents on different Jabber servers with Gabber

A good example of the distinction between the definition of a component within a <browse/> section and that component's reachability is the version query shown in Example 9-16. Regardless of whether the conference component at gnu.mine.nu was listed in the <browse/> section of qmacro.dyndns.org's JSM, the user dj was able to make a version query by specifying the component's address (a valid and resolvable hostname) in the IQ-get's to attribute.

Example 9-16. A Conferencing component responds to a version query

```
SEND: <iq type='get' to='conf.gnu.mine.nu'>
         <query xmlns='jabber:iq:version'&sol;>
      </iq>

RECV: <iq type='result' to='dj@qmacro.dyndns.org/study'
         from='conf.gnu.mine.nu'>
         <query xmlns='jabber:iq:version'>
           <name>conference</name>
           <version>0.4</version>
           <os>Linux 2.2.13</os>
         </query>
      </iq>
```

Polling the RSS sources

Next, we need some way of "interrupting" the process of checking for incoming elements and dispatching them to the callbacks, while we retrieve the RSS data and check for new items. Since we're writing this component in Perl, we could use the alarm() feature to set an alarm and have a subroutine invoked, to poll the RSS sources, when the alarm goes off. However, this recipe uses the Jabber::Connection library, which negates the needs for an external alarm. Instead, we need to take the following steps each time we want to poll the RSS sources:

1. Try to retrieve the source from the URL.

2. Attempt to parse the source's XML.

3. Go through the items, until we come across one we've seen before; the ones we go through until then are deemed to be new. (We need a special case the first time around, so that we don't flood everyone with every item of a source the first time it is retrieved.)

4. For new items, look in the registration database for the users that have registered for that source, construct a headline message like the one shown in Example 9-7, and send it to those users.

5. Remember the first of the new items, so that we don't go beyond it next time.

Other Differences Between Client and Component Programming

There are many differences between programming a component and programming a client. We're already aware of many of the major ones, described earlier in the section "The newsagent script as a component." There are, however, also more subtle differences that we need to bear in mind.

Components, unlike clients, *do not* connect to the JSM. They connect as a *peer* of the JSM. This means not only that they cannot partake of IM features made available by JSM's modules (see the section "Component Connection Method" for a list of these modules) but also that they must do more for themselves. This isn't as bad as it seems. Take store and forward, for example, a feature provided by the JSM's *mod_offline* module. While a message sent to a component won't be stored and forwarded if that component is not connected, a message sent from a component to a client *will* get stored and forwarded if the client is offline, because the message will be routed to the JSM (as specified by the [hostname] in the address), which can decide what action to take. Messages can be passed directly to the client if the user is online or can be stored and forwarded later when they're back online.

When constructing an element as a client, we should not specify a `from` attribute before it is sent; this is added by the JSM as it arrives to prevent JID spoofing. If a component does not connect through the JSM, no "from-stamping" takes place; the component itself must stamp the element with a `from` attribute.

The addressing of a component is also slightly different. Client addresses reflect the fact that they're connected to the JSM, always having the form of (with the *resource* being optional):

    [user]@[hostname]/[resource]

While the basic address form of a *component* is simply:

    [hostname]

This doesn't mean to say that the address of a component cannot have a *user* or a *resource* part. It's just that *all* elements addressed to:

    anything@[hostname]/anything

will be routed by *jabberd* to the component. This means the component can play multiple roles and have many personalities. We'll see an example of this in the script, where we construct an "artificial" [user]@[hostname] address for the `from` attribute of a <message/> element, to convey information.

The component will respond to IQ queries in the `jabber:iq:register` namespace. It is customary, although by no means mandatory, for components to respond to queries in a set of common IQ namespaces. We see that both the JUD and Conferencing components, for example, respond to IQ queries in the `jabber:iq:time` and `jabber:iq:version` namespaces. Example 9-16 shows a typical version query on a Conferencing component. This responsiveness is simply to provide a basic level of administrative information. We want the component to conform to the customs, so we'll make sure it also responds to queries in these namespaces.

The RSS News Agent Script

The RSS news agent script (*newsagent*) is written in Perl and is shown here in Example 9-17.

Example 9-17. The RSS news agent script, written in Perl

```perl
my $NAME     = 'RSS News Agent';
my $ID       = 'rss.qmacro.dyndns.org';
my $VERSION  = '0.1';
my $reg_file = 'registrations';
my %reg;

my %cache;

my %sources = (
  'jonudell' => 'http://udell.roninhouse.com/udell.rdf',
  'slashdot' => 'http://slashdot.org/slashdot.rdf',

  # etc ...
);

tie (%reg, 'MLDBM', $reg_file) or die "Cannot tie to $reg_file: $!\n";

my $c = new Jabber::Connection(
  server    => 'localhost:5999',
  localname => $ID,
  ns        => 'jabber:component:accept',
);

unless ($c->connect()) { die "oops: ".$c->lastError; }

$SIG{HUP} = $SIG{KILL} = $SIG{TERM} = $SIG{INT} = \&cleanup;

debug("registering RSS beat");
$c->register_beat(1800, \&rss);

debug("registering IQ handlers");
$c->register_handler('iq',\&iq_register);
$c->register_handler('iq',\&iq_version);
$c->register_handler('iq',\&iq_browse);
$c->register_handler('iq',\&iq_notimpl);
```

Example 9-17. The RSS news agent script, written in Perl (continued)

```perl
$c->auth('secret');

$c->start;

sub iq_register {
  my $node = shift;
  debug("[iq_register]");
  return unless my $query = $node->getTag('', NS_REGISTER);
  debug("--> registration request");

  # Reg query
  if ($node->attr('type') eq IQ_GET) {
    $node = toFrom($node);
    $node->attr('type', IQ_RESULT);
    my $instructions = "Choose an RSS source from: ".join(", ", keys %sources);
    $query->insertTag('instructions')->data($instructions);
    $query->insertTag('text');
    $c->send($node);
  }

  # Reg request
  if ($node->attr('type') eq IQ_SET) {

    # Strip JID to user@host
    my $jid = stripJID($node->attr('from'));

    $node = toFrom($node);
    my $source;

    # Could be an unregister
    if ($query->getTag('remove')) {
      delete $reg{$jid};
      $node->attr('type', IQ_RESULT);
    }

    # Otherwise it's a registration for a source
    elsif ($source = $query->getTag('text')->data
           and exists($sources{$source})) {
      my $element = $reg{$jid};
      $element->{$source} = 1;
      $reg{$jid} = $element;
      $node->attr('type', IQ_RESULT);
    }

    else {
      $node->attr('type', IQ_ERROR);
      my $error = $node->insertTag('error');
      $error->attr('code', '405');
      $error->data('Not Allowed');
    }

    $c->send($node);
```

Example 9-17. The RSS news agent script, written in Perl (continued)

```perl
  }
  return r_HANDLED;
}

sub iq_version {
  my $node = shift;
  debug("[iq_version]");
  return unless my $query = $node->getTag('', NS_VERSION)
            and $node->attr('type', IQ_GET);
  debug("--> version request");
  $node = toFrom($node);
  $node->attr('code', IQ_RESULT);
  $query->insertTag('name')->data($NAME);
  $query->insertTag('version')->data($VERSION);
  $query->insertTag('os')->data('uname -sr');
  $c->send($node);
  return r_HANDLED;
}

sub iq_browse {
  my $node = shift;
  debug("[iq_browse]");
  return unless my $query = $node->getTag('', NS_BROWSE)
            and $node->attr('type', IQ_GET);
  debug("--> browse request");
  $node = toFrom($node);
  $node->attr('type', IQ_RESULT);
  my $rss = $query->insertTag('service');
  $rss->attr('type', 'rss');
  $rss->attr('jid', $ID);
  $rss->attr('name', $NAME);
  $rss->insertTag('ns')->data(NS_REGISTER);
  $c->send($node);
  return r_HANDLED;
}

sub iq_notimpl {
  my $node = shift;
  $node = toFrom($node);
  $node->attr('type', IQ_ERROR);
  my $error = $node->insertTag('error');
  $error->attr('code', '501');
  $error->data('Not Implemented');
  $c->send($node);
  return r_HANDLED;
}

sub rss {
  debug("[rss]");

  # Create NodeFactory
  my $nf = new Jabber::NodeFactory;
```

Example 9-17. The RSS news agent script, written in Perl (continued)

```perl
# Go through each of the RSS sources
foreach my $source (keys %sources) {

  # Retrieve attempt
  my $data = get($sources{$source});

  # Didn't get it? Next one
  unless (defined($data)) {
    debug("Cannot retrieve $source");
    next;
  }

  # Parse the RSS
  my $rss = XML::RSS->new();
  eval { $rss->parse($data) };

  if ($@) {
    debug("Problems parsing $source");
    next;
  }

  my @items = @{$rss->{items}};

  # Check new items
  debug("$source: looking for new items");
  foreach my $item (@items) {

    # Stop checking if we get to items already seen
    last if exists $cache{$source} and $cache{$source} eq $item->{link};

    debug("$source: new item $item->{title}");

    # Create a headline message
    my $msg = $nf->newNode('message');

    $msg->attr('type', 'headline');
    $msg->attr('from', join('@', $source, $ID));
    $msg->insertTag('subject')->data($item->{title});
    $msg->insertTag('body')->data($item->{description});

    my $xoob = $msg->insertTag('x', NS_XOOB);
    $xoob->insertTag('url')->data($item->{link});
    $xoob->insertTag('desc')->data($item->{description});

    # Deliver to all that want it
    foreach my $jid (keys %reg) {

      my $registration = $reg{$jid};

      if (exists($registration->{$source})) {
        $msg->attr('to', $jid);
        debug("Sending to $jid");
```

Example 9-17. The RSS news agent script, written in Perl (continued)

```
        $c->send($msg);
      }
    }

    # Prevent all items counted as new the
    # first time around
    last unless exists($cache{$source});
  }

  # Remember the latest new item
  $cache{$source} = $items[0]->{link};
  }
}

sub cleanup {
  debug("Cleaning up");
  untie %reg;
  $c->disconnect;
  exit;
}

sub toFrom {
  my $node = shift;
  my $to = $node->attr('to');
  $node->attr('to', $node->attr('from'));
  $node->attr('from', $to);
  return $node;
}

sub stripJID {
  my $JID = shift;
  $JID =~ s|/.*$||;
  return $JID;
}

sub debug {
  print STDERR "debug: ", @_, "\n";
}
```

Reviewing the RSS News Agent Script Step by Step

Now that we know what the *newsagent* script looks like in its entirety, let's review the script piece by piece.

Module declarations and variable definitions

We start out by using the Jabber::Connection library, which is defined as follows:

```
use strict;
use Jabber::Connection;
use Jabber::NodeFactory;
use Jabber::NS qw(:all);
use MLDBM 'DB_File';
use LWP::Simple;
use XML::RSS;
```

The `Jabber::Connection` library consists of the following three modules:

`Jabber::Connection`

> This module is used to manage the connection to the server and parses and dispatches incoming elements.

`Jabber::NodeFactory`

> This module allows us to manipulate elements, which are generically called *nodes*.

`Jabber::NS`

> The last module provides us with a list of constants that reflect namespaces and other common strings used in Jabber server, client, and component programming.

Next we need a way of storing the registration information between invocations of the component script, and for that we'll use the Multi-Level Database Manager module, `MLDBM`. `MLDBM` is a useful wrapper that can be placed around the `DB_File` module. `DB_File` provides access to Berlekey Database (Berkeley DB, at *http://www.sleepycat.com*) facilities using the `tie()` function. While you can't store references (i.e., complex data structures) via `DB_File`, you can with the `MLDBM` wrapper.

We will use the `LWP::Simple` module to grab the RSS sources by URL and the `XML::RSS` module to parse those sources once retrieved:

```
my $NAME     = 'RSS News Agent';
my $ID       = 'rss.qmacro.dyndns.org';
my $VERSION  = '0.1';
my $reg_file = 'registrations';
my %reg;

my %cache;

my %sources = (
  'jonudell' => 'http://udell.roninhouse.com/udell.rdf',
  'slashdot' => 'http://slashdot.org/slashdot.rdf',
  # etc ...
);
```

We start by declaring a few variables. We will see later in the script that `$NAME`, `$ID`, and `$VERSION` will be used to reflect information in response to IQ queries. The variable `$reg_file` defines the name of the DB file to which we will be tying the registration hash, %reg. %cache is the RSS item cache, which holds items we've already seen so we know when we've come to the end of the new items in a particular source.

We define the RSS sources in %sources. These can be defined differently, perhaps outside of the script, but this gives you a general idea of how these should look. There are a couple of examples here; add your own favorite channels to taste.

To make persistent any data we store in the %reg hash, we can use the magic of the tie() function:

```
tie (%reg, 'MLDBM', $reg_file) or die "Cannot tie to $reg_file: $!\n";
```

It works by binding (tie'ing) the operations on the hash (add, delete, and so on) to Berlekey DB operations, using the MLDBM module to stringify (and reconstruct) complex data structures so they can be stored and retrieved.

Connecting to the Jabber server

Now we're ready to connect to the Jabber server as a component. Despite what's involved (described in the section "The newsagent script as a component") it's very easy to make the connection to the Jabber server using a library such as Jabber::Connection:

```
my $c = new Jabber::Connection(
  server    => 'localhost:5999',
  localname => $ID,
  ns        => 'jabber:component:accept',
);
```

We construct a Jabber::Connection object, specifying the details of the connection we wish to make. The server argument is used to specify the hostname, and optionally the port, of the Jabber server to which we wish to connect. In the case of a component, we must always specify the port (which is 5999 in this example, as shown in Example 9-8). The same constructor can be used to create a client connection to the Jabber server, in which case a default port of 5222 (the standard port for client connections) is assumed if none is explicitly specified. The local-name argument is used to specify the component's name, which in this case is rss.qmacro.dyndns.org. In the same way that a default port of 5222 is assumed if none is specified, a default stream namespace of jabber:client is assumed if no ns argument is specified. Since we want to connect as a component using the TCP sockets connection method, we must specify the appropriate namespace: jabber:component:accept.

This constructor call results in a stream header being prepared; it looks like the one shown in Example 9-12.

The actual connection attempt, including the sending of the component's stream header, is done by calling the connect() method on the connection object in $c:

```
unless ($c->connect()) { die "oops: ".$c->lastError; }
```

This will return a true value if the connect succeeded (success is measured in whether the socket connection was established and whether the Jabber server sent a stream header in response). If it didn't succeed, we can retrieve details of what happened using the lastError() method.

We're connected. Before performing the authenticating handshake, we're going to do a bit of preparation:

```
$SIG{HUP} = $SIG{KILL} = $SIG{TERM} = $SIG{INT} = \&cleanup;
```

The idea is that the component will be run and stopped only in certain circumstances. If it is stopped, we want to clean things up before the script ends. Most importantly, we need to make sure the registration data is safe, but also we want to play nicely with the server and gracefully disconnect. This is done in the cleanup() function.

Preparing the RSS event function and element handlers

Jabber::Connection offers a simple way of having a function execute at regular intervals. It avoids the need for setting and resetting alarms. It is the register_beat() function:

```
debug("registering RSS beat");
$c->register_beat(1800, \&rss);
```

Calling the register_beat() method takes two arguments. The first argument represents the interval, in seconds. The second is a reference to the function that should be invoked at each interval. Here, we're saying we want the rss() function called every 30 minutes (1800 seconds).

Most of the traffic relating to the component will be the headline messages emanating from it. However, we are expecting incoming IQ elements, particularly for registration in the jabber:iq:register namespace. We've also already mentioned that it's customary for components to honor basic "administrative" queries such as version checks. So the list of calls to the register_handler() method here reflects what we want to offer in terms of handling these IQ elements:

```
debug("registering IQ handlers");
$c->register_handler('iq',\&iq_register);
$c->register_handler('iq',\&iq_version);
$c->register_handler('iq',\&iq_browse);
$c->register_handler('iq',\&iq_notimpl);
```

Whereas with `Net::Jabber`'s `SetCallBacks()` function and with `Jabberpy`'s `setIqHandler()` method we specify a single function to act as a handler for incoming `<iq&sol;>` elements, we can specify as many handlers as we want for each element type with the `register_handler()` method in `Jabber::Connection`.

The first argument refers to the element name (the name of the element's outermost tag), and the second refers to a function that will be called on receipt of an element of that name. Each of the handlers for a particular element will be called in the order they were registered. So when an `<iq&sol;>` element is received over the XML stream, `Jabber::Connection` will dispatch it to `iq_register()`, then to `iq_version()`, then to `iq_browse()`, and then to `iq_notimpl()`. That is, unless one of those handler functions decides that the element has been handled once and for all and that the dispatch processing for that element should stop there. In this case, that handler simply returns a special value (defined in `Jabber::NS`), and the dispatching stops for that element. The handlers can also cooperate, in that the dispatcher will pass whatever one handler returns into the next handler in the list and so on, so that you can effectively share data across handler events for a particular element, building up a complex response as you go.

This *contextual response chain* model works in a similar way to how the *mod_auth_** authentication modules work in the JSM. Each one that wishes to express its interest in authenticating a user adds its "stamp" to the response to an IQ-get in the `jabber:iq:auth` namespace, before that response is returned to the client.

 Indeed, the author of the `Jabber::Connection` library has taken the (heart)beat idea—the handler chain idea and even the low-level `NodeFactory` mechanisms—directly from the JSM and the server libraries, in homage to the Jabber server's classic design.

Authenticating handshake and launch of main loop

Once we've set up the handlers, we're ready to make the authenticating handshake. This is simply a call to the `auth()` method:

```
$c->auth('secret');
```

It takes either one or three arguments, depending on whether the authentication is for a client or a component. `Jabber::Connection` decides which authentication context is required by looking at the specified (or default) namespace in the connection constructor call. As we specified the namespace `jabber:component:accept`, the `auth()` method is expecting a single argument, the secret specified in the `<secret&sol;>` tag of the component instance definition. The `auth()` method performs the message digest function and sends the `<handshake&sol;>` element.

It's now appropriate for us to "launch" the component, with the `start()` method:

```
$c->start;
```

This is the equivalent of the `MainLoop()` method in Perl's Tk library and is a method from which there's no exit. Calling `start()` causes the connection object to perform an endless loop, which internally calls a `process()` method on a regular basis, receiving, examining, and dispatching elements received on the XML stream. It also starts and maintains the *heartbeat*, to which the `register_beat()` method is related.

If you wish to have more granular control over your script, you can use the `process()` function directly, just as you would with the `Net::Jabber` and `Jabberpy` libraries. Be aware, however, that a heartbeat is maintained only in the context of the `start()` method.

Handling registration requests

The first of the handlers defined for `<iq&sol;>` elements is the `iq_register()` function. We put it first in the list, as we consider receipt of `<iq&sol;>` elements in the `jabber:iq:register` namespace to be the most common. We want this function to deal with the complete registration conversation. This means it must respond to IQ-get and IQ-set requests.

```
sub iq_register {
  my $node = shift;
  debug("[iq_register]");
```

The element to be handled is the primary piece of data that the dispatcher passes to a callback. The element is received by the `$node` variable, which is a Jabber::NodeFactory::Node object. `Jabber::NodeFactory` is the *wrapper* around the class that actually represents the elements (the nodes). Nodes are created using the `Jabber::NodeFactory` class. The first thing we should do is make sure it's appropriate to continue inside this function, which is designed to handle only `jabber:iq:register`-qualified queries. The namespace `jabber:iq:register` is represented with the constant `NS_REGISTER`, imported from the `Jabber::NS` module:

```
return unless my $query = $node->getTag('', NS_REGISTER);
debug("--> registration request");
```

The `getTag()` method can have up to two arguments. The first can be used to specify the name of the tag you want to get, and the second argument can contain a namespace to narrow down the request. For example, there are two `<x&sol;>` elements in this `<message&sol;>` element:

```
<message to='dj@qmacro.dyndns.org' from='piers@jabber.org' id='2941'>
  <body>Let me know when you're ready to go</body>
  <x xmlns='jabber:x:event'><displayed&sol;></x>
  <x xmlns='jabber:x:delay'
     from='dj@qmacro.dyndns.org'
     stamp='20010831T08:58:30'>Offline Storage</x>
</message>
```

We could distinguish one <x/> element from the other by specifying either the jabber:x:event or the jabber:x:delay namespace in the second argument to the getTag() function.

Although the query tag is normally placed within an <iq/> element that has the name "query," we see from the section "IQ subelements" that it *could* be anything.

```
$node->getTag('', NS_REGISTER)
```

This statement says "get a single child tag of the <iq/> node—regardless of its name—and qualify it with the jabber:iq:register namespace."

If we call the getTag() function in scalar context, and there is more than one tag that matches, only the first one found will be returned. If we call it in list context, all the matching tags are returned. Assuming the call is successful, the variable $query then contains the <query/> tag and all its subtags. So if we received this in $node:

```
RECV: <iq type='set' id='JCOM_5' to='rss.qmacro.dyndns.org'
          from='dj@qmacro.dyndns.org/basement'>
          <query xmlns='jabber:iq:register'>
            <text>Slashdot</text>
          </query>
        </iq>
```

then $query would contain a Jabber::NodeFactory::Node object that represented this bit:

```
<query xmlns='jabber:iq:register'>
  <text>Slashdot</text>
</query>
```

If the jabber:iq:register namespace doesn't qualify any of the child tags, iq_register() returns and the dispatcher calls the next handler in line (iq_version()). However, let's assume that we do have a registration IQ on our hands. The function must handle both IQ-get and IQ-set. We first deal with a potential IQ-get:

```
# Reg query
if ($node->attr('type') eq IQ_GET) {
  $node = toFrom($node);
  $node->attr('type', IQ_RESULT);
```

```
    my $instructions = "Choose an RSS source from: ".join(", ", keys %sources);
    $query->insertTag('instructions')->data($instructions);
    $query->insertTag('text');
    $c->send($node);
}
```

The `attr()` method called on a node will return the value of the node's attribute
of the name specified as the first argument. We test to see if IQ's `type` attribute is
get (`IQ_GET`). If it is, we need to return an IQ-result as shown in Example 9-14.

Rather than create a new element from scratch, to return in response, we simply
"convert" the incoming element by making necessary changes to it, turn it around
and sent it back out as the response. The first thing we do is swap the values for
the `from` and `to` attributes in the `<iq&sol;>` tag (in `$node`) by calling the `toFrom()`
function (see the section "Helper functions") and setting the value for the `type`
attribute to `result` by calling a two-argument version of the `attr()` function, which
turns this:

```
<iq type='set' id='JCOM_5' to='rss.qmacro.dyndns.org'
   from='dj@qmacro.dyndns.org/basement'>
```

into this:

```
<iq type='result' id='JCOM_5' from='rss.qmacro.dyndns.org'
   to='dj@qmacro.dyndns.org/basement'>
```

Notice that the `from` attribute is retained. This is required as the script is a component, and the response won't get stamped with one.

The instructions and an empty `<text&sol;>` tag must be passed back in the
response. The names of the sources are combined into a list, and an `<instruc-
tions/>` tag is inserted into the query node (in `$query`) containing the text.
This is done with two method calls: the first to `insertTag()`, which returns a Jabber::NodeFactory::Node object that represents the newly inserted tag, and the second to `data()`, which inserts (or retrieves) data into (or out of) a node. The line:

```
    $query->insertTag('instructions')->data($instructions);
```

could have been written as:

```
    my $instructions = $query->insertTag('instructions');
    $instructions->data($instructions);
```

Once constructed, the response now looks like this:

```
<iq type='result' id='JCOM_5' from='rss.qmacro.dyndns.org'
   to='dj@qmacro.dyndns.org/basement'>
  <query xmlns='jabber:iq:register'>
    <instructions>
      Choose an RSS source from: jonudell, slashdot [...]
    </instructions>
```

```
      <text&sol;>
    </query>
  </iq>
```

This is sent using the `send()` method of the connection object.

If the query wasn't an IQ-get, then it might be an IQ-set:

```
# Reg request
if ($node->attr('type') eq IQ_SET) {

  # Strip JID to user@host
  my $jid = stripJID($node->attr('from'));

  $node = toFrom($node);
  my $source;
```

In this case, the user is requesting new items for an RSS source she's specified in the `<text&sol;>` field carried in the query part of the IQ-set. The user's JID can be found in the `from` attribute of the element, which is extracted with the `attr()` method. There's one thing we should do before using that JID as a key in storing that user's RSS source preferences. Look at what the JID was in earlier examples:

    dj@qmacro.dyndns.org/basement

As you can see, this JID has a `resource` attached to it. That's fine for returning a response to an IQ request, but we need something less specific. The *resource* part of the JID reflects the client connection of the user at the time the registration request was made. In the future, when we have an RSS item to send to her, she might be connected with a different resource. We want the RSS item to go to the right place, so we use only the `user` and `hostname` JIDs to store preferences and subsequently address the headline messages. The more generic form of the JID can be obtained by calling the `stripJID()` function, described later.

After swapping the `from` and `to` values, we then deal with the two different types of IQ-set requests: a request to receive a specific source or a request to cancel the registration:

```
# Could be an unregister request
if ($query->getTag('remove')) {
  delete $reg{$jid};
  $node->attr('type', IQ_RESULT);
}
# Otherwise it's a registration request for a source
elsif ($source = $query->getTag('text')->data
       and exists($sources{$source})) {
  my $element = $reg{$jid};
  $element->{$source} = 1;
  $reg{$jid} = $element;
  $node->attr('type', IQ_RESULT);
}
```

Sending a <remove/> tag in an IQ-set registration context represents a request to *unregister.* So we honor that by removing any trace of the user's JID from the registration hash and simply changing the type of the <iq/> element to result. Otherwise, we interpret the IQ-set as a request to subscribe to the RSS source that she's specified in the <text/> tag. We extract that source's name into $source, check that it's valid, and add a reference to the user's list of sources in the registration hash %reg. Example 9-18 shows what the registration hash looks like.

Example 9-18. Typical contents of the registration hash

```
(
  'dj@qmacro.dyndns.org' => {
                             'slashdot' => 1
                           }
  'piers@jabber.org'      => {
                             'jonudell' => 1
                             'slashdot' => 1
                           }
  ...
)
```

In case you're wondering what's going on with the $element variable, it's because of a current restriction with MLDBM. Although it allows us to store complex structures via DB_File, those structures can't be directly manipulated, so we have to do it via a *proxy* variable, using $element. The value in the registration hash %reg pointed to by the $jid key is a structure. To manipulate that structure, we need to take a reference to it, in $element. The structure can be manipulated through $element and then placed back into the registration hash by assigning $element as the value corresponding to the $jid key.

Once this is done, we also mark the fact that the request was completed by setting the IQ element's type attribute to result.

Finally, it's worth telling the requester that anything else sent isn't allowed:

```
else {
  $node->attr('type', IQ_ERROR);
  my $error = $node->insertTag('error');
  $error->attr('code', '405');
  $error->data('Not Allowed');
}
```

That is, if we haven't understood what the IQ-set was—it wasn't a <remove/> request nor was it a subscription to a source we recognize—we simply return it with an <error/> tag like this:

```
RECV: <iq type="set" id="jimAgentID657" to="rss.qmacro.dyndns.org"
         from="dj@qmacro.dyndns.org/basement">
       <query xmlns="jabber:iq:register">
         <text>banana</text>
       </query>
      </iq>

SEND: <iq id='jimAgentID657' type='error' from='rss.qmacro.dyndns.org'
         to='dj@qmacro.dyndns.org/basement'>
       <query xmlns='jabber:iq:register'>
         <text>banana</text>
       </query>
       <error code='405'>Not Allowed</error>
      </iq>
```

The <iq/> type is set to error to draw the client's attention to the
<error/> tag. Sending an element back in error is a great example of when
reusing an incoming element to build the outgoing response works very well; we
don't have to reproduce what the error was, as it's already contained in what
we're returning to the user.

In all of the IQ-set cases, we want to send something back:

```
    $c->send($node);
  }
  return r_HANDLED;
}
```

Note that we also return a special value, r_HANDLED. The fact that we've got this far
means that an IQ element was received and that it was a registration-related element. It's been handled, so there's no point in the other callbacks registered to
handle IQ elements to get a look in. So we tell the dispatcher to stop the invocation chain for the element just processed.

Handling version requests

Now that we've seen the iq_register() function, the function to handle jab-
ber:iq:version queries looks pretty straightforward:

```
sub iq_version {

  my $node = shift;
  debug("[iq_version]");

  return unless my $query = $node->getTag('', NS_VERSION)
          and $node->attr('type', IQ_GET);

  debug("--> version request");

  $node = toFrom($node);
  $node->attr('code', IQ_RESULT);
  $query->insertTag('name')->data($NAME);
```

```
$query->insertTag('version')->data($VERSION);
$query->insertTag('os')->data('uname -sr');
$c->send($node);

return r_HANDLED;
}
```

Just as we check for whether the element is appropriate to handle in iq_regis-ter(), we do here, too, this time looking for an IQ-get with a query child tag qual-ified by the NS_VERSION (jabber:iq:version) namespace, which we grab in $query.

Setting the <iq/>'s type to result and flipping the addresses, we then just have to add <name/>, <version/>, and <os/> tags to the query child with appropriate values, to end up with a response like the one shown in Exam-ple 9-16.

If we do this, we deem the IQ to have been handled and return the special r_HAN-DLED value, as before, to stop the dispatching going any further for this element.

Handling browse requests

Next in line to handle the incoming <iq/> element is the iq_browse() func-tion. Of course, if we've already handled the element, iq_browse() won't even get a shot at responding. But if it did, it would proceed along similar lines to the iq_version() function:

```
sub iq_browse {

  my $node = shift;
  debug("[iq_browse]");

  return unless my $query = $node->getTag('', NS_BROWSE)
          and $node->attr('type', IQ_GET);

  debug("--> browse request");

  $node = toFrom($node);
  $node->attr('type', IQ_RESULT);
  my $rss = $query->insertTag('service');
  $rss->attr('type', 'rss');
  $rss->attr('jid', $ID);
  $rss->attr('name', $NAME);
  $rss->insertTag('ns')->data(NS_REGISTER);
  $c->send($node);

  return r_HANDLED;
}
```

The only real difference is that we want this function to handle IQ-gets in the jab-ber:iq:browse namespace and return a browse result. Browsing will be discussed in greater detail in the section "Browsing LDAP" in Chapter 10. For now, though, let's focus on returning a top-level browse result that reflects what might be returned if a similar browse request were made of the JSM, as described in the section "jabber:iq:browse" in Chapter 6. Example 9-19 shows what iq_browse() will return.

Example 9-19. The RSS news agent responds to jabber:iq:browse requests via iq_browse()

```
RECV: <iq type="get" id="browser_JCOM_2" to="rss.qmacro.dyndns.org">
          <query xmlns="jabber:iq:browse"&sol;>
      </iq>

SEND: <iq id='browser_JCOM_2' type='result'
          to='dj@qmacro.dyndns.org/winjab'
          from='rss.qmacro.dyndns.org'>
          <query xmlns='jabber:iq:browse'>
            <service jid='rss.qmacro.dyndns.org'
                 type='rss'
                 name='RSS News Agent'>
              <ns>jabber:iq:register</ns>
            </service>
          </query>
      </iq>
```

Dealing with other requests

There are untold IQ elements that could be sent to the component. While it would be *possible* just to ignore them, we ought to do something and at least respond with something like "not supported." For that, we have iq_notimpl() as a catch-all. If the dispatcher manages to make its way to here, we know that the <iq/> element is not anything we recognize as wanting to respond to.

The following can be used to tell the requester that what they're asking for hasn't been implemented:

```
sub iq_notimpl {
   my $node = shift;
   $node = toFrom($node);
   $node->attr('type', IQ_ERROR);
   my $error = $node->insertTag('error');
   $error->attr('code', '501');
   $error->data('Not Implemented');
   $c->send($node);

   return r_HANDLED;
}
```

As you can see, all this does is set the <iq/> type to error, switches the from and to, and adds an <error/> tag:

```
<error code='501'>Not Implemented</error>
```

The modified element is sent back to the requester. This lets them know that they've requested something that just isn't there or hasn't been implemented yet.

The RSS mechanism

Now that we've set up the functions to handle incoming queries, all that's left is for us to define what happens every time the heartbeat in the `Jabber::Connection` loop ticks past the 30-minute mark. We registered this `rss()` function with the `register_beat()` method earlier in the script:

```
sub rss {

    debug("[rss]");

    # Create NodeFactory
    my $nf = new Jabber::NodeFactory;
```

In the IQ handlers `iq-register()`, `iq-version()`, `iq-browse()`, and `iq-notimpl()`, we avoided the need to build elements from scratch, by simply turning around the incoming request elements and making them into responses, before sending them back. Here, in the `rss()` function, we'll actually be building elements from scratch—headline type <message> elements to be precise. This is the reason we need an instance of the `Jabber::NodeFactory`.

```
    # Go through each of the RSS sources
    foreach my $source (keys %sources) {

        # Retrieve attempt
        my $data = get($sources{$source});

        # Didn't get it? Next one
        unless (defined($data)) {
            debug("cannot retrieve $source");
            next;
        }

        # Parse the RSS
        my $rss = XML::RSS->new();
        eval { $rss->parse($data) };

        if ($@) {
            debug("Problems parsing $source");
            next;
        }
```

The procedure in this function reflects what we described earlier in the section "Polling the RSS sources." Each time `rss()` is called, it goes through each of the sources defined in the list (%sources) and tries to retrieve it with `get()`, a function from the `LWP::Simple` library, and parse it with an instance of `XML::RSS`. Because

XML::RSS uses XML::Parser, which dies if it encounters invalid XML, we wrap the call to the parse() method in eval.

> Ideally we'd use just one instance of XML::RSS for the whole rss() function, but XML::RSS requires us to create a new instance for every source we wish to work with.

```
my @items = @{$rss->{items}};

# Check new items
debug("$source: looking for new items");
foreach my $item (@items) {

    # Stop checking if we get to items already seen
    last if exists $cache{$source} and $cache{$source} eq $item->{link};

    debug("$source: new item $item->{title}");
```

Pulling the items from the RSS source into @items, we look through them, but stop looking if we come across one that we've seen previously (and stored in the %cache).

If we do have a new item to send out, we create a headline message containing the item's details:

```
# Create a headline message
my $msg = $nf->newNode('message');

$msg->attr('type', 'headline');
$msg->attr('from', join('@', $source, $ID));
$msg->insertTag('subject')->data($item->{title});
$msg->insertTag('body')->data($item->{description});

my $xoob = $msg->insertTag('x', NS_XOOB);
$xoob->insertTag('url')->data($item->{link});
$xoob->insertTag('desc')->data($item->{description});
```

We use the node factory in $nf to create a new empty <message/> element, with the newNode() method. This element is built into a full-blown headline message with a jabber:x:oob-qualified <x/> extension containing the RSS item information. We can see that the call insertTag() used here has two arguments. The second is used to specify an optional namespace with which the new node (or tag) will be qualified. This call creates a Jabber::NodeFactory::Node object in $xoob that looks like this:

```
<x xmlns='jabber:x:oob'&sol;>
```

This is then embellished with the usual <url/> and <desc/> tags. What's still missing is the address information. We've specified the from; indeed taking a departure from the values we've specified for the `from` in the IQ responses, here we specify something slightly different with `join('@', $source, $ID)`, which is a `[user]@[hostname]`-style address. For example, the source for Slashdot would be:

```
slashdot@rss.qmacro.dyndns.org
```

This is mostly because it conveys more information than just the component name `rss.qmacro.dyndns.org` would. While the component's address would not normally be seen by a client user in the context of the IQ responses, many Jabber clients that support the headline message type will show the message sender in the headline list display. You can see this in Figure 9-8, where the From column in the headline list clearly shows the RSS source from which the item originated. This has a little bit of future for the component built in, too. If we wanted to extend the component for more interaction with the clients, we could have the client send a message to the `[RSS source]@[componentname]` JID and, on receipt, the component would immediately have context information on which source the message was about, without the client user having to do anything other than specify a JID.

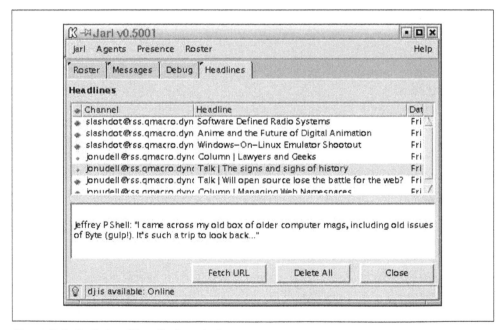

Figure 9-8. Jarl's headline display window

Now that we've built the headline message, which looks like the one in Example 9-9, we can fire it off to each of the users who have registered for that RSS source:

```
# Deliver to all that want RSS headlines
foreach my $jid (keys %reg) {

  my $registration = $reg{$jid};

  if (exists($registration->{$source})) {
    $msg->attr('to', $jid);
    debug("delivering to $jid");
    $c->send($msg);
  }

}
```

The first time we encounter an RSS source, we won't have any record of a "last seen" item in the %cache. So we avoid flooding people with all the items of a new RSS source by jumping out of the item loop if there's no cache info:

```
# Prevent all items counted as new the first time around
last unless exists($cache{$source});
}
```

Finally, we make a mark in the cache for the latest item we've encountered, to prepare the script for the next feed:

```
# Remember the latest new item
$cache{$source} = $items[0]->{link};

  }

}
```

The cleanup() function

The cleanup() function is called if an attempt is made to shut the script down. It unties the registration hash, ensuring no data is lost, and disconnects from the Jabber server:

```
sub cleanup {

  debug("cleaning up");
  untie %reg;
  $c->disconnect;
  exit;

}
```

Helper functions

Any script over a certain size is likely to have some helper functions, and our RSS news agent is no exception. Here we have the function to switch the from and to attribute values of a node (toFrom()), the function to remove the resource from a JID (stripJID()), and something not much better than a debugging-style print statement:

```
sub toFrom {
  my $node = shift;
  my $to = $node->attr('to');
  $node->attr('to', $node->attr('from'));
  $node->attr('from', $to);
  return $node;
}


sub stripJID {
  my $JID = shift;
  $JID =~ s|/.*$||;
  return $JID;
}

sub debug {
  print STDERR "debug: ", @_, "\n";
}
```

Further Ideas

There's only so much that can be included in a demonstration script. There's plenty of room for improvement, even if you don't count rewriting it all from scratch. For example, you could store registrations in a SQL database or, alternatively, use the Jabber server's own xdb component. More importantly, a static list of RSS sources is rather restrictive. How about allowing the user to register their own URLs? Or building an administrative mode that accepts a special IQ from certain JIDs, with which the RSS source list can be maintained?

The browsing response function would be an ideal candidate to be expanded upon. Another level of browsing could be added that would return browse items that reflect the specific user's RSS source registrations. It's probably worth exploring the power of addressing the component to include the RSS source, to extend the interactive facilities. For example, you might want to have the script accept and act upon messages sent to the component's JID, which includes a *username* portion representing the RSS source.

A Simple Headline Viewer

Let's close this chapter on a lighter note by building a complementary script that we can use to keep an eye on the headlines coming in from the RSS news agent. We'll call this program *blv*, for "HeadLine Viewer." Basically, we want to build something that allows the user to watch RSS headlines as they scroll by in a window that doesn't take up a lot of screen real estate.

In the recipes so far, we've had great success building solutions that make use of off-the-shelf clients. But it's time to buck the trend, indeed to make another point. While you can arrange the features of your Jabber-based applications in the direction of standard clients, to take advantage of the installed base of Jabber clients, if you do want to create a client that works differently, a client that fits your needs exactly, then go ahead—it will be surprisingly straightforward. The mantra of "server side complex, client side simple" (with apologies to George Orwell) is there to help us. What's more, we can put into action an idea expressed earlier in the book (in the section "Custom Clients"):

> A Jabber client is a piece of software that implements as much of the Jabber protocol as required to get the job done.

If we're going to build a headline viewer client and know that the information is going to be delivered to us in headline-type <message/> elements, why have the viewer client understand or deal with anything else? To implement a Jabber solution, we pick and choose the parts of the protocol that make sense in the context of that solution. If you want to transport RPC calls in data payloads between two endpoints, why bother with roster management or rich-text chat facilities? If you just want to join a conference room to talk with the other room occupants, why bother with threaded one-on-one conversations? If you need routing and presence capabilities to have your oven know when you've arrived home, why engineer anything else?

What we're going to write here is a simple headline viewer. Nothing more, nothing less. It will know the tiniest thing about presence—as the headlines come in as <message/> elements, it will need to announce its availability to the JSM. We're going to build a Jabber client that will have a session context with the JSM, so we need to tell the JSM that we're available when the client starts. Otherwise, the headlines will be queued by the store-and-forward mechanism for delivery the next time we're available.

We'll leave registration to the RSS news agent to another client that knows about agents (services) and can interact in a jabber:iq:register kind of way. Again, the "one size fits all, one client for everything" philosophy doesn't always have to apply; different features of different programs can get the job done. So while the headline viewer will receive, understand, and display the message headlines, we'll use WinJab or even JIM to manage the RSS source subscriptions. Figure 9-9 illustrates the process of registration with the RSS news agent component, using JIM.

The suggestion of JIM as a client to complement or make up for the lack of features in the headline viewer is deliberately ironic. The role JIM plays is to provide support for core Jabber client features, of which headline messages are not considered to be a part. So while JIM can interact with services and register (and unregister—which will send the <remove/> tag in the query, as described in the

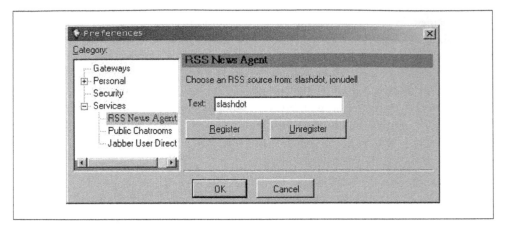

Figure 9-9. Registering with the RSS News Agent, using JIM

section "Handling registration requests"), it doesn't handle headline-type messages, which is perfectly fine. Our headline viewer won't handle chat or normal messages—it's not *supposed* to.

It's worth pointing out that another reason the headline viewer client can remain simple is because the RSS news agent will be doing all the hard work. Unlike other (non-Jabber) headline viewer programs, *hlv* depends upon the RSS news agent. It's that component that will maintain the list of RSS sources. It's also that component that will retrieve those sources at regular intervals and check for new items. All we have to do is sit back and have those new items pushed to us, at which point the client has to make a slight effort to insert the details of those new items into the viewer display.

What the Headline Viewer Is Going to Do

The headline viewer, shown in Figure 9-10, has a scrollable area where headlines are displayed. We can *clear* that area, or select a headline and call up a web browser to *fetch* the story by passing the URL to it.

It's also nice and small, visually and in the amount of code we're going to have to write. We connect to the Jabber server, set up a handler for the incoming headline

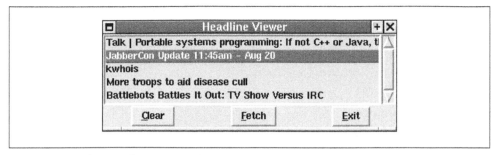

Figure 9-10. The Headline Viewer client

messages, build the display, send our availability, and sit back and watch the news roll in.

Actually, we need to say a few things about the "sitting back" bit. We know that Jabber programming implies an event model. For this example, we're going to use Tk, a widget library for building GUI applications, with bindings for many languages. Tk itself has an event model, which in many ways reflects Jabber's. Table 9-3 shows how Jabber and Tk relate to each other in this programming model.

Table 9-3. Jabber and Tk event model reflections

Jabber	Tk
Establishing connection to server	Constructing widgets
Defining callbacks to handle incoming elements	Defining callbacks to handle UI events
Setting a "heartbeat" function[a]	Setting a command to execute regularly with the repeat() function
Launching the event loop	Starting MainLoop()

[a] See the section "Preparing the RSS event function and element handlers."

Having one program governed by two independent event loops is not what we want to try to achieve. We want Jabber's and Tk's event models to cooperate. This is achievable by using a master/slave relationship between the two models. Tk's repeat() method can be used to invoke a function that calls the Jabber library's process() method. We can hand over control to Tk with MainLoop() and know that the Jabber event model will get a look in because of the Tk event callback we've defined with repeat().

The hlv Script

The *hlv* script, shown in Example 9-20, uses Perl with the `Net::Jabber` library.

Example 9-20. The hlv script, written in Perl

```perl
use Tk;
use Net::Jabber qw(Client);
use strict;

use constant SERVER   => 'gnu.pipetree.com';
use constant PORT     => 5222;
use constant USER     => 'dj';
use constant PASSWORD => 'secret';
use constant RESOURCE => 'hlv';

use constant BROWSER  => '/usr/bin/konqueror';

my @headlines;
my @list;

my $connection = Net::Jabber::Client->new();

$connection->Connect(
  hostname => SERVER,
  port     => PORT,
) or die "Cannot connect ($!)\n";

my @result = $connection->AuthSend(
  username => USER,
  password => PASSWORD,
  resource => RESOURCE,
);

if ($result[0] ne "ok") {
  die "Ident/Auth with server failed: $result[0] - $result[1]\n";
}

$connection->SetCallBacks( message => \&handle_message );

my $main = MainWindow->new( -title => "Headline Viewer" );
$main->geometry('50x5+10+10');
$main->repeat(5000, \&check_headlines);

# Button frame
my $buttons = $main->Frame();
$buttons->pack(qw/-side bottom -fill x/);

# Headline list
my $list = $main->Scrolled(qw/Listbox -scrollbars e -height 40 -setgrid 1/);

# Clear button
my $button_clear = $buttons->Button(
            -text     => 'Clear',
```

Example 9-20. The hlv script, written in Perl (continued)

```perl
                  -underline => '0',
                  -command   => sub
                  {
                    @list = (); $list->delete(0, 'end')
                  },
              );

# Fetch Button
my $button_fetch = $buttons->Button(
                  -text      => 'Fetch',
                  -underline => '0',
                  -command   => sub
                  {
                    system(
                      join(" ", (BROWSER, $list[$list->curselection], "&"))
                    )
                  },
              );

# Exit button
my $button_exit = $buttons->Button(
                  -text      => 'exit',
                  -underline => '0',
                  -command   => [$main => 'destroy'],
              );


$button_clear->pack(qw/-side left -expand 1/);
$button_fetch->pack(qw/-side left -expand 1/);
$button_exit->pack(qw/-side left -expand 1/);

$list->pack(qw/-side left -expand 1 -fill both/);

$connection->PresenceSend();

MainLoop();

$connection->Disconnect;
exit(0);

sub check_headlines {
  $connection->Process(1);
  while (@headlines) {
    my $headline = pop @headlines;
    $list->insert(0, $headline->{title});
    unshift @list, $headline->{link};
  }
}

sub handle_message {
  my $msg = new Net::Jabber::Message($_[1]);
  return unless $msg->GetType eq 'headline';
```

Example 9-20. The hlv script, written in Perl (continued)

```perl
my ($oob) = $msg->GetX('jabber:x:oob');
push @headlines, {
                    link => $oob->GetURL(),
                    title => $msg->GetSubject(),
                };
}
```

Reviewing the hlv Script Step by Step

The script starts with the declarations of the libraries we're going to use, along with some constants:

```perl
use Tk;
use Net::Jabber qw(Client);
use strict;

use constant SERVER   => 'gnu.pipetree.com';
use constant PORT     => 5222;
use constant USER     => 'dj';
use constant PASSWORD => 'secret';
use constant RESOURCE => 'hlv';

use constant BROWSER  => '/usr/bin/konqueror';
```

The *hlv* script will connect to Jabber as a client, so we need to specify that in the use statement to have the appropriate Net::Jabber modules loaded. We're going to be connecting to the Jabber server at *gnu.pipetree.com*, although, as we said, the RSS news agent might live somewhere else. It just so happens that in this scenario, there's a reference to the component in *gnu.pipetree.com*'s JSM <browse/> section, so we can carry out registration conversations with it (using JIM, for example).

If the Fetch button is clicked when an item in the list is selected (see Figure 9-10), we want to jump to the story by launching a web browser. The constant BROWSER used here refers to the browser—in this case, Konqueror, the browser of choice for KDE users—on the local machine.

```perl
my @headlines;
my @list;
```

We declare two arrays: @headlines, which we'll use to hold the items as they arrive contained in the headline <message/> elements on the XML stream, and @list, to hold the URLs that relate to those items in @headlines.

After connecting to and authenticating with the Jabber server, we set up the callback to take care of incoming <message/> elements (this is very similar to the way the coffee monitor script connects and authenticates in the section "The setup_Jabber( ) function"):

```
my $connection = Net::Jabber::Client->new();

$connection->Connect(
  hostname => SERVER,
  port     => PORT,
) or die "Cannot connect ($!)\n";

my @result = $connection->AuthSend(
  username => USER,
  password => PASSWORD,
  resource => RESOURCE,
);

if ($result[0] ne "ok") {
  die "Ident/Auth with server failed: $result[0] - $result[1]\n";
}
```

This is the `handle_message()` function:

```
$connection->SetCallBacks( message => \&handle_message );
```

Now it's time to build the GUI. We start by creating a main window, giving it a title and geometry, and establishing the cooperation between the two event models with the `repeat()` method:

```
my $main = MainWindow->new( -title => "Headline Viewer" );
$main->geometry('50x5+10+10');
$main->repeat(5000, \&check_headlines);
```

The `repeat()` function will arrange Tk's main event loop to hiccup every five seconds (the first argument is measured in milliseconds) and call the `check_headlines()` function.

Next, we build a frame to hold three buttons—Clear, Fetch, and Exit—and a scrollable list to contain the titles as they're received:

```
# Button frame
my $buttons = $main->Frame();
$buttons->pack(qw/-side bottom -fill x/);

# Headline list
my $list = $main->Scrolled(qw/Listbox -scrollbars e -height 40 -setgrid 1/);
```

Defining the buttons, one at a time, brings our attention to the Tk UI event model, in that we define the handlers using the `-command` argument of the `Button()` method. The handlers' jobs are quite small, so we can get away with writing them inline:

```
# Clear button
my $button_clear = $buttons->Button(
            -text       => 'Clear',
            -underline  => '0',
            -command    => sub
            {
               @list = (); $list->delete(0, 'end')
            },
         );
```

If called, the Clear button clears the scrollable display by calling the `delete()` method on the `$list` object and emptying the corresponding array of URLs.

The Fetch button extracts the URL from the highlighted item in the scrollable list using the `curselection()` method to retrieve the index value. The `@list` array is then used to look up the URL by launching the browser (in this case, Konqueror) in the background. Many browsers accept a URL as the first argument; if your choice of browser doesn't, you'll need to modify this call slightly.

```
# Fetch Button
my $button_fetch = $buttons->Button(
            -text       => 'Fetch',
            -underline  => '0',
            -command    => sub
            {
               system(
                 join(" ", (BROWSER, $list[$list->curselection], "&"))
               )
            },
         );
```

If clicked, the Exit button uses a `destroy()` function to, well, destroy (or close) the main window. This causes Tk's main event loop to come to an end, passing control back to the statement in the script following the one with which that main event loop was launched (with `MainLoop()`):

```
# Exit button
my $button_exit = $buttons->Button(
            -text       => 'Exit',
            -underline  => '0',
            -command    => [$main => 'destroy'],
         );
```

Having created all the buttons and packed everything into the window with the `pack()` method:

```
$button_clear->pack(qw/-side left -expand 1/);
$button_fetch->pack(qw/-side left -expand 1/);
$button_exit->pack(qw/-side left -expand 1/);

$list->pack(qw/-side left -expand 1 -fill both/);
```

we announce to the JSM that we're available:

```
$connection->PresenceSend();
```

All that remains for us to do is start Tk's main event loop. We include a call to the
Net::Jabber Disconnect() method for when the Exit button is clicked and control
returns to the script, so we can gracefully end the Jabber connection:

```
MainLoop();

$connection->Disconnect;
exit(0);
```

We defined the check_headlines() function as the function to invoke every five
seconds:

```
sub check_headlines {
  $connection->Process(1);
  while (@headlines) {
    my $headline = pop @headlines;
    $list->insert(0, $headline->{title});
    unshift @list, $headline->{link};
  }
}
```

To check for any messages that have arrived on the XML stream, we can call the
Process() method on the connection object. If there are any messages waiting, the
handle_message() function is called to handle them:

```
sub handle_message {
  my $msg = new Net::Jabber::Message($_[1]);
  return unless $msg->GetType eq 'headline';

  my ($oob) = $msg->GetX('jabber:x:oob');
  push @headlines, {
                      link => $oob->GetURL(),
                      title => $msg->GetSubject(),
                    };
}
```

We can see fairly easily what the GetX() method does, if we remember that a
headline message, complete with an <x/> extension qualified by the jab-
ber:x:oob namespace, looks like this:

```
<message type='headline' to='dj@qmacro.dyndns.org'>
  <subject>JabberCon Update 11:45am - Aug 20</subject>
  <body>JabberCon Update - Monday Morning</body>
  <x xmlns='jabber:x:oob'>
    <url>http://www.jabbercentral.com/news/view.php?news_id=998329970</url>
    <desc>JabberCon Update - Monday Morning</desc>
  </x>
</message>
```

It returns, in list context, all the <x/> elements contained in the element represented by $msg that are qualified by the jabber:x:oob namespace. We're expecting there to be only one, which is why we plan to throw all but the first array item away with the ($oob) construction. After the call to GetX(), the object in $oob represents this part of the message:

```
<x xmlns='jabber:x:oob'>
  <url>http://www.jabbercentral.com/news/view.php?news_id=998329970</url>
  <desc>JabberCon Update - Monday Morning</desc>
</x>
```

The item's details, including the URL and title, are pushed onto the @headlines list, and the headline-type message-handling function has done its job. Control passes back to the check_headlines() script to immediately after the call to the Process() method.

The handle_message() function may have been called multiple times, depending on how many elements had arrived, so the @headlines array might contain more than one item. We run through the array, sending off each headline in turn, inserting the title into the scrollable list object and the URL into the corresponding position in the @list array:

```
$list->insert(0, $headline->{title});
unshift @list, $headline->{link};
```

That's really all there is to the code. The features are minimal, but the hlv script gets the job done. There's just enough programming to be able to receive and display RSS items.

The "just enough" philosophy demonstrated in this recipe can be appropriate in non-GUI applications of Jabber as well. Taking away the visual element of hlv to leave the mechanism for receiving and understanding jabber:x:oob information, we're left with a Jabber-aware "stub" that can be put to many uses; collection and aggregation of news stories comes immediately to mind. Along the same lines, we can see that the way we gave presence to the coffee pot in the section "Connecting Devices to Jabber" was just a melding of a stub, which understood Jabber presence, with a loop mechanism that connected to the MINDSTORMS device.

It's possible to build extremely powerful solutions using Jabber's *protocol* and the building blocks that the protocol represents (described in Chapter 6), without having any relation to a user interface. We'll see such a solution in the section "XML-RPC over Jabber."

10

Pointers for Further Development

The previous two chapters have demonstrated how Jabber can be used to build applications and solutions in many functional areas. They expanded upon and indeed went beyond the theme of instant messaging (IM) to employ the fundamental features of contextual messaging, presence, and request/response sequences, in a wide range of scenarios.

While these scenarios have in some ways been inward looking, they are natural progressions that originated inside the IM world and matured into applications and solutions that retain much of the messaging flavor. Let's consider what else Jabber has to offer as a messaging and routing mechanism.

This chapter explores some "outward looking" scenarios, to give you pointers and ideas for the future. With *Demo::JBook*, we consider the possibility of "Jabber without Jabber"—in other words, using Jabber as an *infrastructure*, in this case as a data store, without focus on any particular Jabber client or IM functionality. We also explore how Jabber is the perfect transport partner for procedure calls formalized in XML: *JabberRPCRequester* and *JabberRPCResponder* are scripts that exchange method calls and responses encoded in XML-RPC.

Using Jabber as a conduit to foreign systems is also a theme of this chapter. With *ldapr*, we build a script that reflects the hierarchy and contents of an LDAP data store, allowing that store to be navigated from a Jabber client. Finally, we look to the business world, employing Jabber in a tiny but crucial role as a conduit between SAP systems and their users.

A Simple Jabber-Based Address Book

With the availability of many different off-the-shelf Jabber clients and the use of these clients as generic tools to interact with diverse Jabber-based services, it's easy to lose sight of the fact that Jabber can also be used to contribute to *infrastructure* solutions. That is, applications and utilities can be built using the Jabber protocols, in conjunction with Jabber server-based services, without the need for a Jabber client.

By way of illustration, let's build a simple two-level address book using Jabber services. We'll call it *Demo::JBook*. We'll use this address book to look up details of our friends and colleagues while we're on the move. The ideal platform for this is going to be a web browser, in that it's accessible from personal workstations, airport web consoles, cybercafés, and personal digital assistants (PDAs) that offer access to the Internet.

The point of this illustration is not to show that there's a single solution to the problem of disconnected, incompatible, and unsynchronized directory information (because, despite any answers that you may get to the contrary—no such solution exists). Instead, the goal is to show that it's possible to make use of Jabber services and get to information stored and managed by those services without having to use a Jabber client.

Using the JUD and vCards

The two levels in our address book are going to reflect two distinct (but related) mechanisms in Jabber. We're going to base our address book on the Jabber User Directory (JUD) component and supply further information, in a "drill-down" action, using vCards.

The JUD

> Our address book will act as a query frontend for a user directory in the form of a JUD. It doesn't matter *which* JUD we use; obviously, that depends on how the application is to be deployed. On one hand, it might be appropriate to point it at your company's internal JUD, if you have one. On the other hand, it might also be just as appropriate to point it at one of the larger public JUDs, such as the one connected to the Jabber server running on *jabber.org* (which is *users.jabber.org*).

vCards

> Every Jabber entity—users, components, and servers—has the potential to have a vCard. We saw in Chapter 4 that the Jabber server itself, and many of the components connected to it, had a vCard definition. While the vCard standard is still fluid, the implementation within Jabber, as described in the section "The vcard-temp Namespace" in Chapter 6, is enough to be useful.

The key to the application is that both the Jabber mechanisms that it relies upon—the JUD and vCards—can be accessed independently of the availability of the users that the information stored in those mechanisms represents. The JUD runs as an independent component and manages the directory information using its own data store. With the default JUD and XML Database (XDB) component configurations, this data store will be in the Jabber server's spool directory in a file called *jud/global.xdb*.

Users interact with the JUD to manage their information, using IQ elements qualified by the `jabber:iq:register` namespace. User vCard information is also stored at the server side, and users manage the vCard contents using IQ elements qualified by the `vcard-temp` namespace. Again, with the default configuration, the vCard information, stored along with the rest of the user data relevant to the Jabber server in user-specific spool files, will be held in the Jabber server's spool directory in files called *[hostname]/[user].xml*.

What Demo::JBook Will Do

The JUD can be queried using a normal Jabber client. In Figure 10-1, we can see the search form of Jabber Instant Messenger (JIM).

The search fields are not fixed; instead, they're dynamically generated, according to the result of an initial IQ-get in the `jabber:iq:search` namespace. Just as an IQ-get in the `jabber:iq:register` namespace (as illustrated in the section "Presence-Sensitive CVS Notification") is used for registering users, the `jabber:iq:search` namespace is is used for search requests. This is illustrated in Example 10-1, where an IQ-get is sent to the JUD at `jud.gnu.mine.nu`.

Example 10-1. An IQ-get to a JUD in the jabber:iq:search namespace

```
SEND: <iq type="get" id="9138" to="jud.gnu.mine.nu">
         <query xmlns="jabber:iq:search"&sol;>
      </iq>

RECV: <iq from='jud.gnu.mine.nu' id='9138'
          to='qmacro@jabber.org/study' type='result'>
        <query xmlns='jabber:iq:search'>
          <first&sol;>
          <last&sol;>
          <instructions>
            Fill in a field to search for any matching Jabber users.
          </instructions>
        </query>
      </iq>
```

In response to the IQ-get request, the JUD sends back a list of fields with which the directory can be searched, along with some simple instructions.

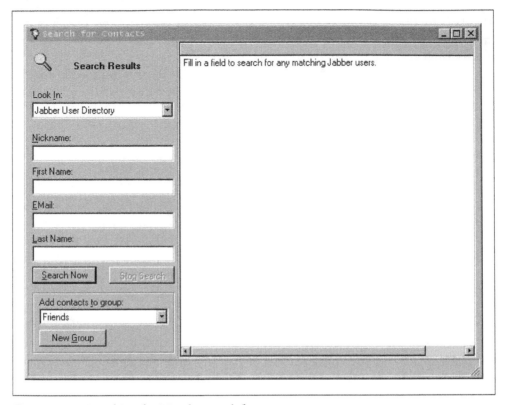

Figure 10-1. Searching the JUD: the search form

The actual search follows the same registration pattern (using the `jabber:iq:register` namespace) that we saw in the section "Presence-Sensitive CVS Notification." After receiving a list of possible search fields, a search request is made with an IQ-set, as shown in Example 10-2. The results, returned in an IQ-result from the JUD, are listed with each entry contained in an `<item&sol;>` tag. The search results are shown in Figure 10-2.

Example 10-2. The JUD search request and response

```
SEND: <iq type="set" id="2627" to="users.jabber.org">
        <query xmlns="jabber:iq:search">
          <last>adams</last>
        </query>
      </iq>

RECV: <iq from='users.jabber.org' id='2627'
          to='qmacro@jabber.org/study' type='result'>
        <query xmlns='jabber:iq:search'>
          <item jid='qmacro@jabber.org'>
            <nick>qmacro</nick>
            <first>DJ</first>
```

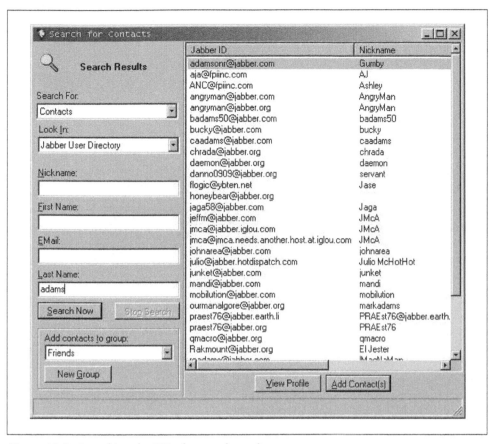

Figure 10-2. Searching the JUD: the search results

Example 10-2. The JUD search request and response (continued)

```
          <email>dj.adams@gmx.net</email>
          <last>Adams</last>
      </item>
      <item jid='qmacro@jabber.com'>
        <nick>dj</nick>
        <first>DJ</first>
        <email>dj.adams@gmx.net</email>
        <last>Adams</last>
      </item>
      <item jid='joseph@gnu.mine.nu'>
        <nick>joseph</nick>
        <first>Joseph</first>
        <email>joseph@pipetree.com</email>
        <last>Adams</last>
      </item>

      ... (more items) ...
```

Example 10-2. The JUD search request and response (continued)

```
    </query>
  </iq>
```

Searching a JUD

The first level that we'll build into *Demo::JBook* is the ability to query a JUD. The address book is to be browser-based, so we'll generate HTML on the fly according to the search fields we receive in response to our IQ-get. It should look something like that shown in Figure 10-3.

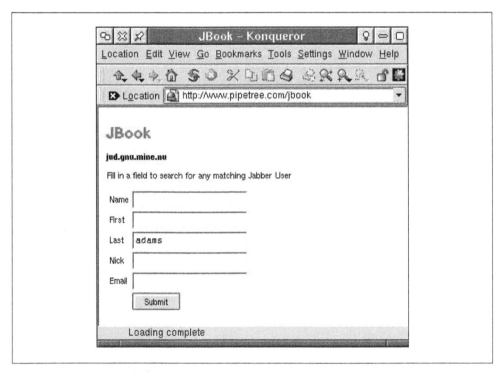

Figure 10-3. JUD search form in HTML

The items returned in the search results don't really provide much information:

```
<item jid='joseph@gnu.mine.nu'>
  <nick>joseph</nick>
  <first>Joseph</first>
  <email>joseph@pipetree.com</email>
  <last>Adams</last>
</item>
```

Here, we have the user's first and last names, his nickname, and his email address. One of the functions of the JUD is to determine which fields are storable.

JUD Fields

The fields in a JUD that are used to store the directory data are determined either by a hardcoded list in the JUD source itself or a configurable list that's stored and maintained separate from the JUD code. The list fields allowed for searching a JUD may or may not be used for storing the information; it may be a subset (it makes no sense, of course, for it to be a superset). For example, if the fields used to store information in a JUD are:

```
<name&sol;>
<email&sol;>
<first&sol;>
<last&sol;>
<nick&sol;>
<text&sol;>
```

it may be that the fields available for searching may be just:

```
<first&sol;>
<last&sol;>
```

as shown in Example 10-1.

In case you're wondering how to discover the fields that can be used to populate the information in the JUD, an IQ-get can be used in the jabber:iq:register namespace to qualify a *registration* conversation with the JUD, which is where the information is "registered," or stored. This is shown in Example 10-3.

Example 10-3. An IQ-get to a JUD in the jabber:iq:register namespace

```
SEND: <iq type='get' to='jud.gnu.mine.nu'>
        <query xmlns='jabber:iq:register'&sol;>
      </iq>

RECV: <iq from='jud.gnu.mine.nu'
          to='qmacro@jabber.com/study' type='result'>
        <query xmlns='jabber:iq:register'>
          <nick&sol;>
          <first&sol;>
          <email&sol;>
          <last&sol;>
          <text&sol;>
          <name&sol;>
          <instructions>
             Fill in all of the fields to add yourself to the JUD.
          </instructions>
        </query>
      </iq>
```

We can see in Figure 10-4 how the results will typically be rendered.

Figure 10-4. JUD search results as rendered in Demo::JBook

Retrieving vCard information

As well as registering with a JUD, it's possible that a user has maintained more information about himself—in his vCard. Depending on the Jabber client used, various user information can be stored in a personal vCard, which is stored on the server side. In Figure 10-5, we see the JIM client's vCard maintenance window, titled User Profile.

The result of entering information and clicking the OK button in Figure 10-5 can be seen in Example 10-4, where an IQ-set in the `vcard-temp` namespace is made to store the information (some of the vCard tags have been omitted to keep the example short). Notice how no `to` attribute is specified in the IQ-set and how the result appears to come from the sender (`qmacro@jabber.com/study`). The storage of personal—user-specific—vCard information is a function of the Jabber Session Manager (JSM), which is where the `<iq&sol;>` element will be routed automatically, as it is coming in over a client connection (defined by the `jabber:client` stream-level namespace). This is further discussed in the section "IQ attributes."

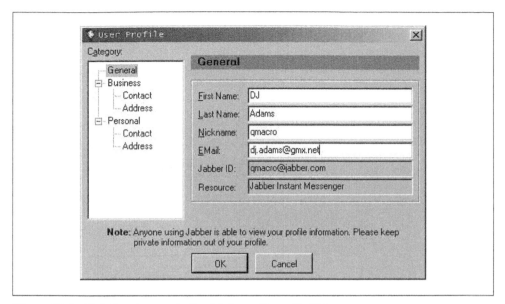

Figure 10-5. Updating personal vCard information with JIM

Example 10-4. Setting vCard information in the vcard-temp namespace

```
SEND: <iq type="set">
        <VCARD version="3.0" xmlns="vcard-temp">
          <N>
            <GIVEN>DJ</GIVEN>
            <FAMILY>Adams</FAMILY>
            <MIDDLE&sol;>
          </N>
          <NICKNAME>qmacro</NICKNAME>
          <EMAIL>
            <INTERNET&sol;>
            <PREF&sol;>
            dj.adams@gmx.net
          </EMAIL>

          ...

        </VCARD>
      </iq>

RECV: <iq type='result' from='qmacro@jabber.com/study'
        to='qmacro@jabber.com/study'&sol;>
```

As well as being storable, the information in a personal vCard is also retrievable by anyone, anytime. The idea of a personal vCard is that the information it contains is permanently available. Because the vCard data is stored server side, it can be retrieved anytime the user is online.

The key (literally and metaphorically) of each of the search result items returned is a JID. We can see this in Example 10-2, where each <item/> tag has a `jid` attribute. You won't be surprised to know that the key to accessing someone's vCard is his JID too. So we have a great way for *Demo::JBook* to jump from level 1, which displays JUD search results, to level 2 by retrieving and displaying a vCard via the JID. The results of jumping from a JUD result entry to a vCard display for the selected user, via the JUD, can be seen in Figure 10-6.

Figure 10-6. A vCard as displayed in Demo::JBook

Using Demo::JBook as an Apache Handler

The *Demo::JBook* application is going to exist as an Apache *mod_perl* handler, that is, we'll use the power of Perl's integration into the Apache web server to write an Apache module in Perl. You can find out more about *mod_perl* at *http://perl.apache.org*.

Being a *mod_perl* module, *Demo::JBook* exists in the form of a Perl module and is configured in Apache to service calls to http://[hostname]/jbook. The configuration can be comfortably placed in the main Apache configuration file, *httpd.conf*, or, as is common in *mod_perl* installations, in an extra file usually called *perl.conf*, which is linked to *httpd.conf* as follows:

```
<IfModule mod_perl.c>
  Include conf/perl.conf
</IfModule>
```

The configuration for *Demo::JBook* is placed in the *perl.conf* file, as shown in Example 10-5.

Example 10-5. Configuring the module as a handler in Apache

```
require conf/startup.pl

...

<Location /jbook>
  SetHandler perl-script
  PerlHandler Demo::JBook
</Location>
```

The `PerlHandler` directive refers to the *Demo::JBook* module, which is the *JBook.pm* file that exists in the *Demo/* directory. The module will be invoked to handle calls to the relative URL */jbook*. You can add the location of the *Demo::JBook* module to *mod_perl*'s list of directories in the `BEGIN` section of the *startup.pl* script, in the *conf/* directory, like this:

```
BEGIN {
  use Apache ();
  use lib '[the directory location of Demo::JBook]';
}
```

The Demo::JBook Script

Before taking the *Demo::JBook* script apart, let's have a look at the script in its entirety, shown in Example 10-6. Written in Perl, *Demo::JBook* uses the `Jabber::Connection` library.

Example 10-6. The Demo::JBook script, written in Perl

```
package Demo::JBook;

use strict;

use Jabber::Connection;
use Jabber::NodeFactory;
use Jabber::NS qw(:iq :misc);

use constant SERVER   => 'gnu.mine.nu';
use constant USER     => 'jbook';
use constant PASS     => 'pass';
use constant RESOURCE => 'jbook';
use constant JUD      => 'jud.gnu.mine.nu';
```

Example 10-6. The Demo::JBook script, written in Perl (continued)

```
sub handler {

  my $r = shift;
  my @a = $r->args;

  my $nf = Jabber::NodeFactory->new;

  $r->content_type('text/html');
  $r->send_http_header;

  $r->print("<html><head><title>JBook</title></head><body>");
  $r->print("<h1><a href='/jbook'>JBook</a></h1>");

  # Connect to the Jabber server
  my $c = Jabber::Connection->new(server => SERVER);
  unless ($c->connect) {
    $r->print("Sorry, no connection to Jabber available at ".SERVER);
    $r->print("</body></html>");
    return;
  }

  $c->auth(USER, PASS, RESOURCE);


  # No arguments: Instructions
  if (scalar @a == 0) {

    # Construct IQ-get in iq:search namespace
    my $iq = $nf->newNode('iq');
    $iq->attr('to', JUD);
    $iq->attr('type', IQ_GET);
    $iq->insertTag('query', NS_SEARCH);

    # Send the IQ-get
    my $result = $c->ask($iq);

    if ($result->attr('type') eq IQ_ERROR) {
      $r->print("sorry, no connection to JUD available at ".JUD);
      $r->print("</body></html>");
      $c->disconnect;
      return;
    }

    my $info = $result->getTag('', NS_SEARCH);

    # Display the results in HTML
    $r->print("<p><strong>".JUD."</strong></p>\n");
    $r->print("<p>".$info->getTag('instructions')->data."</p>\n");
    $r->print("<form><table>\n");
    foreach my $field ($info->getChildren) {
      next if $field->name eq 'instructions';
      $r->print("<tr>");
```

Example 10-6. The Demo::JBook script, written in Perl (continued)

```perl
      $r->print("<td>".ucfirst($field->name)."</td>");
      $r->print("<td><input type='text' name='".$field->name."'></td>");
      $r->print("</tr>\n");
    }
    $r->print("<tr><td></td><td><input type='submit'></td></tr>\n");
    $r->print("</table></form>\n");

  }


  # Multiple arguments: JUD lookup
  elsif (scalar @a > 1) {

    # Treat the arguments as a hash
    my %a = @a;

    # Construct an IQ-set
    my $iq = $nf->newNode('iq');
    $iq->attr('to', JUD);
    $iq->attr('type', IQ_SET);
    my $query = $iq->insertTag('query', NS_SEARCH);

    while (my($name, $val) = each(%a)) {
      $query->insertTag($name)->data($val) if $val;
    }

    # Make call
    my $result = $c->ask($iq);

    if ($result->attr('type') eq IQ_ERROR) {
      $r->print("sorry, cannot query JUD");
      $r->print("</body></html>");
      $c->disconnect;
      return;
    }

    my $info = $c->ask($iq)->getTag('', NS_SEARCH);

    my $items = 0;

    $r->print("<p><strong>".JUD."</strong></p>\n");
    $r->print("<table border='1'>\n");

    foreach my $item ($info->getChildren) {

      # Heading
      unless ($items) {
        $r->print("<tr>");
        foreach my $tag ($item->getChildren) {
          $r->print("<th>".ucfirst($tag->name)."</th>");
        }
        $r->print("</tr>\n");
```

Example 10-6. The Demo::JBook script, written in Perl (continued)

```
    }

    $r->print("<tr>");
    my $flag = 0;
    foreach my $tag ($item->getChildren) {
      unless (length($tag->data) == 0 or $flag++) {
        $r->print("<td><a href='/jbook?".$item->attr('jid')."'>");
        $r->print($tag->data."</a></td>");
      }
      else {
        $r->print("<td>".$tag->data."</td>");
      }
    }
    $r->print("</tr>\n");

    $items++;
  }
  $r->print("</table>\n");

  $r->print("<p>$items results found</p>");

}


# Single argument: vCard lookup
else {

  # Construct query
  my $iq = $nf->newNode('iq');
  $iq->attr('to', $a[0]);
  $iq->attr('type', IQ_GET);
  $iq->insertTag('vcard', NS_VCARD);

  # Make call and retrieve results
  my $result = $c->ask($iq);

  if ($result->attr('type') eq IQ_ERROR)  {
    $r->print("sorry, cannot retrieve vCard for $a[0]");
    $r->print("</body></html>");
    $c->disconnect;
    return;
  }

  my $vcard = $result->getTag('', NS_VCARD);

  print ("<strong>$a[0]</strong>\n");

  # Display each of the top-level tags if they contain data
  foreach my $tag ($vcard->getChildren) {
    print "<br&sol;>".$tag->name." : ".$tag->data."\n" if $tag->data;
  }
```

Example 10-6. The Demo::JBook script, written in Perl (continued)

```
    }

    $r->print("</body></html>");
    $c->disconnect;

    return;

}

1;
```

Taking Demo::JBook Step by Step

Now that we've got a hold on the scope and scale of *Demo::JBook*, let's take the script apart—step by step—to see how it works.

Declarations

Because *Demo::JBook* is an Apache handler, it exists as a Perl module—hence the package declaration at the top of the file:

```
package Demo::JBook;

use strict;

use Jabber::Connection;
use Jabber::NodeFactory;
use Jabber::NS qw(:iq :misc);

use constant SERVER   => 'gnu.mine.nu';
use constant USER     => 'jbook';
use constant PASS     => 'pass';
use constant RESOURCE => 'jbook';
use constant JUD      => 'users.jabber.org';
```

This code exists within the *Demo::JBook* package that was declared as the handler for the `http://[hostname]/jbook` location, shown in Example 10-5. We're going to make full use of the `Jabber::Connection` library and bring in all three of its modules for managing the Jabber server connection, for dispatching elements that arrive (`Jabber::Connection`), for building and manipulating elements (`Jabber::NodeFactory`), and using common Jabber programming constants (`Jabber::NS`). In the case of `Jabber::NS`, we need only a few namespaces to manage our JUD and vCard queries, so the `:iq` and `:misc` tags will be used to refer a collection of constants in `Jabber::NS`.

The constants `SERVER`, `USER`, `PASS`, and `RESOURCE` define the connection to the Jabber server. This connection doesn't have to be made to the JUD that will be queried by *Demo::JBook*. By way of illustration, we have *jabber.org*'s JUD (`users.jabber.org`) specified as the value for the `JUD` constant. For the purpose of this example, this will be the JUD that *Demo::JBook* will query.

You can use the *reguser* script, described in the section "User Registration Script," to create the *Demo::JBook* user. See the section "Presence" for an example of how this can be done.

General handler preparation

Following the script's declarations, it's time to define the handler function that Apache will call to handle incoming requests to the `http://[`*hostname*`]/jbook` location. The name of the handler must be `handler()`:

```
sub handler {

  my $r = shift;
  my @a = $r->args;

  my $nf = Jabber::NodeFactory->new;

  $r->content_type('text/html');
  $r->send_http_header;

  $r->print("<html><head><title>JBook</title></head><body>");
  $r->print("<h1><a href='/jbook'>JBook</a></h1>");

  # Connect to home Jabber server
  my $c = Jabber::Connection->new(server => SERVER);
  unless ($c->connect) {
    $r->print("Sorry, no connection to Jabber available at ".SERVER);
    $r->print("</body></html>");
    return;
  }

  $c->auth(USER, PASS, RESOURCE);
```

The *mod_perl* mechanism hands the `handler()` function an argument that is stored in a variable called $r. This is the HyperText Transfer Protocol (HTTP) *request* that has been made, which is handled by the function.

Calling the `args()` method on our request object gives us a list of arguments. These arguments follow the question mark in a typical HTTP GET request. In Figure 10-3, the URL in the Location bar is `http://www.pipetree.com/jbook`. In this URL, there is neither a question mark nor any arguments. The assignment to @a here:

```
  my @a = $r->args;
```

would leave @a empty.

The first part of the URL containing the hostname is truncated by the size of the browser window.

However, if the URL in the Location bar (shown in Figure 10-4) contained question marks and/or arguments, such as:

```
http://www.pipetree.com/jbook?name=&first=&last=adams&nick=&email=
```

the arguments that @a would receive follow the question mark and are separated in pairs with ampersands and further separated with equals signs. So here, @a would receive the arguments:

```
name, (blank), first, (blank), last, adams, nick, (blank), email, (blank)
```

In the final URL example, shown in Figure 10-6:

```
http://www.pipetree.com/jbook?dj@gnu.mine.nu
```

the array received by @a is just a single element:

```
dj@gnu.mine.nu
```

The content of @a defines which stage of the script takes the appropriate action. Queries will be generated in the form of IQ-gets and IQ-sets to retrieve information from the JUD as well as to retrieve personal vCards. To do this, we need to create an instance of a node factory, so we can build elements:

```
my $nf = Jabber::NodeFactory->new;
```

After retrieving the request arguments and creating a node factory instance, it's time to generate some HTML that will be common to all of *Demo::JBook*'s features. The print() method will be used on the request object $r to send a response back to the requesting web browser:

```
$r->print("<html><head><title>JBook</title></head><body>");
$r->print("<h1><a href='/jbook'>JBook</a></h1>");
```

Next, we need to create a connection to the Jabber server for each request:

```
# Connect to home Jabber server
my $c = Jabber::Connection->new(server => SERVER);
unless ($c->connect) {
  $r->print("Sorry, no connection to Jabber available at ".SERVER);
  $r->print("</body></html>");
  return;
}

$c->auth(USER, PASS, RESOURCE);
```

It will be much more efficient to create a persistent connection that could be used
to serve further requests. One way to do this is to fork a daemon that connects to
the Jabber server, acting as a proxy for this script. Rather than make direct requests
to the Jabber server, *Demo::JBook* is used to send the IQ elements to the daemon,
which in turn uses its persistent Jabber connection to make queries on
Demo::JBook's behalf. A setup like this is shown in Figure 10-7.

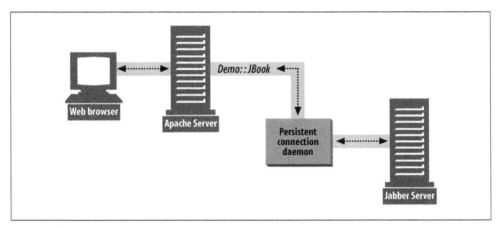

Figure 10-7. Using a persistent connection to Jabber

State 1: Build the JUD query form

Based upon how many arguments we have in the @a array, as described earlier,
we can build the response, which will represent one of three states:

* JUD query form
* JUD query results
* vCard display

If *Demo::JBook* is called without arguments (i.e., `http://[hostname]/jbook`), which
we test for like this:

```
if (scalar @a == 0) {
```

then we want to build and present the JUD search form. This form—the fields that
the form consists of—will be specific to the particular JUD that will be searched.

We construct an IQ-get to send to the JUD to ask for a list of search fields and
instructions. What we're looking for is something like the IQ-get shown in Example 10-1, like this:

```
SEND: <iq type="get" to="users.jabber.org">
        <query xmlns="jabber:iq:search"&sol;>
      </iq>
```

To construct this, we start with a new node (*element*) created by using the node factory:

```
my $iq = $nf->newNode('iq');
$iq->attr('to', JUD);
$iq->attr('type', IQ_GET);
$iq->insertTag('query', NS_SEARCH);
```

In previous recipes, we've called methods in the Jabber libraries (Jabberpy, JabberBeans, Net::Jabber, and Jabber::Connection) to send an element to the Jabber server. Typically, such a method is called a send() method. Here, we don't use a send() method. Instead, we use Jabber::Connection's ask(). Like Net::Jabber's SendAndReceiveWithID() method, and Jabberpy's method of the same name, ask() not only *sends* the element to the Jabber server, it waits for a reply.

A *reply*—in Jabber terms—is a *response* in the form of an element that comes back along the stream, *with a matching* id *attribute*. In this case, we're making an IQ-get and are expecting a response back from the recipient of that IQ-get. One way of expecting and handling the response would be to use a predefined callback specified for <iq/> elements and send our IQ-get with the send() method. However, this means that the script receives the response in an element callback that's somewhat independent of our call to send(). As well as catching the response in the callback, we also need some way of matching it up with the original request. Not to mention getting back on track with the flow of execution that represented the logical sequence of events that we were in the middle of following when we called send().

There's an easier way, if we want to make a request and wait for the response to that request before continuing on in the script. This way makes use of the ask() method.

What the ask() method does is avoid the need to catch responses in callbacks and match them up with their originating requests. It send()s the element to the Jabber server and blocks until an element with a matching id attribute value is received. Other elements that might be received while waiting for the response are duly dispatched as normal. It's not as if elements get queued up if the response takes a moment or two to arrive. When the matching element arrives on the stream, it is passed directly back to the caller of the ask() method, in the same form as if it had been handed to a callback—in object form, as an instance of a Jabber::NodeFactory::Node object, in this case.

```
my $result = $c->ask($iq);
```

So here, $result receives the response to the <iq/> element just sent. This response will look something like this:

```
RECV: <iq from='users.jabber.org' id='43'
          to='jbook@gnu.mine.nu/jbook' type='result'>
      <query xmlns='jabber:iq:search'>
        <nick&sol;>
        <first&sol;>
        <email&sol;>
        <last&sol;>
        <instructions>
           Fill in a field to search for any matching Jabber users.
        </instructions>
      </query>
    </iq>
```

It's addressed to the JID that the script is using, jbook@gnu.mine.nu/jbook. But
hold on—there's something that doesn't look quite right here, that is, when compared to the example of the IQ-get we just sent. Indeed—there's an id attribute in
the response. We didn't specify one in the Perl code that built the <iq/> element. The ask() method did it for us. Knowing that it's going to have to check the
id attribute on every incoming element to find a match for the element it's just
sent off for us, the ask() method makes sure that the outgoing element actually
has an id attribute. If it doesn't, it adds one, giving it a unique value. That way, it
stands a fighting chance of returning to the caller something this side of the end of
time.

 Talking of time, if you're uneasy about calling blocking functions in
general, you can always set an alarm() to interrupt the call after a
certain length of time.

For more information on matching requests and responses, see the section
"Request/Response" in Chapter 2.

Now let's move on to the response to IQ-get, which we now have in $result.
While we're expecting an IQ-result in response to IQ-get, the request might not
have been succesful, and we simply bail out gracefully if it isn't, ending our connection with the Jabber server:

```
if ($result->attr('type') eq IQ_ERROR) {
    $r->print("Sorry, no connection to the JUD available at ".JUD);
    $r->print("</body></html>");
    $c->disconnect;
    return;
}
```

Otherwise, we're expecting a result, containing the search fields and some instructions. These will be contained within the query tag qualified by the jab-
ber:iq:search namespace (the tag is usually called query, but here, as elsewhere

in the script, we're not taking any chances and are looking for "the first (hopefully the only!) occurrence of a child tag qualified by the `jabber:iq:search` namespace."

```
my $info = $result->getTag('', NS_SEARCH);
```

An HTML form is built from the instructions and the search fields; the instructions are retrieved with:

```
$info->getTag('instructions')->data
```

which retrieves the `<instructions&sol;>` tag and extracts its contents.

The `getChildren()` method is called upon our `<query&sol;>` tag to discover what fields are available. For all those fields, barring the "instructions" one, we create an input text field:

```
# Display the results in HTML
$r->print("<p><strong>".JUD."</strong></p>\n");
$r->print("<p>".$info->getTag('instructions')->data."</p>\n");
$r->print("<form><table>\n");
foreach my $field ($info->getChildren) {
  next if $field->name eq 'instructions';
  $r->print("<tr>");
  $r->print("<td>".ucfirst($field->name)."</td>");
  $r->print("<td><input type='text' name='".$field->name."'></td>");
  $r->print("</tr>\n");
}
$r->print("<tr><td></td><td><input type='submit'></td></tr>\n");
$r->print("</table></form>\n");

}
```

Once the form has been built, the work for this stage is complete—the form is relayed to the user, who will submit a completed form, thereby invoking the next state.

State 2: Query the JUD

The submission of the HTML form will cause a number of name/value pairs to be passed as part of the HTTP GET request. These names and values are captured into the `@a` array as described earlier. If we have more than one entry in `@a`, we know it's a form submission and must respond to that by querying the JUD and returning the results. In this case, as we know that the contents of `@a` are name/value pairs, we can view those contents as a hash, using a new variable `%a`:

```
elsif (scalar @a > 1) {
  my %a = @a;
```

Now, `%a` will contain entries where the keys are the names of the search fields and the values are the values entered in the form.

In the same way that we constructed an IQ-get to query the JUD for the search fields and instructions, we construct an IQ-set to perform the actual query:

```
my $iq = $nf->newNode('iq');
$iq->attr('to', JUD);
$iq->attr('type', IQ_SET);
my $query = $iq->insertTag('query', NS_SEARCH);
```

Using the information in %a, we insert tags for each of the search fields for which a value was specified in the form. For example, if only the value adams was specified, in the field representing the <last/> search field, as shown in Figure 10-3, we would only want to insert:

```
<last>adams</last>
```

as a child of the IQ-set's <query/> tag:

```
while (my($name, $val) = each(%a)) {
  $query->insertTag($name)->data($val) if $val;
}
```

Also in a similar way to handling state 1, we make the call by using the ask() method; the response will be received into the $result variable as an object representation of the IQ-result (or IQ-error) element:

```
my $result = $c->ask($iq);
```

We deal simply with any error situation:

```
if ($result->attr('type') eq IQ_ERROR) {
  $r->print("Sorry, cannot query the JUD");
  $r->print("</body></html>");
  $c->disconnect;
  return;
}
```

otherwise proceeding to extract the <query/> tag from the search result. This tag will contain the <item/>s representing the JUD entries found to match the search criteria submitted (see the response in Example 10-2):

```
my $info = $c->ask($iq)->getTag('', NS_SEARCH);
```

We want to display a simple table of results, with each table row representing an <item/>:

```
my $items = 0;

$r->print("<p><strong>".JUD."</strong></p>\n");
$r->print("<table border='1'>\n");

foreach my $item ($info->getChildren) {
```

During the first iteration of the `foreach` loop, that is, on our first child tag of `<query&sol;>`, we take the opportunity to write out a heading row, using the HTML `<th&sol;>` (table heading) tags:

```
unless ($items) {
  $r->print("<tr>");
  foreach my $tag ($item->getChildren) {
    $r->print("<th>".ucfirst($tag->name)."</th>");
  }
  $r->print("</tr>\n");
}
```

The main part of our loop translates the information found in each `<item&sol;>` tag:

```
<item jid='joseph@gnu.mine.nu'>
  <nick>joseph</nick>
  <first>Joseph</first>
  <email>joseph@pipetree.com</email>
  <last>Adams</last>
</item>
```

into HTML table rows, with one table cell (`<td&sol;>`) for each item field:

```
$r->print("<tr>");
my $flag = 0;
foreach my $tag ($item->getChildren) {
  unless (length($tag->data) == 0 or $flag++) {
    $r->print("<td><a href='/jbook?".$item->attr('jid')."'>");
    $r->print($tag->data."</a></td>");
  }
  else {
    $r->print("<td>".$tag->data."</td>");
  }
}
$r->print("</tr>\n");
```

In this section of the code, we also make the link between the first and second level of the address book. The JID, specified in each `<item&sol;>` tag's `jid` attribute, is the key to the JUD entry that the item represents and also the key to the vCard of the user that has that JID. For each of the item lines in the table, we need to build a selectable link to lead the user to the second level, which allows him to view the vCard. This is what we want each link to look like:

```
http://www.pipetree.com/jbook?dj@gnu.mine.nu
```

That is, a single argument, representing the JID, specified after the question mark. The condition:

```
unless (length($tag->data) == 0 or $flag++)
```

serves to ensure that the link is made on a single, nonempty field in the JUD item. When registering with a standard JUD, none of the fields are compulsory, so it's quite possible for there to be missing values returned in the search results. So we want to make sure that the `<a href='...'>...</a>` link that we build actually surrounds some value; otherwise, it wouldn't be clickable. The `$flag` variable just ensures we build only one link and not a link for every nonempty field.

Finally, the number of items found is displayed with:

```
    $items++;
  }
  $r->print("</table>\n");

  $r->print("<p>$items results found</p>");


}
```

State 3: Retrieve a vCard

If we receive a single argument in the request, we'll take it to be a JID, passed from the link in the table build in the previous state, and immediately build an IQ-get to retrieve the vCard. The JID is to be found in the first element in the `@a` array—`$a[0]`.

```
    else {

      my $iq = $nf->newNode('iq');
      $iq->attr('to', $a[0]);
      $iq->attr('type', IQ_GET);
      $iq->insertTag('vcard', NS_VCARD);
```

Notice how the name of the query tag in this query is not query, but vcard. See the section "The vcard-temp Namespace" in Chapter 6 for details.

The retrieval query is in the form of an IQ-get, rather than an IQ-set. As we needed to send information in our JUD query (the search criteria), an IQ-set was appropriate. Here, an IQ-get is appropriate as we're not including any information to qualify our request; all we need to send is this:

```
<iq type='get' to='dj@gnu.mine.nu'>
  <vcard xmlns='vcard-temp'&sol;>
</iq>
```

After sending the `<iq&sol;>` element, waiting for the response, and checking for any errors, we extract the vCard detail and display it:

```
my $result = $c->ask($iq);

if ($result->attr('type') eq IQ_ERROR)  {
   $r->print("Sorry, cannot retrieve the vCard for $a[0]");
   $r->print("</body></html>");
   $c->disconnect;
   return;
}
```

The structure of the vCard namespace is rather complicated and long-winded, and it's common for many of the fields to remain unfilled. So to keep the script simple, we're going to display all the top-level fields that aren't empty:

```
my $vcard = $result->getTag('', NS_VCARD);

print ("<strong>$a[0]</strong>\n");

foreach my $tag ($vcard->getChildren) {
   print "<br&sol;>".$tag->name." : ".$tag->data."\n" if $tag->data;
   }

}
```

General handler close

Once we've dealt with the possible states, we send the closing HTML statements common to all three of them, and disconnect from the Jabber server:

```
$r->print("</body></html>");
$c->disconnect;

return;
```

At this stage, there's nothing more for the module to do. Having discerned the state from the arguments in the URL (and thereby the appropriate action) and having carried out that action, the module ends, handing control back to its *mod_perl* host. Remembering that *Demo::JBook* is an Apache handler in the form of a Perl module, we need to ensure that the module itself returns a true value (as with any Perl module):

```
}

1;
```

Notes for Improvement

The *Demo::JBook* script is merely an example. On top of tightening up the error and exception handling, there are a few other things that you might want to consider doing to improve upon it:

Jabber connectivity

As mentioned already, you'll probably want to improve the connection efficiency to the Jabber server by holding a socket open and sharing this connection across multiple calls to the handler.

Choice of JUD

The JUD to be queried is fixed; you may prefer to allow the user to select which JUD will be searched. What's more, selection of more than one JUD would allow a powerful search across public Jabber user directories.

Key handling

We've seen how a JUD is queried in Example 10-2. Some JUDs use the simple key-based security and pass an additional `<key&sol;>` tag containing random data—a sort of session key, as described in the section "jabber:iq:register" and the section "jabber:iq:search." Any `<key&sol;>` tag received from the JUD in response to an IQ-get must be sent back verbatim to the JUD in the subsequent IQ-set. Otherwise the search will fail, and you'll get a response similar to that shown in Example 10-7.

Visual impact

Last but not least, the visual impact of the end result as shown here (in Figure 10-3, Figure 10-4, and Figure 10-6) lacks a certain something. You might want to do something about that—give it a grander design, make it more pleasing, or at least interesting, to the eye. The HTML has been kept deliberately basic in this recipe, so as not to cloud the real theme of "Jabber without Jabber."

Example 10-7. Failure to return a key could cause a search to fail

```
RECV: <iq from='users.jabber.com' id='jud33'
          to='jbook@gnu.mine.nu/jbook' type='error'>
        <query xmlns='jabber:iq:search'>
        <error code='405'>Keys do not match.</error>
        </query>
      </iq>
```

XML-RPC over Jabber

XML-RPC is an easy way to get software that's running on different operating systems to be able to make and respond to procedure calls (the "RPC" part of the name stands for "Remote Procedure Call") over the Internet.

The basis of XML-RPC is straightforward and is described at XML-RPC's home page (*http://www.xml-rpc.com*). The procedure calls, each consisting of the name of the procedure (or *method*) to call and a set of arguments to go with that call and the corresponding responses, each consisting of a set of results, are encoded in an XML-based format. The requests and responses, so encoded, are exchanged over HTTP, carried as the payloads of POST requests.

Example 10-8 shows a typical request in XML-RPC encoding. It's calling a procedure called `examples.getStateName`, and passing a single integer parameter with the value 41.

Example 10-8. An XML-RPC request

```
<?xml version="1.0"&quest;>
<methodCall>
  <methodName>examples.getStateName</methodName>
  <params>
    <param>
      <value><i4>41</i4></value>
    </param>
  </params>
</methodCall>
```

Example 10-9 shows a typical response to that request. The response consists of a single string value "South Dakota."

Example 10-9. An XML-RPC response

```
<?xml version="1.0"&quest;>
<methodResponse>
  <params>
    <param>
      <value><string>South Dakota</string></value>
    </param>
  </params>
</methodResponse>
```

The choice of the word "payload" to describe the encoded requests and responses is significant: each request, headed with an XML declaration (`<?xml version="1.0"&quest;>`) and encapsulated as a single tag (`<methodCall&sol;>`), and each response, also headed with an XML declaration and encapsulated as a single tag (`<methodResponse&sol;>`), are succinct, fully formed, and complete parcels that have meaning independent of their HTTP carrier.

While the XML-RPC specification stipulates that these parcels be carried over HTTP, we could take advantage of the power and simplicity of the *encoding* and carry procedure calls and responses over Jabber.

Jabber-RPC

Jabber-RPC is the name given to the marriage of encoding from the XML-RPC specification and Jabber as the transport mechanism. As well as building upon a stable specification, Jabber-RPC brings advantages of its own to the world of procedure calls over the Internet. Many of the potential XML-RPC responders are HTTP servers behind corporate firewalls or one-way Network Address Translation (NAT) mechanisms and are therefore unreachable from the Internet. Substituting

Jabber as a transport gives calls a better chance of reaching their destination. If a Jabber-RPC responder—a program that connects to a Jabber server, is addressable by a JID, and can receive (and respond to) XML-RPC–encoded calls—is connected to a Jabber server visible to the Internet, then request calls have to make it only to that Jabber server, and internal packet routing within the server will allow the parcels to reach their destinations behind the firewall, whether those destinations are client-based or component-based responders.

It should be clear by now that the idea of Jabber-RPC is to transport the XML-RPC–encoded parcels in an extension, an attachment, to an IQ element. Just as the details for a search attempt (for example of a Jabber User Directory) are carried in an IQ-set extension qualified by the `jabber:iq:search` namespace (as shown in Example 10-2), so the Jabber-RPC method calls are carried in an IQ-set extension qualified by a namespace of its own. This namespace is a new one and is `jabber:iq:rpc`.*

Similarly, as the results of a JUD search are returned in an IQ-result, so Jabber-RPC method responses are returned in an IQ-result. Example 10-10 shows a simple Jabber-RPC–based method call and response, using the same XML-RPC–encoded parcels as shown in Example 10-8 and Example 10-9.

Example 10-10. A Jabber-RPC request/response conversation

```
SEND: <iq type='set' to='responder@company-a.com/jrpc-server' id='1'>
         <query xmlns='jabber:iq:rpc'>
           <methodCall>
             <methodName>examples.getStateName</methodName>
             <params>
               <param>
                 <value><i4>41</i4></value>
               </param>
             </params>
           </methodCall>
         </query>
      </iq>

RECV: <iq type='result' to='requester@company-b.com/jrpc-client'
             from='responder@company-a.com/jrpc-server' id='1'>
         <query xmlns='jabber:iq:rpc'>
           <methodResponse>
             <params>
               <param>
                 <value><string>South Dakota</string></value>
               </param>
             </params>
           </methodResponse>
```

---

* This was decided during a session at the JabberCon conference in August 2001 and has since been approved as a draft protocol. More details are available at *http://www.pipetree.com/jabber/jrpc.html.*

Example 10-10. A Jabber-RPC request/response conversation (continued)

```
    </query>
  </iq>
```

It's clear that the parcels of XML-RPC encoding lend themselves very well to being transported in a meaningful way over Jabber and that Jabber's ultimate flexibility makes this possible.

The only major difference between the payloads as carried in an HTTP POST and the payloads as carried in an `<iq&sol;>` element is that there's no XML declaration. It's not possible of course, when you consider the *context* of the IQ elements. They're document fragments in the XML stream between the requester (or responder) and the Jabber server. As explained in the section "XML Streams," these documents are fanfared with their own XML declaration, and any further declaration within the document is illegal from an XML point of view.

Jabber-RPC Requesters and Responders

A quick word about Jabber-RPC requesters and reponders. Connection to a Jabber server is possible in two main ways, as we've seen in the recipes so far: as a client via the JSM or as a component connected directly to the *jabberd* backbone. At the simplest level, all a Jabber-RPC requester or responder is, is something that makes a Jabber connection, sends and receives IQ elements, and uses a *standard* XML-RPC library to encode, decode, and service the requests and responses.

It doesn't matter whether the requesters and responders are built as clients or components. One could argue that the Jabber client model fits more naturally into the role of a requester, and the Jabber component model fits more naturally into the role of a responder, but this isn't a requirement. Indeed, if you're not the Jabber server administrator and don't have access to the server configuration (to be able to insert a `<service&sol;>` stanza for a new component—see the section "The newsagent script as a component"), building a Jabber-RPC responder as a Jabber client may be the path of least resistance.

Building a Requester and a Responder

Let's have a look at the power and flexibility of Jabber-RPC and how to build requesters and responders. We're going to build a client-based requester, in Python, and a client-based responder, in Java. There are two great XML-RPC library implementations for Python and Java that we'll use to do the legwork for us. Figure 10-8 shows what we want to build.

To keep things fairly simple, we'll just implement and call something similar to the getStateName() function already shown in the examples: getCountyName().

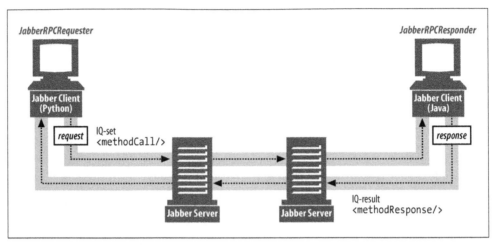

Figure 10-8. The Jabber-RPC requester and responder

The responder: JabberRPCResponder

We'll start up the Java client-based Jabber-RPC responder (imaginatively called *JabberRPCResponder*) specifying a handler class that is to service the XML-RPC–encoded method calls, get it to connect to a Jabber server, and listen for incoming Jabber-RPC requests. It will use the Helma XML-RPC library (at *http://xmlrpc.helma.org*) to service incoming requests using the handler class.

Being a Java script, we'll use the JabberBeans library. We'll need to extend the library's capabilities to handle extensions in the new jabber:iq:rpc namespace.

The requester: JabberRPCRequester

The Python client-based Jabber-RPC requester will also start up and connect to a Jabber server. We'll use a different server than the one the responder is connected to; after all, the whole point of XML-RPC and Jabber-RPC is to make the RPC world a smaller and bigger place at the same time, through the power of the Internet. We're going to use the Pythonware XML-RPC library (*http://www.pythonware.com/products/xmlrpc/index.htm*) to encode a getCountyName() request and decode the response.

JabberRPCResponder

Let's look at the Jabber-RPC responder first. There is a single script, called *JabberRPCResponder*, but there are also a number of supporting classes that we need. Let's take things one at a time.

The RPCHandler class

The Helma XML-RPC library implementation allows you to build XML-RPC responders independent of any particular transport by using an instance of the XmlRpc-Server object, which represents an abstraction of an XML-RPC server. You can then construct a class—the *handler class*—containing your methods to be callable via XML-RPC. The calling of these methods is coordinated by the XmlRpcServer object, which you tell about your handler class using the addHandler() method.

This is what the handler class, called RPCHandler, looks like:

```
// RPCHandler: A class of XML-RPC-callable methods

public class RPCHandler
{

  // Note: This is a "traditional" list of counties!

  private String county[] = {"Bedfordshire", "Berkshire",
      "Buckinghamshire", "Cambridgeshire", "Cheshire",
      "Cornwall", "Cumberland", "Derbyshire", "Devon", "Dorset",
      "Durham", "Essex", "Gloucestershire", "Hampshire", "Herefordshire",
      "Hertfordshire", "Humberside", "Huntingdonshire",
      "Kent", "Lancashire", "Leicestershire",
      "Lincolnshire", "London", "Middlesex", "Norfolk",
      "Northamptonshire", "Northumberland", "Nottinghamshire",
      "Oxfordshire", "Rutland", "Shropshire",
      "Somerset", "Staffordshire", "Suffolk", "Surrey", "Sussex",
      "Warwickshire", "Westmorland", "Wiltshire", "Worcestershire",
      "Yorkshire"};

  public RPCHandler()
  {}

  public String getCountyName(int c)
  {
    return county[c - 1];
  }

}
```

The class has three elements:

The list of counties

> The names of counties are stored in a simple array, county[].

The constructor

> We don't need to do anything in the constructor, RPCHandler(), as there's no requirement to manipulate objects directly, so the constructor remains empty.

The single available method

All public methods in the class are available through the `XmlRpcServer` object. Here we have a single method for the purposes of this recipe: `getCounty-Name()` returns the name of the county for the index given.

When we examine the *JabberRPCResponder* script (in the section "The Jabber-RPCResponder script") we'll see how the `XmlRpcServer` object is instantiated and how this `RPCHandler` class is used.

The IQRPC classes

`JabberBeans` deals with Jabber element extensions—`<query&sol;>` and `<x&sol;>` tags—using individual helper classes. We've seen this in the `HostAlive` recipe in the section "Dialup System Watch," where the `IQAuthBuilder` class is used to construct an authorization extension:

```
<query xmlns='jabber:iq:auth'>
  <username>alive</username>
  ...
</query>
```

The helper classes are oriented around namespaces. Because we have a new namespace to deal with (`jabber:iq:rpc`), `JabberBeans` needs to have helper classes to handle extensions in that namespace.

We need a minimum of two helper classes. We need a class that represents an extension—a `<query&sol;>` tag—in the `jabber:iq:rpc` namespace. If we are going to construct IQ elements containing such Jabber-RPC extensions, we also need a class to *build* those extensions. The class that represents the `jabber:iq:rpc` extension is called `IQRPC`, and the class that is the builder for the extensions is called `IQRPCBuilder`.

For an example we're already familiar with, look at the steps leading up to the authorization phase in the *HostAlive* script (and indeed our *JabberRPCResponder* script, which is shown in the next section); the authorization IQ element is constructed as follows:

```
InfoQueryBuilder iqb = new InfoQueryBuilder();
IQAuthBuilder iqAuthb = new IQAuthBuilder();

iqb.setType("set");

iqAuthb.setUsername(user);
iqAuthb.setPassword(pass);
iqAuthb.setResource(resource);

iqb.addExtension(iqAuthb.build());
```

If we bear in mind that this is what we want to end up with:

```
<iq type='set'>
  <query xmlns='jabber:iq:auth'>
    <username>...</username>
    <password>...</password>
    <resource>...</resource>
  </query>
</iq>
```

then we can understand what's going on:

- The <query/> tag in the jabber:iq:auth namespace is built with an *authorization builder*, iqAuthb, which is an instance of IQAuthBuilder.

- Values for the tags within <query/>, such as <username/> and <password/>, are set using methods belonging to that builder class.

- The actual extension is generated with a call to the build() method.

Using addExtension(), the newly generated extension is added to the container representing the <iq/> element being constructed by the *IQ builder* iqb, an instance of InfoQueryBuilder.

Figure 8-3 shows the relationship between these builders and the things they create. (For a review of what's required to authenticate with a Jabber server, see the section "User Authentication.")

Although necessary, the IQRPC classes aren't the focus of this recipe and can be found in Appendix B. They are essentially modified copies of the classes for the jabber:iq:time namespace: IQTime and IQTimeBuilder. They just need to be compiled and made available in the $CLASSPATH. Putting them in the same directory as the *JabberRPCResponder* script will work fine.

The JabberRPCResponder script

Example 10-11 shows the *JabberRPCResponder* script in its entirety. In the next section we'll take it piece by piece.

Example 10-11. The JabberRPCResponder Script, written in Java

```
import org.jabber.jabberbeans.*;
import org.jabber.jabberbeans.Extension.*;
import org.jabber.jabberbeans.util.JID;
import java.net.InetAddress;
import java.util.Enumeration;
import java.io.*;
import helma.xmlrpc.*;

public class JabberRPCResponder implements PacketListener
{
  private String server   = "gnu.mine.nu";
```

Example 10-11. The JabberRPCResponder Script, written in Java (continued)

```
private String user     = "server";
private String pass     = "pass";
private String resource = "jrpc-server";

private XmlRpcServer responder;

private ConnectionBean cb;


// Constructor
public JabberRPCResponder()
{
  responder = new XmlRpcServer();
  responder.addHandler("examples", new RPCHandler());
}

// Main program
public static void main(String args[])
{
  JabberRPCResponder server = new JabberRPCResponder();
  try
  {
    server.start();
  }
  catch (Exception e)
  {
    System.out.println("Cannot start server: " + e.toString());
  }
}

public void start() throws Exception
{
  cb = new ConnectionBean();
  InetAddress addr;

  cb.addPacketListener(this);

  // Connect
  cb.connect(addr=InetAddress.getByName(server));

  // Authenticate
  InfoQueryBuilder iqb = new InfoQueryBuilder();
      IQAuthBuilder iqAuthb = new IQAuthBuilder();

  iqb.setType("set");

  iqAuthb.setUsername(user);
  iqAuthb.setPassword(pass);
  iqAuthb.setResource(resource);

  iqb.addExtension(iqAuthb.build());
```

Example 10-11. The JabberRPCResponder Script, written in Java (continued)

```
            InfoQuery iq = (InfoQuery)iqb.build();

    cb.send(iq);

    // Send presence
    PresenceBuilder pb = new PresenceBuilder();
    cb.send(pb.build());

}


// Packet listener interface:

public void receivedPacket(PacketEvent pe)
{
    Packet packet = pe.getPacket();
    System.out.println("RECV:" + packet.toString());

    if (packet instanceof InfoQuery)
    {
        Enumeration e = ((InfoQuery)packet).Extensions();
        if (e.hasMoreElements())
        {
            Extension ext = (Extension)e.nextElement();

            String request = ext.toString();
            String id = ((InfoQuery)packet).getIdentifier();
            JID from = ((InfoQuery)packet).getFromAddress();

            ByteArrayInputStream bis =
                new ByteArrayInputStream(request.getBytes());
            String result = new String(responder.execute(bis));

            String response = result;
            int pos = result.lastIndexOf("&quest;>");
            if (pos >= 0)
            {
                response = result.substring(pos + 2);
            }

            IQRPCBuilder iqrpcb = new IQRPCBuilder();
            iqrpcb.setPayload(response);

            InfoQueryBuilder iqb = new InfoQueryBuilder();

            iqb.setType("result");
            iqb.setIdentifier(id);
            iqb.setToAddress(from);
            iqb.addExtension(iqrpcb.build());

            InfoQuery iq;
            try {
```

Example 10-11. The JabberRPCResponder Script, written in Java (continued)

```
            iq = (InfoQuery)iqb.build();
      }
      catch (InstantiationException ie)
      {
        System.out.println("Build failed: " + ie.toString());
        return;
      }

      cb.send(iq);

    }
  }
}

public void sentPacket(PacketEvent pe)
{
  Packet packet = pe.getPacket();
  System.out.println("SEND:" + packet.toString());
}

public void sendFailed(PacketEvent pe)
{
  Packet packet = pe.getPacket();
  System.out.println("failed to send:" + packet.toString());
}

}
```

Looking at JabberRPCResponder Step by Step

Now let's examine the *JabberRPCResponder* script step by step so we can see how it works:

```
import org.jabber.jabberbeans.*;
import org.jabber.jabberbeans.Extension.*;
import org.jabber.jabberbeans.util.JID;
import java.net.InetAddress;
import java.util.Enumeration;
import java.io.*;
import helma.xmlrpc.*;
```

We need to bring in the jabberbeans classes as shown, as well as some core Java features that we'll see used in the script a bit later: an InetAddress to represent the Jabber server's hostname, an Enumeration interface to access the extensions in the incoming IQ elements, and java.io features for feeding the XML-RPC–encoded requests to the XmlRpcServer object. We also bring in the classes from the Helma XML-RPC library.

```
public class JabberRPCResponder implements PacketListener
{
  private String server   = "gnu.mine.nu";
  private String user     = "server";
  private String pass     = "pass";
  private String resource = "jrpc-server";

  private XmlRpcServer responder;

  private ConnectionBean cb;
```

The definition of our `JabberRPCResponder` class looks similar to that of the `HostAlive` class in the section "Dialup System Watch." However, rather than merely connecting to a Jabber server and sending packets off down the stream, we want to *listen* for incoming packets—in this case, IQ elements carrying `jabber:iq:rpc`-qualified payloads—and handle them. Accordingly, we specify that our main class implements `PacketListener`, a JabberBeans interface that Jabber clients use to receive notification of incoming packets. The interface describes three methods: `receivedPacket()`, `sentPacket()`, and `sendFailed()`. We'll define our `receivedPacket()` method, described later in this section, to catch and process the incoming Jabber-RPC requests.

We're going to use an `XmlRpcServer` object, in `responder`, to provide the translation services between our `RPCHandler` class that contains the methods we want to "expose," and the XML-RPC–encoded requests and responses.

Naturally, we also need a JabberBeans `ConnectionBean`, which we'll hold in `cb`.

```
public JabberRPCResponder()
{
  responder = new XmlRpcServer();
  responder.addHandler("examples", new RPCHandler());
}
```

The `JabberRPCResponder` class constructor, `JabberRPCResponder()`, will be called in the `main()` method later in the script. It is used to create an instance of the Helma `XmlRpcServer` object, and associate our `RPCHandler` class with it, as a *handler* for method calls. The `addHandler()` method takes two arguments: the first is the method prefix name, such as `examples` in the `methodName` specification:

```
<methodName>examples.getCountyName</methodName>
```

and the second is the object—an instantiation of our handler class—which contains the methods that the `XmlRpcServer` will use to "service" requests. In other words, the `XmlRpcServer` object will determine that a call to `examples.getCountyName` should be handled, as `getCountyName`, by the `RPCHandler` object.

The `main()` method is quite short:

```
public static void main(String args[])
{
  JabberRPCResponder server = new JabberRPCResponder();
  try
  {
    server.start();
  }
  catch (Exception e)
  {
    System.out.println("Cannot start server: " + e.toString());
  }
}
```

We instantiate our `JabberRPCResponder` object into `server` and call the `start()` method. Various functions in `start()` can raise exceptions; we take care of them all here with a simple `catch` clause and abort if necessary, rather than include all of `start()`'s functions here and have multiple `try` and `catch` statements:

```
public void start() throws Exception
{
  cb = new ConnectionBean();
  InetAddress addr;

  cb.addPacketListener(this);

  // Connect
  cb.connect(addr=InetAddress.getByName(server));

  // Authenticate
  InfoQueryBuilder iqb = new InfoQueryBuilder();
        IQAuthBuilder iqAuthb = new IQAuthBuilder();

  iqb.setType("set");

  iqAuthb.setUsername(user);
  iqAuthb.setPassword(pass);
  iqAuthb.setResource(resource);

  iqb.addExtension(iqAuthb.build());

        InfoQuery iq = (InfoQuery)iqb.build();

  cb.send(iq);

  // Send presence
  PresenceBuilder pb = new PresenceBuilder();
  cb.send(pb.build());

}
```

Most of the content of this `start()` function should be fairly familiar. We instantiate a `ConnectionBean` and will use that, in `cb`, throughout the script to send elements to the Jabber server. Our `PacketListener` is added as a listener to the
`ConnectionBean`, causing a method of that interface (`packetReceived()`) to be
invoked when an incoming element appears on the stream managed by that `Con-
nectionBean`.

In the same way as described in the section "The HostAlive Script" in Chapter 8,
we build our IQ element to authenticate, and send it to the server with the `Con-
nectionBean`'s `send()` method. We also send an initial availability, in the form of a
simple `<presence&sol;>` element to the server.

Having connected to and authenticated with the server and sent initial availability,
we can sit back and relax. All the subsequent activity will be initiated by the
arrival of IQ elements on the stream. As described already, these will be made
known (and available) in the form of calls to the `receivedPacket()` method of the
`PacketListener` interface:

```
// Packet Listener interface:

public void receivedPacket(PacketEvent pe)
{
   Packet packet = pe.getPacket();
   System.out.println("RECV:" + packet.toString());
```

The method receives a `PacketEvent` object, which represents both the *event* of a
packet (an element) arriving and the packet itself, which we retrieve into `packet`
with the `getPacket()` method. For debugging purposes, we print out what we get.

Now to determine what has actually arrived:

```
if (packet instanceof InfoQuery)
{
   Enumeration e = ((InfoQuery)packet).Extensions();
   if (e.hasMoreElements())
   {
      Extension ext = (Extension)e.nextElement();
```

We check to see if the element is an IQ element, and, if so, we retrieve the extensions—the `<query&sol;>` tags—that the element contains. Calling the `Extensions()`
method on the `packet` object returns an `Enumeration` of those tags.

We're expecting only one tag, and we pull that into `ext` using the `nextElement()`
method on our `Enumeration`.

For the sake of simplicity, we're not checking here whether the `<query&sol;>` tag received is qualified by the `jabber:iq:rpc` namespace. You might wish to do that in your version.

```
String request = ext.toString();
String id = ((InfoQuery)packet).getIdentifier();
JID from = ((InfoQuery)packet).getFromAddress();
```

We can pull the extension into string form, with the `toString()` method, ready for passing to our `XmlRpcServer` object. At this stage, `ext` contains the complete XML-RPC–encoded parcel, starting with the `<methodCall>` opening tag:

```
<methodCall>
  <methodName>examples.getCountyName</methodName>
  <params>
    <param>
      <value><i4>14</i4></value>
    </param>
  </params>
</methodCall>
```

So that we can send a response back to the requester, we need two other things from the incoming element besides the actual request payload. In general, when an `<iq&sol;>` element is sent, representing a request, either as an IQ-get or an IQ-set, the sender is expecting the response, either an IQ-result or an IQ-error, with the *same value* in the `id` attribute. This is so the responses, once received, can be matched up with the original requests. So we need to store the `id` value, available to us through the `getIdentifier()` method of the `packet` object. We also need the JID of the sender, retrieved with the `getFromAddress()` method, so we can specify it in the `to` attribute of the IQ-result we'll be sending back.

Now it's time to service the request:

```
ByteArrayInputStream bis =
    new ByteArrayInputStream(request.getBytes());
String result = new String(responder.execute(bis));
```

With the `execute()` method of our `XmlRpcServer` object in `responder`, we convert the `<methodCall&sol;>` into a `<methodResponse&sol;>`, in effect. The decoding of the XML-RPC–encoded request, the determination of which method in which class to call (in our case it will be the `getCountyName()` method in our `RPCHandler` class), the calling of that method, and the encoding of the result into an XML-RPC–encoded response are all done magically and transparently for us by `XmlRpcServer` (thank goodness, or this recipe would be unbearably long!).

There's a bit of jiggling about required before we can make the `execute()` call, though. The method is expecting an `InputStream` object, and we've got a `String`.

Not to worry, we just convert it with a `ByteArrayInputStream`, which can take a byte array (from `request.getBytes()`) and produce an `InputStream` object bis. Similarly, `execute()` produces a byte array, so that is converted to a `String` by wrapping the call with `String()`.

The incoming XML-RPC–encoded request, being carried in the IQ element, will not include an XML declaration. Luckily, the `XmlRpcServer` does not mind that one is not present before decoding and dispatching the request. It will, however, include one on the encoded response it emits. So we must check for that and strip it off if there is one:

```
String response = result;
int pos = result.lastIndexOf("&quest;>");
if (pos >= 0)
{
  response = result.substring(pos + 2);
}
```

Now we have everything we need to return the XML-RPC–encoded response to the requester. It's time to call on the services of our `IQRPC` classes:

```
IQRPCBuilder iqrpcb = new IQRPCBuilder();
iqrpcb.setPayload(response);
```

We create an instance of the `IQRPCBuilder` and call the single method `setPayload()` to load the XML-RPC–encoded response into the <query/> tag, which is qualified by the `jabber:iq:rpc` namespace. This is effectively the "extension" in JabberBeans parlance:

```
InfoQueryBuilder iqb = new InfoQueryBuilder();

iqb.setType("result");
iqb.setIdentifier(id);
iqb.setToAddress(from);
iqb.addExtension(iqrpcb.build());

InfoQuery iq;
try {
        iq = (InfoQuery)iqb.build();
}
catch (InstantiationException ie)
{
  System.out.println("Build failed: " + ie.toString());
  return;
}

cb.send(iq);

      }
    }
  }
```

After creating an IQ element container using an `InfoQueryBuilder` and setting the appropriate attributes, we generate the `<query&sol;>` tag (`iqrpcb.build()`) and add it to the IQ element container with `addExtension()`.

The `<iq&sol;>` is then generated—it now contains our payload—and sent back to the server, where it will be routed to the original requester.

That's pretty much all there is to it. We have a couple of other methods belonging to the `PacketListener` interface:

```
public void sentPacket(PacketEvent pe)
{
  Packet packet = pe.getPacket();
  System.out.println("SEND:" + packet.toString());
}

public void sendFailed(PacketEvent pe)
{
  Packet packet = pe.getPacket();
  System.out.println("Failed to send:" + packet.toString());
}

}
```

We fill these methods with debugging-style output statements for our convenience.

JabberRPCRequester

Now that we've got our Jabber-RPC responder all set up, it's time to turn our attention to our requester, *JabberRPCRequester*, shown in Example 10-12. This is a Python script that uses the `Jabberpy` library and Pythonware's `xmlrpclib` library. It's a pretty simple affair.

Example 10-12. The JabberRPCRequester script, written in Python

```
import jabber
import xmlrpclib
import string
import sys

Server   = 'qmacro.dyndns.org'
Username = 'client'
Password = 'pass'
Resource = 'jrpc-client'
Endpoint = 'server@gnu.mine.nu/jrpc-server';
Method   = 'examples.getCountyName';

county   = string.atoi(sys.argv[1])

con = jabber.Client(host=Server)
try:
    con.connect()
```

Example 10-12. The JabberRPCRequester script, written in Python (continued)

```
except IOError, e:
    print "Couldn't connect: %s" % e
    sys.exit(0)

con.auth(Username,Password,Resource)

request = xmlrpclib.dumps(((county),),
    methodname=Method);

iq = jabber.Iq(to=Endpoint, type='set')
iq.setQuery('jabber:iq:rpc')
iq.setQueryPayload(request)

result = con.SendAndWaitForResponse(iq)

if result.getType() == 'result':
    response = str(result.getQueryPayload())
    parms, func = xmlrpclib.loads(response)
    print parms[0]
else:
    print "Could not complete call"

con.disconnect()
```

Looking at JabberRPCRequester Step by Step

After importing the libraries that we will need:

```
import jabber
import xmlrpclib
import string
import sys
```

we specify a number of parameters:

```
Server   = 'qmacro.dyndns.org'
Username = 'client'
Password = 'pass'
Resource = 'jrpc-client'

Endpoint = 'server@gnu.mine.nu/jrpc-server';
Method   = 'examples.getCountyName';
```

The script connects to the Jabber server defined in Server, with the username defined in Username. The resource that will be passed in the authentication request is jrpc-client. There is as much significance in this name as there is in the name of the resource used by *JabberRPCResponder* (jrpc-server): none. It's just a useful naming convention to adopt when writing requesters and responders.

A single parameter, which will be interpreted as the index of the county to retrieve via the call to `examples.getCountyName`, is expected.

```
county = string.atoi(sys.argv[1])
```

The method expects an integer, so we convert it directly. This has a favorable secondary effect when we come to XML-RPC encode the request; if we hadn't called the `string.atoi()` function and left `county` as a string, this is what the XML-RPC–encoded parcel would have looked like:

```
<methodCall>
  <methodName>examples.getCountyName</methodName>
  <params>
    <param>
      <value><string>1</string></value>
    </param>
  </params>
</methodCall>
```

However, this is what we really want:

```
<methodCall>
  <methodName>examples.getCountyName</methodName>
  <params>
    <param>
      <value><int>1</int></value>
    </param>
  </params>
</methodCall>
```

In the same way as in the previous Python recipes, we connect to the Jabber server and authenticate:

```
con = jabber.Client(host=Server)
try:
    con.connect()
except IOError, e:
    print "Couldn't connect: %s" % e
    sys.exit(0)

con.auth(Username,Password,Resource)
```

Now all we have to do is compose our XML-RPC–encoded request and send it on its way to the Jabber-RPC responder, which in our case, identified here by the JID in the `Endpoint` variable, is our *JabberRPCResponder* script.

It's time to call on the services of the XML-RPC library. We use the `dumps()` function to build an XML-RPC encoding, passing the single parameter (in a tuple, which is required by dumps()) representing the county index and the name of the method to call:

```
request = xmlrpclib.dumps((((county),),
    methodname=Method);
```

We build the IQ-set containing a `<query&sol;>` element in the `jabber:iq:rpc` namespace, by creating an instance of an `Iq` object, and calling methods to specify that namespace (`setQuery()`) and insert the XML-RPC encoding as the payload (`setQueryPayload()`):

```
iq = jabber.Iq(to=Endpoint, type='set')
iq.setQuery('jabber:iq:rpc')
iq.setQueryPayload(request)
```

At this stage, we need to send it off and wait for a response. You have probably noticed that, unlike in previous Python recipes, this script hasn't defined or registered a callback to handle incoming elements. This is because we're approaching the task in a slightly different way in this script. The method used to send the element to the Jabber server—`SendAndWaitForResponse()`:

```
result = con.SendAndWaitForResponse(iq)
```

is the rather verbose cousin of the `Jabber::Connection` library's `ask()` method, as described in the section "State 1: Build the JUD query form." It does "exactly what it says on the tin," namely, send the element off to the server and block until an element is received that is deemed, by a matchup of the `id` attribute values on both elements, to be the response. If no `id` attribute exists on the outgoing element, it is stamped with one (with a value unique within the current usage of the `jabber` class). Both are also relations of `Net::Jabber`'s `SendAndReceiveWithID()`.

So `result` receives an element object. It's an IQ element, as that is what a response to an IQ element will be. If the call *transport* (as opposed to the call itself) is successful, the response will be an IQ-result. If not, for example, if the `Endpoint` that we specified doesn't exist, then the response will be an IQ-error.

```
if result.getType() == 'result':
    response = str(result.getQueryPayload())
    parms, func = xmlrpclib.loads(response)
    print parms[0]
else:
    print "Could not complete call"
```

Conversely, while the call transport might have succeeded, the call itself might have failed, for example, if we had specified a nonexistent method name in `Method`. However, for our purposes, we're going to assume that the call was successful. So we grab the payload (i.e., the contents of the `<query&sol;>` tag) and string it with `str()`.

The `loads()` function of `xmlrpclib` is used to extract the details from an XML-RPC–encoded parcel; it will produce two values, which we capture in `resp` and `func`. The first is the set of parameters, common to either a request or a response, and the second is the method name, if it exists in the encoding. We want to decode a `<methodResponse&sol;>` here, so there's no method name present, but there should be a set of parameters.

We take the first (and only) element from the set of parameters in `resp` and print it out.

Jabber-RPC in Perl

Exciting as this recipe might be, it's not very visual. There are no screenshots of note to show, just a couple of STDOUTs from two scripts started at the command line. To fix this "problem," we're going to round this recipe off with a quick look at Jabber-RPC in Perl. Based on the `Jabber::Connection` library is a fairly new Perl library called `Jabber::RPC`, which sports two modules: `Jabber::RPC::Client.pm` and `Jabber::RPC::Server.pm`.

If you're slightly perplexed about what it takes to extend Jabber support in Java, take a look at Example 10-13 and Example 10-14. The first is an implementation, in Perl, of the *JabberRPCResponder* and all its class periphery. The second is an implementation of our *JabberRPCRequester*.

Example 10-13. A Jabber-RPC Responder in Perl

```
use strict;
use Jabber::RPC::Server;

my @county = ("Bedfordshire", "Berkshire",
     "Buckinghamshire", "Cambridgeshire", "Cheshire",
     "Cornwall", "Cumberland", "Derbyshire", "Devon", "Dorset",
     "Durham", "Essex", "Gloucestershire", "Hampshire", "Herefordshire",
     "Hertfordshire", "Humberside", "Huntingdonshire",
     "Kent", "Lancashire", "Leicestershire",
     "Lincolnshire", "London", "Middlesex", "Norfolk",
     "Northamptonshire", "Northumberland", "Nottinghamshire",
     "Oxfordshire", "Rutland", "Shropshire",
     "Somerset", "Staffordshire", "Suffolk", "Surrey", "Sussex",
     "Warwickshire", "Westmorland", "Wiltshire", "Worcestershire",
     "Yorkshire");

sub getCountyName {
    my $county = shift;
    return $county[$county - 1];
}

my $server = new Jabber::RPC::Server(
  server    => 'gnu.mine.nu',
```

Example 10-13. A Jabber-RPC Responder in Perl (continued)

```
    identauth => 'server:pass',
    resource  => 'jrpc-server',
    methods   => {'examples.getCountyName' => \&getCountyName},
);

$server->start;
```

Example 10-14. A Jabber-RPC Requester in Perl

```
use strict;
use Jabber::RPC::Client;

my $client = new Jabber::RPC::Client(
    server    => 'qmacro.dyndns.org',
    identauth => 'client:pass',
    resource  => 'jrpc-client',
    endpoint  => 'dj@localhost/jrpc-server',
);

print $client->call('examples.getCountyName', $ARGV[0])
      || $client->lastFault;
```

That's it. There's no more code than that. So don't lose heart. Just use Perl; you know it makes sense.

Browsing LDAP

Browsing, a relatively new Jabber feature (introduced in the section "Browsing" and described through its associated namespace in the section "jabber:iq:browse), is an extremely powerful and flexible beast. Whereas many of the standard Jabber namespaces such as jabber:iq:oob, jabber:iq:auth, and jabber:iq:register busy themselves with providing context for relatively narrow areas of information (out-of-band information exchange, authentication, and registration, respectively), jabber:iq:browse is a namespace that qualifies, and therefore defines, a flexible container that can be used to carry all sorts of information—information that is wrapped in meaning and context and that can have virtually unlimited levels of hierarchy. What's more, it can deliver information in a standard way that can be understood by Jabber clients.

As of this writing, the only Jabber client to implement browsing is WinJab.

Put another way, it means that we can extend the scope of Jabber deployment to areas outside what we traditionally see as the "Jabber world." The power and simplicity of the Jabber browsing namespace design means that we can adapt its use to whatever purpose we have in mind. As we push out the Jabber protocol and give entities within our networks the gift of speech and presence (in other words, give them a JID and graft on a Jabber connection stub), we will want to identify those entities as something more than a collection of hazy objects that sit behind Jabber addresses.

- Want to find out about dictionaries that are reachable by Jabber? Browse to a directory and pull out those JIDs—the dictionaries' addresses—that are identified as *keyword/dictionary* JID-types.

- Want to allow your users to navigate an information hierarchy outside the Jabber space but from within the comfort of their Jabber client? Build a "reflector" that navigates the hierarchy on behalf of your Jabber users and transforms it into a Jabber browsing context—by formulating the information in `jabber:iq:browse` terms.

Jabber browsing is one of those oddities that is so simple and so ultimately flexible that it's sometimes better to demonstrate it than to talk about it. Let's have a look at what browsing can do by building *ldapr*, a "reflector" for information in a database accessed by the Lightweight Directory Access Protocol (LDAP).

Building the Reflector

We're going to build the reflector as a component that connects directly to the Jabber backbone. This makes sense, as it's a service that we'll probably want to run continuously (and perhaps start up and shut down in conjunction with the Jabber server itself), rather than something more transient like a client-based 'bot, for example.

Before we go any further, have a look at Figure 10-9.

This figure shows WinJab's browser window, which, when first opened, requests the top-level browse information from the Jabber server that WinJab is connected to (`cicero`, in this case). This is the information in the `<browse&sol;>` section of the JSM component custom configuration, as described in the section "Browsable service information," which looks like:

```
<browse>
  <conference type='public' jid='conf.cicero' name='Public Chat'&sol;>
</browse>
```

We can see just one icon, representing the Public Chat conference service.

Figure 10-9. Basic browsing in WinJab

WinJab sensibly uses this location—the Jabber server (specifically the JSM) itself—as a starting position for browsing navigation. From the description of jabber:iq:browse in the section "jabber:iq:browse," we know that each element within a <browse/> section is identified with a JID, in the jid attribute. Here, the Public Chat has a JID of conf.cicero. If we click on the element's icon in WinJab's browser window, it would make a further browse request—an IQ-get with an empty extension qualified by the jabber:iq:browse namespace—*to that JID*. Thus is a browse hierarchy descended. Example 10-15 shows what that browse request might look like.

Example 10-15. Browsing to the Public Chat service

```
<iq type='get' to='conf.cicero' id='82A'>
  <query xmlns='jabber:iq:browse'&sol;>
</iq>
```

Identifying ldapr in the browsing hierarchy

This is exactly where our reflector service, in the form of a script called *ldapr*, will fit in. In the same way as we described our RSS news agent (*newsagent*) in the JSM configuration's <browse/> section, we'll now describe *ldapr*. We add it, like this:

```
<browse>
  <conference type='public' jid='conf.cicero' name='Public Chat'&sol;>
  <service type='x-ldap' jid='ldap.cicero' name='LDAP Reflector'&sol;>
</browse>
```

There are a couple of things to note in the definition:

service/x-ldap

> The LDAP reflector is a service, so we use the `service` category for the tag name used to describe it. While there are already many subtypes defined within the `jabber:iq:browse` namespace (such as `irc`, `aim`, and `jud`), none of them matches what this service is going to offer, so in the same way as we invent Multipurpose Internet Mail Extensions (MIME) subtypes in the `x-` space, we specify `x-ldap` for the `type` attribute here.

ldap.cicero

> Each component has a JID. In browsing, the JID is the key to navigation. When the icon representing this service is clicked, it's to this JID that the browse request is sent. To provide a smooth navigational path through the hierarchy, it's up to the component to return browse data items that are identified by JIDs appropriate for further navigation. We'll see what this means in the next section.

Navigating into the LDAP hierarchy

Having our reflector component defined in the JSM's `<browse&sol;>` list makes for a smooth transition into the reflection. We're going to navigate the LDAP hierarchy in a similar way to what was described in the section "Descending the browse hierarchy from an LDAP reflector." On receipt of an initial browse request, *ldapr* must return the top level of the LDAP hierarchy it has been set up to reflect:

```
<iq type='get' to='ldap.cicero' id='7'>
  <query xmlns='jabber:iq:browse'&sol;>
</iq>
```

Figure 10-10 shows the LDAP hierarchy we've discussed in the section "Descending the browse hierarchy from an LDAP reflector." It's part of an imaginary structure devised to represent people and departments in an organization. The base distinguished name, or *base DN* (an LDAP term meaning the common suffix used in the identifiers of all elements in a particular LDAP structure), is `dc=demo,dc=org`. A DN, or *distinguished name*, can be thought of as a key for a particular element. Levels within the LDAP structure are identified with DNs of ever-increasing lengths, as they get more specific the deeper the hierarchy is descended.

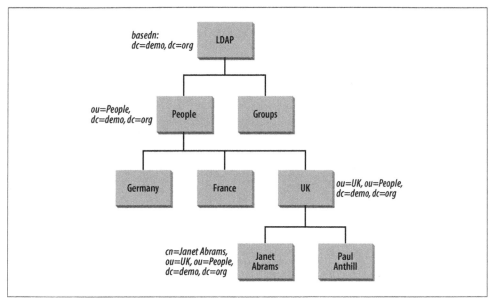

Figure 10-10. The LDAP hierarchy

If ldapr were to reflect this hierarchy, we want the response to an initial browse request to return information about the People and Groups nodes. In Example 10-16, we see what this response looks like.

Example 10-16. An initial browse request elicits a reflection of the People and Groups nodes

```
SEND: <iq type="get" id="B88" to="ldap.cicero">
          <query xmlns="jabber:iq:browse"&sol;>
      </iq>

RECV: <iq id='B88' type='result'
          to='dj@cicero/basement' from='ldap.cicero'>
        <query xmlns='jabber:iq:browse'>
          <item jid='ldap.cicero/ou=People' name='ou=People'&sol;>
          <item jid='ldap.cicero/ou=Groups' name='ou=Groups'&sol;>
        </query>
      </iq>
```

In the response, we're returning a single level of the LDAP hierarchy. The People and Groups nodes are represented by <item/> tags, within the generic container tag <query/>.

This is in slight contrast to the browse <iq/> elements shown in the section "Descending the browse hierarchy from an LDAP reflector," in which, effectively, two levels of hierarchy are returned:

```
RECV: <iq type='result' id='B89'
        to='dj@cicero/basement' from='ldap.cicero'>
      <item name='root entry' xmlns='jabber:iq:browse' jid='ldap.cicero'>
        <item name='ou=People' jid='ou=People@ldap.cicero'&sol;>
        <item name='ou=Groups' jid='ou=Groups@ldap.cicero'&sol;>
      </item>
    </iq>
```

It's really up to you to decide how many levels of information you want each browse response to emit. It depends on circumstances (will the requester be able to interpret multiple levels of hierarchy?) and the type of application scenario in which you're wanting to employ Jabber browsing. In this case, despite the difference in appearance, WinJab will interpret the information correctly whichever way you play it.

No Query Tag?

This last example looks slightly odd, because the familiar <query/> tag, usually the container for information within various IQ namespaces, is conspicuously absent. It's actually still there in spirit, in the form of the first <item/> tag, which takes the <query/> tag's role in carrying the xmlns='jabber:iq:browse' namespace declaration.

So, we've got our first two LDAP levels back. Figure 10-11 shows how they're displayed in WinJab's browser window. The JID we've just browsed to— ldap.cicero—is shown in the Jabber Address field. The *People* and *Groups* nodes are represented by <item/> tags within the jabber:iq:browse-qualified result; these are translated into folder icons in the browser window.

The browser displays folder icons for these nodes because we've described them using jabber:iq:browse's generic "holder" tag <item/>. While the namespace describes many categories to represent many different things (service, conference, user, and so on), there's not really a category that fits the "LDAP hierarchy node" description. So we plump for the generic <item/>, reserved specially for such occasions.

To navigate to the next level in the hierarchy, all we do is click on one of the icons now displayed to us. WinJab will send this next browse request to the JID that's associated with the icon we click. In the case of the People icon, we know

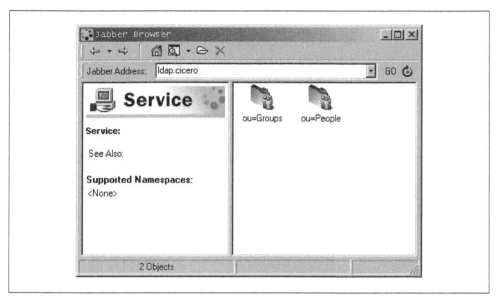

Figure 10-11. Showing the first hierarchy level in WinJab's browser

from the browse result shown in Example 10-16 that the JID is `ldap.cicero/ou=People`. This is what that browse request and response look like:

```
SEND: <iq type="get" id="B105" to="ldap.cicero/ou=People">
        <query xmlns="jabber:iq:browse"&sol;>
      </iq>

RECV: <iq id='B105' type='result'
          to='dj@cicero/basement' from='ldap.cicero/ou=People'>
        <query xmlns='jabber:iq:browse'>
          <item jid='ldap.cicero/ou=UK, ou=People' name='ou=UK'&sol;>
          <item jid='ldap.cicero/ou=France, ou=People' name='ou=France'&sol;>
          <item jid='ldap.cicero/ou=Germany, ou=People' name='ou=Germany'&sol;>
        </query>
      </iq>
```

The results of this browse request are shown in Figure 10-12. Again, notice the JID displayed in the Jabber Address window—it's the JID that we've just browsed to. The JIDs that are assigned to the items displayed here reflect the next level in the hierarchy. And so it goes on.

What the reflector is actually doing

Each of the JIDs that are browsed to look like this:

```
[component name]/[relative LDAP DN]
```

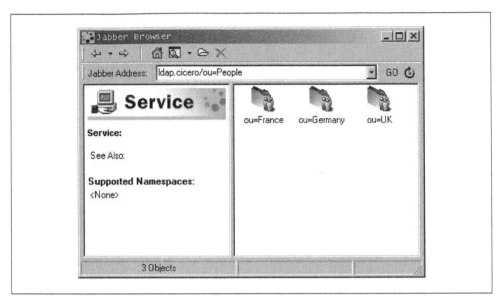

Figure 10-12. Showing the first hierarchy level in WinJab's browser

such as:

```
ldap.cicero/ou=UK, ou=People
```

The *hostname* part of the JID—[component_name]—is the name of the LDAP reflector component, and the *resource* part of the JID—[relative_LDAP_DN]—reflects the DN of the node (minus the base DN suffix) within the LDAP structure that the <item/> with that JID represents.

The crucial bit is that the [component_name] part remains the same (ldap.cicero) across every call. This means that *all* of the jabber:iq:browse requests made in the navigation sequence go to the component, in this case, the *ldapr* script.

Once the component receives these requests, it disassembles the JID, extracting the resource part, and uses it to query the LDAP server on the Jabber client's behalf. It then builds a response, in the form of an IQ-result containing the all-important jabber:iq:browse-qualified extension, containing the results of the LDAP query.

JIDs are used to *convey information* to the component, as well as to have the request delivered to the right place.

Using JID Parts to Convey Information

The example from the section "Descending the browse hierarchy from an LDAP reflector showed the information being conveyed as the *user* part of the JID:

```
<item name='ou=People' jid='ou=People@ldap.yak'&sol;>
```

This is perfectly fine, as long as the information we want to convey doesn't contain characters deigned illegal for that part of the JID. There are far fewer restrictions on how the resource part of a JID may be constructed. So it should usually be your first choice of location for piggybacking information:

```
<item jid='ldap.cicero/ou=People' name='ou=People'&sol;>
```

The ldapr script

While the explanation might be long, the actual script, shown in Example 10-17, is relatively short. Written in Perl, the *ldapr* script uses the `Jabber::Connection` library.

Example 10-17. The ldapr script, written in Perl

```perl
use strict;
use Jabber::Connection;
use Jabber::NodeFactory;
use Jabber::NS qw(:all);
use Net::LDAP;

my $ldapsrv = 'cicero';
my $basedn  = 'dc=demo,dc=org';

my $ldap = Net::LDAP->new($ldapsrv) or die $@;

debug("connecting to Jabber");
my $c = new Jabber::Connection(
  server    => 'localhost:9389',
  localname => 'ldap.cicero',
  ns        => 'jabber:component:accept',
);

unless ($c->connect()) { die "Oops: ".$c->lastError; }

debug("registering IQ handlers");
$c->register_handler('iq',\&iq_browse);
$c->register_handler('iq',\&iq_notimpl);

debug("authenticating");
$c->auth('pass');
```

Example 10-17. The ldapr script, written in Perl (continued)

```perl
debug("waiting for requests");
$c->start;


sub iq_browse {

  my $node = shift;
  return unless $node->attr('type') eq IQ_GET
        and my $query = $node->getTag('', NS_BROWSE);

  my ($obj) = $node->attr('to') =~ /\/(.*)$/;
  debug("request: $obj");

  my $result = $ldap->search(
    base   => $obj ? join(',', $obj, $basedn) : $basedn,
    filter => "(objectclass=*)",
    scope  => 'one',
  );

  if ($result->code) {
    debug("search error: ".$result->error);
  }
  else {
    foreach my $entry ($result->all_entries) {
      my $e = strip($entry->dn, $basedn);
      debug("found: $e");
      my $item = $query->insertTag(isUser($e) ? "user" : "item");
      $item->attr('jid', join('/', $ID, $e));
      $item->attr('name', [split(/,/, $e)]->[0]);
    }
  }

  $node = toFrom($node);
  $node->attr('type', IQ_RESULT);

  $c->send($node);

  return r_HANDLED;

}


sub iq_notimpl {

  my $node = shift;
  $node = toFrom($node);
  $node->attr('type', IQ_ERROR);
  my $error = $node->insertTag('error');
  $error->attr('code', '501');
  $error->data('Not Implemented');
  $c->send($node);
  return r_HANDLED;
```

Example 10-17. The ldapr script, written in Perl (continued)

```perl
}


sub strip {

  my ($fqdn, $basedn) = @_;
  my @fqdn = split(/,/, $fqdn);
  my @basedn_elements = split(/,/, $basedn);
  return join(',', @fqdn[0 .. ($#fqdn - scalar @basedn_elements)]);
}


sub toFrom {
  my $node = shift;
  my $to = $node->attr('to');
  $node->attr('to', $node->attr('from'));
  $node->attr('from', $to);
  return $node;
}

sub isUser {

  my $rdn = shift;
  return $rdn =~ /^cn/ ? 1 : 0

}


sub debug {

  print STDERR "debug: ", @_, "\n";

}
```

Looking at ldapr Step by Step

Taking the script step by step, we start on familiar ground:

```perl
use strict;
use Jabber::Connection;
use Jabber::NodeFactory;
use Jabber::NS qw(:all);
use Net::LDAP;

my $ldapsrv = 'cicero';
my $basedn  = 'dc=demo,dc=org';
```

After declaring the modules we want to use (the only one we haven't seen so far is the Net::LDAP module that we'll need to connect to and query an LDAP server), we define a couple of variables. $ldapsrv is the name of the LDAP server that *ldapr* is going to be reflecting, and $basedn is the base distinguished name that will be used as the suffix in all of the LDAP queries.

If you don't have an LDAP server of your own, a number of public ones are available that you could point this script at. The two variables $ldapsrv and $basedn go together—make sure you specify the correct base DN for the LDAP server you want to reflect.

Depending on the configuration, some LDAP servers will require you to *bind* to them with a username and password before you can perform searches. To do this, you'll need to include an extra step in this script, using the bind() method in Net::LDAP.

Having opened our connection to the LDAP server:

```
my $ldap = Net::LDAP->new($ldapsrv) or die $@;
```

we then proceed to connect to the Jabber server as a component. We're connecting to localhost:9389, which means this component script is going to run on the same host as the Jabber server, and connect to it on port 9389:

```
debug("connecting to Jabber");
my $c = new Jabber::Connection(
  server    => 'localhost:9389',
  localname => 'ldap.cicero',
  ns        => 'jabber:component:accept',
);

unless ($c->connect()) { die "cannot connect: ".$c->lastError; }
```

We'll also need a <service/> stanza in the Jabber server's configuration file to describe this component. The stanza in Example 10-18 would be appropriate. Refer to the section "The newsagent script as a component" for more details on connecting to Jabber as a component.

Example 10-18. A component instance definition for ldapr

```
<service id='ldap.cicero'>
  <accept>
    <ip>localhost</ip>
    <port>9389</port>
    <secret>secret</secret>
  </accept>
</service>
```

The script isn't going to do much apart from reflect jabber:iq:browse queries as LDAP searches. Consequently, it doesn't need to be able to handle anything apart from incoming IQ elements:

```
debug("registering IQ handlers");
$c->register_handler('iq',\&iq_browse);
$c->register_handler('iq',\&iq_notimpl);
```

The iq_browse() function is where all the work will be done. As in the newsagent recipe (the section "Presence-Sensitive CVS Notification)," we also have a "catchall" function (iq_notimpl()) that cleans up any "stray" IQ elements that it doesn't know about. Furthermore, because we aren't registering any handlers for <message/> or <presence/> elements, the dispatcher in Jabber::Connection will just throw them away, leaving *ldapr* blissfully ignorant of them—which is what we want.

After authenticating with the server by calling the auth() method to send the <handshake/> element:

```
debug("authenticating");
$c->auth('secret');
```

it's time to set the main event loop going. With a call to start(), we hand over control to Jabber::Connection, safe in the knowledge that we have a function (iq_browse()) to deal with the incoming requests that we're supposed to deal with, and that we don't care a hoot about anything else:

```
debug("waiting for requests");
$c->start;
```

Performing the actual reflection

Now, let's move on to the meat of the script. The main handler, iq_browse(), starts by making sure it has an IQ element:

```
sub iq_browse {

  my $node = shift;
  return unless $node->attr('type') eq IQ_GET
      and my $query = $node->getTag('', NS_BROWSE);
```

What we're looking for is an IQ-get with a jabber:iq:browse-qualified query extension. If there isn't one, we exit out of the function, and dispatching continues to the iq_notimpl() function, because we didn't return the special value represented by m_HANDLED.

If we do get a valid request, we first extract the relative DN from the *resource* part of the JID specified in the IQ-get's to attribute—the JID. If the request was sent to

ldap.cicero/ou=UK, ou=People, then we extract the relative DN ou=UK, ou=People
into $obj like this:

```
my ($obj) = $node->attr('to') =~ /\/(.*)$/;
debug("request: $obj");
```

Armed with a specification of what part of the LDAP hierarchy needs to be
searched, the next step is to call the search() method on the LDAP object in
$ldap:

```
my $result = $ldap->search(
  base   => $obj ? join(',', $obj, $basedn) : $basedn,
  filter => "(objectclass=*)",
  scope  => 'one',
);
```

As you can see, we're specifying three parameters in the search() method:

base

> This is the point within the LDAP hierarchy from which to start looking. We
> must specify this as a full DN, so we append the base DN (dc=demo,dc=org) to
> the relative DN received in the request to make an absolute DN:
>
> ```
> ou=UK, ou=People, dc=demo, dc=org
> ```

filter

> Specifying (objectclass=*) effectively means "look for anything."

scope

> There may be many levels below the point in the hierarchy that we're going
> to start searching from. Specifying 1 for the scope parameter tells the search to
> descend only one level. After all, we want to return only one level back to the
> requester in the reflection.

If the search failed for some reason (e.g., if a relative DN specified in the request
didn't exist in the hierarchy),* then don't bother checking the results. Instead, a
warning debug message with the error details is issued:

```
if ($result->code) {
  debug("search error: ".$result->error);
}
```

---

* This is an easy error to simulate using WinJab's browser window, as the Jabber Address bar is
(thankfully) editable.

However, if the search succeeded, the results should be translated into the `jab-ber:iq:browse` extension:

```
else {
  foreach my $entry ($result->all_entries) {
    my $e = strip($entry->dn, $basedn);
    debug("found: $e");
    my $item = $query->insertTag(isUser($e) ? "user" : "item");
    $item->attr('jid', join('/', $ID, $e));
    $item->attr('name', [split(/,/, $e)]->[0]);
  }
}
```

Calling the `all_entries()` method on the search results returns a list of LDAP entries, in the form of objects. Calling the `dn()` method on one of these objects (in `$entry`) returns us its full DN. Searching with a `base` of:

```
ou=UK, ou=People, dc=demo, dc=org
```

in the demonstration database would return two entries:

```
cn=Janet Abrams, ou=UK, ou=People, dc=demo, dc=org
cn=Paul Anthill, ou=UK, ou=People, dc=demo, dc=org
```

The task of this section of the `iq_browse()` function is to turn the information, in the form of these two entries, into something like this:

```
<iq id='B25' type='result' to='dj@cicero/basement'
    from='ldap.cicero/ou=UK, ou=People'>
  <query xmlns='jabber:iq:browse'>
    <user name='cn=Janet Abrams'
          jid='ldap.cicero/cn=Janet Abrams, ou=UK, ou=People'&sol;>
    <user name='cn=Paul Anthill'
          jid='ldap.cicero/cn=Paul Anthill, ou=UK, ou=People'&sol;>
  </query>
</iq>
```

which in turn should be rendered into something like the contents of WinJab's browser window as shown in Figure 10-13.

The function `strip()` takes two arguments and strips away a base DN from a fully qualified DN to leave the significant, relative part. Calling `strip()` on this:

```
cn=Janet Abrams, ou=UK, ou=People, dc=demo, dc=org
```

when specifying the base DN in `$basedn`, would return this:

```
cn=Janet Abrams, ou=UK, ou=People
```

For each of the entries found, we insert a tag into the `<query&sol;>` extension. The name of the tag is either `item`, if the entry is simply an LDAP hierarchy node, or `user` (a valid `jabber:iq:browse` category), if the entry points to a person. We make

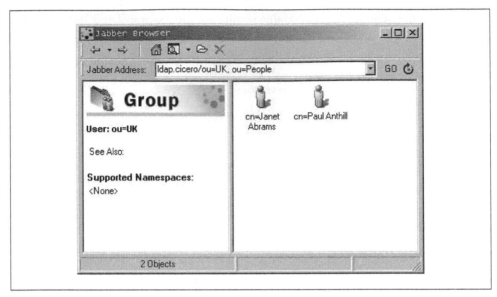

Figure 10-13. Showing the third level of hierarchy in WinJab's browser window

the decision on the basis of the first part of the DN—if it's cn=, then it's a reference to a person. The isUser() function makes this decision for us.

Once inserted, we embellish the <item/> or <user/> tag with name and jid attributes. The jid attribute is crucial, as it represents the path to further descend within the LDAP hierarchy on the next request. It is given the whole of the relative DN as a value. The name attribute is simply given the most significant portion of the DN as a value.

Whether we found something or not, we still want to return a result to the requester:

```
$node = toFrom($node);
$node->attr('type', IQ_RESULT);

$c->send($node);
```

So we swap around the to and from attributes (remembering we're a component, and not a client) change the IQ element's type from get to result, and send it back.

We end the function by telling the dispatcher that the element has been handled:

```
return r_HANDLED;

}
```

Supporting functions

The rest of the script consists of minor functions that play roles in assisting the core `iq_browse()`.

The `iq_notimpl()` function is exactly the same as in the newsagent script in the section "Presence-Sensitive CVS Notification"; it serves to catch stray IQ elements that in this case aren't IQ-gets containing a `jabber:iq:browse` query, and send them back with a "Not Implemented" error. With IQs, this is preferable to not responding at all, as responses are usually expected, even if those responses are IQ-errors. It's different with `<message&sol;>` and `<presence&sol;>` elements, as they can be seen as "one-way" and valid fodder for an element-sink.

```
sub iq_notimpl {

    my $node = shift;
    $node = toFrom($node);
    $node->attr('type', IQ_ERROR);
    my $error = $node->insertTag('error');
    $error->attr('code', '501');
    $error->data('Not Implemented');
    $c->send($node);
    return r_HANDLED;

}
```

The `strip()` function, as described already, removes a base DN from a fully qualified DN:

```
sub strip {

    my ($fqdn, $basedn) = @_;
    my @fqdn = split(/,/, $fqdn);
    my @basedn_elements = split(/,/, $basedn);
    return join(',', @fqdn[0 .. ($#fqdn - scalar @basedn_elements)]);
}
```

As well as sharing the `iq_notimpl()` function with the *newsagent* script, *ldapr* also shares the `toFrom()` function, which flips around the values of the `to` and `from` attributes of an element:

```
sub toFrom {
    my $node = shift;
    my $to = $node->attr('to');
    $node->attr('to', $node->attr('from'));
    $node->attr('from', $to);
    return $node;
}
```

The `isUser()` function, also described earlier, makes an arbitrary distinction between LDAP nodes that it thinks are `People` and those that it thinks aren't:

```
sub isUser {

  my $rdn = shift;
  return $rdn =~ /^cn/ ? 1 : 0

}
```

Last but not least, we have a simple `debug()` function, which in this case is simply an abstraction of the classic "print to STDERR" method:

```
sub debug {

  print STDERR "debug: ", @_, "\n";

}
```

Building an ERP Connection

To some extent, SAP's R/3, an Enterprise Resource Planning (ERP) system, has until recently been a monolithic piece of software, both from an actual and psychological perspective.

The drive to replace disparate and incompatible business system "islands" with an integrated software solution that covered business processes across the board was strong in the 1980s and 1990s. With good reason. For example, SAP delivered the ability for companies to manage their different end-to-end processes coherently, without requiring custom-built interfaces between logistics and financial accounting packages. The flow of information was automatic between the application subsystems that were standard within SAP's R/2 and R/3 products.

The upside to this was, of course, the seamless integration of data and functions within the SAP universe, a universe vast enough to offer application coverage for pretty much every conceivable business function.

The downside was, ironically, the universe itself. All-encompassing as SAP's products were, and indeed they were forever changing and expanding to meet business demands, it was never enough, if you wanted to break out of the mould formed by the omnipresent standard proprietary client called SAPGUI. Sure, these days, with a huge installed base of R/2 and R/3 systems in production around the world, there are a multitude of ways to get data in and out of SAP systems, but despite the varied successes of alternative client initiatives, user interaction with the business processes remains largely orientated around the SAPGUI.

This recipe is extremely simple compared to the others in this chapter. It breaks out of the SAPGUI mold and the monolithic software culture to use open source tools and technologies to add value to our SAP business processes. The point of this recipe is not particularly what the script looks like or how it's written, but what it does and how it does it.

Building an Order Approval Notification Mechanism

We're going to use a standard Jabber client as an SAP R/3 client—obviously not to replace SAPGUI, rather to allow someone who perhaps has a single R/3-related task to perform and connects only to SAP occasionally. In stark contrast to the SAPGUI client, an off-the-shelf Jabber client is much smaller. It takes up less screen space, memory, and CPU and generally for focused access is a great way for someone to play his part in business processes from the comfort of familiar communication surroundings—his IM client.

Of course, the available Jabber clients don't have any built-in R/3 functionality per se, but as clients that can receive messages and recognize URLs,* they provide enough horsepower for us to achieve our goal.

That goal is to notify a supervisor whenever a sales order is placed that requires his approval. The notification will arrive in the form of a <message/> element, carrying some descriptive text and, crucially, a URL, which points to an Apache-based handler. When invoked, the handler pulls the relevant information for the order out of R/3, requests verification of the viewer's identity, and offers a chance to approve the order with the click of a button.

Effectively we're building a miniworkflow scenario: in one direction a notification is transmitted out of the bounds of the SAP universe to the approver, and in the other direction the notification process is turned around in a one-step approval cycle via Apache. Figure 10-14 shows this scenario and where our Jabber client and script, called *approv*, fits in.

The goal here is to get the notification message out of R/3 and send it to the supervisor's JID along with a URL that he can follow back into the R/3 system to carry out the approval process. The return process via Apache is outside this recipe's scope and has been left as an exercise for you.

Getting the notification out of R/3

As we've already mentioned, there are many ways of getting data in and out of SAP. We're going to use a generic, lowest common denominator feature of the R/3 Basis system to invoke a script and pass it parameters.

---

* This recognition is a client feature, not necessarily related to the XHTML namespace described in the section "The XHTML Namespace."

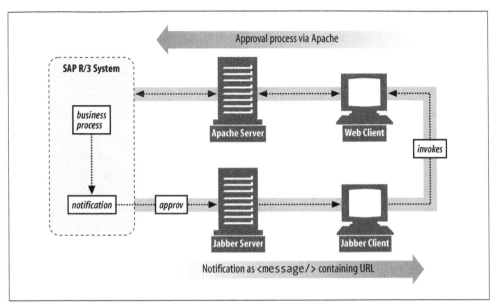

Figure 10-14. An external order approval workflow

 At this stage, if you're squeamish about R/3 Basis or SAP's ABAP language or are of another ERP persuasion, it's time to look away. What we're going to do here is not rocket science, nor is the general process specific to R/3. We're just going to call a script, at the operating system level, from within an application inside R/3.

The function group SXPT encompasses a number of function modules related to the definition, management, and execution of operating system commands. Each of these commands is described within sets of configuration parameters that define how and where they can be invoked. Using the program *RSLOGCOM*, you can create definitions for these operating system commands manually.

We need to define such a command that refers to the *approv* script. Figure 10-15 shows the *RSLOGCOM* definition of *approv* as an external command that is called ZNOTIFY.

Once *approv* has been defined this way, it can be invoked by passing parameters with a call to a function module in the SXPT function group (SXPG_EXECUTE_COM-MAND). Example 10-19 shows how the script might be invoked using this function module in ABAP. Code like this could typically be installed in a *customer exit*—a place in a standard R/3 application where custom processing can be added without having to go through the involved process of creating and carrying out a modification request.

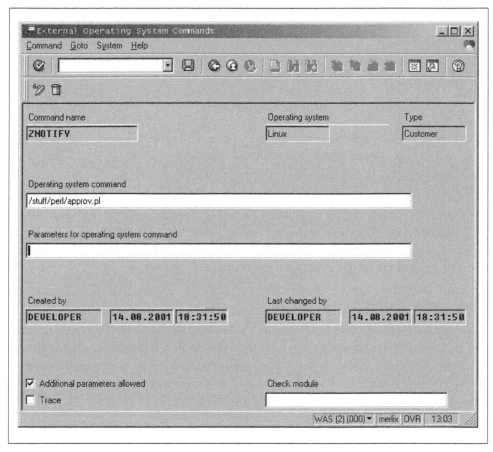

Figure 10-15. Defining approv as an external command with RSLOGCM

Example 10-19. Calling approv, via ZNOTIFY, from within R/3

```
data: sxpg_exec_protocol
      like btcxpm occurs 0 with header line,

      sxpg_add_parms
      like SXPGCOLIST-PARAMETERS,

      sxpg_target_system
      like RFCDISPLAY-RFCHOST value 'gnu.mine.nu'.

concatenate ordernumber approver
  into sxpg_add_parms separated by space.

call function 'SXPG_COMMAND_EXECUTE'
  exporting
    commandname         = 'ZNOTIFY'
    additional_parameters = sxpg_add_parms
    operatingsystem     = sy-opsys
```

Example 10-19. Calling approv, via ZNOTIFY, from within R/3 (continued)

```
    targetsystem          = sxpg_target_system
    stdout                = 'X'
    stderr                = 'X'
    terminationwait       = 'X'
  table
    exec_protocol         = sxpg_exec_protocol
  exception
    others                = 1.

if sy-subrc <> 0.
  raise notification_failed.
endif.
```

We pass two parameters to *approv* via the SXPG_COMMAND_EXECUTE: the number of
the order that needs approving (from ordernumber) and the JID of the approver
(from approver). The SXPG mechanism invokes the *approv* script with the two
parameters, and the notification starts its journey.

The approv Script

As mentioned already, the *approv* script (shown in Example 10-20) is rather small
and insignificant. Its purpose is to take the order number it receives, wrap it in a
descriptive message that includes a URL, and send it to the approver's JID. Written
in Perl, the *approv* script uses a minimum set of features from the Jabber::Connec-
tion library.

Example 10-20. The approv script, written in Perl

```
use strict;
use Jabber::Connection;

my ($order, $approver) = @ARGV;
my $c = new Jabber::Connection(server => 'qmacro.dyndns.org');
die "Cannot connect: ".$c->lastError unless $c->connect();
$c->auth('approv','secret','approv');

$c->send(<<EO_MSG);
<message to='$jid'>
<subject>Order Approval Required</subject>
<body>
An order ($order) requiring your approval has been placed.
Please visit http://qmacro.dyndns.org/approv?$order to
approve.

Thank you.
</body>
</message>
EO_MSG

$c->disconnect;
```

The script receives the two parameters passed from R/3 into the $order and $approver variables. Having connected to the Jabber server at qmacro.dyndns.org and authenticated as the user approv, it sends off a formatted message to the approver, before disconnecting.

The script itself is extremely simple and is not of primary importance. What is crucial here is the role that Jabber is playing. The <message/> element of Jabber's protocol is used to span the R/3 world with the IM world, enabling a business process cycle to take place *outside* the normal boundaries of R/3 interaction. On a simple level, that's all it takes to merge the ERP business process world with the world of IM.

The return path to R/3, via the Apache-based CGI application, is initiated when the user clicks on the URL in the message, as shown in Figure 10-16.

Figure 10-16. Receipt of an order approval request in Jarl

Here we see that Jarl has recognized the *http://* address and has rendered it as an active link. That's all it has to do. There's no attempt on Jarl's part to make an HTTP request to the Apache server and render the HTML received. Focusing on "the right tools for the right job," we should leave that role to a web browser, as indeed Jarl does, starting up the browser of our choice.*

---

* Specified in Jarl's configuration options.

Taking This Further

The journey through the recipes in the last three chapters of the book has taken us from the simplest CVS notification mechanism with the *cvsmsg* script (the section "CVS Notification via Jabber") through a fairly involved RSS component (the section "An RSS News Agent") to the transporting of XML-RPC–encoded requests and responses with our *JabberRPCRequester* and *JabberRPCResponder* scripts (the section "Browsing LDAP").

This chapter, and indeed the book, ends on a simple note, in the form of the *approv* script. Not without reason, we've completed the circle of script and application complexity. While we can build very useful and successful applications that are naturally complex, a Jabber-powered solution doesn't necessarily have to be. To employ the Jabber philosophy, the technology, and the protocol elements to build bridges between previously separate systems, and to span different areas of technology, open and proprietary alike, using Jabber's open, extensible, and flexible protocol, is what it's all about.

Finally, it's hopefully clear from the diversity of recipes shown in this part of the book that deploying solutions with Jabber, as noted in the Preface, really *is* fun!

A

The jabber.xml Contents

This appendix contains the contents of the default *jabber.xml* configuration file installed with Version 1.4.1 of the Jabber server (see Example A-1). The contents have been extended with the addition of Conferencing and local Jabber User Directory (JUD) components. Each "section" of the configuration has been separated from the next with comment-style dividing lines, and the configuration has been set up for the host on which we installed our Jabber server in Chapter 3—yak.

The structure and contents of this *jabber.xml* configuration are discussed in the section "A Tour of jabber.xml" in Chapter 4.

Example A-1. Version 1.4.1 jabber.xml with JUD and conferencing

```
<jabber>

  <!----------------------------------->

  <service id="sessions">

    <host><jabberd:cmdline flag="h">yak</jabberd:cmdline></host>

    <jsm xmlns="jabber:config:jsm">
      <filter>
          <default&sol;>
          <max_size>100</max_size>
          <allow>
              <conditions>
                  <ns&sol;>
                  <unavailable&sol;>
                  <from&sol;>
                  <resource&sol;>
                  <subject&sol;>
                  <body&sol;>
```

Example A-1. Version 1.4.1 jabber.xml with JUD and conferencing (continued)

```
                <show&sol;>
                <type&sol;>
                <roster&sol;>
                <group&sol;>
            </conditions>
            <actions>
                <error&sol;>
                <offline&sol;>
                <forward&sol;>
                <reply&sol;>
                <continue&sol;>
                <settype&sol;>
            </actions>
        </allow>
    </filter>
    <vCard>
      <FN>Jabber Server on yak</FN>
      <DESC>A Jabber Server!</DESC>
      <URL>http://yak/</URL>
    </vCard>
    <register notify="yes">
      <instructions>Choose a userid and password to register.</instructions>
      <name&sol;>
      <email&sol;>
    </register>
    <welcome>
      <subject>Welcome!</subject>
      <body>Welcome to the Jabber server on yak</body>
    </welcome>
    <!--
    <admin>
      <read>support@yak</read>
      <write>admin@yak</write>
      <reply>
        <subject>Auto Reply</subject>
        <body>This is a special administrative address.</body>
      </reply>
    </admin>
    -->
    <update><jabberd:cmdline flag="h">yak</jabberd:cmdline></update>
    <vcard2jud&sol;>
    <browse>
      <service type="jud" jid="jud.yak" name="yak User Directory">
        <ns>jabber:iq:search</ns>
        <ns>jabber:iq:register</ns>
      </service>
      <conference type="public" jid="conference.yak" name="yak Conferencing"&sol;>
    </browse>

  </jsm>

  <load main="jsm">
```

Example A-1. Version 1.4.1 jabber.xml with JUD and conferencing (continued)

```
        <jsm>./jsm/jsm.so</jsm>
        <mod_echo>./jsm/jsm.so</mod_echo>
        <mod_roster>./jsm/jsm.so</mod_roster>
        <mod_time>./jsm/jsm.so</mod_time>
        <mod_vcard>./jsm/jsm.so</mod_vcard>
        <mod_last>./jsm/jsm.so</mod_last>
        <mod_version>./jsm/jsm.so</mod_version>
        <mod_announce>./jsm/jsm.so</mod_announce>
        <mod_agents>./jsm/jsm.so</mod_agents>
        <mod_browse>./jsm/jsm.so</mod_browse>
        <mod_admin>./jsm/jsm.so</mod_admin>
        <mod_filter>./jsm/jsm.so</mod_filter>
        <mod_offline>./jsm/jsm.so</mod_offline>
        <mod_presence>./jsm/jsm.so</mod_presence>
        <mod_auth_plain>./jsm/jsm.so</mod_auth_plain>
        <mod_auth_digest>./jsm/jsm.so</mod_auth_digest>
        <mod_auth_0k>./jsm/jsm.so</mod_auth_0k>
        <mod_log>./jsm/jsm.so</mod_log>
        <mod_register>./jsm/jsm.so</mod_register>
        <mod_xml>./jsm/jsm.so</mod_xml>
      </load>

  </service>

  <!--------------------------------->

  <xdb id="xdb">

    <host&sol;>

    <load>
      <xdb_file>./xdb_file/xdb_file.so</xdb_file>
    </load>

    <xdb_file xmlns="jabber:config:xdb_file">
      <spool><jabberd:cmdline flag='s'>./spool</jabberd:cmdline></spool>
    </xdb_file>

  </xdb>

  <!--------------------------------->

  <service id="c2s">

    <load>
      <pthsock_client>./pthsock/pthsock_client.so</pthsock_client>
    </load>

    <pthcsock xmlns='jabber:config:pth-csock'>
      <authtime&sol;>
      <karma>
        <init>10</init>
```

Example A-1. Version 1.4.1 jabber.xml with JUD and conferencing (continued)

```
        <max>10</max>
        <inc>1</inc>
        <dec>1</dec>
        <penalty>-6</penalty>
        <restore>10</restore>
      </karma>
      <ip port="5222"&sol;>
    </pthcsock>

  </service>

  <!---------------------------------->

  <log id='elogger'>
    <host&sol;>
    <logtype&sol;>
    <format>%d: [%t] (%h): %s</format>
    <file>error.log</file>
    <stderr&sol;>
  </log>

  <!--------------------------------->

  <log id='rlogger'>
    <host&sol;>
    <logtype>record</logtype>
    <format>%d %h %s</format>
    <file>record.log</file>
  </log>

  <!--------------------------------->

  <service id="dnsrv">

    <host&sol;>

    <load>
      <dnsrv>./dnsrv/dnsrv.so</dnsrv>
    </load>

    <dnsrv xmlns="jabber:config:dnsrv">
        <resend service="_jabber._tcp">s2s</resend>
        <resend>s2s</resend>
    </dnsrv>

  </service>

  <!---------------------------------->

  <service id="s2s">

    <load>
```

Example A-1. Version 1.4.1 jabber.xml with JUD and conferencing (continued)

```
      <dialback>./dialback/dialback.so</dialback>
    </load>

    <dialback xmlns='jabber:config:dialback'>
      <legacy&sol;>
      <ip port="5269"&sol;>
      <karma>
        <init>50</init>
        <max>50</max>
        <inc>4</inc>
        <dec>1</dec>
        <penalty>-5</penalty>
        <restore>50</restore>
      </karma>
    </dialback>

  </service>

  <!-------------------------------->

  <service id='conf'>

    <host>conference.yak</host>

    <load>
      <conference>./conference-0.4.1/conference.so</conference>
    </load>

    <conference xmlns="jabber:config:conference">
      <public&sol;>
      <vCard>
        <FN>yak Chatrooms</FN>
        <DESC>This service is for public chatrooms.</DESC>
        <URL>http://yak/chat</URL>
      </vCard>
      <history>20</history>
      <notice>
        <join> has become available</join>
        <leave> has left</leave>
        <rename> is now known as </rename>
      </notice>
      <room jid="kitchen@conference.yak">
        <name>The Kitchen</name>
        <notice>
          <join> has entered the cooking melee</join>
          <leave> can't stand the heat</leave>
          <rename> now answers to </rename>
        </notice>
      </room>
    </conference>

  </service>
```

Example A-1. Version 1.4.1 jabber.xml with JUD and conferencing (continued)

```
<!----------------------------------->

<service id="jud">

  <host>jud.yak</host>

  <load>
    <jud>./jud-0.4/jud.so</jud>
  </load>

  <jud xmlns="jabber:config:jud">
    <vCard>
      <FN>JUD on yak</FN>
      <DESC>yak User Directory Services</DESC>
      <URL>http://yak/</URL>
    </vCard>
  </jud>

</service>

<!----------------------------------->

<io>

  <karma>
    <heartbeat>2</heartbeat>
    <init>64</init>
    <max>64</max>
    <inc>6</inc>
    <dec>1</dec>
    <penalty>-3</penalty>
    <restore>64</restore>
  </karma>

  <rate points="5" time="25"&sol;>

</io>

<!----------------------------------->

<pidfile>./jabber.pid</pidfile>

<!----------------------------------->

</jabber>
```

B

The IQRPC Classes for JabberRPCResponder

This appendix contains the two IQRPC classes, IQRPC and IQRPCBuilder. They are required for the Java *JabberRPCResponder* script in the section "XML-RPC over Jabber."

They're essentially modified copies of two existing and equivalent classes for the jabber:iq:time namespace, IQTime and IQTimeBuilder.

The IQRPC Class

```
// IQRPC.java

import org.jabber.jabberbeans.*;
import org.jabber.jabberbeans.Extension.*;

public class IQRPC
    extends XMLData
    implements QueryExtension
{
    private String payload;

    public IQRPC(IQRPCBuilder builder)
    {
        payload=builder.getPayload();
    }

    public String getPayload()
    {
        return payload;
    }

    public void appendItem(StringBuffer retval)
    {
```

```
            retval.append("<query xmlns=\"jabber:iq:rpc\">");
            retval.append(payload);
            retval.append("</query>");
        }
    }
```

The IQRPCBuilder Class

```java
// IQRPCBuilder.java

import org.jabber.jabberbeans.*;
import org.jabber.jabberbeans.Extension.*;

public class IQRPCBuilder
    implements ExtensionBuilder
{
    private String payload;

    public IQRPCBuilder()
    {
        reset();
    }

    public void reset()
    {
        payload=null;
    }

    public String getPayload()
    {
        return payload;
    }

    public void setPayload(String value)
    {
        payload=value;
    }

    public Extension build()
    {
        return new IQRPC(this);
    }
}
```

Index

Symbols

@ (at symbol) in JIDs, 122
/ (forward slash) in JIDs, 122

A

A2A (application-to-application), 10
  store and forward, 13
A2P (application-to-person), 10
  applications, 15
  store and forward, 13
accept tag, 48
accounts, registering for, 33, 211-219
  preventing, 67
address book, Jabber-based, 362-386
administration, 68
  modules, enabling, 222
administrator user/group, 28, 68-70
agents
  information about
    requesting, 74
    returning, 169-171
agents tag, 170
AIM Transport jabber:iq:gateway utility, 181
AIX, 27
algorithm, NIST SHA-1 message digest, 223
alias tag, 83, 134
aliases for Jabber server, 83
allow tag, 65, 102
allow/deny tags, 103

announcements, 70
  from administrators, 122
  serverwide, 74
Apache, Demo::JBook application as
    handler of, 370
applications
  A2P/P2A, 15
  Demo::JBook
    as Apache handler, 370
application-to-application (see A2A)
application-to-person (see A2P)
approv script, 425-429
architecture, Jabber server, 40-50
ask attribute, 193
asynchronous
  connections, 12
  conversations, 6
at symbol (@) in JIDs, 122
attachments, 15
  autoupdate, 173
  headline message type and, 139
  qualified by namespaces, 168
  roster information, 204
  tags for, 16
  URLs, 203
attributes
  ask, 193
  code, 142

We'd like to hear your suggestions for improving our indexes. Send email to *index@oreilly.com*.

About the Author

DJ Adams is a beer drinker and Perl programmer, so it naturally follows that he is a proud member of the London and Niederrhein Perl Monger groups. If pressed at parties, he will admit to being an SAP technical consultant during the day and, if pressed further, will also admit to using open source technologies to solve real business problems. (These admissions are less likely to be an issue these days, as he hardly ever gets invited to parties.) He is the author of *sjabber*, the groupchat client, Jabber::Connection, a Perl library for Jabber, and Jabber::RPC, an implementation of Jabber-RPC. In his spare time, DJ writes the "Fun with Jabber" series of online tutorials and contributes to O'Reilly's OpenP2P site (*http://www.openp2p.com*).

DJ has been fascinated by open source tools and technologies for a good part of his working life, and he has implemented many solutions based on mixing and matching software in large-scale business environments. He holds a degree in Classics and, at the drop of a hat, will argue in favor of Latin and Ancient Greek as the best grounding for odd computer languages and protocols, on a sliding scale of vehemence directly related to how long he's been in the pub.

Colophon

Our look is the result of reader comments, our own experimentation, and feedback from distribution channels. Distinctive covers complement our distinctive approach to technical topics, breathing personality and life into potentially dry subjects.

The animal on the cover of *Programming Jabber* is a bare-throated bellbird (*Procnias nudicollis*). This particular type of bellbird can be found from Central America to Argentina, though other types can be found in New Zealand and Australia. Bellbirds are named for their distinctive bell-like call. The call of the bare-throated bellbird in particular resembles a loud, scratchy gong.

The bare-throated bellbird is the national bird of Paraguay. It finds its home in the moist, tropical climates of the rain forest. Due to deforestation, the already-rare bird is at risk of extinction.

Catherine Morris was the production editor and proofreader and Norma Emory was the copyeditor for *Programming Jabber*. Tatiana Apandi Diaz, Claire Cloutier, and Sue Willing provided quality control. Interior composition was done by Derek Di Matteo and Catherine Morris. Nancy Crumpton wrote the index.

Ellie Volckhausen designed the cover of this book, based on a series design by Edie Freedman. The cover image is a 19th-century engraving from the Dover Pictorial Archive. Emma Colby produced the cover layout with QuarkXPress 4.1 using Adobe's ITC Garamond font.

David Futato designed the interior layout based on a series design by Nancy Priest. The print version of this book was created by translating the DocBook XML markup of its source files into a set of gtroff macros using a filter developed at O'Reilly & Associates by Norman Walsh. Steve Talbott designed and wrote the underlying macro set on the basis of the GNU *troff* –*gs* macros; Lenny Muellner adapted them to XML and implemented the book design. The GNU groff text formatter version 1.11.1 was used to generate PostScript output. The text and heading fonts are ITC Garamond Light and Garamond Book; the code font is Constant Willison. The illustrations that appear in the book were produced by Robert Romano and Jessamyn Read using Macromedia FreeHand 9 and Adobe Photoshop 6. This colophon was written by Linley Dolby.

Whenever possible, our books use a durable and flexible lay-flat binding.

Lightning Source UK Ltd.
Milton Keynes UK
UKOW05f1942220316

270684UK00001B/13/P